DOPING IN SPORT AND THE LAW

This unique international legal and cross-disciplinary edited volume contains analysis of the legal impact of doping regulation by eminent and well known experts in the legal fields of sports doping regulation and diverse legal fields which are intrinsically important areas for consideration in the sports doping landscape. These are thoughtful extended reflections by experts on theory and policy and how they interact with law in the context of doping in sport. It is the first book to examine the topical and contentious area of sports doping from a variety of different but very relevant legal perspectives which impact the stakeholders in sport at both professional and grass roots levels. The World Anti-Doping Code contains an unusual mix of public and private regulation which is of more general interest and fully explored in this work. Each of the 14 chapters addresses doping regulation from a legal perspective such as tort, corporate governance, employment law, human rights law, or a scientific area. Legal areas are generally considered from an international and not national perspective. Issues including fairness, logic and the likelihood of compliance are explored. It is vital reading for anyone interested in the law, regulation and governance of sport.

Doping in Sport and the Law

Edited by
Ulrich Haas and Deborah Healey

•HART•
OXFORD • LONDON • NEW YORK • NEW DELHI • SYDNEY

HART PUBLISHING
Bloomsbury Publishing Plc
Kemp House, Chawley Park, Cumnor Hill, Oxford, OX2 9PH, UK

HART PUBLISHING, the Hart/Stag logo, BLOOMSBURY and the Diana logo are trademarks of Bloomsbury Publishing Plc
First published in Great Britain 2016
Reprinted 2017

First published in hardback, 2016
Paperback edition, 2019

A catalogue record for this book is available from the British Library.

Library of Congress Cataloging-in-Publication Data

Names: Haas, Ulrich, editor. | Healey, Deborah, 1955– editor.

Title: Doping in sport and the law / edited by Ulrich Haas and Deborah Healey.

Description: Oxford ; Portland, Oregon : Hart Publishing, 2016. | Includes bibliographical references and index.

Identifiers: LCCN 2016016038 (print) | LCCN 2016016210 (ebook) | ISBN 9781509905881 (hardback : alk. paper) | ISBN 9781509905898 (Epub)

Subjects: LCSH: Doping in sports—Law and legislation. | World Anti-Doping Agency. World Anti-Doping Code.

Classification: LCC K3702 .D666 2016 (print) | LCC K3702 (ebook) | DDC 344.04/46088796—dc23

LC record available at https://lccn.loc.gov/2016016038

ISBN: HB: 978-1-50990-588-1
PB: 978-1-50992-678-7
ePDF: 978-1-50990-590-4
ePub: 978-1-50990-589-8

Typeset by Compuscript Ltd, Shannon

FOREWORD

The greatest peacetime event in the world's history takes place every four years under the banner of Sport. It is the Olympic Games. It has survived two world wars, boycotts from leading sporting nations and even the fact that its blue ribbon event, the 100 meters Men's Sprint, was won by successive drug cheats from Ben Johnson in Seoul in 1988 through to Justin Gatlin in Athens in 2004. Johnson cheated at the Games, whilst the remainder were exposed in other major events.

By the mid-90s the growing disquiet in the sporting world with the recognition that drug cheating was tainting the venerable Olympic brand and the exposure annually of drug cheats in the Tour de France cycle event eventually left the IOC with little option other than to address the issue of performance- enhancing drugs in sport. Starting with the Los Angeles Olympics in 1984, the Olympic Games moved rapidly from amateur to professional with massive financial rewards for event organisers, host cities and athletes. The biggest single threat to ongoing success was universally recognised as drug cheating.

The IOC convened a conference in Lausanne in 1999 to which it invited not only the top officials of world sport and leading athletes but also representatives of the governments of the world. All who attended and spoke at that conference recognised the inherent values and good qualities embedded in the 'spirit of sport'.

Like many other nationalities, Australians understand and pay homage to the special place occupied by sport. Blessed by our outdoor climate we not only participate but we turn up to watch the elite compete at local, national and international level. Like others we worship the superstars and we support them being rewarded financially. We are also passionate about fair play and proper contests, the very essence of integrity in sport. These were the sentiments that drove the outcome of the Lausanne conference on doping in sport.

To the credit of the delegates in Lausanne, they resolved to establish an independent, international organisation that would develop a set of rules that would be applied harmoniously to all athletes, in all sports, in all countries of the world. The World Anti-Doping Agency, WADA, was established as a unique partnership between sports represented by the IOC and 193 Governments around the world by the time the set of rules were approved and became known as the World Anti-Doping Code (the Code) in 2003. WADA was registered as a Swiss Foundation under Swiss law and was entrusted with the management and custodianship of the Code.

In the dozen or so years since the adoption of the Code it hasn't been as simple as the original concept of the founding fathers might have hoped. They did recognise that it had to be a living document and it has been significantly amended twice through worldwide consultation and ratification at world conferences. But there were many factors that were always present and bound to surface in the implementation of anti-doping programs worldwide. They included sovereign rights of nations to make and enforce their own laws for the benefit of their own citizens; the different privacy laws in national or continental systems or lack of them; the different legal systems; the enshrinement of the Code in national legislation and also in the criminal codes in some nations; the ratification and implications of the UNESCO Convention on Doping in Sport and the use of contract law, employment law, workplace and safety law and human rights laws, to name just a few. These and other similar laws were always going to come into play and so they should if justice is not only seen to be done but is done.

Coupled with the Code's interaction with national and international law and human rights are some of the Code's peculiar legal principles such as strict liability. To establish a rule violation it is not necessary to establish with an athlete's positive sample the presence of intent, fault, negligence or knowing use. Further, the standard of proof, namely to the comfortable satisfaction of the tribunal, sits somewhere between the civil 'balance of probabilities' and the criminal 'beyond reasonable doubt' standard. Most lawyers (me included) have had trouble in accepting this standard.

It is these differences in the Code and its application that make this book such a valuable contribution to anti-doping administration and practice. So many aspects of the legal framework within which anti-doping sits are examined by a combination of experts, from eminent sports law practitioners to talented and dedicated academics. Many of the chapters offer a critique of the governance structure and 'apparent' harsh regulation and even suggest it is close to impossible for our average athletes to keep up with their obligations under the Code, such as the contents of the prohibited list or for our young athletes to say no to a coach or mentor to the use of a supplement. Most importantly, the book offers guidance to the administrators of sport and at the same time it points out, in a constructive manner, where there are some shortfalls in the system. I found myself agreeing with numerous suggestions, such as a more effective education program for all athletes and a more accountable structure for the WADA Foundation Board and many -but not all- others.

People everywhere love sport and sport heroes. We crave success for our national, state and club teams. We are shattered and disillusioned when a Jobe Watson or a Paul Gallen or a Maria Sharapova is sanctioned for cheating through the use of performance-enhancing drugs. And we are puzzled by a strange set of rules which effectively says if the drug is in your system, guilt is a given and the only room left is to endeavour to reduce the sanction. The 'innocent until proven guilty' principle rarely comes into play. In Australia particularly because of the Essendon and

Cronulla teams doping incidents we are now more aware of the seriousness and consequences of doping but our athletes and officials still have much to learn.

This book will be a significant resource for athletes and officials. It should certainly be read by sport medical officers, coaches and club directors. Nearly all of the content will be easily understood and readily discernable by the average non-lawyer reader and I urge particularly Club officials to use it for guidance and advice. I am confident much of the mystique and complexity will disappear.

John Fahey AC
Former President of WADA

CONTENTS

Part IV: The World Anti-Doping Code: Obligations and Liability

Part V: The World Anti-Doping Code as Regulation: Governance and Compliance

CONTRIBUTORS

Jack Anderson is a professor at Queen's University Belfast where he teaches in torts, the law of obligations, alternative dispute resolution and sports law. His primary research interest is the relationship between sport and law. He has published widely including *Modern Sports Law* (Oxford, Hart Publishing, 2010); *Landmark Cases in Sports Law* (The Hague, Asser, 2013), featuring contributions from 25 leading international sports law academics and practitioners. He is Editor in Chief of the *International Sports Law Journal*. He is a member of a number of sports resolution tribunals in the UK and Ireland.

Narelle Bedford is an assistant professor (Lecturer) at Bond University where she teaches administrative law and Canadian administrative law. Narelle joined Bond University after teaching at the University of Queensland and the National University of Samoa. Prior to those academic positions she was employed in a range of roles by the Australian Government, including by the Australian Attorney-General's Department in the Administrative Law Branch and in the secretariat of the Administrative Law Review Council. She has also worked as an Executive Officer for the Migration and Refugee Tribunals. Narelle was formerly an Australian Diplomat, serving the Department of Foreign Affairs and Trade both in Australia and as Second Secretary in the Australian High Commission in Malaysia. She was also an Associate to the Hon Justice Moore. Her research interests are administrative law, tribunals and merits review and comparative public law. Narelle co-authored with Robin Creyke *Inquisitorial Processes in Australian Tribunals* (The Australasian Institute of Judicial Administration, 2006), which has been cited by the Australian High Court. She has also organised and presented at various conferences on sport in the Pacific region and co-ordinates international sports law moots for Bond law students.

Andrew Byrnes is Professor of Law at the University of New South Wales, Sydney, Australia, where he is also Chair of the Australian Human Rights Centre based in the UNSW Law School. He teaches and writes in the fields of public international law, human rights and international criminal/humanitarian law. His publications include the co-authored *Bills of Rights in Australia: History, Theory and Practice* (UNSW Press, 2009), and articles on gender and human rights, national human rights institutions, economic and social rights, peoples' tribunals, and the incorporation of human rights in Australian law. He has served as co-rapporteur of the International Law Association's Committee on International Human Rights Law and Practice. From November 2012 until September 2014 he was external legal adviser to the Commonwealth Parliamentary Joint Committee on Human Rights which examined various aspects of Australia's national anti-doping in sports legislation in 2013 and 2014.

Paul David QC is a New Zealand barrister who practises across a wide range of legal areas as an adviser and advocate, including sport law. He is a member of the Court of Arbitration for Sport and has been independent counsel to Drug Free Sport New Zealand since 2000. He is the author of the important work *A Guide to the World Anti-Doping Code: A Fight for the Spirit of Sport* (Cambridge University Press, 2008; second edition 2013; third edition 2016). He is a member of the Board of the Australia and New Zealand Sport Law Association.

Ulrich Haas is Professor of Civil Procedure and Civil Law at the University of Zurich. His work and research are concentrated on international civil procedure, including arbitration, company insolvency and sport law. He is the editor of numerous publications in these areas and has worked for many years as a consultant and arbitrator. He is a member of the Court of Arbitration for Sport, the Deutches Sportschiedsgericht and the Deutsche Institution fur Schiedsgerichtsbarkeit eV(DIS). He is also a member of various association courts.

Paul Hayes is a barrister and arbitrator who practises in Melbourne and Sydney (Dever's List) and in London, Kuala Lumpur and Singapore (39 Essex Chambers). He is also a senior fellow in the Faculty of Law at the University of Melbourne (Melbourne Law Masters) and the founder and co-editor of the *Australian and New Zealand Sports Law Journal*. He practises predominantly in commercial and equity litigation/arbitration, sports law, defamation and international law (public and private) and has appeared in a wide variety of cases (ranging from large-scale complex commercial matters to defamation jury trials and sporting disputes) in multiple curial and arbitral jurisdictions, including the Court of Arbitration for Sport.

Deborah Healey is Associate Professor at University of New South Wales where she is Director of Corporate and Commercial in the LLM programme, and a solicitor. She teaches competition law and sports law subjects. She is author of *Sport and the Law* 4th edn (UNSW Press, 2009), which has been continuously in print since 1989, and has authored many other books, book chapters and journal articles. She was in commercial practice for many years and acted for sporting organisations, athletes and sponsors in a wide variety of legal areas, including doping matters before the Court of Arbitration for Sport. She is a Life Member of the Australia and New Zealand Sport Law Association and editor of the *Australia and New Zealand Sport Law Journal*. She has considerable experience as chair and tribunal member across a large number of professional and grassroots sports, including on selection, disciplinary and doping disputes for major professional sports and the Australian Olympic Committee. She is currently a board member of the New South Wales Rugby League and a member of the Independent Appeal Committee of Football Federation of Australia.

Dr Thomas Hickie is a barrister at the NSW Bar and visiting fellow at UNSW Australia. He has also been called to the Bar of England and Wales (Gray's Inn) and was in chambers in London. A former judge of the High Court of Fiji and ex officio justice of the Fiji Court of Appeal, he is currently the Non-Resident Legal Services Commissioner for Fiji. His research and teaching interests are mainly in tort law, criminal law and sports law. He established the undergraduate course in Sport and the Law at UNSW and has lectured and written widely in the area. He regularly advises sporting organisations and athletes and appears before sporting tribunals. He is a member of the Australian Society for Sports History and the Australian and New Zealand Sport Law Association. He is also a past board member of the Lloyd McDermott Aboriginal Development Team (seeking to give talented Indigenous youth a future through education and sport).

Sudarshan Kanagaratnam is a barrister advising in areas of commercial law with substantial experience in sport law both at the bar and in his previous career as a solicitor. He has appeared before sports tribunals and advised major sports in areas including doping.

Dr Jason Mazanov is a senior lecturer with the School of Business at UNSW-Canberra, and a Registered Psychologist. He has a PhD in mathematical health psychology. His primary research interest is aimed at understanding the management of drugs in sport, from alcohol to anabolic steroids, drawing on all the disciplines of social science. Dr Mazanov has appeared in the Australian and international media over 100 times for his expertise on the anti-doping policy. As founding editor of the peer-review journal *Performance Enhancement and Health*, Dr Mazanov has a keen interest in the implications of how performance enhancing technology affects the physical, psychological, social and spiritual health.

Dr Marina Nehme is a senior lecturer in Corporate Law at the Law Faculty, UNSW Australia. Marina teaches corporate law, professional legal ethics and financial services law. She has taught both business and law students in the past. Marina was the recipient of an Australian Learning and Teaching Council citation for excellence in 2011. Her doctoral research on enforceable undertakings was groundbreaking and positioned her as a leading authority on this topic. Her research is primarily in corporate law, regulation, indigenous corporate governance and financial services laws.

Catherine Ordway is a professor of Practice (Sports Management) at La Trobe University; a senior fellow at the University of Melbourne; a visiting lecturer at UNSW; and a visiting scholar at Washington and Lee University, Virginia, USA. Catherine is a senior consultant with Snedden Hall and Gallop Lawyers in SHG Sport. She is an anti-doping tribunal member of the International Cricket Council, the World Baseball-Softball Confederation, SportAccord and the West Indies Cricket Board; the IAAF Doping Control and Medical Delegate for Australia; and a member of the Ethics and Integrity panel for Triathlon Australia. Catherine sits on the *International Sports Law Journal* editorial board and is an expert contributor to the Australian Sports Commission Clearinghouse. She has assisted a wide variety of sports and has been a board member of Australian Canoeing and Capital Football.

Joellen Riley is Dean and Professor of Labour Law at the University of Sydney Law School. She has been teaching and researching in the field of employment and workplace laws since joining the academy in 1998. Her major publications include *The Law of Work* (with Rosemary Owens and Jill Murray) (OUP, 2007 and 2011); *Employee Protection at Common Law* (Federation Press, 2005,), and she has written a number of books on Australian federal workplace legislation. From 2008 until 2012 she was a co-editor of the *Australian Journal of Labour Law*, and she has published widely in academic journals. Prior to her academic career she practised law with a large commercial law firm, and spent some time in journalism.

Alan Sullivan QC has been a barrister for more than 35 years and a Queen's Counsel for 25 years. He has appeared in the Privy Council, the High Court of Australia and other important courts in the Australian States, Papua New Guinea and the Pacific. From 1994 to 1998 he was Chairman, New South Wales Rugby League Judiciary and subsequently of the Australian Rugby League Judiciary. Between 1988 and 2000 he served as a Commissioner, Code of Behaviour for the Australian Cricket Board and since 2000 has served as the Deputy Senior Commissioner for Cricket Australia's Code of Behaviour. He is a member of the Court of Arbitration for Sports, served as the Advocate for the British Olympic Team at the 2000 Sydney Olympics and was a member of the Ad Hoc Panel of the Court of Arbitration for Sports to adjudicate disputes at the 2008 Beijing Olympics and the 2012 London Olympics. Since 2013 he has been Deputy Chairman of the Adjudicatory Chamber of the FIFA Ethics Committee participating in the decisions to sanction many leading FIFA officials.

Professor Prue Vines has been a member of the Faculty of Law at the University of New South Wales, Australia, since 1990. She is the co-convenor of the Private Law Research and Policy Group there. She has also been Visiting Professor at the Law School, University of Strathclyde, Scotland since 2007. Her research interests are in torts (particularly in the duty of care and the attribution of responsibility, and the extent of compensation) and succession law. She has published widely in both those areas. She is a member, inter alia, of the NSW Law Society Specialist Accreditation Committee for Personal Injury, and the book review editor of the *Torts Law Journal*. She has no formal connections to sporting bodies now but played hockey, netball and basketball in community teams until she had children and then ferried them about to the same; she now is a keen kayaker and cyclist.

Dr Greg Weeks is a senior lecturer in the Faculty of Law at the University of New South Wales. He teaches the administrative law and advanced administrative law courses at UNSW and has previously taught torts, contracts and legal ethics at other institutions. Greg's research interests are primarily related to judicial review and state liability and he has published a number of articles and book chapters in these fields; he has recently published a monograph on the remedies available when public authorities fail to adhere to their own soft law instruments: *Soft Law and Public Authorities: Remedies and Reform* (Oxford, Hart Publishing, 2016).

David Weiler BA (Politics) (Hons) (University of Western Ontario), JD (Sydney) is a Sydney-based lawyer specialising in employment and labour law where he provides advice to both state and national level sporting organisations on various issues arising in the workplace. During the 2010 Winter Olympics held in his hometown of Vancouver, he was a member of the in-house legal team responsible for advising the Media Consortium which was made up of Canada's largest private and public broadcasters.

TABLE OF CASES

European Court of Human Rights

European Court of Justice

Court of Arbitration for Sport

Australia

Canada

Germany

New Zealand

Singapore

Switzerland

United Kingdom

United States of America

TABLE OF LEGISLATION

Australia

Germany

New Zealand

TABLE OF CODES AND POLICIES

International

Australia

TABLE OF INTERNATIONAL INSTRUMENTS

Part I

The Evolution of the World Anti-Doping Code

1

The Myth of the Level Playing Field in Sport

DEBORAH HEALEY*

The Special Place of Sport in the Community

The foundational values of sport, such as striving for personal best performance and excellence, coupled with the integrity of competition, ground its special role and standing, and its significant cultural importance in the community. These foundational features and its cultural significance are also the basis of its commercial value.

Doping in sport attacks these foundational values, calling into question the basic purpose and function, and, indeed, the actual relevance, of sport. Doping threatens the universal appeal of sport and its special place in the hearts of fans. In a commercial context, doping threatens the booming sports marketplace.

These views were echoed by David Howman, Chief Executive of the World Anti-Doping Agency (WADA), who recently stated:

> Doping undermines the values of sport. The intrinsic value of sport, often referred to as the 'spirit of sport' is the celebration of the human spirit, body and mind, and is characterised by values such as ethics, honesty, respect for rules, self-respect and respect for others, fair play and healthy competition. If sport is void of these rules (and others) it might be argued that it is no longer sport.[1]

There are a number of practical reasons why we prohibit doping. By eliminating doping, we strive to recreate a level playing field for sport from which the most skilful athletes or teams ultimately emerge as the winners of any particular competition or event. We have come a long way from the days when, to quote Michael Beloff, first Chair of the IAAF Ethics Committee, 'a pacemaker was the most questionable thing that was being done'.[2] Since that time, media rights,

* Associate Professor, Faculty of Law, UNSW Australia.

[1] David Howman, 'Challenges to the Integrity of Sport' (Keynote address to Australia and New Zealand Sports Law Association Annual Conference, Melbourne, 15 October 2015) 1.

[2] Michael Beloff, IBA Global Insight, March 2015, 12.

gambling and big money have wrought changes to the imperatives of athletes and sports and the environment in which sporting events are conducted.

At a very basic level, doping can damage the physical health of athletes. As noted by Howman above, doping affects the integrity of competition. It provides unfair advantages to the drug taker over fellow athletes, so it raises basic issues of fairness. It undermines the commercial value of sport by destroying people's interest in the triumph of the individual. This flows through to undermine the 'brand' of the athlete, the particular contest, the relevant sport itself and ultimately sport as an important cultural aspect of our society. It also undermines attempts at good governance within a sport, its competition and its teams. Addressing issues relating to doping in sport is thus crucial to the continuation of sport as we know it.

The World Anti-Doping Code (hereinafter the Code) and its related rules were implemented in 2004. They form an essential backdrop to consideration of doping in sport and are considered in detail in the chapters of this book. Through an amalgam of contract law, legislation and international treaty, they create a framework for dealing with doping in sport.

Illicit Substances in the Community

Of course, doping is not confined to sport. There appears to be a broader trend towards the use of illicit substances in the community generally, and this has heightened views about the importance of the Code. Again quoting David Howman:

> [W]hen the curtain is drawn, what is revealed is a social problem of steroids in schools and amongst our security forces; the presence of the criminal underworld in trafficking prohibited substances; an unregulated supply of non-sanitized drugs through the internet and from profit-making opportunists (including many in local gyms); amateur athletes doping in recreational sporting events; young people taking steroids in a bid to look good; and, an overall challenge to the values of sport and its integrity through allied activities such as spot-or match-fixing, bribery and corruption.[3]

To this mix must be added the increased use of drugs by 'wellness clinics', which in simple terms seek to improve the performance of individuals in their daily lives.

Some of this conduct is illegal and some is not. All of these examples, however, suggest a growing tolerance within communities to the use of drugs on a daily basis. Nevertheless, this has not been reflected in our treatment of athletes under the regulatory framework of the Code, which might be described as detailed, definite and unforgiving. Arguably this is mainly because of the impact that doping has on the special qualities of sport outlined above, which position sport so favourably within the cultural and commercial life of our community. It is also true that were defences available to athletes, there would often be an excuse of

[3] Howman (n 1) 2.

special case or special circumstances to be made for athletes involved in doping in sport, with others around them seeking to take the blame, which would necessarily result in few contraventions of the Code and few penalties if such arguments were available.

Not all doping in sport is actually illegal. Ingesting products and engaging in methods which are prohibited by the Code are breaches of the Code, and it is the consideration of the Code which is the focus of this book.

Background to this Book

The writing of the book was set against the background of many national and international controversies over the last few years, including the Lance Armstrong affair, which continues to this day in a commercial context; the baseball player Alex Rodrigues; the findings of the Australian Crime Commission Report in Australia; and the controversial issues surrounding the major Australian sports of Australian Football (AFL) and Rugby League (NRL) and various of their participants.

The concept of this book was developed by the editors, and initial draft papers and ideas were workshopped at a Symposium of targeted participants at University of NSW Law in April 2014. The editors thank UNSW Law for funding the Symposium, and the participants for engaging so willingly and ultimately for their contributions to the book.

Doping Regulation: Review of the Basic Assumptions

Chapter one seeks to analyse doping in sport and to explore briefly three major themes, asking basic questions about the implementation and operation of the Code. The chapter assumes that the regulation of doping is essential to the continued place of sport in our society and to the good governance of sporting organisations. It does, however, examine a number of issues about assumptions around the Code and its implementation in the best interests of sports and sporting participants, in the hope that we can continue to improve the framework for addressing doping in sport.

It first examines the basic proposition behind the prohibition on doping in sport which is embodied in the Code, itself an unusual mix of public and private regulation. It poses a number of seminal questions about notions of the 'level playing field' and the idea of pure competition in sport which the Code seeks to enforce. A second basic question is the ability of current scientific testing to determine who is actually doping. The chapter thirdly comments on the Code as regulation.

Finally, the chapter introduces and contextualises the remainder of the chapters. As noted, the Code is a mix of public and private regulation. It does not operate in a legal vacuum—it operates in the context of the legal environment as a whole. The remaining chapters themselves examine the Code through the lens of individual legal disciplines. Both this chapter and the book itself reinforce the truth that the Code itself, despite its complexity, is only part of the legal framework of doping regulation.

The Goal of the Level Playing Field

Anti-doping regulation (and the Code in particular) is based on the idea of the creation of a level playing field to allow pure competition in sport. But what if the level playing field, even in a generalised form, is a pipe dream?

Diverse evidence suggests significant shortcomings in the logic of the level playing field, including, for example, the innate differences in the inherent characteristics of individual athletes. This spans both their physical attributes and their gender identities. In an oft-cited article in the *New Yorker* in 2013, Malcolm Gladwell, celebrated author of influential works such as *The Tipping Point* and *Outliers*, asked whether it was time to reconsider some of the assumptions which underscore doping regulation and the way in which our quest for the level playing field is currently implemented.[4] His major thesis was that: 'Elite sport is a contest among athletes with an uneven set of natural advantages.'[5] He was making the point that we want sport to be fair and take elaborate measures to make sure that no one competitor has an advantage over any other, but that despite this, there can never be a contest among equals due to the physical differences between individual competitors. This is even aside from the myriad performance-enhancing drugs and methods which exist today. And he gives a number of interesting examples in his article.

But physical characteristics are not generally regulated, nor are many forms of corrective surgery which might assist sportspeople to improve their performance. Major League Baseball allows laser surgery and tendon replacement surgery, but not drugs. Oscar Pistorius was ultimately allowed to run with his 'blades', which were deemed not to give him an advantage over other competitors. But surely they enhanced his own personal performance?[6]

[4] Malcolm Gladwell, 'Man and Superman: In Athletic Competitions, What Qualifies as a Sporting Chance?' *New Yorker* (9 September 2013) www.newyorker.com/magazine/2013/09/09/man-and-superman.

[5] ibid.

[6] Which is not to say that the author necessarily disagrees with him competing as an able-bodied athlete in the Olympics.

On another score, sports have traditionally divided their competitions into those for men and those for women. They struggle to deal with issues relating to the integration of athletes across the gender spectrum, including those athletes who appear to be 'men' or 'women', but who have an atypical chromosomal makeup, and others such as those who are transgender, except on what appears to be a mainly ad hoc basis. Circumstances such as these suggest that athletes are not always easily pigeon-holed as 'men' or 'women' for the purposes of competition divided into those categories.[7]

All of these examples emphasise that to a significant extent, that there is no 'typical' athlete. For a level playing field to exist, arguably we would wish for a field of 'typical' athletes.

There are also questions about the ability of regulators under the Code to practically enforce the Code. This current discussion thus moves past the concept of the 'cheating athlete' to objectively consider what it is that the Code can actually achieve in terms of realising its goal, the level playing field. The level playing field is problematic in terms of the limits of scientific testing, and methodology used by WADA, although it is accepted that great efforts have been made to establish fair and appropriate mechanisms and to use cutting-edge technologies.

There is widespread evidence, however, that detection occurs only in the minority of cases. There is evidence that there are some substances which are not detectable, difficult to detect or detectable within a small timeframe only, that the performance of the various laboratories around the world is far from equal, that not all athletes are tested regularly and/or intelligently, and that not all samples collected from athletes are tested for all prohibited substances and prohibited methods. In addition, laboratories can only detect substances they are looking and analysing for. Without inside information of what is being used by the athletes in the field, the testers will—in many instances—not know what to test for, so the cheats are one step ahead of the testers. This creates very difficult issues for the testers.

There is also some evidence that some substances are more detectable when used by athletes of particular ethnicities. The most common urine test for detecting use of illicit testosterone by athletes involves the T/E ratio, and analyses the ratio of testosterone to epitestosterone, which is another hormone. Depending upon the relationship between the two, drug testers determine whether there is possible cheating. The *Mail Online* in 2014, in an article provocatively entitled 'Born to Cheat. How World Class Athletes Can Take Drugs … and Get Away with it', outlined shortcomings with the use of T/E ratios as a signpost to steroid use. While it had been suggested previously that there was a wide range of gene

[7] See, for example, *Dutee Chand v AFI & IAAF* CAS 2014/A/3759, which addresses regulations made to address hyperandrogenism in female athletes. The determination specifically refers to arguments made by the International Association of Athletics Federations (IAAF) about the need to preserve the 'level playing field' (at [503]) in female competition.

variants which may keep the T/E ratio low naturally, the article underlined the depth of the problem with the use of the T/E ratio as an indicator of doping. It cited a study purporting to show that the 'doping with impunity gene' is more widespread in some racial groups than others. For example, it stated that up to 81 per cent of some Asian populations had the 'impunity gene variant': 30–40 per cent of Chinese and Japanese; almost 80 per cent of Koreans; 10 per cent of Caucasians and 7 per cent of Hispanics. More information on this phenomenon is found in the fascinating book *The Sports Gene* by David Epstein.[8] While it may be coincidence, Epstein states that figures show that countries which have higher rates of the gene are returning fewer positive samples.[9] Epstein ultimately states that 'if we want to be technologically savvy about drug-testing, we'd have to have genetically personalised testing'.[10]

None of this is to necessarily suggest that significant numbers of these groups of athletes are doping and 'getting away with it'. Nor does it suggest that we should abandon the anti-doping programme. It does, however, indicate once again the fallacy of the level playing field for competition and, possibly, even for testing for prohibited substances based on current methods. And this is all before one considers contentious theories of racial characteristics of various groups which may give them an advantage in particular sports, or considerations relating to ideas of 'nature or nurture' and 'learned perceptual expertise' which may influence outcomes.[11]

There are also inconsistencies between products and methods which are able to be used and those which are prohibited under the Code. To take the extreme example, why are spectacles allowed to be worn in competition? Surely they are performance-enhancing devices? This example may seem ridiculous, but when pared back, it is difficult to see why it is different from other methods which are contraventions. Why is invasive surgery to correct injury acceptable while blood doping is not? Why does professional baseball allow laser eye surgery when eyesight seems to be the hallmark of all great professional players, and corrective tendon surgery for pitchers, but not drugs to otherwise improve performance? This is not to discuss the rights and wrongs of each of these examples, but rather to emphasise that nothing in sports competition is as simple as the mantra that if we remove doping, there will be a level playing field for competition.

So, to summarise, there are already significant shortcomings in the logical basis for both the creation of a level playing field in sport and the ability of current mechanisms to determine who is actually doping which provide some food for thought in the context of this chapter and the book itself.

[8] David Epstein, *The Sports Gene: Inside the Science of Extraordinary Athletic Performance* (New York, Penguin, 2013).

[9] Nick Harris, 'Born to Cheat. How World Class Athletes Can Take Drugs … and Get Away with it' *Mail Online* (25 August 2013) www.dailymail.co.uk/sport/othersports/article-2401478/How-world-class-athletes-drugs-away-it.html.

[10] ibid.

[11] See Epstein (n 8) 16, 22, 37.

The Code as Regulation

Consideration of why and how athletes dope underscores the dynamic nature of this area of law. The desire to be the very best is strong and this incentivises some competitors to go to their absolute limits. Many seek to go beyond what is naturally physically possible for them in order to achieve fame and fortune. Commercialisation and the resultant promise of fame and fortune are strong motivators for some. The level of expertise required of professional athletes also often means that they have committed everything to their sport and they are ill-equipped to do any other work. This dependency on their sport for their livelihood, particularly when some are used to being very well paid, makes them very vulnerable. Injuries and bad luck may combine to end what is already likely to be a very short career; thus, the incentive to take a prohibited substance to restore the balance which has been tilted by their bad luck can be strong. Other incentives may be more political. Sport is often misused to showcase the supremacy of a country's social, political or economic system, as was the case in the old East German system or may have been with the recent example in Russian athletics. In the well-known East German example, there was a well-established system of state-backed doping.[12]

There is much discussion and scholarship today about regulation. Regulatory theory dictates that the general concept of regulation is broader than it has ever been and there is a lot of discussion about what constitutes good regulation. Traditionally regulation was all about law. Today regulation is considered to encompass governance with control emanating from both public and private sector actors though laws, private agreements and other control mechanisms.[13]

The Code is an example of the modern regulation of the use of prohibited substances—control emanates from both public and private actors and it is an example of a cooperative approach to regulation taken by governments and stakeholders. It is a true attempt to address the areas of technical, social and political risk that are the focus of modern regulation. Regular review, consultation and thorough transparency of the development processes suggest that optimal regulation should be possible. The Code also strives for a solid basis of legitimation within its constituency. An example of this can be found in the way in which the Code was implemented, ie, through three open consultation rounds with all stakeholders. Even though such a procedure may add to the democratic legitimacy of the rules, the downside of such a procedure is that progress will be slow, radical changes will be impossible and, in case of doubt, the force of inertia will always prevail.

[12] See, for example, Epstein (n. 8), 69.

[13] See, generally, Bronwen Morgan and Karen Yeung, *An Introduction to Law and Regulation* (Cambridge, Cambridge University Press, 2007).

But all of these ideas of good regulation are more complicated in the sporting context for reasons bound up with the scientific complexity of the subject matter. These include the wide variety of the contexts in which the Code is implemented; difficulties of detection of the use of prohibited substances; and continual developments in pharmacology which mean that the testers are likely to always be a step behind. Of particular importance to this mix is the motivation of athletes. Athletes striving for better performances coupled with the significant rewards which generally go to winners—and there is usually only one winner—provide very substantial incentive to win at all costs. This is accompanied by the motivation of others—sports, support personnel, player agents, sponsors and competition organisers—for success of an athlete based on his or her reward should the athlete perform well. Difficulties also arise from the fact that the more efficient the anti-doping fight tries to be, the more invasive the anti-doping measures will be in relation to the athlete's personal rights. Gathering urine samples or blood samples, storing the analytical data, requiring the athletes to provide detailed whereabouts information, to be available for testing at all or certain times, or to waive access to state courts when contesting disciplinary measures all touch upon the athletes' basic rights, which must be balanced proportionally with the requirements of an efficient fight against doping.

All of these factors mean that the regulation of the area of doping in sport is particularly complex and difficult. This makes it harder for all to understand the regulation and potentially harder to enforce.

The Code itself

A lot of time, effort and consultation have been invested in developing a 'state of the art' system of regulation to address doping. Nevertheless, there are a number of issues which strongly militate against its ease of use and application, each of which needs to be considered in more detail.

The complexity of the Code means that it is difficult for athletes to fully understand the principles of liability and punishment. While there have been significant efforts in a number of jurisdictions to educate athletes on the Code, the provisions themselves are extremely lengthy and complex. Any level of understanding of the Code beyond its simplest rules is extremely difficult even for the well educated and well informed. In addition, many athletes are so focused on their performance that even in the face of educative processes about the Code, detailed investigation of the Code's provisions, despite their importance, is unlikely until it is too late.

The list of substances and methods prohibited by the code, known as the Prohibited List, continues to be a particular problem for athletes. It contains a very large number of banned substances under their scientific names and a general catch-all provision aimed at other substances with a similar chemical structure or similar biological effect. The reason for the inclusion of the catch-all is obvious because very similar but as yet unlisted products could be developed if it did not exist; however, it does make compliance more difficult even for athletes who have no intention of doping. It also means that athletes are at the mercy of those whom they trust as to what they ingest, even if they have good intentions—ask a young athlete with visions of being a star whether he would take whatever his coach suggests and see what he says. Linked to this are the difficulties arising from the Code itself of absolute liability for truly inadvertent users. While one understands why an athlete's trainer or doctor or a contaminated supplement would always be used as an excuse by an athlete, it does make life very challenging for an athlete relying in good faith on one of these people or on a product contents list with no reason to suspect any risk.

One may alternatively say that if athletes took nothing, they would have nothing to worry about, as the intricacies of the Prohibited List would then pose no problems. The inclusion of many over-the-counter pharmaceuticals and remedies for a host of minor ailments such as a cold or a rash complicates this issue. There have been examples of athletes losing medals and titles because products marketed under the same brand name contained different substances in different jurisdictions and the athletes had presumed that what was acceptable in one jurisdiction could be taken in another.

The complexity of sanctions for teams is also an issue. Whatever governance methods are employed, legal compliance experience indicates that with the best will in the world and sophisticated systems, sports will never be able to make absolutely sure that none of their athletes are doping.

Finally, two points should be made on the overall complexity of the Code. First, one must ask whether this is an example of regulation imposing ever more onerous obligations on organisations and individuals in circumstances where those who comply are increasingly overloaded and those who never intended to comply still don't because they don't believe they will be caught. Second, the costs, time and resources which need to be applied to the implementation and policing of this regulation by sports, many of which do not have substantial resources, should be constantly assessed.

Remaining Chapters

The Code is a mix of public and private regulation. It does not operate in a legal vacuum—it operates in the context of the legal environment as a whole. The remaining chapters of this book themselves examine the Code through the lens of individual legal disciplines

Part I of the book is entitled 'The Evolution of the World Anti-Doping Code'. It contains two chapters: this chapter and chapter two, 'Revising the World Anti-Doping Code', by Professor Ulrich Haas of the University of Zurich. Haas considers the most recent Code redraft (effective 2015) in detail. He argues that despite extensive consultations with stakeholders, paradigmatic change was minor. A number of problematic areas were thoroughly considered by the expert panel and changes were made. The most important amendments are discussed in detail. Haas addresses the contentious issue of cannabis testing, controversies relating to fault and suspension, the treatment of contaminated products, and the difficult area of disciplining support personnel.

Part II of the book is entitled 'The World Anti-Doping and the Athletes'. It focuses on the impact of the Code on athletes from a variety of perspectives. Chapter three, 'Do What I Say, Not What I So: Is This the "Play True" Reality of the World Anti-Doping Code?', is written by Dr Tom Hickie, barrister and adjunct lecturer at UNSW. This chapter critically examines the imposts of the Code itself in the context of recent doping scandals involving professional football in Australia and the well-known Lance Armstrong case. The author notes that the draconian nature of the Code means that fault does not have to be proven for an infringement to occur. In addition, however, anti-doping authorities, including the Australian Sports Anti-Doping Agency, have lobbied for additional investigatory powers somewhat similar to criminal investigatory powers in circumstances in which there may have been no breach of the law, but a breach of the Code. The chapter considers the implications of such legislation.

Chapter four, 'The World Anti-Doping Code and Contract Law', is written by Australian barrister and Court of Arbitration for Sport arbitrator Alan Sullivan QC. It analyses the seminal role that contract law plays in the regulation of doping under the Code. It discusses the extent to which the 2015 Code operates as a contract and between whom. It sets out the way in which the overall Code framework is achieved, examining difficult issues of privity of contract. It analyses the correct methodologies for interpreting the 2015 Code. It notes that despite all the changes in the 2015 version, the Code, as a legal instrument, has not changed in its various iterations. The 2015 Code, like its predecessors, has effect, and almost only has effect, as a contract, albeit a very special form of contract.

In chapter five, 'Human Rights and the International Sports Anti-doping Regime', Professor Andrew Byrnes notes that the exercises of regulatory power that take place under the anti-doping regime have a significant impact on the lives of individual athletes and those associated with them. The anti-doping regime engages many human rights: not only work-related rights, but also the right to respect for private and family life, the right not to have one's reputation unlawfully or arbitrarily interfered with, freedom of association, the right to equality and non-discrimination, and a range of procedural rights (including the right of access to a court and a fair hearing in the determination of one's civil rights and obligations, and subsidiary aspects of those rights). In some cases, the regime may involve the exercise by state sporting or anti-doping authorities of coercive investigative powers more familiar from the investigation of serious criminal offences. Professor Byrnes' chapter explores how human rights standards affect the exercise of power by those who decide whether or not a person should be permitted to engage in or to continue engaging in sport. It examines the ways in which human rights norms have entered into the anti-doping regime. Its focus is not primarily whether particular regulatory rules or procedures are (in)consistent with substantive human rights guarantees; rather, its concern is with the way in which the direct and indirect application of human rights are facilitated or impeded/resisted by the legal structures on which the anti-doping regime is built. In this field, systems of state law both carve out an area for the operation of an area of private globalised law, yet still control that activity by policing the boundaries of that 'autonomous area'. At the same time, those engaged in setting the standards of that privatised area have chosen to explicitly import certain human rights values, partly for policy reasons and partly for strategic reasons, as a means of protection against incursion into their decision-making processes. By taking over the task of policing the implementation of public law values, the regime limits the intervention of external assessors of human rights compatibility, reducing their role to patrolling the outer limits and thus ensuring that considerable deference is shown to those with sports expertise.

Part III of the book is entitled 'The World Anti-Doping Code: Procedural Questions'. The consequences of detection and the application of the Code are catastrophic for an athlete, so doping is generally secretive and well planned. Analytical evidence raises a strong case against an athlete, but a breach of the Code may also be proven by non-analytical evidence. This is the focus of chapter six, 'Issues in the Gathering and Use of Non-analytical Evidence to Establish Anti-doping Rule Violations', by barrister Sudarshan Kanagaratnam, The focus of anti-doping organisations is increasingly on the use of non-analytical evidence as a means of establishing anti-doping rule violations. The Code, in recognition of the importance of non-analytical evidence, places greater emphasis on evidence obtained through investigation and the use of intelligence in the fight against doping. The Australian Parliament has introduced legislation which gives Australian Sports Anti-Doping Authority (ASADA) significant powers aimed at facilitating the gathering of non-analytical evidence and information sharing. Such legislative power, allied with contractual obligations which bind athletes to anti-doping policies, forms the principal means by which anti-doping organisations obtain non-analytical evidence. This chapter examines the powers pursuant to which non-analytical evidence is gathered, the scope of those powers and issues that arise from the way in which the evidence so gathered is used to establish anti-doping rule violations.

Chapter seven, 'Hearings under the World Anti-Doping Code: Observations on Anti-doping Proceedings', is written by New Zealand QC Paul David, who is prosecutor for Drug Free Sport New Zealand (DFSNZ). It outlines the intricacies of prosecuting an anti-doping charge before a doping tribunal in New Zealand on behalf of the national anti-doping organisation, with some reference to other jurisdictions. Observations on the operation of one national anti-doping system provide insights and assistance to those establishing and running the systems for the hearing of anti-doping matters in other jurisdictions. The chapter examines the operation of the current system and discusses its advantages and disadvantages, and the challenges faced by such a system. It concludes that under the New Zealand national anti-doping organisation (DFSNZ), the system developed to afford hearings for anti-doping violations effectively provides the speedy reasoned decisions required.

Chapter eight, 'Doping in Sport: What Role for Administrative Law?', is written by Dr Greg Weeks and Narelle Bedford. It examines the intersection of administrative law and doping in sport. Administrative law is the specialised area of law concerned with challenging government decisions. The chapter explains how administrative law may be applicable to doping decisions at an Australian national level, as doping decisions are made by the ASADA, a body created by and exercising its powers under a Commonwealth Act. The authors detail the different options for challenging a doping decision using administrative law, which include merits review by a tribunal and judicial review or appeal before a court. At an international level, administrative law's fundamental concepts are reflected and embedded into the Court of Arbitration for Sport's Code and Rules, and also the Code. The centrally applicable concept is procedural fairness (sometimes referred to as natural justice or due process), which requires all administrative decisions to be made by an unbiased decision-maker following a fair hearing. The chapter concludes that administrative law principles can provide much beneficial guidance to doping decision-makers that will assist in improved decision-making, as well as providing a possible basis for affected individuals and entities to challenge doping decisions.

Part IV of the book is entitled 'The World Anti-Doping Code: Obligations and Liability' and contains two chapters. The advent of professional sport changed the nature of the legal relationship between many athletes, their teams and their sports. Chapter nine, 'Gladiators: The Rights and Responsibilities of Players as Employees', is written by Professor Joellen Riley and David Weiler. It discusses the employment law implications of doping regulation, including liability of the employer and liability of employees and others. Professional players engaged by football teams are generally regarded as employees, so the doping scandals of recent times raise questions about the respective rights and responsibilities of players as workers who have engaged in—and are victims of—workplace misconduct. This chapter argues that the high level of control that clubs seek to exert over players' lives—both on and off the field—warrants a correspondingly rigorous application of the employer's duty of care towards players, which means a high level of diligence by clubs in instituting supervisory practices to manage these risks.

The issue of negligence by sporting organisations in the administration of prohibited substances is considered in chapter ten, 'Doping as Tort: Liability of Sport Supervisors and the Problem of Consent', by Professor Prue Vines. This chapter considers the situation that arises when an athlete is administered a prohibited substance by a sport supervisor (coach, sports scientist, sports medical practitioner etc). It considers the consequences if a negligence action is brought because of personal injury or economic loss to the athlete. Arguing that the best analogy is not to earlier sport law, but to medical malpractice law, the chapter considers how the requirements of the law of negligence play out in a range of jurisdictions. It argues that the most problematic issue in this context is the question of consent and whether, in a context where the sport supervisor may have a 'godlike' power, it is realistic to argue that athletes voluntarily assumed the risk when they take the advice of their supervisor and take a particular substance. Given that what is prohibited under the Code at any time has varied and that prohibition under the Code will not be determinative of liability in negligence, the liability of sports supervisors may be wider than they are aware of. In particular, they may need to be more aware of the duty to warn of risk than may presently be the case. Again, the effectiveness of warnings may be undermined by the level of reliance of elite athletes on supervisors, so that consent or the voluntariness of the taking of the doping substance may be less real than the law has taken account of so far.

The last part of the book, Part V, is entitled 'The World Anti-Doping Code as Regulation: Governance and Compliance'.

Chapter eleven, 'Governance and Anti-doping: Beyond the Fox and the Hen House', is written by Marina Nehme, Senior Lecturer, UNSW and Catherine Ordway, international anti-doping consultant. It considers the structure and governance of the WADA. It argues that the two core values that guide this Agency are accountability and integrity, with an emphasis on the independent and unbiased judgement of the organisation. The Agency also encourages those organisations with national and sporting responsibility for anti-doping to prioritise structures and accountability independent of political pressures. However, the authors suggest that a closer review of WADA's structure highlights the fact that the focus of the organisation is on external accountability: the Agency is accountable to its funding bodies. This raises a question regarding the internal accountability of the organisation, a concept that has attracted little attention from commentators and academics. The chapter considers the governance of WADA and suggests reform to enhance its transparency, accountability and integrity, canvassing the literature on corporate governance to assess good corporate governance policies and guidelines which WADA might adopt to improve its governance.

Chapter twelve, 'The Chimera of Compliance with the World Anti-Doping Code', is written by Jason Mazanov, Senior Lecturer, School of Business, UNSW-Canberra. It examines the likelihood of code compliance from a psychological perspective and whether the Code as we know it will actually deter doping. Drug control in sport uses a legalistic prohibitionist policy framework to restrict the use of certain substances in an attempt to regulate the rapidly evolving field of sports science. Significant effort has been expended on developing an elegant legal framework that integrates the Code, international treaties, domestic laws and contractual arrangements to regulate both international institutions and individual athletes in a clear and consistent manner. Reports from the WADA suggest that compliance with the Code has advanced considerably since the introduction of the Code 2003 and continues to improve. While there appears to be breadth in Code compliance (eg, the number of Code-compliant countries), actual Code compliance appears to lack depth (eg, anti-doping education). Evidence from the social sciences suggests this is because the elegant legal framework is inaccessible to athletes and support personnel and, as a result, is perceived as irrelevant to the practice of sport. This creates a 'Chimera' of compliance, where the headline success of international compliance exists next to the failure to achieve compliance with the Code where it matters—the daily practice of athletes and support personnel. The experiences of athletes and support personnel are used to inform recommendations for changes to the legal framework to promote compliance with the Code in the daily practice of sport.

Chapter thirteen, 'The Juridification and Criminalisation of Doping: Time to Revive the Spirit of Sport?', is written by Professor Jack Anderson. It examines the recent 'juridification' of sports doping investigations. Juridification is taken to mean the process by which formal legal principles are infusing the conduct and procedural regulation of doping disputes by internal sports dispute resolution mechanisms. It argues that the juridification of sporting disputes is an underplayed factor in the development of sports law more generally. In assessing juridification, the chapter balances two competing conceptual views. The first view is whether an over-juridification of sports doping investigations is severely hindering the ability of first instance decision-makers in sport to eradicate doping as the antithesis of the spirit of sport—a process known in administrative law terms as 'ossification'. The second and competing perspective is that harmonised, legal standards of proof and procedure have not unduly harmed the 'fight' against doping in sport and that, if anything, the integration and harmonisation of such legal principles are a necessity in preventing sports bodies from having to engage in lengthy, costly litigation in the ordinary courts of multiple jurisdictions—what is known in terms of alternative dispute resolution theory as the 'pluralistic' approach. The chapter concludes by briefly assessing whether the objectives of the current anti-doping policy will only ever be realised when the regulatory pursuit of those who dope is supplemented by the criminalisation of doping.

Finally, chapter fourteen, 'The Politics of International Sports Anti-doping Regulation', is written by Paul Hayes, barrister. It notes that the preamble to the 2015 edition of the Code recites the rationale for its existence as seeking to preserve 'what is intrinsically valuable about sport, often referred to as the "spirit of sport"' (essentially, 'fair play'). Against this backdrop, substances that have the potential to enhance sports performance represent a potential health threat to the athlete or that violate the 'spirit of sport' are included on the WADA List of Prohibited Substances, which is updated annually. However, the author questions whether the anti-doping rationale as stated in the Code is the complete rationale for the implementation and enforcement of a strict international anti-doping regulatory regime, which sometimes produces harsh or unjust outcomes for athletes. He argues that the stated rationale expressed in the Code does not explain all of the reasons for the Code's existence in its present form and that there is a broader rationale at work. The broader rationale supporting the existence of a strict international anti-doping regulatory regime also takes into account the commercial objectives of promoters, broadcasters and sponsors of international sporting events to produce 'clean sporting product', particularly with respect to Olympic sport. This chapter examines how it is that commercial interests also influence the development of international sports anti-doping regulation and, in particular, the Code, and that 'clean sport' is not just for the benefit of athletes, but also for the benefit of promoters, broadcasters and sponsors.

Conclusion

This book addresses in detail aspects of the Code and, in particular, its rationale and its interactions with other very important legal and political considerations. The strong conclusion to be drawn from the content is that the Code itself, despite its importance and complexity, is only part of the legal framework of doping regulation. Other laws and regulations will assume great importance in particular cases. Those involved in implementing the Code at all levels should be well aware of this and should take great care to address all legal issues relating to doping in sport to the extent that they affect the sports, the teams and, in particular, the athletes.

2

Revising the World Anti-Doping Code

ULRICH HAAS*

Background to the World Anti-Doping Code 2015

The World Anti-Doping Code (hereinafter the Code) forms the backbone of the global fight against doping, and serves to harmonise and coordinate this fight.[1] At the Fourth World Conference on Doping in Sport in Johannesburg, South Africa in November 2013, the third version of the Code, the World Anti-Doping Code 2015 (2015 Code), after those of 2003 and 2007, was recently adopted. The approval of the 2015 Code concluded a reform process lasting about 18 months.[2] The 2015 Code then entered into force on 1 January 2015, by which date the signatories, in particular the International Federations (IFs), the National Olympic Committees (NOCs) and the National Anti-Doping Agencies (NADOs), needed to implement it into their respective bodies of rules. As was also the case with the 2003 and 2007 iterations, the 2015 Code is the product of three open rounds of consultations that were administered by a commission[3] set up by the World Anti-Doping Agency (WADA). During the different consultation phases, all those interested in the subject could participate in, and contribute to, the reform process. A total of 315 stakeholders entered their comments. By far the greatest number of submissions came from the sports movement (149), regional or national anti-doping agencies (84) and state or supranational organisations (36). A total of 3,987 amendments were proposed. While this figure is indeed high, one must not overlook that such a global reform process is quite like an ocean tanker for which wild changes in direction are hardly possible due to the comparatively

* Professor, University of Zurich.

[1] See Deborah Healey, *Sport and the Law* 4th edn (Sydney, University of New South Wales Press, 2009) 233–35. For the origins of the Code, see Paul David, *A Guide to the World Anti-Doping Code: A Fight for the Spirit of Sport* 2nd edn (Cambridge, Cambridge University Press, 2013) 2–3.

[2] See Olivier Niggli, 'Code Mondial Antidopage: Processus de Révision et Principales Modifications' (2013) 137 *Jurisport* 20.

[3] For this commission's competencies, see ibid 21.

high forces of inertia. Accordingly, the 2015 Code is rather a continuation or further development of existing anti-doping practice, with only little paradigmatic changes. 'Radical' reform proposals have almost unanimously been rejected by the majority of stakeholders. From the large number of submissions, a few important problematic topics are singled out in this chapter.[4]

The Cannabis Challenge

The number of athletes testing positive for cannabis ranks near the top in the statistics of most anti-doping organisations (ADOs).[5] In view of this finding, it is a much-discussed question whether the fight against doping should really be directed against such so-called 'social drugs'. Throughout the reform process, many stakeholders, especially those from among the group of regional and national anti-doping agencies, have supported this position and have pointed out that the scarce resources in the fight against doping should not be spent combating drug abuse. Various related submissions promoted a change in the coordinates of the fight against doping, intending to relieve the ADOs of general drug-related problems. These submissions include broadly rethinking the prohibited list and the consequences of doping, and are explored in greater detail below.

Rethinking the Prohibited List

The definition of doping is centred on factual circumstances involving the 'Presence of a *Prohibited Substance* or its *Metabolites* or *Markers* in an *Athlete's Sample*'[6] and the '*Use* or *Attempted Use* by an *Athlete* of a *Prohibited Substance* or a *Prohibited Method*'.[7] Both these defining elements of an anti-doping rule violation (ADRV) are associated with the so-called Prohibited List in Article 4 of the 2015 Code, which specifies the substances and methods that are forbidden in sports.[8]

[4] For a comprehensive overview, see Antonio Rigozzi, Marjolaine Viret and Emily Wisnosky, 'A New Code for a New Era in the Fight against Doping in Sports: A Summary of the Main Changes in the *2015 WADA Code*' (2014) 5(1) *Global Sports Law and Taxation Reports* 25.

[5] See WADA, '2013 Anti-Doping Testing Figures' (Sport Report, 2013) 19 (Table 12) https://wada-main-prod.s3.amazonaws.com/resources/files/WADA-2013-Anti-Doping-Testing-Figures-SPORT-REPORT.pdf.

[6] 2015 Code art 2.1 (emphasis in original).

[7] 2015 Code art 2.2 (emphasis in original).

[8] See David (n 1) 81–82.

The Specificities of the Prohibited List

The Prohibited List is essentially characterised by two aspects. First, according to the criteria defined by the Code, a particular substance or method can be included in the Prohibited List either if it carries the potential to mask the use or presence of another prohibited substance or method[9] or if it fulfils two of the following three criteria:

— 'potential to enhance sporting performance';
— 'actual or potential health risk to an athlete';
— 'use of the substance or method which violates the *spirit of sport* described in the introduction to' the 2015 Code.[10]

The second characteristic of the Prohibited List is that it differentiates whether a substance is prohibited only inside or also outside competition, ie, the actual sport contests. This is at least somewhat contradictory because the above-mentioned criteria—strictly speaking—do not permit such a differentiation.[11] If the use of a substance is performance enhancing, unethical or harmful, this conclusion applies completely regardless of when the substance was taken. Arguably, the ultimate objective of the Prohibited List's differentiation between in- and out-of-competition is to reasonably limit the number of prohibited substances. To achieve this, the Prohibited List distinguishes whether substances and methods are prohibited exclusively inside or also outside competition. As a result, it therefore comprises two lists of prohibited substances, the list of substances prohibited in-competition being much more comprehensive than the list of substances whose ingestion and use are excluded out-of-competition.

Proposals for Reform

The reform proposals to decriminalise cannabis—in terms of the relevance for anti-doping—draw upon the two above-described features of the Prohibited List. It was proposed, for example, to alter the priority of criteria that determine the inclusion of a substance or method into the Prohibited List by making the criterion 'potential to enhance sport performance' mandatory, unless, of course, the substance at stake is a masking agent. Hence, of the two required list criteria, one, namely the 'potential to enhance sport performance', would necessarily have

[9] 2015 Code art 4.3.2.
[10] Healey (n 1) 238 (emphasis added).
[11] See Bastian Kern, *Internationale Dopingbekämpfung—Der World Anti-Doping Code der World Anti-Doping Agency* (Hamburg, Verlag Dr Kovac, 2007) 385; Clemens Prokop, *Die Grenzen der Dopingverbote* (Nomos Verlagsges, 2000) 239 ff.

to be present to allow the inclusion of a substance in the Prohibited List. According to this proposal, doping would be inconceivable if the ingested substances do not enhance performance. Basically equating doping with prohibited performance enhancing, this proposal has a lot in its favour. First, it sharpens the (as yet vague) concept of 'doping'. Second, the Code already attributes a special significance to the 'performance enhancement' aspect in a number of its provisions.[12]

Although good reasons support this proposal, it fell through in the end, mainly for political reasons.[13] First, among its opponents were government authorities, who were especially against downgrading health and safety concerns in the fight against doping versus the criterion of performance enhancement. Fears were voiced that this would hamper the public commitment to the fight against doping, especially the widely customary financial funding of national anti-doping agencies, health safety often serving as the political justification of such governmental commitment. On the other hand, experts were and are divided as to whether the use of cannabis may not, in particular types of cases (eg, downhill mountain biking), have a disinhibiting effect after all and may consequently, under exceptional circumstances, enhance performance.

Likewise rejected by a majority of stakeholders was the proposal to abolish the Prohibited List's (contradictory) differentiation between in-competition and out-of-competition with the aim of streamlining the List, as this would have necessitated a complete revision of the Prohibited List. Most of the stakeholders did not want to support such a far-reaching step.

Rethinking the Consequences

As a fundamental reform of the Prohibited List had been predominantly rejected, an alternative approach was proposed to mitigate the consequences of doping violations involving the use of cannabis. Here, too, the initial intention was to seek a general solution for all 'social drugs' or 'substances of abuse', that is, a solution not focused exclusively on the problem of cannabis.[14] Accordingly, the draft in the second round of consultations contained roughly the following wording for Article 10.4.3 concerning the sanctioning of doping violations:

> Where the anti-doping rule violation *involves a substance that is identified on the Prohibited List as* a Substance of Abuse, *and the Athlete or other Person* establish no intent to enhance

[12] See, eg, The World Anti-Doping Code 2015 arts 4.2.1, 10.2.3 and comment to art 4.2.2. See also various definitions: at app 1 (definition of 'administration'), (definition of 'trafficking), (definition of 'no significant fault or negligence') and its comment.

[13] See also Antonio Rigozzi, Marjolaine Viret and Emily Wisnosky, 'Does the World Anti-Doping Code Revision Live up to its Promises? A Preliminary Survey of the Main Changes in the Final Draft of the 2015 WADA Code' (2013) *Jusletter* 1, 10 [48].

[14] ibid 26 [140].

> sport performance … [then] the *Anti-Doping Organization* with results management responsibility may allow the *Athlete* the opportunity to participate in a program of rehabilitation, at the *Athlete*'s expense, in lieu of an appropriate part of the period of *Ineligibility* which would otherwise be applicable.[15]

This proposal also failed to find majority acceptance. The primary concern of its critics was that not all ADOs possessed the financial resources to set up a rehabilitation programme, so this provision would encourage the unequal treatment of athletes in their respective countries.

Summary

Overall, cannabis use among athletes, which is widespread in certain circles, raises fundamental questions about the meaning and purpose of the anti-doping campaign. The stakeholders were not able to attain a 'major' solution through a general rebalancing of the coordinates of the fight against doping, either at the level of factual conditions by reforming the Prohibited List, or in terms of the legal consequences by reforming the sanction system. A solution to the problem is to be found, if one is possible, within the known, pre-existing framework. This, however, is unlikely to be feasible without causing ruptures.

Standard Sanctions for Athletes

Unlike its predecessor, the 2015 Code basically provides for two standard sanctions against athletes who have committed an ADRV according to Articles 2.1 or 2.2 of the 2015 Code (the presence or use of a prohibited substance or method). For 'intentional' violations, the 2015 Code stipulates a standard sanction of four years.[16] For unintentional ADRVs, by contrast, the standard sanction is a two-year period of ineligibility.[17] These standard sanctions apply regardless of which prohibited substance or method was used by the athlete. What varies, however, is the burden of proof for intentional ADRVs, depending on whether or not the prohibited substance is a so-called 'specified substance'. By definition, in the Prohibited List, this term denotes substances 'which are more likely to have been consumed by an Athlete for a purpose other than the enhancement of sport performance'.[18]

[15] WADA, World Anti-Doping Code 2015 Draft—Version 2 (3 December 2012) art 10.4.3.

[16] ibid art 10.2.1.

[17] ibid art 10.2.2.

[18] See ibid, comment to art 4.2.2. See also Philippe Fuchs, 'The Sanctioning Process for Specified Substances in the 2015 World Anti-Doping Code—A Fresh Start?' (2013) 8 *Australian and New Zealand Sports Law Journal* 127.

The new regulation in Articles 10.2.1 and 10.2.2 of the 2015 Code contains stricter sanctions compared to the former 2009 Code.[19] The latter also provided for increased periods of ineligibility for both specified and non-specified substances under aggravating circumstances,[20] but the sports federations seldom applied these stricter sanctions in practice.[21] Furthermore, the term 'aggravating circumstances' in Article 10.6 of the 2009 Code was significantly more restrictive than the term 'intentional'. As a prerequisite for 'aggravating circumstances', there need to be further elements of the athlete's personal behaviour, apart from intentionality, which justify the particular reprehensibility of the ADRV. In this respect, the new Code has significantly lowered the threshold for increased sanctions, since henceforth the intentional nature of an offence is sufficient to validate a period of ineligibility of more than two years. In addition, the new Code, unlike Article 10.6 of the previous 2009 Code, no longer provides for a sliding scale on the side of the legal consequences. Instead of varying within a range, the sanction for an intentional ADRV now consists of a fixed four-year period of ineligibility.

Various circumstances gave rise to these stricter sanctions. For one thing, the Armstrong case[22] occurring during the reform process certainly created a favourable climate for aggravated sanctioning.[23] In view of Armstrong's 'doping scheme, more extensive than any previously revealed in professional sports history',[24] the calls for stricter sanctions could hardly be politically denied. Whether, however, the threat of higher standard sanctions would have deterred Armstrong from his doping practices is an issue that was neither raised nor investigated in detail or even answered.[25] For another thing, it was the International Olympic Committee (IOC) that primarily promoted a stricter sanction system.[26] The IOC aspires to optimally protect the values of its own events and thus the economic exploitability of the Olympic Games. Whenever a doping offender whose period of ineligibility is over rejoins the competition, this is an occasion for the media to address the offender's doping history in conjunction with the event in question. In many cases, the doping offender and the related scandal, which is actually a thing of the past, receive more attention than the sporting event itself or the 'clean

[19] With regard to the compatibility of stricter sanctions with human rights, see Jean-Paul Costa, 'Legal Opinion Regarding the Draft 3.0 Revision of the World Anti-Doping Code' (25 June 2013) https://wada-main-prod.s3.amazonaws.com/resources/files/WADC-Legal-Opinion-on-Draft-2015-Code-3.0-EN.pdf. See also Niggli (n 2) 21.

[20] For analysis of this provision, see Adam Lewis and Jonathan Taylor, *Sport: Law and Practice* 3rd edn (Haywards Heath, Bloomsbury Professional, 2014) [C2.176]. See also David (n 1) 305–06.

[21] See Ulrich Haas, 'Mögliche Ansatzpunkte für eine Reform des Welt Anti-Doping Code' in Antonio Rigozzi, Dominique Sprumount and Yann Hafner (eds), *Citius, Altius, Fortius, Mélanges en l'honneur de Denis Oswald* (Basel, Helbing & Lichtenhahn, 2012) 627, 642.

[22] See *United States Anti-Doping Agency v Lance Armstrong* (Decision, United States Anti-Doping Agency, 10 October 2012).

[23] To this effect, *cf* Rigozzi, Viret and Wisnosky (n 13) 21 [113].

[24] See *United States Anti-Doping Agency v Lance Armstrong* (n 22) 5.

[25] See generally Rigozzi, Viret and Wisnosky (n 13) 22 [116].

[26] See also Niggli (n 2) 22.

athletes' competing with the former doping offender. So, if negative coverage on doping, which affects economic interests, is to be kept out of competitive sport, it is natural to raise the bar for the return of former doping offenders as high as possible. The longer the standard period of ineligibility, the less likely it is for the doped athlete to re-enter organised sports. Prior to this, the IOC has tried to permanently exclude doped athletes from participation in the Olympic Games, but has failed before the Court of Arbitration for Sport (CAS).[27] In the first draft of the new 2015 Code, the IOC's intentions were again manifest, as may be seen in that draft's Article 10.15.1:

> Where an *Athlete* or other *Person* has been sanctioned for an anti-doping rule violation other than under Articles 10.3.3 (Filing Failures and Missed Tests), 10.3.4 (Prohibited Association), 10.4 (Specified Substances), or 10.5.2 (No Significant Fault or Negligence), and Article 10.5.3 (Substantial Assistance) is not applicable, then, as an additional sanction, the *Athlete* or other *Person* shall be Ineligible to participate in the next Summer Olympic Games and the next Winter Olympic Games taking place after the end of the period of *Ineligibility* otherwise imposed.[28]

After fierce criticism of this tailor-made rule focused solely on the interests of the IOC, the current wording of the 2015 Code was agreed upon; however, it goes without saying that in many sports, a period of ineligibility of four years is in most cases tantamount to a lifelong ban.

Reduced Sanctions for Athletes

The concept of reduced sanctions follows from the concept of proportionality. This principle holds that where a fundamental right of the athlete is concerned, the scope of any provision curtailing this right 'should be upheld only to the extent necessary to fulfil the aim of the provision and should be proportionate to the aim'.[29] This principle of proportionality is well enshrined in CAS jurisprudence.[30]

Whether any mitigating factors apply to a sanction, and, if so, which ones, depends upon which relevant standard period of ineligibility forms the starting

[27] *United States Olympic Committee v International Olympic Committee* (Award, Court of Arbitration for Sport, Case No CAS 2011/O/2422, 4 October 2011). See also Ulrich Haas, 'Ex-Doper Willkommen? Anmerkung zur Entscheidung des Court of Arbitration for Sport zur Rechtmässigkeit der sog. "Osaka Rule" des Internationalen Olympischen Komitees' (2012) *Jusletter* 13.

[28] WADA, World Anti-Doping Code 2015 Draft—Version 1 (3 December 2012) art 10.4.3.

[29] David (n 1) 246.

[30] *WADA v Jobson Leandro Pereira de Oliveira* (Award, Court of Arbitration for Sport, Case No CAS 2010/A/2307, 14 November 2011) 25–26 [131]; *Hans Knauss v FIS* (Award, Court of Arbitration for Sport, Case No CAS 2005/A/847, 20 July 2005) 9 [16], 13 [29]–[30]; *Doping Authority Netherlands v Nick Zuijkerbuijk* (Award, Court of Arbitration for Sport, Case No CAS 2009/A/2012, 11 June 2010) 11–12 [39]–[43].

point or, in other words, on whether the ADRV is intentional or negligent. In the first case, only non-fault-related reductions come into consideration;[31] in the latter case, 'fault-related' as well as 'non-fault-related' reductions can apply. All of this must be seen against the background of the new 2015 Code's aim to deal flexibly with athletes who accidentally commit an ADRV, whilst 'cracking down' on those who dope intentionally. Two new features of the 2015 Code deal with the essential issue of fault-related reductions: (1) no significant fault; and (2) contaminated products.

No Significant Fault

According to the new 2015 Code, fault-related sanction reduction is inapplicable in cases of negligent ADRV if the athlete's negligence is assessed to be above the No Significant Fault (NSF) threshold. Thus, beyond this threshold, the standard sanction of Article 10.2.2 of the 2015 Code, a two-year period of ineligibility, remains in force, whereas a reduced sanction is possible if the athlete's degree of fault lies below the threshold. This rule applies regardless of which prohibited substance or method is involved. In order to reach the NSF threshold, the athlete is not required to have taken *all* necessary precautions.[32] On the contrary, it is important not to impose exaggerated requirements on what qualifies as NSF, because the degree of fault is ultimately doubly relevant.[33] It determines not only whether a reduced sanction is at all possible but also the length of the specific period of ineligibility within the applicable range. Hence, placing excessive demands on the NSF threshold ultimately leaves little room to reasonably determine the specific and appropriate period of ineligibility within the available range of sanctions. According to CAS jurisprudence, the NSF threshold is already achieved if the athlete 'take[s] the clear and obvious precautions which any human being would take' in the particular situation.[34] This NSF scale is flexible,[35] because what may be expected from a reasonable athlete in a given situation in terms of 'obvious and clear precautions' depends on the actual risk exposure. The greater and more obvious the risk, the more the athlete may be required and expected to observe certain precautions. In the case of products that are, for example, being advertised as performance enhancing or used for therapeutic purposes, the standard for 'clear and obvious precautions' must therefore be comparatively high.[36]

[31] 2015 Code art 10.6.

[32] Lewis and Taylor (n 20) [C2.222].

[33] *Hans Knauss v FIS* (Award, Court of Arbitration for Sport, Case No CAS 2005/A/847, 20 July 2005) 15 [38]. See also Lewis and Taylor (n 20) [C2.209].

[34] *Hans Knauss v FIS* (Award, Court of Arbitration for Sport, Case No CAS 2005/A/847, 20 July 2005) 9 [17]. See also Lewis and Taylor (n 20) [C2.224], discussion of 'reasonable steps'.

[35] See Fuchs (n 18) 138.

[36] For an analysis of CAS jurisprudence, see David (n 1) 291–302.

Contaminated Products

A further significant change concerning fault-related reductions has been introduced by the following provision of Article 10.5.1.2 of the 2015 Code:

> In cases where the *Athlete* or other *Person* can establish *No Significant Fault or Negligence* and that the detected *Prohibited Substance* came from a *Contaminated Product*, then the period of *Ineligibility* shall be, at a minimum, a reprimand and no period of *Ineligibility*, and at a maximum, two years *Ineligibility*, depending on the *Athlete*'s or other *Person*'s degree of *Fault*.

The applicable framework of sanctions primarily depends on the nature of the substance detected in an athlete's sample. If the ADRV concerns a 'specified substance'[37] and the NSF threshold is reached, then the period of ineligibility basically ranges from a reprimand to a two-year period of ineligibility.[38] By contrast, if a non-specified substance is involved, the sanction for the identical ADRV ranges only from one to two years. By imposing different sanctions depending on what prohibited substance or method the athlete is found to have used, a variety of circumstances can be taken into account. For one thing, this differentiation indicates the particular reprehensibility ascribed to the application of certain specific substances and methods in sports.[39] For another, the differentiation also makes allowance for the fact that, precisely in cases of specified substances, there is a 'greater likelihood' of accidental use, that is, for purposes other than to enhance performance.

Admittedly, this is a typologistic approach which in individual cases may lead to injustices, as, for instance, in a CAS proceeding[40] that was based on the following circumstances: Jessica Hardy, the world-class swimmer, had been taking a dietary supplement from manufacturer A over an extended period of eight months prior to the Olympic Games in Beijing. She was aware that sports organisations regularly issue general warnings regarding the use of dietary supplements due to various past discoveries of contaminated products on the market—that is, products containing substances (even if only in traces) prohibited in sports, without any respective information on the packaging or its insert. In view of these general warnings, Hardy had taken several precautions. For example, she had enquired with the manufacturer, which assured her that the composition of its products was tested by an independent expert. She had also made enquiries with other 'experts' to convince herself of the 'reliability' of the product from

[37] 2015 Code arts 2.1–2.2.

[38] ibid art 10.5.1.1.

[39] However, this is a secondary point of view, as indicated in the comment on art 4.2.2 of the 2015 Code, which states: 'The Specified Substances identified in Article 4.2.2 should not in any way be considered less important or less dangerous than other doping substances.'

[40] *World Anti-Doping Agency v Jessica Hardy* (Award, Court of Arbitration for Sport, Case No CAS 2009/A/1870, 21 May 2010). See also Haas (n 21) 634.

manufacturer A. Unfortunately, one of the many packages of food supplement used by her contained clenbuterol, a prohibited, 'non-specified' substance.

The CAS panel in the case considered the NSF threshold to have been attained, and imposed a sanction at the low end of the range, due to the slightness of Ms Hardy's 'residual fault'. Since a 'non-specified' substance was involved, however, the CAS panel, under the 2009 Code, had only limited scope to apply a reduced sanction and had to levy a one-year period of ineligibility.[41] If, instead, a 'specified' substance had been at stake, then—all other factors remaining being equal—a much shorter ineligibility period, or maybe even only a reprimand, might have been possible in this case. Whether, in a case of contaminated food supplements, the sanction can be reduced as far down as a reprimand or only to one year of ineligibility ultimately depends on a random factor—completely outside the athlete's sphere of influence—namely the kind of substance with which the product is contaminated. Such a significant divergence, depending on what kind of prohibited substance is detected in the athlete's sample, is inadequate, considering that the athlete's 'criminal energy' or degree of fault is the same in either case. With the new Article 10.5.1.2 of the 2015 Code, this inequality in treatment has been remedied and a more athlete-friendly range of sanctions is now available, even if the product the athlete has been using is contaminated with a 'non-specified' substance.

The Term 'Contaminated Product'

Reduction of sanctions pursuant to Article 10.5.1.2 of the 2015 Code is linked to the term 'contaminated product', which is defined as '[a] product that contains a *Prohibited Substance* that is not disclosed on the product label or in information available in a reasonable Internet search'.[42] In other words, if the prohibited substance is declared on the product itself or an accompanying package insert, the qualification 'contaminated product' is excluded by definition and Article 10.5.1.2 of the 2015 Code is inapplicable. Another, more difficult matter concerns the conditions under which the prohibited substance is deemed to be disclosed in information sources available in a reasonable Internet search. The problem starts with the issue of what requirements there are for a 'reasonable Internet search'—that is, what language or which search engine is to be used, or what passes as 'reasonable' if Internet access is limited or unavailable etc.[43] Still more doubtful is the point by which the prohibited substance has been revealed by the Internet search.[44] Does the prohibited substance have to be listed by name or is the substance already sufficiently disclosed if the product effects are described and advertised on the website in a way typical for prohibited substances (eg, 'extreme muscle growth')?

[41] *World Anti-Doping Agency v Jessica Hardy* (n 40) 33 [126].

[42] 2015 Code app 1 (definition of 'contaminated product').

[43] See also Rigozzi, Viret and Wisnosky (n 13) 24 [133].

[44] See, eg, Antonio Rigozzi et al, 'Breaking Down the Process for Determining a Basic Sanction under the 2015 World Anti-Doping Code' (2015) 15 *International Sports Law Journal* 3, 40–41 [6.2.3.2].

Better reasons seem to support a narrow interpretation, according to which the prohibited substance needs to be identified or listed by name. However, it does not follow from this that the manner in which a product is advertised on the Internet is of no relevance for assessing the sanction. Rather, it is a factor to be weighed against the athlete's due care requirements when deciding whether or not the athlete's safety precautions measure up to the NSF threshold.

Athlete Support Person

The lack of ability to impose obligations and sanctions on the athletes' entourage (eg, their coaches and physicians) has long been one of the major concerns in the fight against doping.[45] The athlete's entourage plays an eminent role in facilitating doping.[46] This is why the 2015 Code—much more heavily than the previous versions of the 2015 Code—focuses on the athlete's entourage, also referred to as athlete support personnel (ASP).[47] The term 'ASP' is described as follows: 'Any coach, trainer, manager, agent, team staff, official, medical, paramedical personnel, parent or any other *Person* working with, treating or assisting an *Athlete* participating in or preparing for sports *Competition*.'[48] The 2015 Code essentially introduces the following reforms: (1) prohibited association; (2) assisting in violating the prohibition against participation; (3) automatic investigations against ASPs; and (4) strengthening the role model obligations of ASP.

Prohibited Association

Quite often in practice, ASPs, despite having been sentenced to a period of ineligibility or even completely excluded from the sports community due to involvement in doping practices, nonetheless continue unabashedly to provide services to athletes, clubs or federations.[49] Consequently, there is a risk that these people

[45] Rigozzi, Viret and Wisnosky (n 13) 14 [73].

[46] ibid.

[47] For an analysis, see ibid 14–15 [74].

[48] The World Anti-Doping Code 2015 app 1 (definition of 'athlete support personnel').

[49] See, eg, *Emil Hoch v FIS* (Award, Court of Arbitration for Sport, Case No CAS 2008/A/1513, 26 January 2009); *Giuseppe Gibilisco v CONI* (Award, Court of Arbitration for Sport, Case No CAS 2007/A/1428, 9 May 2008); *Danilo Di Luca v CONI* (Award, Court of Arbitration for Sport, Case No CAS 2007/A/1433, 30 April 2008); *CONI v Fabrizio Macchi* (Award, Court of Arbitration for Sport, Case No CAS 2012/A/2992, 11 June 2013); *Ivan Stevic v CONI* (Award, Court of Arbitration for Sport, Case No CAS 2008/A/1684, 23 March 2009); *Marco Cedroni v CONI* (Award, Court of Arbitration for Sport, Case No CAS 2008/A/1618, 22 December 2008).

will continue to aid and abet doping. To make this harder in future and to ostracise such individuals more efficiently, the 2015 Code has introduced a boycott provision in Article 2.10. It considers an ADRV to be established if an athlete or other person subject to the authority of an ADO engages the services of an ASP on whom a period of ineligibility has been imposed,[50] or would have been imposed if the ASP were subject to the authority and jurisdiction of an ADO.[51] The group of persons defined in Articles 2.10.1 and 2.10.2 of the 2015 Code has thus become virtually 'untouchable' for anyone participating in organised sports—athletes, club managers, heads of other national and international sports organisations. They may not establish professional or sport-related contact with such individuals, whether directly or through intermediaries.[52] Any breach of this provision is subject to a two-year period of ineligibility.[53] According to the comment on Article 10.2 of the 2015 Code, prohibited professional or sports-related contact includes:

> [O]btaining training, strategy, technique, nutrition or medical advice; obtaining therapy, treatment or prescriptions; providing any bodily products for analysis; or allowing the Athlete Support Person to serve as an agent or representative. Prohibited association need not involve any form of compensation.

As a central register of these 'untouchables' does not exist, athletes cannot inform themselves as to whether their ASP is serving a period of ineligibility or was engaged in doping conduct that would have constituted an ADRV if the Code were applicable to it. Therefore, a certain safeguard was put in place to protect athletes. It is designed such that an athlete can only become punishable under Article 10.2 of the 2015 Code after having been informed by the responsible ADO that he or she is maintaining 'undue' professional or sports-related contact to an ASP. Only an athlete who continues maintaining the 'undue' contact, despite prior warning, is guilty of an ADRV. In addition, a sanction may only be imposed if an athlete has the possibility to avoid contact with the 'untouchable'. For example, if a club has hired an 'untouchable' to coach a sports team, the athlete may well be under a contractual employment obligation to train with the team and with the coach in question. He or she can hardly be expected to breach his or her employment contract in order to comply with the boycott provision. However, the president of the club that engaged the 'untouchable' can very well be held liable of the ADRV according to Article 2.10 of the 2015 Code.

All doping-related sanctions issued by an ADO against an ASP are documented by that particular ADO. ADOs, however, do not collect data on convictions in criminal or professional proceedings. Organised sports bodies often do not even have access to this kind of information and therefore have no way of knowing whether a given ASP fulfils the factual criteria according to Article 2.10 of the 2015

[50] 2015 Code art 2.10.1.
[51] ibid art 2.10.2.
[52] ibid art 2.10.3.
[53] ibid art 10.3.5.

Code. The ASP is obliged, in order to fill this information gap, at least partially, to 'disclose to his or her *National Anti-Doping Organization* and International Federation any decision by a non-*Signatory* finding that he or she committed an anti-doping rule violation within the previous ten years'.[54]

Assisting in Violating the Prohibition against Participation

The status of an athlete during the period of ineligibility is defined in Article 10.12 of the Code 2015. According to Article 10.12.1, no:

> *Athlete* ... who has been declared *Ineligible* may, during the period of *Ineligibility*, participate in any capacity in a *Competition* or activity ... authorized or organized by any *Signatory*, *Signatory*'s member organization, or a club or other member organization of a *Signatory*'s member organization.

Any transgression on the athlete's part further prolongs the sanction period.[55] Where an ASP assists an athlete in violating the prohibition against participation during ineligibility, the ASP is also subject to sanctioning pursuant to Article 2.9 of the 2015 Code. This derives from the express wording of the last paragraph of Article 10.12.3 of the 2015 Code. Complicity of a person in an ADRV of another person is sanctionable in accordance with Article 2.9 of the 2015 Code with a standard period of ineligibility of two to four years.[56]

Automatic Investigations against ASP

The 2015 Code obliges IFs and ADOs to oversee the activities of ASPs more effectively. As a novelty, the new 2015 Code provides that certain situations require the automatic initiation of investigations against ASPs. This applies if the ASP has provided support to a minor who gets involved in an ADRV, or to 'more than one *Athlete* found to have committed an anti-doping rule violation'.[57]

Supplementing the above provisions, Article 21.2.5 of the 2015 Code stipulates that the ASP is obliged to 'cooperate with *Anti-Doping Organizations* investigating anti-doping rule violations', to which the comment specifies: 'Failure to cooperate is not an anti-doping rule violation under the Code, but it may be the basis

[54] ibid art 21.2.4.
[55] ibid art 10.12.3.
[56] ibid art 10.3.4.
[57] ibid arts 20.3.10, 20.5.9.

for disciplinary action under a stakeholder's rules.' In other words, the comment entrusts the respective ADO with deciding whether or not to back up the ASP's duty to cooperate with disciplinary sanctions. The vagueness of this provision is due the fact that there is little certainty about the extent and scope of the duty to cooperate. This is particularly true concerning the question of whether and to what extent the duty includes assistance in uncovering an ADRV committed by the ASP, which bears upon the criminal law principle of *nemo tenetur se ipsum accusare*, that is, no one need accuse himself. Whether and to what extent this principle imposes limits on the ASP's obligation to cooperate is a legal issue in need of further analysis. On the one hand, it is generally accepted that principles developed for criminal law cannot be applied indiscriminately to doping-related disciplinary proceedings. This is reflected, for example, in the fact that athletes are also obliged—under threat of a doping sanction—to submit doping samples, and thus to cooperate in the detection of doping offences they may have committed.[58] On the other hand, an expert opinion commissioned at the time that the 2009 Code was in force presupposes that *nemo tenetur* in principle also applies to doping-related disciplinary proceedings.[59]

Strengthening the Role Model Obligations of ASP

Whenever ASPs are in possession of prohibited substances or methods without valid justification, they commit, in principle, an ADRV.[60] The standard sanction in this case is four or two years of ineligibility, depending on whether the violation was committed intentionally or not.[61] It must be noted that out-of-competition possession of a substance prohibited only in-competition is allowed. However, since ASPs also serve as role models for athletes, Article 21.2.6 of the 2015 Code states that, even in cases where the possession of a prohibited substance does not constitute an ADRV, an ASP 'shall not *Use* or *Possess* any *Prohibited Substances* or *Prohibited Method* without valid justification'. The comment on Article 21.2.6 of the 2015 Code explains why such a requirement—beyond Article 2.6—has been put in place:

> In those situations where Use or personal Possession of a Prohibited Substance or Prohibited Method by an Athlete Support Person without justification is not an anti-doping rule violation under the Code, it should be subject to other sport

[58] ibid art 2.3.

[59] See Gabrielle Kauffmann-Kohler and Antonio Rigozzi, 'Legal Opinion on the Conformity of Article 10.6 of the 2007 Draft World Anti-Doping Code with the Fundamental Rights of Athletes' (13 November 2007) WADA 36 [100] https://wada-main-prod.s3.amazonaws.com/resources/files/Legal_Opinion_Conformity_10_6_complete_document.pdf.

[60] 2015 Code art 2.6 ('possession of a prohibited substance or method').

[61] ibid art 10.2.

disciplinary rules. Coaches and other Athlete Support Personnel are often role models for Athletes. They should not be engaging in personal conduct which conflicts with their responsibility to encourage their Athletes not to dope.

In addition, the rules relating to ASPs are rounded off by two further provisions specifically addressing the IFs[62] and NOCs,[63] and requiring them: 'To have disciplinary rules in place … to prevent *Athlete Support Personnel* who are *Using Prohibited Substances* or *Prohibited Methods* without valid justification from providing support to *Athletes* within … [their] authority.' In other words, an ASP's infringement of Article 21.2.6 of the 2015 Code does not amount to an ADRV, but the sport organisations are nevertheless called upon to sanction such an infringement based on their general disciplinary rules.[64] The type of disciplinary sanction to be imposed is only suggested in general terms by stating that the ASP is barred from 'providing support to athletes'. The duration of the disciplinary sanction is not specified either, but it is hardly conceivable that an ASP can be banished from professional practice permanently or for a long time on account of personal misconduct that does not even constitute an ADRV.

Access to Justice

The 2015 Code provides for a wide range of decisions which affect the rights of the various involved parties. If, however, third-party rights are impinged upon, possibilities of legal protection must be available. The total exclusion of judicial protection is only permissible in very restricted, exceptional cases requiring special justification.

Exception: Exclusion of All Judicial Protection

The Code recognises only a few cases in which all judicial protection is excluded. For the most part, this concerns 'decisions' of WADA. For instance, WADA decisions pursuant to Article 10.6.1.2 of the Code on 'what it considers to be an appropriate suspension of the otherwise applicable period of *Ineligibility*' cannot be appealed by any other ADO. A further example is Article 4.3.3 of the 2015 Code, according to which:

> *WADA*'s determination of the *Prohibited Substances* and *Prohibited Methods* that will be included on the *Prohibited List*, the classification of substances into categories on

[62] ibid art 20.3.15.
[63] ibid art 20.4.13.
[64] For reservations voiced over art 21.2.6 of the 2015 Code, see Rigozzi, Viret and Wisnosky (n 13) 18 [88].

the *Prohibited List*, and the classification of a substance as prohibited at all times or *In-Competition* only, is final and shall not be subject to challenge by an *Athlete* or other *Person*.[65]

To ensure the equal treatment of all athletes, the content of the Prohibited List, that is, the factual designation of substances and methods fulfilling the various list criteria, is reviewed and reconfirmed by expert determination at annual intervals, after which it is binding on the entire world of organised sports. The expert in this context is the 'List Expert Group', that is, a panel of scientists chosen by WADA for their international expertise.[66] Once every year, this panel, in a transparent procedure, recommends changes to the Prohibited List, which are then adopted by WADA's executive committee so as to become binding for the whole of organised sports.[67] The fact that the Prohibited List cannot be challenged in individual doping proceedings is well justified, not only by the necessity of equal treatment of all athletes but also because the annual List Expert Group assessment is seen as an anticipated expertise, thus eliminating the need for reassessment in individual doping proceedings.[68]

Concentration of Jurisdiction at CAS

To ensure consistent and uniform application, the 2015 Code—just like its predecessors—provides for the concentration of doping-related proceedings at CAS in Lausanne.[69] Strictly speaking, this is a form of compulsory arbitration, the individual only having a choice between accepting the arbitration agreement or refraining from participation in organised sports altogether. In recent years the lawfulness of compulsory doping-related arbitration has been under attack, both before CAS[70] and the state courts.[71] It is beyond question that the legitimisation

[65] See David (n 1) 85. See also *FINA v Kreutzmann* (Award, Court of Arbitration for Sport, Case No CAS 2005/A/921, 18 January 2006) [32].

[66] The members of the Prohibited List Expert Group can be found at WADA, 'Prohibited List Expert Group' (2015) https://www.wada-ama.org/en/node/159.

[67] For more details, see WADA, 'Welcome to the List' (2015) http://list.wada-ama.org.

[68] Ultimately agreeing, see Kern (n 11) 383.

[69] 2015 Code art 13.

[70] *Stichting Anti-Doping Autoriteit Nederland v W* (Award, Court of Arbitration for Sport, Case Nos CAS 2010/A/2311 and 2312, 22 August 2011) 20 [6.13].

[71] See, eg, Oberlandesgericht München (Higher Munich Regional Court), U 1110/14 Kart, 15 January 2015; Landesgericht München [Munich Regional Court], 37 O 28331/12, 26 February 2014. See comments by Laurence Burger and Perréard de Boccard, 'Invalidity of Arbitration Agreement When Lack of Choice to Refuse it' *Kluwer Arbitration Blog* (12 March 2014) http://kluwerarbitrationblog.com/2014/03/12/invalidity-of-arbitration-agreement-when-lack-of-choice-to-refuse-it; Ian Mill, 'Sports Arbitration: A Matter of Choice?' *Sports Law Bulletin* (25 March 2014) http://sportslawbulletin.org/2014/03/25/sports-arbitration-a-matter-of-choice; Richard Happ, René-Alexander

of the decision-making competence of the arbitral tribunal is based on the parties' will, and that this autonomy is somewhat restricted here. However, this alone does not yet invalidate the arbitration agreement in favour of CAS. Indeed, weighty reasons of good administration of justice support a concentration of jurisdiction in favour of arbitration; arbitration is the only way to guarantee a globally consistent and uniform application of the 2015 Code independently of national sports interests.

The factual scope of the arbitration clause in Article 13.1 of the 2015 Code is outlined in detail in Article 13.2, which itemises the various kinds of decision that can be brought before CAS. There remain a small number of gaps:

1. In the event of an ASP's breach of Article 20.4.13 of the 2015 Code, recourse to CAS is not provided for, as discussed above.
2. Ingestion of a prohibited substance by an ASP, unless its possession already constitutes an ADRV, needs to be sanctioned as a general disciplinary offence, which in itself does not represent an ADRV (see above). If a respective disciplinary measure is imposed against the ASP, recourse to CAS is not possible according to Article 13.2 of the Code.
3. The same applies if an ADO provides for a disciplinary sanction in the event that an ASP does not 'cooperate with *Anti-Doping Organizations* investigating anti-doping rule violations';[72] this is because the failure to cooperate constitutes no ADRV and therefore does not fall within the objective scope of the arbitration clause in Article 13.2.
4. A final difficulty arises in the case of Article 10.2 ('prohibited association'). As mentioned above, this is a boycott measure directed, from a formal perspective, at athletes and other persons subject to the authority of an ADO, but in actual fact is addressed to offending ASPs in order to stop them from further providing services to any members of the sports community. Therefore, when an athlete is convicted of an ADRV for breaching Article 10.2, this measure affects not only the athlete's rights but also those of the boycotted ASP. Unlike the athlete, however, the ASP—if operating outside organised sports—is not subject to the Code and thus is not bound by the arbitration clause in Article 13.1 of the 2015 Code either. Other than the athlete, the ASP can challenge the measure before the state courts. For cases involving Article 10.2 of the 2015 Code, this results in a risk of concurrent jurisdiction before arbitral tribunals and state courts, and ultimately of conflicting decisions.

Hirth and Karolin Hoffmann, 'Germany' [2015] *European, Middle Eastern and African Arbitration Review* http://globalarbitrationreview.com/reviews/67/sections/233/chapters/2692/germany; Christian Duve and Karl Ömer Rösch, 'Der Fall Pechstein: Kein Startschuss für eine Neugestaltung der Sportschiedsgerichtsbarkeit' [2014] 12 *SchiedsVZ* 216; Lukas Handschin and Tony M Schütz, 'Bemerkungen zum Fall Pechstein' [2014] 5 SpuRt 179; Ulrich Haas, 'Zwangsschiedsgerichtsbarkeit im Sport und EMRK' (2014) 32(4) *ASA Bulletin* 707.

[72] 2015 Code art 21.2.5.

Scope of Review

The mandate of a CAS panel in doping-related disputes is basically determined by the CAS Procedural Rules (hereinafter the CAS Code). Article R57(1) states: 'The Panel shall have full power to review the facts and the law. It may issue a new decision which replaces the decision challenged or annul the decision and refer the case back to the previous instance.'

The CAS's so-called 'de novo mandate' is limited in two ways. One exception arises directly from the CAS Code itself; Article R57(3) states that: 'The Panel has discretion to exclude evidence presented by the parties if it was available to them or could reasonably have been discovered by them before the challenged decision was rendered.' The second exception derives from CAS jurisprudence, which in some instances interprets the de novo mandate of Article R57(1) of the CAS Code in the narrow sense of a limited cognition.[73] To this effect, for example, a CAS decision states:

> To the extent the exercise of such discretion does not run against the internal rules of the association, the mandatory provisions of the law applicable or even fundamental general principles of law, the Panel finds itself limited by the respect to be paid to the freedom of association to set the way to secure observance by its associates of the association rules ... To [the] extent [that] the sanction is not evidently and grossly disproportionate to the offence, therefore, it is appropriate to let the sanction remain as determined by the Chamber.[74]

Restrictions of the power of review of a CAS panel are problematic both as to their justification and in respect of their consequences. A CAS panel has formulated these concerns as follows:

> CAS Panels in the past have contrary to the clear wording accepted restrictions to Art. R57 of the CAS Code, where the first instance was—in view of the very special circumstances of the case and/or in view of its technical expertise—in a better position to decide the matter (e.g. field of play decisions). However, no such specific situation is given in the case at hand. The rules that are at stake here are based on the WADC, the purpose of which is to ensure the uniform application of anti-doping standards throughout the world and across all sports. The Sole Arbitrator cannot see why a federation would have more expertise in applying these rules of a truly transnational character than CAS Panels or why the danger that someone would adjudicate the matter *'according to its subjective sensitivity'* ... is any different at the CAS level or the level of the federation organs.

[73] For an overview of the problem, see Ulrich Haas, 'Die Kognition des Court of Arbitration for Sport (CAS) in dopingbezogenen Streitigkeiten' in Pascal Mahon and Minh Son Nguyen (eds), *L'activité et l'éspace, Mélanges en l'honneur de Piermarco Zen-Ruffinen* (Basel, Helbing Lichtenhahn, 2012) 51. See also Rigozzi, Viret and Wisnosky (n 13) 35–36 [204]–[211].

[74] *Daniute v International DanceSport Federation* (Award, Court of Arbitration for Sport, Case No CAS 2006/A/1175, 26 June 2007) 13 [47]–[48].

> Furthermore, the Sole Arbitrator is hesitant to follow the Respondent's view that limits to the mandate of CAS Panels must be imposed in order to deter *'the systematic filing of appeals'*. It is rather doubtful whether a literal application of Art. R57 of the CAS Code really results in the (negative) behavioural consequences described by the Respondent. Even if it were so, these consequences would have to be balanced with those resulting from granting (partial) immunity to the decisions by organs of federation, because the latter might have negative behavioural consequences as well. Partial immunity might induce organs of federations (to a certain extent) to misuse their adjudicative powers to the detriment of the athletes. The Sole Arbitrator is of the view that it does not seem particularly helpful to embark in such behavioural speculations (either in favour or against a partial immunity of decisions of federations). Instead, the Sole Arbitrator would like to point at Art. 6(1) of the European Convention of Human Rights (hereinafter referred to as 'ECHR') to which he is indirectly bound (cf. CAS 2011/A/2384 & 2386 [*UCI and WADA v Contador Velasco and SCF*], paras. 17 et seq.; CAS 2010/A/2311 & 2312 [*NADO and KNSB v Lommers*], paras. 6.13 et seq.). According thereto, a person affected by a decision must have, in principle, access to (at least) one instance of justice. It goes without saying that doping sanctions strongly affect the rights of an athlete and that federation instances do not provide for access to justice within the meaning of Art. 6(1) ECHR, since they do not guarantee adjudication of the facts and the law by a truly independent judicial instance. Restrictions to the fundamental right of access to justice should not be accepted easily, but only where such restrictions are justified both in the interest of good administration of justice and proportionality. The Sole Arbitrator fails to see why a restriction of his mandate—contrary to the clear wording of the Art. R57 of the CAS Code—would be in the interest of good administration of justice.[75]

For the future, the new 2015 Code has now clearly established that no restrictions of de novo competence apply at the expense of the CAS panel in doping-related disputes. Article R57(3) of the CAS Code is abrogated in the context of ADRV disputes by Article 13.1.1 of the 2015 Code, which states: 'The scope of review on appeal includes all issues relevant to the matter and is expressly not limited to the issues or scope of review before the initial decision maker.' And, whereas in former CAS case law partial immunity was occasionally granted to doping-related decisions of sports organisation, this jurisprudence has been abolished by Article 13.1.2 of the [2015 Code], which reads: 'In making its decision, *CAS* need not give deference to the discretion exercised by the body whose decision is being appealed.'

From a Quantitative to a Qualitative Anti-doping Policy

Even nowadays, the effectiveness of anti-doping policies is still assessed largely in quantitative terms. Accordingly, the IOC document states: 'Since then [from the

[75] *Mads Glasner v Fédération Internationale de Natation* (Award, Court of Arbitration for Sport, Case No CAS 2013/A/3274, 31 January 2014) 16–17 [64]–[65].

creation of WADA in 1999], the IOC has stepped up the number of tests (from 2,359 at Sydney in 2000 to 5,051 at London in 2012).'[76] However, numbers alone say little about the effectiveness of a particular anti-doping policy as the statistics conceal various aspects.

First, the statistics do not disclose that samples collected from athletes are not tested for all substances included on the Prohibited List. As a matter of fact, laboratories routinely analyse the samples only for a selection of those substances, referred to as the 'standard menu'.[77] Therefore, for instance, an athlete's sample will only be tested for growth hormones (HGH) or erythropoietin (EPO) upon express instruction by the respective ADO that commissioned the sample collection. In endurance sports, unless specifically ordered, no analysis of athletes' samples for EPO will be performed and, as a consequence, no evidence of this prohibited substance will be established. An ADO may not choose to prescribe such additional analyses for a variety of reasons. On the financial side, additional analyses cause additional costs and, with the budget remaining the same, an ADO would consequently have to reduce the number of doping tests undertaken. This, in turn, harbours significant potential for conflict since the testing figures are usually published. On the practical side, some laboratories are not equipped to perform all additional analyses. So, if an ADO primarily relies on such a laboratory, either by choice or by legal obligation, then the samples will not be checked for the respective substances. Finally, ADOs might not be interested in revealing particularly high numbers of positive doping test results (eg, for EPO) in their statistics. They will therefore refrain from commissioning those special analyses from the laboratories in the first place.

Second, the statistics do not show that the various laboratories employ different standards. Though all laboratories are WADA-accredited and have to observe a certain minimum standard for each individual method of analysis, some laboratories are able to exceed that minimum standard by far—at least for some analysis techniques. So whether or not a finding qualifies as adverse may depend on the mere contingency of where an athlete's sample was analysed. The cyclist Alberto Contador, for example, had the 'misfortune' that his sample, taken during the Tour de France 2010, was tested for anabolic steroids in Cologne and not in another laboratory.[78] The Cologne laboratory at the time was able to trace much lower concentrations of clenbuterol than most other laboratories. The choice of laboratory to which a sample is sent for analysis does not necessarily form part of a coherent testing strategy, but is in most cases the result of coincidences, national pride or cost considerations as different laboratories offering analytical services may vary widely with regard to commercial terms.

[76] IOC, 'Factsheet—The Fight against Doping and Promotion of Athletes' Health—Update January 2014' (January 2014) 1, http://www.olympic.org/documents/reference_documents_factsheets/fight_against_doping.pdf.

[77] See also Rigozzi, Viret and Wisnosky (n 13) 8 [41].

[78] See *Union Cycliste Internationale v Alberto Contador Velasco* (Award, Court of Arbitration for Sport, Case Nos CAS 2011/A/2384 and 2386, 6 February 2012).

Third, what the statistics do not reveal is the fact that, increasingly, athletes are not convicted of doping based on sample analysis,[79] but through investigations and intelligence, as happened in the Armstrong case.[80] Accordingly, exclusive emphasis on sample collection can certainly not be taken as proof of an effective anti-doping policy.

The 2015 Code is a decisive step away from quantitative analysis towards a more quality-oriented approach. Various measures contribute to this goal.

Article 5.4 of the 2015 Code stipulates that each ADO should base its test distribution plan on a risk analysis. The test distribution plan lays down the number and categories of tests (in- or out-of-competition; blood or urine samples) that are to be conducted, as well as the testing menu, the sports types or sports disciplines, the athletes and the performance levels to be included in testing. Test distribution plans have to be adequately geared towards the risk of the specific sport or discipline. ADOs are not free in their assessment of whether and to what extent a sport or discipline is susceptible to doping. Instead, the minimum standard applying to risk analysis is specified in a technical document[81] prepared by WADA in collaboration with other stakeholders. Furthermore, Article 5.4.2 of the 2015 Code stipulates that: 'Each *Anti-Doping Organization* shall provide *WADA* upon request with a copy of its current distribution plan.' In this way, WADA can assure itself of the effectiveness of each organisation's anti-doping policy.

Article 6.4.3 of the 2015 Code moreover stipulates that laboratories must not necessarily adhere to the testing menu specified by the ADO. The provision reads:

> As provided in the International Standard for Laboratories, laboratories at their own initiative and expense may analyze *Samples* for *Prohibited Substances* or *Prohibited Methods* not included on the *Sample* analysis menu described in the Technical Document or specified by the *Testing* authority. Results from any such analysis shall be reported and have the same validity and *Consequence* as any other analytical result.

A further move towards a qualitative approach in the fight against doping can be found in Article 5.8 of the 2015 Code. This provision is intended to ensure that ADOs, apart from conducting doping tests, will in the future be able to also perform investigations and gather intelligence in order to take into account the growing importance of circumstantial evidence in the fight against doping.[82] Insights gained through intelligence gathering will also help in designing effective test distribution plans.

[79] See generally WADA, International Standard for Testing and Investigations (January 2015) art 11.2.1.

[80] See also Rigozzi, Viret and Wisnosky (n 13) 3 [7].

[81] See WADA, 'Technical Document for Sport Specific Analysis—TD2014SSA' (1 January 2015) https://wada-main-prod.s3.amazonaws.com/resources/files/wada-tdssa-v2.2-en.pdf.

[82] Richard H McLaren, 'An Overview of Non-analytical Positive and Circumstantial Evidence Cases in Sports' (2006) 16 *Marquette Sports Law Review* 193, 194. See also Rigozzi, Viret and Wisnosky (n 13) 4 [13]–[14].

Finally, according to the second paragraph of Article 6.5 of the 2015 Code, athlete samples that have not been tested positive may at a later point be re-analysed for the presence of prohibited substances if, for instance, improved analysis techniques have been introduced either generally or at the respective laboratory. The provision expressly states:

> Samples may be stored and subjected to further analyses for the purpose of Article 6.2 at any time exclusively at the direction of the *Anti-Doping Organization* that initiated and directed *Sample* collection or *WADA* ... Further analysis of *Samples* shall conform with the requirements of the International Standard for Laboratories and the International Standard for Testing and Investigations.

Part II

The World Anti-Doping Code and the Athletes

3

'Do What I Say, Not What I Do': Is This the 'Play True' Reality of the World Anti-Doping Code?

THOMAS HICKIE*

Introduction—The World Anti-Doping Code: 'Play True' and 'Olympism'

The World Anti-Doping Agency (WADA) was established on 10 November 1999 in Lausanne, Switzerland 'as a foundation under the initiative' of the International Olympic Committee (IOC) 'with the support and participation of intergovernmental organizations, governments, public authorities and other public and private bodies fighting doping in sport'.[1] Just over three years later, at Copenhagen on 5 March 2003, the final version of the World Anti-Doping Code (hereinafter the Code) was agreed upon, which came into effect on 1 January 2004.[2] A revised Code was adopted by WADA's Foundation Board in November 2007, taking effect from 1 January 2009.[3] A further review of the Code was adopted by WADA's Foundation Board on 15 November 2013 that took effect as from 1 January 2015.[4]

* Barrister, Sydney.

[1] WADA, 'Who are We', 'The Agency's History', www.wada-ama.org/en/who-we-are.

[2] Larry D Bowers, 'The International Antidoping System and Why it Works' (2009) 55(8) *Clinical Chemistry* 1456.

[3] ibid.

[4] See WADA, World Anti-Doping Code Final Draft 2015, 2, https://wada-main-prod.s3.amazonaws.com/resources/files/wada-redline-2015-wadc-to-2009-wadc-en.pdf, and WADA, 'World Anti-Doping Code 2015', https://wada-main-prod.s3.amazonaws.com/resources/files/wada-2015-world-anti-doping-code.pdf.

As to the current status of the WADA Foundation Board, according to its website, 'the 38-member Foundation Board is WADA's supreme decision-making body. It is composed equally of representatives from the Olympic Movement and governments'.[5] The IOC is a private organisation based in Lausanne.[6] 'WADA is a Swiss private law Foundation' whose 'seat is in Lausanne, Switzerland, and its headquarters are in Montreal, Canada',[7] with regional offices in Cape Town, Tokyo and Montevideo.[8] For a private organisation and a private law foundation respectively, both the Olympic movement and WADA certainly have enormous influence.

The logo of both the WADA and its Code contain the slogan 'play true'.[9] According to WADA's website, 'the "play true" tag line encapsulates WADA's core values and is intended as a guiding principle for all athletes at every level of competition'.[10] The preamble to the 2015 Code states that the 'fundamental rationale for the World Anti-Doping Code' is 'to preserve what is intrinsically valuable about sport … it is the essence of Olympism; it is how we play true'.[11] This is further defined in the preamble to the Code by the statement that 'the spirit of sport … is reflected in values' such as 'ethics, fair play and honesty', and 'respect for rules and laws'.[12] However, neither the slogan 'play true' nor the term 'Olympism' is defined in the body of the Code or in its Appendix of 'Definitions'.[13]

The underlying premise of the Code[14] for sport is that fault does not have to be proved. Apart from the arguable unfairness of imposing absolute liability which prevails in much of the Code (that is, all that has to be proven is the ingestion of a banned substance, such that an athlete's explanation only goes to mitigation of penalty),[15] the Code may soon be heading in an even more questionable

[5] WADA, 'Who are We', 'Governance', https://www.wada-ama.org/en/governance.

[6] See, for example, 222; John Horne and Garry Whannel, *Understanding the Olympics*', Routledge, Abingdon, 2012, 37; 'Company overview of International Olympic Committee', Bloomberg Business, www.bloomberg.com/research/stocks/private/snapshot.asp?privcapId=5363066; Gus Lubin and Lawrence Delevingne, 'Olympics, Inc: Inside The Secretive, $6 Billion World of the International Olympic Committee', *Business Insider*, www.businessinsider.com/olympics-inc-inside-the-business-of-the-ioc/?r=AU&IR=T.

[7] WADA, 'Who are We', 'Governance', 'Statutes', https://www.wada-ama.org/en/governance.

[8] WADA, 'Regional Offices', www.wada-ama.org/en/regional-offices.

[9] See WADA website and WADA, World Anti-Doping Code, www.wada-ama.org/en.

[10] WADA, 'Who are We', 'Logo Story', www.wada-ama.org/en/who-we-are.

[11] 'World Anti-Doping Code' n 4, 14.

[12] ibid 14.

[13] See ibid 11–128 and 'Appendix One Definitions', 130–42.

[14] World Anti-Doping Authority, World Anti-Doping Code (1 January 2015).

[15] Absolute liability is where liability is imposed regardless of fault and no defences exist. This is in contrast to the onus normally on the prosecution required by the domestic criminal drug laws of Western democratic countries, which generally require the prosecution to prove a particular state of mind of the accused. It is important, however, to differentiate between parts of the Code where absolute liability applies. There are a few anti-doping rule violations (ADRVs) where 'fault' is a condition. For example, the attempted use of a prohibited substance in art 2.2 (see the comment in the Code to this article), as well as arts 2.3–2.5. The principle of strict liability applies only to the *presence* of a prohibited substance (art 2.1) and the *use* of a prohibited substance—see the definitions in

direction if the lead taken by Australia's anti-doping body is 'pushed' by WADA to be adopted elsewhere. In 2013, the Australian Sports Anti-Doping Authority (ASADA) successfully lobbied the Australian Federal Government to pass legislation giving the Chief Executive Officer (CEO) of ASADA the equivalent of criminal coercive powers. While preserving the right against self-incrimination, the legislation has made it a federal 'civil' offence for an athlete or support person to refuse to attend an interview with ASADA and/or produce documents.[16] This chapter considers the implications of such legislation.

The Australian Crime Commission Sees its Charter as Overlooking Fair Play in Australian Sport

The legislation passed by the Australian Parliament giving the CEO of ASADA the equivalent of criminal coercive powers was a direct consequence of a report released by the Australian Crime Commission (ACC) on 7 February 2013 entitled 'Organised Crime and Drugs in Sport: New Generation Performance and Image Enhancing Drugs and Organised Criminal Involvement in Their Use in Professional Sport'.[17] As the ACC report noted: 'In early 2012, the ACC, with the assistance of ASADA, began a project to consider the extent of use of PIEDs by professional athletes, the size of this market and the extent of organised criminal involvement.'[18] 'PIED' is an acronym for performance and image enhancing drugs.[19]

Apparently, 'data from the ACC's 2010–11 Illicit Drug Data Report indicated that the market for Performance and Image Enhancing Drugs (PIEDs) has

app 1 of the Code. As to the *consequences*, the concept of strict liability only applies to disqualification, not to periods of ineligibility. Under art 10, there is no period of ineligibility without fault. The rules are, however, harsh. This is particularly true for the onus of proof. The author thanks one of the co-editors for clarifying this issue.

[16] See Australian Sports Anti-Doping Authority Amendment Act 2013 (Cth) www.austlii.edu.au/au/legis/cth/num_act/asaaaa2013535. The legislation amended the Australian Sports Anti-Doping Authority Act 2006 (Cth). The specifics of the legislation will be discussed later in this chapter.

[17] Australian Crime Commission, 'Organised Crime and Drugs in Sport: New Generation Performance and Image Enhancing Drugs and Organised Criminal Involvement in Their Use in Professional Sport' (February 2013) https://www.crimecommission.gov.au/sites/default/files/organised-crime-and-drugs-in-sports-feb2013.pdf; see also Michael Gordon, 'This is the Blackest Day in Australian Sport' *Sydney Morning Herald* (8 February 2013) www.smh.com.au/national/this-is-the-blackest-day-in-australian-sport-20130207-2e1i3.html; Press Association, 'Australian Doping Report Represents "Blackest Day in Australian Sport"' *The Guardian* (7 February 2013) www.theguardian.com/sport/2013/feb/07/australian-doping-report-blackest-day.

[18] Australian Crime Commission (n 17) 4 (citations omitted).

[19] ibid.

expanded' in Australia.[20] Presumably, this was a shorthand way of saying that the Australian Crime Commission's officers, while working with Australian Customs and others, had noted a significant 'spike' in the number of PIEDs being imported into and/or in use in Australia. Whether this had links with the ongoing battle in the courts between the ACC (and its state counterparts) working at the behest of governments both at a national and a state level in their attempts to outlaw various bikie gangs (including their sources of income) was unstated.[21] According to the ACC's February 2013 report, 'the ACC has now identified use of these substances, which are prohibited by the World Anti-Doping Agency (WADA), by professional athletes in a number of sports in Australia. Widespread use has been identified or is suspected in a number of professional sporting codes'.[22]

So even though such substances may not have been illegal under Australian domestic law, they became of interest to the ACC because they were prohibited by WADA (a private body) based in Switzerland. Was this not a strange state of affairs? The ACC Report further noted:

> The PIEDs market does not rival the established markets for methylamphetamine, cocaine or heroin in terms of the risk and harms they pose to the Australian community, but it does currently, and has the potential to increasingly pose harm to the sector and the broader community out of all proportion to the relative size of the market. This is because of the special status of sport for Australia and Australians, and the enduring significance of concepts such as fairness and integrity in Australian sport …
>
> There are clear parallels between what has been discovered in Australia and the USADA investigation into Lance Armstrong, which underlines the transnational threat posed by doping to professional sport, both from a 'fair play' perspective and as a broader integrity issue.[23]

When and how the Australian Crime Commission came to decide that 'fairness and integrity in Australian sport' came within its charter is unstated. Also, does sport in Australia really have a 'special status' compared with many other countries? If so, what does that mean and did it justify the intervention of the ACC? Further, what was not explicitly stated in the ACC's report was that failing to abide by the loose and undefined concept of 'fair play' is not a federal criminal offence in Australia. What seems to be implied (and thus have attracted the interest of the ACC without it specifically saying so) was that somehow 'organised crime' (again an undefined and broad term) was involved in supplying PIEDs.

To discuss the alleged 'transnational threat posed by doping to professional sport' would require not just a separate publication, but a stringent analysis as

[20] ibid.

[21] See, eg, *X7 v Australian Crime Commission* (2013) 248 CLR 92; *Lee v New South Wales Crime Commission* (2013) 251 CLR 196. See also, eg, Mark Solomons, 'Challenge to Qld Anti-bikie Laws to Reach High Court within Weeks' *ABC News* (9 January 2014) www.abc.net.au/news/2014-01-09/challenge-to-qld-anti-bikie-laws-to-reach-high-court/5191620.

[22] ibid 4.

[23] Australian Crime Commission n 17, 36.

to the arbitrariness of WADA's prohibited list such that some drugs are demonised, while others, such as painkillers, are freely available—a code under which blood doping is banned, but athletes undergoing routine surgery does not raise a question. Indeed, it was reported in 2014 that 'stem cells placed into the knees' of some football players in Australia had 'helped resurrect their careers'.[24] Also, the arbitrary differentiation between banning and allowing the use of some substances depending upon whether the use has taken place 'in' or 'out-of-competition' is not persuasive. Surely it is likely that a substance is either bad for one's health and/or it is 'performance enhancing', whether it is taken 'in' or 'out-of-competition'?[25]

The Australian Sports Anti-Doping Authority Amendment Bill 2013 (Cth)

The day before the release of the ACC report on 7 February 2013 concerning the use of PIEDs by athletes in Australia, the Australian Sports Anti-Doping Authority Amendment Bill 2013 (hereinafter the Australian Sports Anti-Doping Bill) was introduced into the Australian Senate.[26] The Bill proposed to give additional investigative powers to the CEO of ASADA. A Senate inquiry into the Bill was then established. It heard evidence from a range of advocates of the new powers such as John Coates, the President of the Australian Olympic Committee (AOC), who was 'pushing for athletes to face jail for refusing to cooperate with doping investigations'.[27]

In response, Brendan Schwab, the General Secretary of the Australian Athletes' Alliance, made the point on the Australian radio programme *AM* that the 'whole concept that athletes would face a criminal penalty for a breach of contract is ridiculous and absurd, and needs to be looked at in that context' and that 'the threat of jail terms for those who refuse to be interviewed by Australia's anti-doping agency infringes the basic civil rights of sportspeople'.[28] He further noted that 'everyone should be under no illusion that the powers … under the existing anti-doping codes which have been agreed to by the athletes are extreme'.[29]

[24] Michael Carayannis, 'State of Origin: Stem Cells Give New Life to Worn-Out Knees' *Sydney Morning Herald* (25 May 2014) www.smh.com.au/rugby-league/league-news/state-of-origin-stem-cells-give-new-life-to-wornout-knees-20140525-zrnjs.html.

[25] The author thanks one of the co-editors for highlighting this issue.

[26] Rhonda Jolly, *Bills Digest*, No 92 of 2012–13 *19 March 2013) 4, www.aph.gov.au/Parliamentary_Business/Bills_Legislation/bd/bd1213a/13bd092.

[27] 'Coates Fronts Senate Inquiry' *ABC News* (1 March 2013) www.abc.net.au/news/2013-03-01/coates-fronts-senate-enquiry/4547506.

[28] ABC Radio, 'Jailing Doping Athletes "Draconian" and "Ridiculous"' *AM* (2 March 2013) www.abc.net.au/news/2013-03-02/jailing-doping-athletes-draconian-and-ridiculous/4549278.

[29] ibid.

It also needs to be asked whether the contractual agreement between the AOC and an athlete constitutes a fair bargain. Is an individual athlete really on an equal footing when bargaining with the AOC? In fact, is there any 'bargaining'? The reality is that an athlete is presented with the standard contract and either has to accept it (including its many draconian terms) or reject it and thus be excluded from participating in the Olympic Games. This appears to be particularly problematic where it is now a requirement that an athlete must also sign a statutory declaration 'declaring they haven't taken performance enhancing drugs' prior to acceptance into the team.[30]

As the AOC's President, John Coates, told the Australian radio programme *PM* in November 2012 when 'floating' the idea of having athletes sign statutory declarations:

> They volunteer to be members of our team and they volunteer to be members of our team on our conditions. They always have.
>
> If they say, 'Well that's a breach of my privacy', then we say, 'Well we don't want you in the team' …
>
> Statutory declarations signed under the Oaths Act of each of the respective states and territories—false content in those, or false swearing, carries with it quite onerous criminal convictions and sanctions.[31]

It was subsequently reported in February 2013 that:

> Coates circulated the final details of the profound 'Ethical Behaviour Bylaw' amendment to his executive on the same day the Australian Crime Commission tabled its devastating findings about widespread banned drug abuse in elite sport. Within a day, Coates reported unanimous approval …
>
> The AOC's draft statutory declaration informs athletes they are 'strongly encouraged to seek independent legal advice' before signing. The document outlines that making a false declaration about their doping history is a 'criminal offence and may attract significant penalties'. It cites penalties of up to two years' imprisonment if the offence is dealt with summarily, and up to five years' imprisonment if the offence is dealt with on indictment.[32]

Further, apart from amending its own by-laws affecting athletes involved with Olympic sports, the AOC was urging non-Olympic 'domestic sporting codes to follow suit'.[33] Coates stated: 'I would encourage them to look at what we've done, even down at a club level.'[34]

[30] The author thanks the anonymous peer reviewer of this chapter for highlighting this point. See also ABC Radio, 'AOC Wants Statutory Declarations from Athletes on Drugs' *PM* (2 November 2012) www.abc.net.au/pm/content/2012/s3624618.htm.

[31] ibid.

[32] Samantha Lane, 'Olympic Committee Takes Hardest Line' *Sydney Morning Herald* (9 February 2013) 3.

[33] ibid.

[34] ibid.

If the AOC was already requiring athletes under its jurisdiction to sign statutory declarations, what was the pressing need for the Australian Government to continue to proceed with legislation proposing to provide the CEO of ASADA with the equivalent of criminal coercive powers, particularly when one notes that ASADA's role has been to oversee that athletes conform to WADA's questionable absolute liability Code and arbitrary 'Prohibited List'?[35] Further, considering that a breach of the Code is, in effect, a contractual dispute between an athlete and a sports organiser, was not the proposed legislation somewhat excessive? Indeed, in late 2015, when ASADA was criticised for 'compelling athletes to give up their common law right to silence' by having 'inserted a provision in its 2015 anti-doping policy that requires athletes to give up the right, otherwise they cannot compete at the 2016 Rio Olympics',[36] ASADA issued a media release in response noting:

> ASADA does not mandate any sport to abrogate athletes of their privilege against self-incrimination in anti-doping investigations.
>
> Under ASADA's legislation, sports determine their own anti-doping policies, which are contractual arrangements with their members.[37]

The ASADA Peptides Saga

The 2013 Senate Inquiry took place at a time when ASADA was seeking publicly to persuade players in two of the leading male football competitions, the Australian Football League (AFL) and the National Rugby League (NRL), to admit to having taken supplements allegedly banned under the Code.[38] The NRL brought 'charges' against the Cronulla-Sutherland District Rugby League Football Club for allegedly 'exposing players to significant potential risks to health' and 'exposing players to possible breaches of the NRL Anti-Doping Rules'.[39] However, as the NRL's own media outlet, NRL.com, explained, the breach notice and proposed penalty against

[35] As WADA's website notes, the Prohibited List 'is an International Standard identifying substances and methods prohibited in-competition, out-of-competition and in particular sports'. See WADA, '2015 List of Prohibited Substances and Methods', http://list.wada-ama.org.

[36] Tracey Holmes, 'ASADA Stripping Athletes' Legal Right to Silence by Inserting Provision in Policy, Sports Lawyer Says' *ABC News* (29 November 2015) www.abc.net.au/news/2015-11-29/asada-stripping-legal-right-to-silence-lawyer-says/6984008.

[37] ASADA, 'Media Correction: ABC Report about ASADA's Legislative Powers Inaccurate' (29 November 2015) https://www.asada.gov.au/news/media-correction-abc-report-about-asadas-legislative-powers-inaccurate.

[38] See Lexi Metherell, 'Questions over ACC's Handling of Doping Scandal' *The World Today*, ABC Radio (11 February 2013) www.abc.net.au/worldtoday/content/2013/s3687464.htm?site=hobart.

[39] Sally Whyte, 'What We Have Learnt from AFL, NRL Drugs Scandals' *Crikey* (19 December 2013) www.crikey.com.au/2013/12/19/what-we-have-learnt-from-the-afl-and-nrl-supplement-scandals/?wpmp_switcher=mobile. See also 'NRL Fines Cronulla $1 Million, Bans Coach Shane Flanagan for 12 Months over Supplements' *ABC News* (17 December 2013) www.abc.net.au/news/2013-12-17/sharks-fined-1m-flanagan-banned-over-supplements/5161310.

the Cronulla Club were in relation to 'preliminary findings against the Club for breach of the NRL Code of Conduct', *not* for the Club actually breaching the NRL's anti-doping rules.[40]

Similarly, the AFL used the supplements scandal as the basis for later imposing fines against Essendon Football Club for allegedly bringing the game into disrepute.[41] Among the 15 'grounds' supporting 'the laying of the charge' by the AFL against the Essendon Football Club in 2013 were allegations that the Club '(a) engaged in practices that exposed players to significant risks to their health and safety as well as the risk of using substances that were prohibited by the *AFL Anti-Doping Code* and the *World Anti-Doping Code*'[42] and '(f) failed to devise or implement any adequate system or process to ensure that all substances provided to and used by players were safe and were compliant with the *AFL Anti-Doping Code* and the *World Anti-Doping Code*'.[43]

It further stated in relation to attribution of conduct that the conduct of eight named individuals was 'conduct engaged in by the Club'.[44] One of those eight named persons was a biochemist, Dr Stephen Dank, who had been contracted to the Essendon Club.[45] Dr Dank subsequently refused to be interviewed by the AFL and denied the allegations.[46] It was reported by the AFL's media news website some 15 months later, in November 2014, that Dr Dank was 'set to sue [the] AFL'.[47] Dr Dank had also been named in 'media reporting of his involvement in the Cronulla Sharks supplements scandal'.[48] Indeed, two former players with the Cronulla Sharks, Isaac Gordon and Josh Cordoba, were reported in early 2014 as 'taking the Sharks to court for negligence' and were considering 'whether to add Dank as a defendant'.[49] Further unspecified legal action was foreshadowed by Dr Dank in March 2015 'after the AFL Anti-Doping Tribunal absolved

[40] NRL.com, 'Sharks Fined $1m, Flanagan Suspended' (17 December 2013) www.nrl.com/sharks-fined-1m,-flanagan-suspended/tabid/10874/newsid/75768/default.aspx.

[41] See 'Australian Football League Notice of Charge Rule 1.6' from Andrew Dillon, General Counsel, to Essendon Football Club, 13 August 2013, 1, www.afl.com.au/staticfile/AFL%20Tenant/AFL/Files/EssendonFC-notice-of-charges.pdf.

[42] 'Australian Football League Notice of Charge Rule 1.6' from Andrew Dillon, General Counsel, to Essendon Football Club, 13 August 2013, 2 [1] para (a).

[43] ibid 2 [1] para (f).

[44] ibid 4 [11].

[45] ibid 4 [11].

[46] Nick McKenzie, 'The Science of Stephen Dank' *Real Footy, The Age* (24 August 2013) 4, www.theage.com.au/afl/afl-news/the-science-of-stephen-dank-20130823-2shhd.html.

[47] Mitch Cleary, 'Stephen Dank Says He Can Help Clear Players Facing Bans, is also Set to Sue AFL' (17 November 2014) www.afl.com.au/news/2014-11-17/i-can-clear-players-dank.

[48] Paul Bibby, 'Sharks Supplements Scandal: Sports Scientist Stephen Dank Loses Defamation Appeal' *Sydney Morning Herald* (28 August 2014) www.smh.com.au/nsw/sharks-supplements-scandal-sports-scientist-stephen-dank-loses-defamation-appeal-20140828-109eh7.html.

[49] Brendan Hills, 'Stephen Dank Has 11 Days to Hand over Papers about Supplement Program to Former Sharks Players Who are Considering Legal Action' *Sunday Telegraph* (26 January 2014) www.dailytelegraph.com.au/news/nsw/stephen-dank-has-11-days-to-hand-over-papers-about-supplement-program-to-former-sharks-players-who-are-considering-legal-action/story-fni0cx12-1226810393408.

34 Essendon 2012-listed players of doping violations'.[50] Then, in early April 2015, it was announced that Dr Dank 'has reportedly said he will sue ASADA and its chief executive Ben McDevitt for defamation in the wake of the Essendon supplement saga'.[51] By mid-April 2015, Dr Dank was reported as saying: 'I've got 12 litigations in Sydney against the media and about 20 to be launched in Melbourne ... There will be a body count.'[52] As at the end of 2015, although some of Dr Dank's defamation actions had been struck out, it was understood that many were still pending.[53]

Whatever the eventual outcome of the WADA/ASADA versus Essendon peptides dispute (as well as the various associated legal actions), there are two features of this episode worthy of particular note. First, it is clear that unless a player had specific scientific training, any players in a similar situation in the future would probably have no idea as to whether the supplements administered to them were legal or illegal, and would need to rely instead on advice provided to them by their club. In the Essendon case, this was particularly so because some substances were not specifically named in the codes prevailing at the time of the Essendon allegations, that is, 'in the period from about August 2011 to about July 2012'.[54] Indeed, in the 2012 Code, under the heading 'peptide hormones, growth factors and other prohibited substances', five types of substances were listed.[55] The list then concluded with a general 'catch-all' phrase: 'and other substances with similar chemical structure or similar biological effect(s)'.[56]

Second, on 9 November 2015, nearly three years after the announcement in February 2013 of 'the blackest day in Australian sport', followed by the AFL fining the Essendon FC for allegedly 'bringing the game into disrepute' in August that year, it was announced that two charges had been brought against the Essendon FC 'by WorkSafe Victoria for breaching the Occupational Health and Safety (OHS) Act over its handling of the 2012 supplements program' and that 'the club said it

[50] AAP, 'Essendon ASADA Investigation: Sports Scientist Stephen Dank Says Saga was Stage-Managed by AFL, Foreshadows More Legal Action' *ABC News* (31 March 2015) www.abc.net.au/news/2015-03-31/unrepentant-dank-foreshadows-more-legal-action/6363252.

[51] 'Stephen Dank to Reportedly Sue ASADA, Ben McDevitt for Defamation in Wake of Essendon Supplements Saga' *ABC News* (2 April 2015) www.abc.net.au/news/2015-04-02/stephen-dank-to-sue-asada-chief-ben-mcdevitt-reports/6368224.

[52] Roy Masters, 'Controversial Scientist Stephen Dank Insists Drug Documents were Left at Essendon' *The Age* (13 April 2015) www.theage.com.au/afl/afl-news/controversial-scientist-stephen-dank-insists-drug-documents-were-left-at-essendon-20150413-1mk388.html.

[53] For example, by 6 November 2015, there were 17 judgments from the Supreme Court of New South Wales (NSW) listed on both Austlii and the 'NSW Case Law' websites involving Dr Dank and defamation proceedings (14 from a single judge in the Supreme Court and two from the NSW Court of Appeal).

[54] See World Anti-Doping Agency, 'The World Anti-Doping Code—The 2012 Prohibited List: International Standard' (as at 24 August 2011), which was to 'come into effect on 1 January 2012', https://wada-main-prod.s3.amazonaws.com/resources/files/WADA_Prohibited_List_2012_EN.pdf.

[55] ibid 4.

[56] ibid.

had accepted the charges'.[57] Interestingly, it was also reported that 'WorkSafe said it had also completed an investigation in the AFL, but said it 'could not be established to the requisite standard that the AFL breached the OHS Act'. As was noted in *The Age* the following day,

> [Despite the] millions of dollars incurred by the club in fines and legal fees [and] with 32 past and present players still facing doping charges following an appeal by the World Anti-Doping Agency ... only now, as a result of the two charges levelled at and accepted by the Bombers following a lengthy WorkSafe investigation, has the club faced sanction in *a court of law*.[58]

Is this not the real crux of the whole peptides saga? Was it not the Essendon FC rather than the individual players who should have been bearing the brunt of the WADA/ASADA investigation?

Players Being Compelled to Answer an ASADA Investigation

Despite sports doping being a civil investigation, players could be compelled to be interviewed about matters arising from the playing contracts applicable in both the AFL and NRL. As the 'summary' to the judgment handed down by the Full Court of the Federal Court of Australia in *Hird v Chief Executive Officer, Australian Sports Anti-Doping Authority* found:

> The legislative scheme enabled ASADA to benefit lawfully from the AFL's use of its compulsory contractual powers, including by requiring Essendon players and personnel to attend interviews at which both AFL and ASADA representatives were present and to answer questions.[59]

Further, in the judgment itself, it was found that:

> The CEO did not unlawfully facilitate the abrogation of the interviewees' common law rights to the privileges against self-incrimination or exposure to penalty by engaging the AFL to participate in ASADA's investigation and relying upon the exercise of the AFL's compulsory contractual powers. The appellant and the 34 Players entered into a contractual arrangement with the AFL, which the appellant accepted at trial required them to cooperate not only with the AFL but also with ASADA, including by attending interviews and answering questions.[60]

[57] ABC News, 'Essendon Football Club Charged by WorkSafe over 2012 Supplements Program' (9 November 2015) www.abc.net.au/news/2015-11-09/essendon-charged-by-worksafe-over-2012-supplements-program/6923672.

[58] Caroline Wilson, 'Essendon Doping Saga: Bombers Face First Sanction in a Court of Law' *The Age* (9 November 2015) www.theage.com.au/afl/afl-news/essendon-doping-saga-bombers-face-first-sanction-in-a-court-of-law-20151109-gkupmx.html (emphasis added).

[59] (2015) 227 FCR 95, 99.

[60] ibid 101 [8] (the Court).

If ASADA could already use standard playing/participation contacts to be involved in compulsory 'backdoor' interviews, what was the pressing need for the Australian Parliament to pass the Australian Sports Anti-Doping Bill in June 2014, which proposed giving further investigative powers to the CEO of ASADA?

Whether there was a consistent policy position adopted by the Federal Parliament (or just the Gillard Labor Government) to whittle away (or allow to be whittled away) procedural protections in criminal and quasi-criminal matters is unclear. What is clear is that only 12 months earlier, in 2013, when the NSW Parliament abolished the right to silence in serious criminal matters heard in that state, there had been no attempt by the Federal Parliament to pass legislation in relation to Commonwealth criminal offences either confirming or overriding what had just been passed in NSW.[61] What is also clear is that 12 months later, the two federal Labor Governments in power arguably went even further than the conservative NSW State Government by extending the erosion of the right to silence to include sport-related civil doping disputes.

First, the Gillard Labor Government drafted the Australian Sports Anti-Doping Bill, which gave the CEO of ASADA the equivalent of criminal coercive powers.[62] This was later amended to make it a federal 'civil' offence for a player to refuse to be *interviewed* by ASADA. This was passed by the Australian Senate on 24 June 2013.[63] It was then referred back to the House of Representatives.

In the meantime, a new Prime Minister, Kevin Rudd, was sworn in on 27 June 2013 followed by a new cabinet.[64] On the same day, the Australian Sports Anti-Doping Bill was passed by the House of Representatives and was given the Royal Assent two days later.[65] Presumably, the policy intricacies of drugs in sport were not high on the new government's agenda as they dealt with more pressing matters such as how to turn around the poor opinion polls before a soon to be announced federal election.

It must be of concern that a system that starts with the presumption of guilt rather than innocence (and with private interviews) is now at the forefront of

[61] In 2013, the NSW Parliament passed the Evidence Act 1995 (NSW) s 89A, which abolished the right to silence in serious criminal matters, and which (by virtue of the Judiciary Act 1903 (Cth) s 79) applies 'to proceedings in a State court exercising federal jurisdiction': Evidence Act 1995 (NSW) s 4, Notes, para 4. There was no attempt by the Gillard Labor Government to have the Federal Parliament pass legislation under the Criminal Code Act 1995 (Cth) sch 1 (hereinafter the Commonwealth Criminal Code) or via the Commonwealth Evidence Act, either overriding or conforming to the NSW legislation in relation to Commonwealth criminal offences.

[62] See especially the Australian Sports Anti-Doping Bill sch 1 item 9, inserting the Australian Sports Anti-Doping Authority Act 2006 (Cth) ss 13A–13D, www.austlii.edu.au/au/legis/cth/consol_act/asaaa2006455.

[63] See Australian Sports Anti-Doping Authority Amendment Bill 2013, www.aph.gov.au/Parliamentary_Business/Bills_Legislation/Bills_Search_Results/Result?bId=s902.

[64] Rudd took over as Prime Minister from Gillard when she 'was dumped as Labor leader by 57 votes to 45 in a caucus ballot at 7pm on Wednesday [26 June 2013]'. See Phillip Coorey, 'Rudd's Revenge, Gillard Gone' *Australian Financial Review* (27 June 2013) www.afr.com/news/politics/national/rudds-revenge-gillard-gone-20130626-je5mc.

[65] Australian Sports Anti-Doping Authority Amendment Bill 2013 www.aph.gov.au/Parliamentary_Business/Bills_Legislation/Bills_Search_Results/Result?bId=s902.

Australian sport. Further, not only must one question the reliability of such evidence obtained from such private compulsory interviews, but is it not also abhorrent to the general concept of 'fair play', the philosophy supposedly underpinning the Code? If WADA is so concerned about trumpeting fair play and a level playing field, should not that same philosophy extend to upholding 'fair play' and the human rights values which underpin our common law system?

There is also a vicious sting in the tail of the new legislation. Although there is a statutory protection preserving the right against self-incrimination,[66] this protection is limited. A person is still required to comply with a notice to produce. That is, pursuant to section 13D(2): 'A person is not excused from producing a document or thing as required by a disclosure notice given to the person on the ground that the document or thing might tend to incriminate the person or expose the person to a penalty.'[67] Further, although what a person may say in any ASADA interview or document or thing produced cannot be used against him or her in any subsequent legal proceeding, this protection is again limited. It will not apply to any charges laid under the Commonwealth Criminal Code for providing false and misleading information or false or misleading documents,[68] each of which carries a penalty of 12 months' imprisonment.[69] Nor does the protection apply to any disciplinary proceedings under the anti-doping procedures.[70] So although the abrogation of the right not to incriminate oneself was not passed as part of the amended ASADA legislation, that abrogation still exists under contract law (just not backed by criminal penalties),[71] as the ASADA versus Essendon saga demonstrated. The abrogation also applies in relation to complying with a 'notice to produce' issued by the CEO of ASADA pursuant to the new legislation (with criminal sanctions for providing false and misleading information or documents).

Interestingly, similar investigative bodies (where the rules of evidence do not apply and legislation provides statutory 'protections' against 'evidence' obtained by such bodies being used in any subsequent legal proceedings) have not always proven to be so protective.[72] Also, the recent pursuit in 2014–15 by the NSW

[66] Australian Sports Anti-Doping Authority Act 2006 (Cth) s 13D(1) states: 'An individual is excused from complying with a requirement to answer a question or to give information if the answer to the question or the information might tend to incriminate the individual or expose the individual to a penalty.'

[67] Australian Sports Anti-Doping Authority Act 2006 (Cth) s 13D(1A), as amended by the Australian Sports Anti-Doping Authority Amendment Act 2013 (Cth) sch 1 item 9.

[68] Australian Sports Anti-Doping Authority Act 2006 (Cth) s 13D(2)(e).

[69] Commonwealth Criminal Code ss 137.1(1), 137.2(1).

[70] The author thanks one of the reviewers for this point.

[71] The author also thanks one of the reviewers for clarifying this point.

[72] See the judgments from the High Court of Australia in *X7* (n 21) and *Lee* (n 21). In *X7*, the High Court halted the Australian Crime Commission from continuing with a secret hearing, whereas four months later in *Lee*, the bench split 4:3, with the majority allowing the NSW Crime Commission to continue with its investigation.

Independent Commission Against Corruption (ICAC) of NSW prosecutor Margaret Cunneen, her son and his girlfriend for allegedly attempting to pervert the course of justice (following the latter's innocent involvement in a traffic accident and Cunneen's alleged advice to fake chest pains in order to avoid a roadside alcohol breathalyser test, even though the girlfriend later recorded a zero alcohol blood reading) has provided a further cautionary tale. Not only did the High Court find in favour of Ms Cunneen and her relatives, holding that ICAC was acting outside of its powers,[73] this was then followed by allegations 'that ICAC leaked … messages from Ms Cunneen's mobile phone to her boss, [the] Director of Public Prosecutions'.[74] The concerns about what statutory safeguards one has when being pursued by such bodies was, strangely enough, aptly summed up by the ICAC Commissioner herself in a private talk she gave to the NSW Bar Association as part of a continuing professional development seminar on 24 February 2014 (prior to the Cunneen investigation), when she observed: 'inquisitorial litigation is fantastic … You are not confined by the rules of evidence. You have a free kick', 'it's just, you know, like pulling wings off butterflies' and 'you know exactly what you expect that witness to say and very often they have already given evidence in a compulsory examination'.[75] There have also been further allegations of ICAC leaking stories to selected journalists while 'ICAC gags those it is investigating'.[76]

In relation specifically to the ASADA legislation, it is also of concern that representatives from organisations other than ASADA could be present at private interviews, and those other organisations could then conceivably use that information to delist a player.[77] This is despite the fact that section 13D(2) and (3) of the Australian Sports Anti-Doping Authority Act were inserted as part of the 2013 amendments to specifically protect against self-incrimination.[78]

[73] *Independent Commission against Corruption v Cunneen* (2015) 318 ALR 391.

[74] Sharri Markson and Chris Merritt, 'Caught on Tape: Another ICAC Raid Goes beyond Search Warrant' *The Australian* (28 October 2015) 6. See also Sharri Markson, 'ICAC's Margaret Cunneen SMS Leak Sparked Prosecutor Feud' *The Australian* (23 October 2015) www.theaustralian.com.au/business/legal-affairs/icacs-margaret-cunneen-sms-leak-sparked-prosecutor-feud/story-e6frg97x-1227579201538.

[75] David Levine, Office of the Inspector of the Independent Commission against Corruption (NSW), *Annual Report 2014–2015* (October 2015) 24–5, www.oiicac.nsw.gov.au/assets/oiicac/reports/annual-reports/Annual-Report-2014-2015.pdf; Mark Coultan, 'It Can Be a Lot of Fun: Latham' *The Australian* (21 April 2015) 8. See also Evidence to Committee on the Independent Commission Against Corruption, Parliament of New South Wales, Sydney, 7 August 2015, 16–18 (Megan Latham, ICAC Commissioner) https://www.parliament.nsw.gov.au/prod/parlment/committee.nsf/0/4cd9755b1e757 11bca257ea30080a411/$FILE/Corrected%20transcript%20-%207%20August%202015.pdf.

[76] Sharri Markson, 'Independence in Doubt as Fairfax Goes Easy on ICAC' *The Weekend Australian* (12–13 December 2015) 21.

[77] NRL.com, 'What are the Latest Developments in the ASADA Investigation?' www.nrl.com/portals/nrl/RadEditor/Documents/nrl.comFAQs24713.pdf. See also 'NRL Expecting Same Treatment as AFL Players in ASADA Doping Investigation' *ABC News* (22 July 2013) www.abc.net.au/news/2013-07-22/nrl-expecting-level-asada-playing-field/4836194.

[78] See Australian Sports Anti-Doping Authority Act 2006 (Cth) s 13D(2)–(3), as inserted by the Australian Sports Anti-Doping Authority Amendment Act 2013 (Cth) sch 1, item 9.

Are Youths to Be Compelled to Answer an ASADA Investigation?

What about the many sporting participants who are under 18 years of age? Are they to be subject to this legislation? Even the NSW Government's 2013 draconian legislation, which undermines an accused's right to silence in serious criminal proceedings, specifically states that it does not apply 'to a defendant who, at the time of the official questioning, is under 18 years of age or is incapable of understanding the general nature and effect of a special caution'.[79] While it could be argued that the protection provided in the NSW legislation for youths is justified because it deals with serious criminal consequences (rather than limitations on the ability to participate in sport),[80] surely it is not that simple, particularly as an ASADA investigation has the potential to affect a youth's future career both in and out of sport and thus his or her employment.

Cases involving youths have been at the forefront of some arguably heavy-handed anti-doping arbitrations and anti-doping zealotry. Such incidents as the suspension in 1995 of the 14 year-old US swimmer Jessica Foschi[81] and the disqualification at the Sydney 2000 Olympic Games of the 16-year-old Romanian gymnast Andreea Răducan are cautionary tales indeed. One is also reminded of the furore following the ASADA investigators appearing at two schoolboy rowing regattas in Sydney in 2007 and demanding students to 'strip and provide urine samples', even though it was reported that the participants were 'mainly 17-year-old boys'.[82] The allegations against ASADA also included that 'one boy … was forced to stand naked for 20 minutes'.[83]

The reported hype from ASADA alleged that the 'reaction [of a coach and parents] was it's about time that someone from ASADA came in and conducted testing' and officials from ASADA had 'attended the meet based on a tip-off from a parent of a competitor'.[84] Yet, as ASADA later had to concede, despite the alleged 'tip-off', 'all tests had turned out negative'.[85] ASADA's then chief executive (the position which has now been given the equivalent of criminal coercive powers by the Australian Federal Parliament) was, however, unrepentant. At the time, he was reported as saying that 'ASADA routinely checked minors for drugs and despite their age, young athletes had to expect anti-doping measures as part of competition'.[86]

[79] Evidence Act 1995 (NSW) s 89A(5)(a).

[80] The author thanks one of the reviewers for making this point.

[81] *Foschi v Fédération Internationale de Natation Amateur (FINA)* (Award, Court of Arbitration for Sport, Case No CAS 96/156, 13 June 1997).

[82] AAP, 'Officials Defend Schoolboy Drug Tests' *The Age* (4 April 2007) www.theage.com.au/news/sport/schoolboys-forced-to-strip-for-drugs-test/2007/04/04/1175366277503.html.

[83] ibid.

[84] ibid.

[85] ibid.

[86] ibid.

This was a strange claim, as was explained by the headmasters from two of the schools whose rowing students ASADA had attempted to test. First, 'parents, and only parents, can give permission for these sort of things to happen to their child'. Second, 'the ASADA officials could not provide any evidence that they had undergone the necessary background checks to work with children',[87] which was a requirement of NSW state law. This is now regulated in NSW pursuant to the Child Protection (Working with Children) Act 2012 (NSW).[88] Each state and territory has similar legislation. Section 41 of the NSW Act purports to bind the Crown in all its capacities to the extent that it is possible (that is, 'in so far as the legislative power of the Parliament of New South Wales permits'), but it is unclear whether this applies to Commonwealth officials (of which ASADA's staff are part).[89]

Conclusion: A Quasi-criminal Future?

According to the 'summing-up' speech delivered by the then Australian Minister for Sport in the Australian Senate just after that legislative chamber had passed the Australian Sports Anti-Doping Bill, the Bill had provided 'ASADA with the powers it needs to combat doping in sport in 2013 and beyond'. Part of her speech noted the impact of the legislation:

> While this legislation won't force individuals to self-incriminate in interviews, interviewees will now have to produce documents, materials and things relating to anti-doping investigations.
>
> This legislation will also force those people who work with athletes at the fringes, but not directly employed by clubs, to attend ASADA interviews.
>
> Individuals who defy ASADA could face a civil penalty of more than $5000 for every day they refuse to cooperate. This is a tough but appropriate penalty for individuals who refuse to cooperate with an anti-doping investigation.
>
> The amendments put forward by the Government and Senator Di Natalie [of The Greens political party] add further checks and balances on ASADA and ensure all powers are used responsibility [sic].[90]

[87] ibid.

[88] See Child Protection (Working with Children) Act 2012 (NSW) www5.austlii.edu.au/au/legis/nsw/consol_act/cpwca2012388/s41.html.

[89] ibid s.41.

[90] Kate Lundy, 'Australian Sports Anti-Doping Authority Amendment Bill 2013' (Summing-up Speech, Senate, Australian Parliament, 24 June 2013) http://pandora.nla.gov.au/pan/38983/20140908-1403/www.katelundy.com.au/2013/06/25/australian-sports-anti-doping-authority-amendment-bill-2013/index.html.

The speech was later posted on the Minister's website together with a photograph (without a caption) of the Minster sitting alongside the President of the AOC[91] and the words '[s]hare this page'.[92]

So a Bill that undermines such a fundamental human right as the right to silence was eventually passed with the support of The Greens in the Senate on the basis that at least it 'won't force individuals to self-incriminate'. While one may well say 'Isn't that democracy?', the objection is to the substance of the legislation, not the process,[93] and the arguable naiveté of some of those who supported it. Indeed, according to The Greens' website, the party claims to 'believe that … [u]niversal human rights are fundamental and must be respected and protected in all countries and for all people'[94] and that: 'Unlike the two old parties, the Greens have a proud history of standing up for what is right, not just what is easy or what polls well.'[95] It remains to be seen whether such lofty statements will provide much comfort to those athletes, officials, medical and other associated personnel who are pursued by ASADA in its private 'interviews'.

Some countries have already 'enacted sports-specific laws that criminalise the use of a World Anti-Doping Code (WADC) Prohibited Substance (most notably Austria, France and Italy)'.[96] And make no mistake, criminal sanctions are being considered as an option by those involved in administering world sport. As WADA Director General David Howman asked rhetorically at the 2015 Australian and New Zealand Sports Law Association Conference:

> Should doping become a criminal matter like in Italy and other countries? Is the real deterrence the fear of losing one's liberty, not being out of sport for a few years?[97]

He observed that 'imposing sanctions often relies on governmental processes, not sport tribunals'.[98] Indeed, he suggested that 'a world sports integrity agency could be established with the same governance as WADA'.[99]

As such, we are seeing sports doping matters move from being civil contractual law disputes to the murky area of quasi-criminal investigations, reinforcing

[91] ibid.

[92] ibid. Whilst (as noted by one of the anonymous peer reviewers of this chapter) 'share this page' is generally a standard social media link that appears at the end of many web pages and there is no basis to 'imply that there was something special about the appearance of the message on this particular webpage', perhaps politicians and their staffers might carefully think about how they use such social media links.

[93] The author thanks one of the reviewers for making this point.

[94] The Greens, 'Human Rights', http://greens.org.au/policies/human-rights.

[95] The Greens, 'Home', http://greens.org.au.

[96] Jaan Murphy, 'Where in the World is Doping a Crime? (Doping in Sports pt 6)' *Flagpost* (24 April 2013) www.aph.gov.au/About_Parliament/Parliamentary_Departments/Parliamentary_Library/FlagPost/2013/April/Where_in_the_world_is_doping_a_crime_doping_in_sports_pt_6.

[97] David Howman, 'Challenges to the Integrity of Sport' (speech delivered at the ANZSLA Annual Conference, Melbourne, 15 October 2015) 8, https://anzsla.com/sites/default/files/David%20Howman%20Presentation.pdf.

[98] ibid 17.

[99] ibid 20.

the argument expressed more recently by Moller and Dimeo 'that sport is essentially deteriorating under the current anti-doping campaign executed by an un-coordinated alliance between the WADA, law enforcement authorities, sports organizers and the media'.[100] The concern is 'not to advocate termination of the anti-doping rules altogether'.[101] Rather, 'it appears about time to move away from the moral crusade approach in favour of a more level-headed and rational strategy which takes the nature of sport into account to avoid throwing the baby out with the bath water'.[102]

On 30 January 2014, just seven months after the Australian legislation was passed, it was reported that Darren Hibbert, an employee of a sports nutrition company, 'has become the first person to be fined for failing to co-operate with the Australian Sports Anti-Doping Authority under the body's new powers'.[103] Apparently, he was fined twice for 'failing to comply with two interview notices'.[104] On the first occasion, he attended but 'declined to be interviewed … claiming ASADA had not produced the correct legal documentation' and, for the second, he did not attend as he was ill and provided a doctor's certificate explaining his absence.[105] As Hibbert explained:

> The first interview was called off because the disclosure notices weren't above board legally … There's meant to be three signatures to sign off on them.
>
> They still fined me. For the second interview, I wasn't well, I had gastro. I provided a doctor's certificate to reschedule the meeting but they fined me for not turning up to that as well.
>
> So they have fined me for turning up to the first one … and fined me for the second one as well, even though I supplied a doctor's certificate to say I wasn't well [enough] to attend.
>
> I was prepared to co-operate with them, but after they did that, I'm not prepared to co-operate with them now. They have done their dash now, I'm not going to speak to them.[106]

In addition, apart from the fines, it was reported that despite Hibbert maintaining that 'he never supplied athletes with banned performance-enhancing substances',[107] he had been 'stood down' by his employer: 'This is affecting my job as well, because my boss blames me for getting [the company] caught up in this

[100] Verner Møller and Paul Dimeo, 'Anti-doping—The End of Sport' (2014) 6 *International Journal of Sport Policy and Politics* 259, 260.

[101] ibid.

[102] ibid 271.

[103] Adrian Proszenko, 'ASADA Fines Darren Hibbert over Interviews on NRL Supplements' *League HQ*, *Sydney Morning Herald* (30 January 2014) www.smh.com.au/rugby-league/league-news/asada-fines-darren-hibbert-over-interviews-on-nrl-supplements-20140129-31n5a.html.

[104] ibid.

[105] ibid.

[106] ibid.

[107] ibid.

controversy … Now he says my contract has been put on hold *until I can prove my innocence*.'[108]

On that note, perhaps it is appropriate to conclude with three quotes. The first, from the nineteenth-century French novelist Gustave Flaubert, explaining why he gave up studying law: 'The Law leaves me in a state of moral castration which is almost inconceivable.'[109] The second is from Anne Amos, who, in her 2008 PhD thesis, concluded: 'anti-doping policy is not fundamentally a rational system: instead it has been driven much more by emotional factors … than rational argument'.[110] And, finally, the words of Horace Rumpole—John Mortimer QC's fictional London barrister—and upon whose insight our politicians might care to reflect, if not 'share this page':

> When London is nothing more than a memory, and the Old Bailey has sunk back into the primeval mud, my country will be remembered for three things: the British breakfast, *The Oxford Book of English Verse*, and the presumption of innocence. That is the 'golden thread' which runs through the whole history of our criminal law so that … no man shall be convicted if there is reasonable doubt as to his guilt.[111]

[108] ibid (emphasis added).

[109] Stephen Romer, 'Passion Play: Stephen Romer on the Explosive Energies of the Larger than Life Gustave Flaubert in Geoffrey Wall's *Flaubert: A Life*' *The Guardian* (24 November 2001) www.theguardian.com/books/2001/nov/24/biography.highereducation.

[110] Anne Amos, 'Anti-doping Policy: Rationale or Rationalisation?' (PhD thesis, Faculty of Law, University of Sydney, 2008) ii.

[111] See 'Rumpole and the Golden Thread' *Rumpole of the Bailey* (directed by Donald McWhinnie, Thames Television, 1983), adapted from John Mortimer, *Rumpole and the Golden Thread* (Harmondsworth, Penguin, 1983).

4

The World Anti-Doping Code and Contract Law

ALAN SULLIVAN*

Introduction

The World Anti-Doping Code 2015[1] came into force on 1 January 2015. It is the third-generation World Anti-Doping Code (hereinafter the Code), replacing the 2009 Code, which, in turn, superseded the original 2003 Code.

This chapter discusses two topics: first, the extent to which the 2015 Code operates as a contract, and between whom and how; and, second, how the 2015 Code should be construed or interpreted.

Despite all the changes in the 2015 version, the Code, as a legal instrument, has not changed in term of its various iterations. Like its predecessors, it has effect, and almost only has effect, as a contract, albeit a very special form of contract.

The 2015 Code as a Contract

The Code has been described 'as a kind of international law of sport in the anti-doping area'.[2] It is one of the main elements of the world anti-doping programme which 'encompasses all of the elements needed to ensure optimal harmonization and best practice in international and national anti-doping programs'.[3]

The 2015 Code 'is the fundamental and universal document upon which the World Anti-Doping Program in sport is based'.[4]

* Queen's Counsel, Sydney.

1 World Anti-Doping Agency, World Anti-Doping Code (1 January 2015).

2 Paul David, *A Guide to the World Anti-Doping Code: A Fight for the Spirit of Sport* 2nd edn (Cambridge University Press, 2013) 52.

3 See 2015 Code 12.

4 ibid 11.

The Code's Operation as a Contract Binding on Signatories

In the main, the Code operates as a result of the voluntary agreement of signatories to it. It functions much:

> [T]he same way as voluntary international instruments in areas such as international trade or commerce. The voluntary rules which govern the operation *of* bankers' documentary credits and the conventions which govern the carriage of goods by sea [such as the Hague-Visby Rules][5] are good examples. The Uniform Customs and Practice for Documentary Credits function by agreement or incorporation, and might, like the Code, be described as a body of international law which has been generally adapted so as to bring about a common approach in a particular area of activity. In the case of the Code, the aim is to provide a common, harmonised [international] approach to the regulation of doping in sport.[6]

To date, hundreds of international sporting organisations have adopted the Code, including all sporting associations associated with the Olympic Games and the Commonwealth Games. There are very few major or even minor sports, which have not adopted the Code, even though those sports may not yet be included in the Olympic Games programme. Thus, sports such as cricket, netball, squash and surfing have adopted the Code. Even organisations in which one might think doping might not be the most pressing concern, such as the World Flying Disc Federation, the World Draughts Federation and the International Federation of Cheerleading, are signatories to the Code.[7]

It is not only sporting organisations which have adopted the Code. Already over 100 governments have implemented or agreed to implement the Code by individually ratifying the International Convention against Doping in Sport 2005,[8] the first global international treaty against doping in sport which was unanimously adopted by 191 governments at the United Nations Education, Scientific and Cultural Organization General Conference in October 2005 and came into force in February 2007. The Convention has been ratified by governments at record speed.[9]

One of the ways Australia has implemented the Code has been by enactment of legislation such as the Australian Sports Anti-Doping Authority Act 2006 (Cth)

[5] International Convention for the Unification of Certain Rules of Law relating to Bills of Lading, signed 25 August 1924, 120 LNTS 187 (entered into force 2 June 1931), as amended by the Protocol to Amend the International Convention for the Unification of Certain Rules of Law Relating to Bills of Lading, signed 23 February 1968, 1412 UNTS 127 (entered into force 23 June 1977), as amended by the Protocol to Amend the International Convention for the Unification of Certain Rules of Law Relating to Bills of Lading, signed 21 December 1979, 1412 UNTS 146 (entered into force 14 February 1984).

[6] David (n 2) 52. See also 2015 Code 16–17.

[7] WADA, 'Code Signatories' (2015) https://www.wada-ama.org/en/what-we-do/the-code/code-signatories.

[8] Opened for signature 19 October 2015, 2419 UNTS 43649 (entered into force 1 February 2007).

[9] See WADA, 'UNESCO Convention Nears 100 Ratifications' (2008) 3 *Play True* 31.

(hereinafter the ASADA Act) and by making, pursuant to that Act, the Australian Sports Anti-Doping Authority Regulations 2006 (Cth) (hereinafter the ASADA Regulations). In so doing, Australia has, perhaps, done more than is required by the Convention.[10]

As between signatories to the 2015 Code, there is no doubt that it operates as a contract. By signing the declaration of acceptance,[11] a signatory promises to implement and comply with the Code.[12]

The 2015 Code itself spells out the sanctions for a signatory who breaches the contract. Article 23.6 provides:

> Non-compliance with the *Code* by any *Signatory* may result in consequences in addition to ineligibility to bid for *Events* as set forth in Article 20.1.8 (International Olympic Committee), 20.3.11 (International Federations) and 20.6.6 (Major Event Organisations), for example: forfeiture of offices and positions within *WADA*; *Ineligibility* or non-admission of any candidature to hold any International Event in a country; cancellation of *International Events*; symbolic consequences and other consequences pursuant to Olympic Charter.

Legal Effect upon Sporting Organisations Other than as a Contract

There are other sporting organisations that are not signatories to the Code but may be bound by it and bound to implement it independently of contract. Typically, this will be because a legislature of a country in which the sporting organisation is domiciled or operates may have legislated to require the sporting organisation to have the 2015 Code as part of its rules. In Australia, the ASADA Act requires a national anti-doping scheme to be prescribed by delegated legislation.[13]

Regulation 3 of the ASADA Regulations prescribes the national anti-doping scheme as set out in Schedule 1 to those Regulations (hereinafter the NAD Scheme).

Clause 2.04 of the NAD Scheme requires 'a sporting administration body' (SAB) to have in place and comply with the mandatory provisions of the Code.[14]

In turn, a SAB is defined as 'a national sporting organisation for Australia',[15] and that definition takes one back to the ASADA Act, which makes it clear that such an

[10] As to those obligations, see 2015 Code art 22.

[11] Governments signed the Copenhagen Declaration on Anti-Doping in Sport of 3 March 2003 to show their acceptance: 2015 Code art 22.

[12] ibid art 23.

[13] ASADA Act s 9.

[14] As all provisions of the 2015 Code are 'mandatory in substance', this means, in effect, that the whole of the Code is: see 2015 Code 16.

[15] NAD Scheme cl 2.02.

organisation is one 'responsible for administering the affairs of the sport, or of a substantial part or section of the sport, in Australia'.[16]

Thus, in Australia, at least, peak national sporting bodies, even if they are not signatories to the 2015 Code, may be compelled to make its provisions part of their rules and to comply with and enforce them.

Yet, it is respectfully suggested that it is debatable as to how effective clause 2.04 is where the sporting organisation itself is not a signatory to the Code. No sanction is prescribed for its breach and there are no express enforcement provisions. Arguably it is a 'duty of imperfect obligation'—namely, it specifies a norm of conduct for breach of which there may be no legal sanction.[17]

Therefore, Australian national sporting organisations that are not signatories to the Code may fall between the cracks when it comes to the enforcement of the Code. They are not contractually bound to implement the Code and the legislative requirement to do so may be somewhat of a toothless tiger.[18]

However, the recent decision of the Full Federal Court of Australia in *Hird v Chief Executive Officer of the Australian Sports Anti-Doping Authority*[19] demonstrates the significance and importance of legislative action to supplement and augment the contractual powers of a sporting organisation and vice versa.

The peak body controlling the sport of Australian Rules Football in Australia is the Australian Football League (AFL). Essendon is a club licensed to field a team in the elite competition conducted by the AFL and Mr James Hird was the head coach of that team.

It was common ground in the case that Mr Hird, as coach, and the Essendon players were all contractually bound by the AFL Rules, the AFL Regulations, the AFL Player Rules and the AFL Anti-Doping Code. In his capacity as senior coach of Essendon, Mr Hird had supervised the preparation, training and performance of personnel who participated as players for Essendon in the 2012 season. During that season, the players were allegedly participants in a 'supplements program' in circumstances where the AFL suspected that substances prohibited under the Code had been administered to them.

In early February 2013, the CEO of the Australian Sports and Anti-Doping Authority (ASADA) and the AFL agreed to conduct a 'joint investigation' into the participation of the Essendon players and personnel in the supplements programme. The investigation, from ASADA's point of view, was part of a wider investigation by ASADA under the ASADA Act, the NAD Scheme and the ASADA Regulations.

[16] ASADA Act s 4 (definition of 'national sporting organisation').

[17] See, eg, in the context of the disqualification of judges for bias, *Ebner v Official Trustee in Bankruptcy* (2000) 205 CLR 337, 360 [70] (Gleeson CJ, McHugh, Gummow and Hayne JJ).

[18] However, such bodies may depend upon, or desire, government funding or assistance, and such needs may be more persuasive in ensuring compliance than any legal sanction.

[19] *Hird v Chief Executive Officer of the Australian Sports Anti-Doping Authority* (2015) 22 FCR 95.

The problem, of course, for ASADA with those legislative powers and that investigation was that it had no powers of compulsion to require the Essendon players and/or personnel to participate in any such investigation. Any powers it had under the relevant legislation were confined to powers in respect of the AFL.

To overcome this problem, ASADA and the AFL reached an agreement where, in effect, the AFL would use its compulsory contractual powers in respect of its players and personnel to require them to share information with ASADA, and to require them to attend interviews and the like at which ASADA representatives were present.

As the primary judge recorded:

> There is no dispute that in carrying out the investigation with the co-operation of the AFL, the CEO and ASADA obtained the benefit they did not otherwise have under the Act or the NAD Scheme. Whilst CEO and ASADA had no power to compel and sanction, it obtained the benefit of what the AFL had, namely the contractual power of the AFL:
>
> (a) to compel Essendon players and personnel to participate in an AFL investigation and to attend an interrogative interview; and
> (b) to direct, under threat of AFL sanction, that an Essendon player or personnel respond and answer every question asked of him or her.
>
> In the course of the investigation, ASADA and the AFL agreed to use the powers of compulsion available to the AFL under the AFL Player Rules … and the AFL Anti-Doping Code … in order to compel Essendon players and personnel to attend interviews and answer questions, and effectively disclose (to the extent lawful) information collected in the course of the investigation.
>
> The CEO admitted that the AFL's compulsory powers enabled the AFL to compel Essendon players and personnel to provide information as directed by the AFL, including by attending interviews (at which ASADA and the AFL were present), in circumstances where interviewees were not then able to claim the privileges against self-incrimination or self-exposure to a penalty.[20]

The primary judge found that ASADA had not acted improperly in carrying out the joint investigation with the AFL or in using the information so obtained by it for its purposes. Mr Hird appealed from those findings. The appeal was unsuccessful. The Full Federal Court in dismissing the appeal embarked upon a detailed and important consideration of the ASADA Act, the ASADA Regulations, the NAD Scheme and of their interrelationship with the contractual rules of the AFL, which were relevantly based on the 2009 Code.[21]

Whilst Mr Hird's case may only be of significance in jurisdictions where there is legislation in place similar to that of Australia, it does indicate how the combined effect of contractual power and legislative power may be much more effective in

[20] *Essendon Football Club v Chief Executive Officer of the Australian Sports Anti-Doping Authority* (2014) FCR 1, 9–10 [10]–[12] (Middleton J).

[21] *Hird* (n 19) 127–42 [93]–[158], 145–54 [168]–[199] (the Court).

detecting and penalising anti-doping rule violations than the exercise of merely contractual power on the one hand or of legislative power on the other. As the judgment makes plain, that is what the Code is all about. The Full Court said:

> [T]he provisions of the ASADA Act and the NAD Scheme contemplate close cooperation between ASADA and a SAB [ie, a peak sporting body such as the AFL], particularly in ASADA's anti-doping investigations. Cooperation of this kind is also within the contemplation of the international instruments to which the ASADA Act, the 2006 Regulations and the NAD Scheme refer. Even without reference to these international instruments, we would conclude that the ASADA Act and the NAD Scheme, particularly cll 2.04 and 3.27 of the NAD Scheme and s 22 of the ASADA Act … authorised ASADA to conduct an investigation in cooperation with the AFL. The effect of the international instruments is to confirm that this ordinary meaning of the relevant provisions is their intended meaning. The provisions regarding the need for cooperation in these international instruments confirm that the ASADA Act and the NAD Scheme contemplated that ASADA and the SABs would work closely together to combat doping in sport, particularly in ASADA's anti-doping investigations. There is nothing in the legislative regime that supports the appellant's proposition that ASADA was required to conduct its investigation under cl 3.27 independently of a SAB, in the sense that it could not require a SAB to cooperate with its investigations by working alongside it.[22]

In summary, so far as sporting organisations are concerned, the primary way they are bound to include the Code as part of their rules is by contact. However, in places such as Australia, a national sporting organisation which is not a signatory to the Code and thus not contractually bound to implement it may also become bound technically, but query how effectively, to include the Code as part of its rules and implement it by legislation.

The Code as a Binding Contract for Athletes

But sporting organisations themselves are not, of course, the main targets of the Code. The main targets are the athletes who have allegedly committed anti-doping rule violations (ADRVs) and the support personnel who force, encourage or assist them to do that.

Such individuals are not themselves signatories to the Code. Nor, in Australia, does rule 2.04 of the NAD Scheme apply to them. How then do they become bound by the provisions of the Code? The answer, of course, is by contract.

The 2015 Code seeks to achieve contractual submission by athletes to its provisions by requiring signatories to 'establish rules and procedures to ensure that all *Athletes* or other *Persons* … are informed of and agree to be bound by anti-doping

[22] ibid 140 [149] (the Court).

rules'.[23] Likewise, it asserts that: 'Athletes … accept these rules as a condition of participation and shall be bound by these rules.'[24]

Typically, the way in which a sporting organisation complies with this obligation imposed by the Code is for the national peak body to require its constituent member organisations to agree to be bound by and comply with the national body's rules, including its anti-doping rules. In turn, those constituent member organisations, by a series of cascading agreements, pass such obligations down the line until the athlete or support person ultimately signs a registration form or application for membership or accreditation acknowledging that he or she agrees to be bound by the relevant rules of the organisation, including the anti-doping policy.

Then there arises a chain or series of interlocking documents which will constitute a multi-partite contract binding the athlete to accept and comply with the organisation's anti-doping rules and thus, in effect, with the Code.[25]

A question might arise as to whether such a contract is legally binding or justiciable in a court of law. But, generally, there is not much doubt that it will be so regarded. The principal focus of the 2015 Code is to prevent doping by athletes who participate at an international or national level.[26] Such athletes will usually be professional or semi-professional. Moreover, exposure at such a level offers them the opportunity of sponsorship, travel, participation in major world sporting events and public recognition. Also the sporting organisations with which the athletes 'contract' will, in all likelihood, have a virtual monopoly in controlling the right of the athlete to participate or compete in a particular sport. Finally, often the sporting body will be an incorporated body, making its constitution, by-laws and rules a statutory contract or analogous to one.

By reason of the combination of some or all of these typical features, a court will generally have little reluctance in imputing, objectively, to the parties an intention that the contract between them is a legally enforceable one.[27]

As Mance LJ observed in *Modahl v British Athletic Federation*:

> The submission that no one can have intended this [ie, to create a legally enforceable relationship] in a sporting context seems unrealistic in relation to the modern sporting scene, which, whatever the labels of amateurism, has aspects affecting substantially the career, livelihood and prosperity of participants.[28]

[23] 2015 Code 16. See also roles and responsibilities imposed on signatories: arts 20.1.6, 20.2.6, 20.3.3–20.3.5, 20.4.2, 20.4.5, 20.4.7.

[24] ibid 16.

[25] See *Raguz v Sullivan* (2000) 50 NSWLR 236; *Rose v Boxing NSW Inc* [2007] NSWSC 20 [46]–[51] (Brereton J); *International Rugby Board v Troy* (Award, Court of Arbitration for Sport, Case No CAS 2008/A/1664, 6 August 2009).

[26] See 2015 Code app 1 (definition of 'athlete').

[27] See generally Alan Sullivan, 'The Role of Contract in Sports Law' (2010) 5 *Australian and New Zealand Sports Law Journal* 3, 6–11 and the cases referred to therein.

[28] *Modahl v British Athletic Federation* [2002] 1 WLR 1192, 1222 [105].

Thus, generally speaking, there will be no problem in finding that an athlete who has signed the document agreeing to be bound by his or her association's rules is legally bound by those rules, including the incorporated anti-doping rules.

However, that is not always the case. What happens if, by accident, inadvertence or oversight, an athlete does not sign such a document but still participates in the sport? What happens when a sporting club brings in an outsider, such as a 'sports scientist', as a 'consultant' and that person is neither an employee of the organisation nor signs anything agreeing to be bound by its rules?

In such circumstances, the question becomes whether the 2015 Code has sufficient 'reach' to enable sanctions to be imposed for alleged ADRVs by such people. Regrettably, there is no definitive 'one-size-fits-all' answer to that question. In any particular case, the answer will depend on the ordinary principles of contractual formation adapted to the sporting context and applied to the facts of the specific case.

Even where there is no traditional offer and acceptance or where a person has not signed a document acknowledging to be bound by the rules, parties may become bound by a contract whenthey intend and contemplate becoming bound by such a contract. This is an objective inquiry that needs to be answered idiosyncratically on the facts of each case.[29]

As stated by McHugh JA in *Integrated Computer Services Pty Ltd v Digital Equipment Corporation (Australia) Pty Ltd*:

> [A] contract may be inferred from the acts and conduct of parties as well as or in the absence of their words ... The question in this class of case is whether the conduct of the parties viewed in the light of the surrounding circumstances shows a tacit understanding or agreement. The conduct of the parties, however, must be capable of proving all the essential terms of an express contract.[30]

The critical need to examine the facts of the case to determine whether a contract can be inferred and, if so, what are its terms and who are its parties is illustrated by the differing outcomes in two of the so-called 'yacht race contract' cases, *Clarke v Earl of Dunraven*[31] and *Forbes v Australian Yachting Federation*.[32]

In the former case, the House of Lords had no difficulty inferring a contract between competitors in a yacht race to abide by the rules for that race, merely by reason of the fact of those competitors entering into the race with knowledge of those rules. In *Forbes*, Santow J of the New South Wales Supreme Court was not so easily persuaded. He distinguished *Clarke v Earl of Dunraven* and concluded

29 *Eccles v Bryant* [1948] Ch 93, 104 (Lord Greene MR); *Brambles Holdings Ltd v Bathurst City Council* (2001) 53 NSWLR 153, 176–79 [71]–[79] (Heydon JA).

30 *Integrated Computer Services Pty Ltd v Digital Equipment Corporation (Australia) Pty Ltd* (1988) 5 BPR 11,110, 11,117; *Kriketos v Livschitz* (2009) 14 BPR 26,717, 26,719 [14] (Allsop P), 26,736–7 [115]–[117] (McColl JA).

31 *Clarke v Earl of Dunraven* [1897] AC 59.

32 *Forbes v Australian Yachting Federation* (1996) 131 FLR 241.

that, on the facts before him, there was no contract between the participants in the relevant regatta and the organiser of that regatta.[33]

Notwithstanding the decision in *Forbes*, the approach adopted in *Clarke v Earl of Dunraven* appears to have been subsequently viewed sympathetically by Australian courts[34] and seems to accord most with common sense and sporting experience. The approach is most likely to be more influential than *Forbes* in any future deliberations on this subject.

In the case of a contract comprising or including anti-doping rules, the need for the conduct of the parties to be capable of proving all of the essential elements of an express contract[35] necessarily means that the relevant conduct must show, on the balance of probabilities, that a person has agreed to participate in the particular sport at least in the knowledge that anti-doping rules exist and are intended to apply in respect of such participation. Such conduct may be hard to prove absent evidence of attendance at meetings or the like where the anti-doping policy was mentioned or discussed, or evidence of notoriety of the existence of such rules in the sport. It is notorious, for instance, that anti-doping rules, the Code, apply in respect of Olympic sports. It would be easy to infer that an athlete or support person who participates in such a sport was aware that he or she was doing so in circumstances where anti-doping rules applied in respect of such participation.[36] But in other areas of sport, such an inference may be much harder to draw.

A Possible Non-contractual Basis for Enforcing the Code

Where an athlete has not signed a document undertaking to be bound by anti-doping rules or where his or her conduct is not sufficient to infer such a contract, there remains one further possibility for holding that the person is nevertheless bound by the anti-doping rules. This possible basis is best illustrated by the decision of the Privy Council in *Stephen v Naylor*,[37] which is often cited as authority for the

[33] See ibid 285.

[34] See, eg, *Raguz v Sullivan* (2000) 50 NSWLR 236, 250–51 [65]–[67] (Spigelman CJ and Mason P); *Brambles Holdings Ltd* (n 29) 176–79 [71]–[80] (Heydon JA).

[35] See *Integrated Computer Services Pty Ltd* (n 30) 11,117 (McHugh JA); *Kriketos v Livschitz* (n 30) 26,719 [14] (Allsop P), 26,736–7 [115]–[117] (McColl JA).

[36] See International Olympic Committee, Olympic Charter (at 2 August 2015), a publicly available document. It provides, inter alia, that to be eligible for participation in the Olympic Games, all competitors, support staff and officials must respect and comply with the Code: r 40. Furthermore, it provides that the Code is mandatory for the entire Olympic Movement: r 43.

[37] *Stephen v Naylor* (1937) 37 SR (NSW) 127. It should be noted that at the time this decision was handed down, the Privy Council stood at the apex of the Australian legal system, with the consequence that its decisions were binding on all courts below it in the Australian legal hierarchy. See,

proposition that those in control of a sport or pastime can exercise disciplinary powers over persons whose conduct brings their actions within the 'purview' of the sporting organisation's rules, even if there is no contractual or statutory basis for exercising those powers.[38]

It is desirable to briefly outline the facts of *Stephen v Naylor.* Mr Rufus Naylor had been, prior to the events in question, a bookmaker, but at the material time, his case was that he desired and was entitled to go on to the racecourse as a member of the public for his own purposes, which included attending to his business of betting large sums on horses racing there. The racing club in question, the Australian Jockey Club (AJC), suspected that Mr Naylor was a party to serious irregularities in connection with the ownership of a horse, which had run in a race under its control. Mr Naylor was thereupon summoned to an inquiry and it was conceded that he gave deliberately false evidence at the inquiry. In consequence, he was disqualified under the Rules of Racing, which had no statutory force. That disqualification was then used by the AJC in the exercise of powers conferred by its by-laws, which were in fact a form of delegated legislation, to exclude him indefinitely from racecourses controlled by the AJC.

Naylor's main contention was that he was not subject to the Rules of Racing and that they were therefore ineffective to bring about his disqualification and consequent exclusion from the racecourse. That submission was accepted in the Full Court of the Supreme Court of New South Wales, but was ultimately rejected by the Privy Council. In delivering the judgment of the Privy Council, Lord Roche said:

> The by-law is clear enough and gives power to exclude disqualified persons. The question then is what is a disqualified person. The dictionary to which reference is to be made, as everyone knew, is the Rules of Racing. The meaning there given is clear and includes one in the respondent's case. *It is not a question whether he consented to any adjudication or submitted to any jurisdiction.* The Club properly undertook to regulate racing within its territorial limits and properly announced the rules by which it would regulate it and properly also to satisfy the claims of justice gave an opportunity to anyone whose conduct called for enquiry in connection with racing within those limits to attend and proffer explanations. Disqualification is a well-known and legitimate and indeed a necessary safeguard to be adopted to secure the absence from the racecourse of persons who had been found guilty of conduct gravely detrimental to the interest of racing. The exercise of such a jurisdiction may as to some matters and things such as licensing, arise out of consent, but in others such as the present, it seems no more to depend upon consent than

eg, *Skelton v Collins* (1966) 115 CLR 94, 104 (Kitto J); *Viro v The Queen* (1978) 141 CLR 88, 118 (Gibbs CJ). However, appeals to the Privy Council were finally abolished in 1986: Australia Act 1986 (Cth) s 11; Australia Act 1986 (UK) c 2. It remains an open question in Australia whether Privy Council holdings in Australian appeals at the time when the Privy Council was part of the Australian judicial hierarchy remain binding on Australian courts: see, eg, *Footes v Southern Cross Mine Management Pty Ltd* (2007) 234 CLR 52, 84 [96] (Kirby J).

[38] See, eg, Anthony J Crocker, 'Bringing the "Strangers" within the Rules of Racing' (2012) 7 *Australian and New Zealand Sports Law Journal* 33, 33.

> does the disqualification of a horse. A horse is disqualified because improper things are done to it. The respondent was disqualified because he impeded by lying the course of a necessary and proper enquiry and he has to suffer *not because he consented to be bound by the rules, but because he permitted himself so to act as to bring his actions within their purview*.[39]

If this passage is read in isolation and if *Stephen v Naylor* is truly authority for the proposition referred to above, by analogy and/or extension, it might be argued that an athlete who participates in a sport where there are known anti-doping rules may be subject to those rules even if he or she cannot be said to have contracted to be bound by them. It is at least arguable that such an athlete who takes prohibited substances 'permits himself so as to act as to bring his actions within' the purview of the relevant sporting body's anti-doping rules.

However, properly understood, *Stephen v Naylor* is not authority for the proposition that persons whose conduct brings their action within the 'purview' of a sporting association's rules can therefore become subject to that sporting association's disciplinary actions in the absence of a contractual or statutory basis. Rather, although their Lordships' reasoning is opaque, the decision is explained by the fact that their Lordships found that it was the operation of the by-laws which was critical and that those by-laws were statutory in nature.[40]

In its reasoning in *Stephen v Naylor*, the Privy Council effectively treated the 'Rules of Racing' as a 'dictionary' to explain the powers conferred by the by-laws. Their Lordships then went one step further. They rejected the notion that 'disqualifications' had to be dealt with, to be effective, in the statutory by-laws as opposed to the Rules of Racing. They did so in these words:

> Their Lordships see nothing to warrant the conclusion that the matter or others proper to be dealt with by Rules of Racing must be dealt with by by-law and it is in their opinion both convenient and legitimate *to enable by by-law* that such a disqualification as this resulting from violation of the Rules of Racing may be a ground of exclusion from the racecourse.[41]

These passages, in my respectful view, clearly demonstrate that the Privy Council was, in effect, saying that the relevant rules of racing were given statutory effect by the way in which the relevant by-law was framed.[42] The statutory power in the by-laws to exclude people who were disqualified necessarily extended to the right of the AJC to have rules providing for the disqualification of people.

So viewed, the reasoning in *Stephen v Naylor* could not be applied or relied upon to successfully argue that the Code could apply to a person in the absence

[39] *Stephen v Naylor* (n 37) 139–40 (emphasis added).

[40] See also Crocker (n 38).

[41] (*Stephen v Naylor* (n 37) 140 (emphasis added).

[42] By-law (IX)(3) prohibited entry to the racecourse of any person 'under disqualification' by the AJC. But the by-laws themselves did not deal with 'disqualification'. This was dealt with in the club's 'Rules of Racing', which did not have any statutory force by themselves. Rule 171(h) gave the club power to disqualify any person 'who has given at any inquiry … any evidence which … is false or misleading'.

of a contractual or statutory basis. If, however, contrary to this view, *Stephen v Naylor* is authority for the proposition referred to above,[43] then there must be great doubt as to whether or not it was correctly decided or reasoned. If it stands for a broader proposition that a sporting organisation's rules apply to a person who, by his or her actions, brings himself or herself within the purview of those rules, even though not contractually bound by them, then it seems inconsistent with legal principle. On what basis can it be said that 'rules' are enforceable against strangers when there is no relevant contractual, proprietary or statutory power? As Denning LJ, as he then was, put it colourfully but accurately: 'The jurisdiction of a domestic tribunal … must be founded on a contract, express or implied. Outside the regular courts of this country, no set of men can sit in judgment on their fellows except so far as Parliament authorizes it or the parties agree to it.'[44]

Further, whilst *Stephen v Naylor* may or may not be still binding on Australian courts, it almost certainly will not be regarded as binding in disputes arising in respect of the Code, even if the overall contract between the athlete and the sporting body is governed by Australian law, because of the requirement of those hearing such disputes to adopt an international or global approach to the resolution of the problem rather than simply applying the local law.[45]

In short, it is extremely difficult to see any argument based on *Stephen v Naylor* succeeding so that a person becomes subject to the Code or to anti-doping rules derived from it in the absence of contract.

Turning to the other theme of this chapter, to the extent that the 2015 Code does form a contract between the relevant parties, how is that contract to be interpreted?

Interpreting the Code

Ordinarily, one interprets or construes a contract by first ascertaining its proper law as determined by the express agreement of the parties or by forming a conclusion from the facts as to the system of law with which the contract has its most natural connection.[46] Having determined the proper law of the contract,

[43] See Crocker (n 38).

[44] *Lee v Showmen's Guild of Great Britain* [1952] 2 QB 329, 341.

[45] 2015 Code art 24.3. Furthermore, the Code states: 'These sport-related rules and procedures, aimed at enforcing anti-doping rules in a global and harmonised way, are distinct in nature from the criminal and civil proceedings. They are not intended to be subject to or limited by any national requirements and legal standards applicable in such proceedings, although they are intended to be applied in a manner which respects the principles of proportionality and human rights. When reviewing the facts and the law of a given case, all courts, arbitral hearing panels and other adjudicating bodies should be aware of and respect the distinct nature of the anti-doping rules in the *Code* and the fact that those rules represent the consensus of a broad spectrum of stakeholders around the world with an interest in fair sport': at 17.

[46] *Bonython v Commonwealth* (1950) 81 CLR 486, 498 (Lord Simons).

the principles of construction applicable according to that system of law are then applied to interpret or construe the contract.

But that orthodox approach cannot be applied in respect of the Code. Indeed the Code expressly forbids it. Article 24.3 of the 2015 Code states: 'The Code shall be interpreted as an independent and autonomous text and not by reference to the existing law or statutes of the Signatories or governments.'

In practice, one rarely confronts the Code directly. Rather, in virtually every case, the dispute will arise in respect of the anti-doping rules of a sporting organisation that is a signatory to the Code or is otherwise bound by it. However, even in this circumstance, Article 24.3 of the Code will be a consideration because a signatory to the Code is obliged to include in its anti-doping rules a provision in the form of Article 24 of the Code, without substantive change.[47]

Article 24 of the Code deals with the interpretation of the Code. It contains a number of important provisions as follows:

(a) whilst the official text of the Code shall be published in English and in French, in the event of any conflict, the English version is to prevail;[48]
(b) 'comments annotating various provisions of the Code shall be used to interpret the Code';[49]
(c) headings used in the various parts of the Code and to the articles of the Code are for convenience only and are not to be taken into account for the purposes of interpretation;[50]
(d) the Code is generally not to be interpreted so as to apply retroactively to matters pending before the date the Code is accepted by the signatory and implemented in its rules;[51] and
(e) '[t]he Purpose, Scope and Organization of the World Anti-Doping Program and the *Code* and Appendix 1, Definitions and Appendix 2, Examples of the Application of Article 10, shall be considered integral parts of the *Code*'.[52]

Some of the provisions of Article 24 of the *2015* Code mirror, or are substantially similar to, the approach to construction which would be taken anyway in common law countries. Thus, for instance, the requirement in Article 24.2 that the numerous comments annotating various provisions of the Code shall be used to interpret the Code differs little in substance from the general law principle that the courts may take into account published explanatory notes in interpreting the

[47] 2015 Code art 23.2.2.
[48] ibid art 24.1.
[49] ibid art 24.2. Moreover, anti-doping rules of signatories to the Code must expressly acknowledge the Commentary and endow it with the same status in those anti-doping rules as it has in the Code: art 23.2.2.
[50] ibid art 24.4.
[51] ibid art 24.5.
[52] ibid art 24.6.

contract that they are intended to explain.[53] However, at least one other provision of Article 24 of the Code does seem to alter the general law position. At general law, a heading or marginal note to a clause may be taken into account in construing the clause. But it cannot override the clear words in the clause or create an ambiguity where, but for the heading, none would otherwise exist.[54] Article 24.4, however, is much more emphatic than the general law position. It makes it plain that the headings cannot be used in construing the clause at all. It states that the headings are not 'to affect in any way the language of the provisions to which they refer'.

But, undoubtedly, the most significant provision of Article 24 of the 2015 Code is Article 24.3. As Paul David in his very useful and helpful book *A Guide to the World Anti-Doping Code* states, in my view, correctly:

> This important provision emphasises for tribunals, which have to consider the interpretation of the Code, that general principles of interpretation are to be applied, rather than particular principles of interpretation and law derived from one particular national legal system or another. The focus in interpreting the Code should, accordingly, be on the principles of interpretation which are common to all legal systems. If that approach is adopted, it is more likely that the Code will be interpreted and applied in a consistent manner.[55]

Such an approach to interpretation of the Code or of anti-doping rules of a sporting organisation based on its provisions is consistent with the international nature of the text as a code which is intended to function outside the constraints of a particular legal system.[56] It is also consistent with the way in which common law courts have treated the interpretation of international treaties or conventions, which, in my opinion, is an analogous situation.

The approach of courts to the interpretation of international treaties or conventions is that they should be interpreted 'uniformly by contracting states'.[57] Moreover, such international treaties should not 'be interpreted by reference to presumptions and technical rules of interpretation applied in construing domestic statutes or contracts',[58] but rather should be interpreted in a manner which emphasises uniformity and achieves comity, and is consistent with 'broad principles of general acceptation'.[59]

[53] See, eg, Kim Lewison and David Hughes, *The Interpretation of Contracts in Australia* (Thomson Reuters, 2012) 72–73 [3.07] and the cases discussed therein.

[54] ibid 205–06 [5.13] and the cases referred to therein.

[55] David (n 2) 126.

[56] See 2015 Code 17.

[57] *Povey v Qantas Airways Ltd* (2005) 223 CLR 189, 202 [25] (Gleeson CJ, Gummow, Hayne and Heydon JJ); *LK v Director-General, Department of Community Services* (2009) 237 CLR 582, 596 [36] (the Court).

[58] *Povey v Qantas Airways Ltd* (n 58) 211 [60] (McHugh J). See also *Applicant A v Minister for Immigration and Ethnic Affairs* (1997) 190 CLR 225, 251–56 (McHugh J).

[59] *Fothergill v Monarch Airlines Ltd* [1981] AC 251, 281–84 (Lord Diplock); *JI MacWilliam Co Inc v Mediterranean Shipping Co SA* [2005] 2 AC 423, 437; *El Greco (Australia) Pty Ltd v Mediterranean Shipping Co SA* (2004) 140 FCR 296, 326–27 [142] (Allsop J).

There are some differences in the principles of interpretation of contracts between common law and civil law jurisdictions.[60] Further, the 2015 Code envisages the Court of Arbitration for Sport (CAS) as the final 'court of appeal' in respect of anti-doping disputes arising under it.[61] CAS is comprised of experienced lawyers knowledgeable in sport, drawn from many countries around the world, some of which are governed by the common law and some of which are governed by civil law. The composition of CAS panels varies infinitely. Sometimes there is a majority of civil lawyers on them; sometimes there is a majority of common lawyers. It is possible, therefore, that the Code, or provisions of anti-doping rules derived from the Code, could be interpreted differently if the governing law was held to be, say, English law, as opposed to German law, and the interpretation exercise was to be approached in accordance with that law. That would be undesirable and contrary to the purpose and object of the Code. It is also possible that even if this mistake is not made, CAS panel members may subconsciously apply the interpretation rules applicable in their own countries to interpreting the Code. That would also be wrong and contrary to the purpose and object of the Code.

Given these potential substantive differences and the possible differences of approach of those who will be interpreting the 2015 Code, it is critically important to identify the global 'broad principles of general acceptation' of construction which should govern the interpretation of the Code in conjunction with Article 24 of the 2015 Code itself. What then are the 'broad principles of general acceptation' in the international community applicable to the interpretation of anti-doping rules derived from the Code?

Subject to one qualification, these principles have been accurately summarised as follows:

> The general principles of contractual interpretation are a well-established feature of contract law in most, if not all, jurisdictions ... [T]he essential applicable principles involve ascertaining the intentions of the parties to the agreement in the objective sense, by reference to the natural ordinary meaning of the words used in the contract. The court or arbitrator has to consider what a reasonable person in the position of the parties to the contract would have understood the contract to mean at the time it was entered into. The meaning will be considered against the general ... background or factual matrix of the contract. *Where there is doubt as to the meaning of the words, the court or arbitrator may consider how a suggested interpretation fits with the purpose of the contract.*[62]

[60] In particular, civil law jurisdictions take a much more relaxed approach to the admissibility of extrinsic evidence as an aid to interpretation such as the subsequent conduct of parties. See, eg, Stefan Vogenauer, 'Interpretation of Contracts: Concluding Comparative Observations' in A Burrows and E Peel (eds), *Contract Terms* (Oxford, Oxford University Press, 2007) 123, 135. Even within the common law world there are the same differences between jurisdictions—compare *Agricultural and Rural Finance Pty Ltd v Gardiner* (2008) 238 CLR 570, 582 [35] (Gummow, Hayne and Kiefel JJ); *Gibbons Holdings Ltd v Wholesale Distributors Ltd* [2008] 1 NZLR 277 [52].

[61] 2015 Code art 13.

[62] David (n 2) 123–24 (emphasis added).

The above emphasised part should be differed from for two reasons. First, both in civil and common law jurisdictions, the purpose of the contract must be considered in any construction exercise and not only where there is 'doubt as to the meaning of the words'. Second, to ignore the purpose where, on the face of it, there appears to be no doubt as to the meaning of the words appears to be contrary to the express approach adopted in the 2015 Code. The express requirement to take into account the comments in interpreting the words of the Code, Article 24.2, strongly suggests that even clear words may have to give way to the 'purpose' or 'intent' of the drafters of the Code, as reflected in those comments.

Moreover, whilst in civil law jurisdictions, great weight is attached to the wording of the contract, nevertheless courts are willing to deviate from the wording of the contract if other circumstances strongly militate in favour of a different result. Civil courts are much more receptive to the reception of extrinsic evidence as an aid to interpretation than common law courts.[63] The extrinsic evidence to which a civil court would have regard would include, of course, evidence of the purpose or object of the contract.

Currently, the situation appears to be the same in common law countries, especially in Australia. The current view in Australia is that the purposes and object of a contract are to be taken into account in the construction exercise even if the relevant words appear to be otherwise clear and unambiguous.[64]

Finally, on this aspect, personal experience—sitting for more than a decade with civil lawyers on the Court of Arbitration for Sport and for the past couple of years in the Adjudicatory Chamber of the Fédération Internationale de Football Association (FIFA) Ethics Committee—confirms that the 'broad principles of general acceptation' are seen as being as set forth as mentioned. There has been remarkably little difference in views expressed on contractual interpretation. All panel members seem to go about it in much the same way. There is no doubt that the actual language employed and the comments attached to the Code are regarded as of the most fundamental importance.

There are, however, perhaps two potential problems with an 'international approach' to the construction of the Code and the associated desire or urging to maintain consistency on an international basis. First, it gives perhaps undue weight to the decision of the first court, tribunal or panel to consider a matter. Second, such an approach assumes that it is easy, or relatively easy, to ascertain what courts, tribunals or CAS panels in other jurisdictions have said about a particular provision. Article 13 makes CAS the final 'court of appeal' for most disputes involving the Code. It is CAS's decisions, therefore, which are most influential in respect of interpretation of the Code. However, not all CAS awards are made public. If all parties agree, the CAS award, and the reasons for it, will remain

[63] Vogenauer (n 60) 132, 134–38, 150.

[64] *Electricity General Corporation v Woodside Energy Ltd* (2014) 251 CLR 640, 656–57 [35] (French CJ, Hayne, Crennan and Kiefel JJ); *Mainteck Services Pty Ltd v Stein Heurtey SA* (2014) 310 ALR 113, 130 (Leeming JA); *Newey v Westpac Banking Corporation* [2014] NSWCA 319 [89] (Gleeson JA); *Stratton Finance Pty Ltd v Webb* (2014) 245 IR 223, 232 [41] (the Court).

confidential.[65] Further, even when the CAS award is a public one, it can be somewhat difficult to obtain or access copies of relevant CAS awards.[66]

Regrettably, there is no single place where one can quickly, reliably and efficiently search for CAS awards on the Code or derivative anti-doping rule violations of various national sporting bodies. The CAS website, which is improving, is by no means a perfect research tool for such a task. There are many CAS awards published on that website, but doing an efficient search of them for cases relating to specific provisions of the Code is not easy.

The World Anti-Doping Agency website also contains CAS decisions where it is a party. It also contains very useful links to websites of other sporting bodies which contain decisions of CAS and other tribunals relating to anti-doping matters. But it too is not comprehensive.

More recently, the *Australian and New Zealand Sports Law Journal* has begun to publish a reports section publishing CAS awards arising from incidents in Australia and New Zealand, or involving athletes from those countries.

However, there is not one consistent and reliable library of all CAS awards involving the Code. It seems to me that it is essential to establish such a library, which is readily accessible to lawyers, sporting organisations and athletes, if the aims of the Code are to be achieved and if it is to be interpreted and applied in a globalised and harmonised way.

Usually the task of interpreting the Code will be a disguised or masked one in the sense that one will be, in fact, interpreting the anti-doping rules of a domestic sporting organisation in which there will be no specific reference to the Code.[67] In this context, the anti-doping rules of a domestic sporting organisation may be

[65] CAS, Code of Sports-Related Arbitration (at 1 March 2013) r 59.

[66] A unique consideration which arises by virtue of the Code's purpose of having a consistent, harmonised approach to anti-doping matters and, to that end, largely entrusting to CAS the task of interpreting and applying the Code is that is necessitates CAS operating in a way quite different from other international arbitral bodies. The orthodox view is that one of the great advantages of international arbitration, as opposed to having disputes determined by a domestic court, is privacy. Thus, awards in such cases, being private in nature, have absolutely no value as precedents. By definition, they will never be in the public arena and are not intended to govern, or to be relied upon by, parties other than the parties to the particular arbitration agreement. Yet, the achievement of a common and harmonic approach to interpretation application of the Code demands that not only are CAS awards made public but also that they are readily available in the public arena and that, in effect, a doctrine of precedent is established in respect of such awards. In effect, this means, at least when adjudicating on disputes in respect of the Code, CAS is operating at least as much like a court as an arbitral body. This is especially so as the rights of appeal from a CAS decision to the Swiss Federal Tribunal are extremely limited. Essentially, CAS decisions can only be appealed against: (a) if the panel was constituted irregularly; (b) if the panel erroneously held that it had or did not have jurisdiction; (c) if the panel ruled on matters beyond the claims submitted to it or failed to rule on one of the claims; (d) if the principle of equal treatment of the parties, the principle of a fair hearing is violated; (e) if the award is incompatible with Swiss public policy.

See Loi Fédérale sur le Droit International Privé du 18 décembre 1987 (Federal Law on Private International Law of 18 December 1987) (Switzerland) art 190(2). See generally Stephan Netzle, 'Appeals against Arbitral Awards by the CAS' (2011) 2 *CAS Bulletin* 21–22.

[67] However, in essence, the anti-doping rules of that sporting organisation will mirror the provisions of the Code because the sporting organisation has complied with its obligations under art 23 of the 2015 Code.

part of its overall rules and the provenance of the anti-doping section of the rules will not be obvious on its face.

Article 8 of the Code contemplates that prior to an appeal to CAS, there will be a hearing before a domestic tribunal. The people comprising that tribunal may be completely unfamiliar with the Code. Or it may be that an urgent approach is made to a court of law for an injunction or the like, to restrain an imposition of a provisional suspension or the like, based on a breach of anti-doping rules. In any such case, the question of construction or interpretation of the anti-doping rules, and hence the Code, may arise to be determined by people who are unfamiliar with the Code. This is where problems may arise with the approach to construction by such a body.

A basic principle of construction of a contract is that the words of any particular provision must be construed in the light of the contract as a whole.[68] Yet it would be a cardinal sin to interpret the anti-doping rules of a sporting organisation, where those rules are based on the Code, in the light of the overall body of rules of the sporting organisation.[69] In particular, it would be wrong to construe words or expressions used in the anti-doping rules by reference to the way in which words or expressions are employed in other parts of the rules of such a sporting organisation.

Article 23 of the 2015 Code requires signatories to implement its core provisions 'without substantive change'. Thus, significant textual, linguistic and styling differences may be found in the rules of sporting bodies between those parts of the rules which relate to doping offences and those which do not. It is important, therefore, when construing the anti-doping rules of a sporting body derived from the Code, only to have regard to the anti-doping provisions and not to the rules as a whole.[70] Thus, it is important when appearing before a court or tribunal unfamiliar with the Code to explain its unique features and provenance so that such an understandable mistake in the interpretation exercise is not committed.

Further, when construing anti-doping rules based on the Code, one also has to abandon the accepted principle of construction that regard may be had to the relevant background facts or circumstances actually known to the particular parties to the contract.[71]

In the case of an ADRV, the 'parties' to the contract will be the sporting organisation concerned and the athlete. Yet neither of those parties had anything

[68] See, eg, *Australian Broadcasting Commission v Australasian Performing Rights Association Ltd* (1973) 129 CLR 99, 109 (Gibbs J).

[69] See 2015 Code 17.

[70] For an illustration of the problems which may arise if provisions derived from the Code are sought to be construed in the light of provisions not so derived, see *Berger v World Anti-Doping Authority* (Award, Court of Arbitration for Sport, Case No CAS 2009/A/1948, March 2010) 265–75 [58]–[61].

[71] *Electricity General Corporation* (n 64) 656–57 [35] (French CJ, Hayne, Crennan and Kiefel JJ); *QBE Insurance Australia Ltd v Vasik* (2010) 16 ANZ Insurance Cases ¶61-851, 78,341 [35] (Allsop P); *The Movie Network Channels Pty Ltd v Optus Vision Pty Ltd* [2010] NSWCA 111 [92]–[106] (Mcfarlan JA).

whatsoever to do, in all likelihood, with the creation of the anti-doping rules. Rather, those anti-doping rules are simply copied from the Code, which represents 'the consensus of a broad spectrum of stakeholders around the world with an interest in fair sport'.[72]

It would be neither sensible nor profitable, in those circumstances, to construe the ADRV in question by reference to facts actually known at the time the contract was entered into by either the sporting organisation concerned or by the athlete.

There is much to be said for the view that, in construing the Code, the only surrounding circumstances, including the purpose and object of the provision in question, which can be used as an aid to construction are those which one can know without evidence from the terms of the document itself. It would be an impossible task to ascertain the surrounding circumstances actually known to all of the stakeholders involved in the preparation of the 2015 Code. It would be, literally, impossible to embark upon the exercise of seeking to find out whether any such circumstances existed.[73]

Once more, anyone tasked with construing anti-doping rules based on the 2015 Code must adjust his or her approach to construction to accommodate its unique characteristics.

Conclusions

There can be no doubt that, first and foremost, the 2015 Code derives its status, authority and effect in respect of both sporting organisations and athletes by reason of it being a contract. But it is a contract with a difference. In many ways, it is more akin to an international convention or an international set of trade rules.

[72] See 2015 Code 17.

[73] By analogy, there is judicial support for the proposition that, in such circumstances, the only circumstances that should be used as an aid to construction—save, perhaps, in exceptional cases—are those which can be seen from the terms of the document itself. In *Phoenix Commercial Enterprises Pty Ltd v City of Canada Bay Council* [2010] NSWCA 64 [166], Campbell JA had to consider the situation of a contract in the form of a lease which was a long-term one capable of assignment and subject to indefeasibility principles. In such circumstances, especially because of the virtual impossibility of an assignee being in a position to know the surrounding circumstances which were actually known to the original parties, Campbell JA held, with the agreement of the other two members of the Court, that the only relevant surrounding circumstances, for the construction exercise, were those which could be gleaned from the terms of the document itself. Likewise, in *Owners of Strata Plan No 3397 v Tate* (2007) 70 NSWLR 344, the Court of Appeal held in the context of corporate constitutions and strata plan by-laws that there should be a 'tight' rein on having recourse to evidence of surrounding circumstances and that, ordinarily, caution should be exercised in going beyond the language of the contract: 360–62 [65]–[71] (McColl JA). Moreover, such an approach is also consistent with that adopted in respect of international conventions or treaties where similar issues arise and primacy is therefore given to the text: see generally Vienna Convention on the Law of Treaties, opened for signature on 23 May 1969, 1155 UNTS 331 (entered into force 27 January 1980) arts 31–32.

It is a contract which is intended to have worldwide effect and to be interpreted without regard to the laws of any particular country or any particular system of laws. Moreover, it contains its own specific rules of interpretation, some of which differ, in any event, from accepted rules of construction in common law countries.

All of this means that accepted principles of construction of contracts require modification or adaptation in respect of the 2015 Code. It would be a mistake to interpret the 2015 Code or the anti-doping rules of domestic sporting organisations based on the 2015 Code entirely in accordance with the accepted principles of construction in Australia.

5

Human Rights and the Anti-Doping *Lex Sportiva*—The Relationship of Public and Private International Law, 'Law Beyond the State' and the Laws of Nation States

ANDREW BYRNES*

> [The provisions of the Code] are not intended to be subject to or limited by any national requirements and legal standards applicable to such proceedings, although they are intended to be applied in a manner which respects the principles of proportionality and human rights.[1]

> These Olympic people seem to elevate themselves by a process of self-levitation.[2]

> [S]ports law is now far from being amenable to an exhaustive explanation based on structures of private law alone, but rather presents a mixed nature, in which a regulatory framework based on private autonomy interacts constantly with public law norms. Such a phenomenon takes place at the national level especially, a level at which the sports legal regime has always been characterized by a tight dialectic between public and private law.[3]

Introduction

Sport—whether professional or otherwise—is big business for professional athletes and their support personnel, sports administrators, manufacturers of sporting

* Professor of Law, Australia Human Rights Centre and Faculty of Law, UNSW Australia.

1 World Anti-Doping Authority, World Anti-Doping Code (1 January 2015) 17 (hereinafter the Code).

2 Transcript of Proceedings, *Zhu v Treasurer (NSW)* [2004] HCATrans 200 (15 June 2004) 2591 (Gummow J).

3 Lorenzo Casini, 'The Making of a *Lex Sportiva* by the Court of Arbitration for Sport' (2011) 12 *German Law Journal* 1317, 1318.

equipment, advertisers, the gambling industry and communities. Sport also has important social and cultural as well as political dimensions.[4] The power enjoyed by those who administer sport and those who participate in it vary, though their relationship is an asymmetrical one, with most athletes and participants enjoying less power than the institutions which govern their sport and determine whether they can participate in it for profit or pleasure.

Human rights are reflected in many ways in the mythology, practice and regulation of sport.[5] The human right to engage in sport and to do so without discrimination is recognised and proclaimed in various human rights treaties and other human rights instruments[6]—'a fundamental right for all', according to the United Nations Educational, Scientific and Cultural Organization (UNESCO)[7]—and is affirmed in other documents such as the Olympic Charter.[8] The professional practice of sports directly engages the right to work of athletes and associated support personnel, and the related right to enjoy just and favourable conditions of work, and other rights, while the right to enjoy sports as a non-professional participant or spectator is recognised as one aspect of the right to participate in cultural life.[9]

The exercises of regulatory power that take place under the umbrella of the international sports anti-doping regime have a significant impact on the lives of individual athletes and those associated with them professionally and personally. They involve subjecting athletes and others to stringent rules of behaviour as a condition of participation in national and international sports events. Depending on the level at which the athletes perform, they may also involve significant intrusions into their daily lives and those of their families, who are subjected

[4] See Jack Anderson, *Modern Sports Law: A Textbook* (Oxford, Hart Publishing, 2010) 1–20.

[5] For a different, unsentimental perspective on human rights and sport, see Richard Giulianotti, 'Human Rights, Globalization and Sentimental Education: The Case of Sport' (2004) 7(3) *Sport in Society* 355.

[6] See generally Human Rights Council, *Progress Report of the Human Rights Council Advisory Committee on the Study on the Possibilities of Using Sport and the Olympic Ideal to Promote Human Rights*, 27th session, Agenda Items 3 and 5, UN Doc A/HRC/27/58 (25 August 2014); Human Rights Council, *Final Report of the Human Rights Council Advisory Committee on the Possibilities of Using Sport and the Olympic Ideal to Promote Human Rights for All and to Strengthen Universal Respect for Them*, 30th session, Agenda Items 3 and 5, UN Doc A/HRC/30/50 (17 August 2015).

[7] UNESCO, International Charter of Physical Education and Sport, UNESCO Res 1/5.4/2, 20th session (21 November 1978) art 1 heading; UNESCO, *Report on the Progress of the Revision of the International Charter of Physical Education and Sport*, 196th session, Agenda Item 9 (18 March 2015) annex ('International Charter of Physical Education, Physical Activity and Sport') art 1 heading. Sport is seen as both an end in itself and a means to many other noble ends: see United Nations Sport for Development and Peace. Sport for Development and Peace: The UN System in Action. (2011) www.un.org/wcm/content/site/sport/home.

[8] International Olympic Committee, Olympic Charter (2 August 2015) 'Fundamental Principles of Olympism', Principle 4, www.olympic.org/Documents/olympic_charter_en.pdf.

[9] International Covenant on Economic, Social and Cultural Rights, opened for signature 16 December 1966, 993 UNTS 3 (entered into force 3 November 1976) art 15(1)(a). See Committee on Economic, Social and Cultural Rights, *General Comment No 21: Right of Everyone to Take Part in Cultural Life (Art 15, Para 1(a), of the International Covenant on Economic, Social and Cultural Rights)*, 43rd session, UN Doc E/C.12/GC/21 (21 December 2009) paras 11, 16, 31, 37.

to rules and potential penalties that may be viewed at first sight as incompatible with fundamental principles of due process and proportionality. They may further involve the termination or significant restriction of their ability to earn a livelihood through sport or support activities, limitations on their access to legal remedies in relation to disputes, the transmission of their personal data across national boundaries, and the publication of the details of disciplinary findings that are likely to do significant reputational damage. In some cases, the regime may involve the exercise by state sporting or anti-doping authorities of coercive investigative powers more familiar in the context of the investigation of serious criminal offences, even though anti-doping rule violations are, for the most part, violations of civil law obligations. Some of these powers are backed by significant financial or other penalties in the event of non-cooperation.

The sanctioning of athletes and others for failure to comply with anti-doping rules or other regulations thus engages many human rights protected by international treaties and national constitutions or legislation.[10] Not only work-related rights are affected, but also the right to respect for private and family life, the right not to have one's reputation unlawfully or arbitrarily interfered with, freedom of association, the right to equality and non-discrimination, and a range of procedural rights, including the right of access to a court and a fair hearing in the determination of one's civil rights and obligations.[11]

The literature is replete with examples of rulings by national and international sports associations and of the Court of Arbitration for Sport (CAS) which appear to be harsh and to involve the application of stringent standards in an inflexible way, in many cases punishing athletes who do not appear to have been at fault and who have been innocent victims of mistakes that seem reasonably avoidable only in retrospect. Among the aspects of the regime criticised on human rights grounds are: the widespread use of a strict liability standard; the imposition of uniform periods of suspension as punishment, regardless of the differential impact on athletes in different sports;[12] the extension of limitation periods to well beyond

[10] Human rights (values) are also promoted by other non-human rights statutes such as competition law and by the policing of the application of the rules of associations and the contracts (eg, the right to a fair hearing by disciplinary tribunals) or common law doctrines. See, eg, the protection of the right to work through common law's restriction on unreasonable restraint of trade: *Eastham v Newcastle United Football Club Ltd* [1964] Ch 413; *Buckley v Tutty* (1971) 125 CLR 353; *Hughes v Western Australian Cricket Association Inc* (1986) 19 FCR 10; *Pilkadaris v Asian Tour (Tournament Players Division) Pte Ltd* [2012] SGHC 236; *Carberry v Drice* [2011] QSC 16. See generally JRS Forbes, 'Private Tribunals and Restraint of Trade' in *Justice in Tribunals* 4th edn (Sydney, Federation Press, 2014) 48.

[11] For an overview, see Antonio Rigozzi, Gabrielle Kaufmann-Kohler and Giorgio Malinverni, 'Doping and Fundamental Rights of Athletes: Comments in the Wake of the Adoption of the World Anti-Doping Code' (2003) 3 *International Sports Law Review* 39. Of course, the human rights of other athletes are also affected when athletes use prohibited substances, and these must be taken into account when assessing the reasonableness of the measures taken to identify and sanction those athletes engaged in illegal doping activities.

[12] See, eg, Barrie Houlihan, 'Civil Rights, Doping Control and the World Anti-doping Code' (2004) 7(3) *Sport in Society* 420, 427–28.

those that apply in other civil cases; the intrusiveness of the whereabouts regime for certain groups of athletes;[13] the rights of athletes who are children;[14] and the requirement that disputes can be finally determined on the merits only by an arbitral body, which, because of the dominance of sporting associations and official bodies in determining its makeup, might not satisfy the requirements of an independent and impartial tribunal.

All these rules and procedures have been adopted and are justified as part of a stringent regime that is required to eradicate (or at least limit) the extent of doping in sport. Supporters point to the broad international consensus among states, sporting associations and athlete representatives that there is a pressing need to address the problem with vigour through universal, uniform and robust standards. Critics, on the other hand, suggest that the regime has been designed and is implemented with excessive, almost missionary zeal, that in certain respects it is not supported by a significant number of athletes, and that it is disproportionate in design and impact in a number of respects. They question whether the regime is effective and whether its encroachment on a number of human rights can in fact be justified.

This chapter explores how human rights standards and values directly or indirectly affect the exercise of power by those involved in adjudicating upon allegations of violations of anti-doping rules. It examines the ways in which human rights norms and values have entered into the anti-doping regime. Its focus is not primarily on whether particular regulatory rules or procedures are (in)consistent with substantive human rights guarantees. Rather, its concern is how the application of human rights is facilitated or impeded by the legal structures on which the anti-doping regime is built. In this field, systems of state law carve out an area for the operation of a body of largely autonomous private globalised law to which norms of public law (such as human rights) have little or no direct application. Yet, at the same time, state laws may provide some limited protection against encroachment on rights by policing the outer limits of what can legitimately be undertaken within that 'autonomous area', thus providing an incentive for those administering the 'private law' to ensure that a certain level of respect for human rights values is guaranteed.

[13] As Kreft puts it: 'One of the points where the usual restraints do not apply is athletes' whereabouts information. The whereabouts policy entails a regulation unthinkable in the case of police or other state and international repressive systems where basic human rights have to be respected. Of course there are recent and significant exceptions such as the war on terrorism. Does the war on doping deserve to be such an exception?' Lev Kreft, 'The Elite Athlete—In a State of Exception?' (2009) 3(1) *Sport, Ethics and Philosophy* 3, 11–12. See also Oskar MacGregor et al, 'Anti-doping, Purported Rights to Privacy and WADA's Whereabouts Requirements: A Legal Analysis' (2013) 1(2) *Fair Play: Revista de Filosofía, Ética y Derecho del Deporte* 13; James Halt, 'Where is the Privacy in WADA's "Whereabouts" Rule?' (2009) 20 *Marquette Sports Law Review* 267; Dag Vidar Hanstad and Sigmund Loland, 'Elite Athletes' Duty to Provide Information on Their Whereabouts: Justifiable Anti-doping Work or an Indefensible Surveillance Regime?' (2009) 9 *European Journal of Sport Science* 3.

[14] See Houlihan (n 12) 431–33.

Furthermore, those engaged in setting the standards and values of that autonomous body of law have chosen to explicitly import certain human rights norms and values, partly for policy reasons and partly for strategic reasons. Furthermore, the regime's principal adjudicatory body, the CAS, has also added to the protections enjoyed by athletes, though within the significant constraints imposed by the Code and other relevant regulations.

As a result of these various moves, the international sports anti-doping regime limits the occasion for the intervention of external assessors of human rights compatibility in the form of national or international human rights instances, reducing their role to patrolling the outer limits, and leaving the primary task of ensuring and assessing the enjoyment of human rights by those affected to the bodies involved in the administration of the *lex sportiva* (in particular, the various national associations and the CAS). As a consequence, while a level of protection of human rights is provided, this is limited by the constraints of the Code and generally involves the adoption of interpretation of rights guarantees favourable to upholding the compatibility of the stringent and at times draconian provisions of the Code itself. Overall, one sees a regulatory system-friendly interpretation articulated largely by those internal to the system that contrasts with much more critical assessments made by those outside the system (as well as by many athletes' organisations and advocates within the system).

The Anti-Doping Regime as an Example of the Interaction of Formal Law-Making and 'Informal' Law-Making beyond the State

The international anti-doping regime provides a striking example of the way in which 'law-making' and 'law enforcement' can take place 'outside' (or at least beyond) the state, and yet be simultaneously supported by the actions and institutions of the state.[15] In this field, standards regulating the behaviour of athletes and support persons are established and given effect through the actions of a combination of state and international public institutions, and various private and non-state actors operating at the international and national levels. Anti-doping standards and disciplinary procedures are a combination of 'private law' and state-based or state-endorsed norms: they derive their force from the 'private law' of

[15] Though, as Casini notes, not necessarily 'law without a State', drawing on the work of Gunther Teubner, '"Global Bukowina": Legal Pluralism in the World Society' in Gunther Teubner (ed), *Global Law without a State* (Aldershot, Dartmouth Publishing, 1997) 3, cited in Casini (n 3) 1318 fn 5. See Ralf Michaels, 'The True *Lex Mercatoria*: Private Law beyond the State' (2007) 14 *Indiana Journal of Global Legal Studies* 447. See also the excellent discussion by Klaus Dieter Wolf, 'The Non-existence of Private Self-regulation in the Transnational Sphere and its Implications for the Responsibility to Procure Legitimacy: The Case of the *Lex Sportiva*' (2014) 3 *Global Constitutionalism* 275.

contract within state systems, but also from 'private law outside the state', bodies of rules and procedures with which state law intersects as a result of contractual links.[16]

The actors involved in the creation and administration of the international anti-doping regime include national and international non-governmental sporting organisations (the International Olympic Committee, national Olympic committees, international and national sporting federations), and national governments. Those who engage in sport—whether for leisure, as professional athletes, or as support persons for these groups—are affected by the anti-doping regime and also have input into its form and content.

The roles played by national governments are diverse. They operate in traditional diplomatic fora through the adoption of treaties and other international instruments that set policy and embody binding and non-binding calls for action.[17] States also contribute to the funding and are members of multi-partite international private bodies such as the World Anti-Doping Agency (WADA), which set anti-doping standards. States also support and interact with the anti-doping regime through the activities of transnational networks of government anti-doping agencies, and domestic parliaments may provide support for the anti-doping regime through the enactment of national legislation.

State courts are also involved in the anti-doping regime, sometimes supporting and sometimes impeding its operation. Often their role will be to maintain the boundaries within which the 'private' law of the anti-doping regime operates by enforcing arbitration clauses and recognising the arbitral awards that result. Conversely, in other cases (though much less frequently), their intervention may involve frustrating the actions of anti-doping bodies by refusing to recognise their decisions or penalties on substantive or procedural grounds, sometimes drawing on human rights, constitutional or other public law norms to ground their decisions.

Anti-doping norms and procedures are thus sourced in or regulated by public international law, private international law, 'informal' standards that receive direct or indirect endorsement by the state, contract law (including the rules regulating the membership of sporting organisations and conditions for participation

[16] See, eg, Matthew J Mitten and Hayden Opie, '"Sports Law": Implications for the Development of International, Comparative, and National Law and Global Dispute Resolution' in Robert CR Siekmann and Janwillem Soek (eds), *Lex Sportiva: What is Sports Law?* (The Hague, TMC Asser Press, 2012) 173, 177–85, 193–206 (originally published in Matthew J Mitten and Hayden Opie, '"Sports Law": Implications for the Development of International, Comparative, and National Law and Global Dispute Resolution' (2010) 85 *Tulane Law Review* 269).

[17] Andreas Wax, 'Public International Sports Law: A "Forgotten" Discipline?' in Siekmann and Soek (n 16) 287, 294–97, also published in Andreas Wax, 'Public International Sports Law: A "Forgotten" Discipline?' (2010) 3–4 *International Sports Law Journal* 25 (noting the range of issues in addition to doping which the public international law of sport addresses). See also Andreas Wax, *Internationales Sportrecht: Unter besonderer Berücksichtigung des Sportvölkerrechts* (Berlin, Duncker & Humblot, 2009).

in sporting events), constitutional and administrative law, as well as employment law, competition law and tort law.[18]

Whether it is meaningful and helpful to designate these standards and procedures (or a subset of them) as part of a *lex sportiva*[19] (whatever the motivations for and consequences of such a classification),[20] there is clearly a large and growing body of largely self-contained and self-referential norms, institutions and procedures and jurisprudence regulating doping in sport.

The Legal Framework of the Anti-Doping Regime and the Relevance of Human Rights Law

The international anti-doping regime has been structured in a way which minimises, even if it cannot entirely eliminate, the direct application of positive human rights law to the conduct of doping investigations, proceedings and the imposition of penalties. There are at least two dimensions to this: the grounding of the anti-doping regime in the private law of contract and associations, bolstered by national and international arbitration law; and the conceptual underpinnings of human rights law and its primary focus on the actions of the state.

The broad policy framework of the international anti-doping regime has been endorsed by states in the form of the 2005 International Convention against Doping in Sport adopted under the auspices of UNESCO,[21] and the Copenhagen Declaration on Anti-Doping in Sport.[22] Under the UNESCO Convention, states parties commit themselves to the principles of the Code and to take appropriate measures to support anti-doping efforts,[23] including through facilitating the work

[18] Lorenzo Casini, 'The Making of a *Lex Sportiva* by the Court of Arbitration for Sport' in Armin von Bogdandy and Ingo Venzke (eds), *International Judicial Lawmaking: On Public Authority and Democratic Legitimation in Global Governance* (Heidelberg, Springer International Publishing, 2012) 439, 439–44, also available in Casini (n 3) 1317–21.

[19] See the various views in Robert CR Siekmann, 'What is Sports Law? *Lex Sportiva* and *Lex Ludica*: A Reassessment of Content and Terminology' (2011) 11(3–4) *International Sports Law Journal* 3; Ken Foster, 'Is There a Global Sports Law?' in Siekmann and Soek (n 16) 35; James AR Nafziger, '*Lex Sportiva*' in Siekmann and Soek (n 16) 53; Michael J Beloff, 'Is There a *Lex Sportiva*?' in Siekmann and Soek (n 16) 69; Robert CR Siekmann, *Introduction to International and European Sports Law* (The Hague, TMC Asser Press, 2012) 1–33; Casini (n 3); Franck Latty, *La lex sportiva: Recherche sur le droit transnational* (Leiden, Martinus Nijhoff Publishers, 2007) 41–46; Anne Röthel, 'Lex mercatoria, lex sportiva, lex technica—Private Rechtsetzung jenseits des Nationalstaates?' (2007) 62 *JuristenZeitung* 755.

[20] Alfonso Valero, 'In Search of a Working Notion of *Lex Sportiva*' (2014) 14 *International Sports Law Journal* 3.

[21] International Convention against Doping in Sport, opened for signature 19 October 2005, 2419 UNTS 201 (entered into force 1 February 2007) (hereinafter the UNESCO Convention).

[22] World Anti-Doping Agency, Copenhagen Declaration on Anti-Doping in Sport (at 5 March 2003). See also Anti-Doping Convention, opened for signature 16 November 1989 [1994] ATS 33 (entered into force 1 March 1990) (also known as the Council of Europe Anti-Doping Convention).

[23] UNESCO Convention, especially arts 4–5.

of WADA and other organisations operating in compliance with the Code, and to cooperate in the technical and cross-border measures needed to effectively implement the Code.[24] The UNESCO Convention is thus a form of suppression convention, identifying a mischief and obliging states parties individually and collectively to take steps to eliminate it through prohibition backed by sanctions, in this case through endorsing the Code, which in effect requires prohibitions to be incorporated into contracts and disciplinary sanctions imposed under those contractual arrangements.

There is no explicit reference to 'human rights' in the substantive provisions of the UNESCO Convention; a formulaic reference in the preamble to human rights[25] and references to the importance of sport in relation to health, education and culture, which might also have been articulated in human rights terms, are all that is to be found in the treaty.[26] Thus, human rights do not loom large in the text of the Convention, either because it was taken for granted that they would be observed in the process of its implementation or because they were simply not seen as particularly relevant—the focus of the Convention is on stimulating measures to implement fully the regime represented by the Code and endorsed in the treaty.

It is sometimes asserted that the Convention requires states parties to give effect to all provisions of the Code. In fact, states parties commit themselves to 'the principles of the Code' as the basis for undertaking action at the national and international levels.[27] A range of different types of concepts and standards are referred to as 'principles' in the 2015 Code (and earlier codes); they include broad principles such as human rights, proportionality, due process and natural justice, and respect for the privacy of athletes, along with such 'principles' as the coordination of anti-doping results, public transparency, the 'principle for education and information programs', and 'principles for the analysis of samples' and 'for conducting results management'. It is far from clear whether the obligations under the Convention in relation to these principles necessarily require the adoption of the Code in all its detail (as indeed the Code itself appears to recognise in various places).[28]

[24] ibid art 16.

[25] ibid preamble.

[26] The Convention also contains a savings clause in the form of art 6, which can be read as preserving a state's obligations in relation to human rights, to the extent that they apply to actions that they undertake to carry out under the UNESCO Convention. Article 6 provides: 'This Convention shall not alter the rights and obligations of States Parties which arise from other agreements previously concluded and consistent with the object and purpose of this Convention. This does not affect the enjoyment by other States Parties of their rights or the performance of their obligations under this Convention.'

[27] International Convention against Doping in Sport, opened for signature 19 October 2005, 2419 UNTS 201 (entered into force 1 February 2007) arts 3(a), 4(1).

[28] See the comments in *Pechstein v International Skating Union*, Oberlandesgericht München, U 1110/14 Kart, 15 January 2015 [84]–[86] (the UNESCO Convention did not oblige states parties to ensure that athletes accepted arbitration clause in favour of CAS as part of their contracts with their sporting associations).

As a practical matter, of course, the implementation of the detailed provisions in the Code has in practice become a requirement for sports associations. States will often require associations to adopt the Code or equivalent rules as a condition for funding; membership of sporting associations in international federations or national Olympic committees is in effect dependent on such compliance; and athletes are required to accept the provisions of the Code or equivalent rules if they wish to be members of their sporting associations and/or to participate in particular events.

International Human Rights Obligations: Their Nature, Scope and Application to the Anti-Doping in Sports Regime

The international human rights law framework essentially involves the imposition of obligations on states, not on non-state actors. All states parties to the UNESCO Convention are also bound under human rights treaties or the customary international human rights law to respect and protect human rights and fundamental freedoms, including those engaged by the operation of the Code and associated national procedures. In the first place, states are obliged to *respect* human rights—that is, not to encroach directly upon the enjoyment of rights through their own acts or omissions. However, states are also obliged to *protect* human rights—that is, to take appropriate step to endeavour to ensure that the human rights of a person are not violated by other non-state actors.

International human rights obligations and the corresponding obligations under most national constitutions thus have their most important direct impact in relation to the exercise of power by the state against the citizen, rather than applying directly to inter-citizen relations through a doctrine of horizontal effect.[29] As a matter of international law, the question of the responsibility of the state in relation to the actions of private parties towards each other (including those that might infringe human rights) has traditionally come under the rubric of the state's obligation of due diligence or its obligation to 'protect'. In other words, the acts of private individuals are not as such directly attributable to the state, and the obligation of the state is to take all feasible/reasonable/appropriate measures to prevent or punish the infringement of the rights of one private actor by another private

[29] CAS has noted on various occasions the primarily vertical operation of international human rights guarantees, binding the state in relation to individuals. See, eg, *Adamu v Fédération Internationale de Football Association (FIFA)* (Award, Court of Arbitration for Sport, Case No CAS 2011/A/2426, 24 February 2012) [65]–[67]; *Diakite v Fédération Internationale de Football Association (FIFA)* (Award, Court of Arbitration for Sport, Case No CAS 2011/A/2433, 8 March 2012) [23]–[24]; *Football Club Girondins de Bordeaux v Fédération Internationale de Football Association (FIFA)* (Award, Court of Arbitration for Sport, Case No CAS 2012/A/2862, 11 January 2013) [105]–[108].

actor. It must be said, though, that this approach has tended to downplay the role of the state in providing a background system of law for 'voluntary' interaction in the market/private sphere, which is given effect through the ultimate backing of state power by means of the enforcement of private obligations through the courts.

Neither WADA (despite its hybrid status)[30] nor most national anti-doping organisations or international and national sporting federations are state or public bodies; they are non-state entities incorporated under national law with private law status. The UNESCO Convention does not require states parties themselves to take over the administration of anti-doping investigations and sanctioning or to delegate the power of the state to the institutions that are engaged in it. While in some cases, national anti-doping agencies may be given statutory powers to assist in the investigation of alleged anti-doping violations by compelling testimony and the production of evidence, the hearings and adjudication take place in most cases before the 'private' tribunal of sporting associations or before the private arbitral tribunal that is CAS.

Most sporting organisations are private law entities, whether they are unincorporated associations or bodies incorporated under relevant associations or corporations legislation. Depending on the legal system, the power of sporting associations to enforce their rules and the Code against their members lies in contract, associations or institutional law, or in a *sui generis* relationship that recognises the athlete's membership of the organisation as giving rights to enforceable obligations under the law.[31]

Accordingly, in most instances, the institutions which operate the anti-doping system within individual countries are not exercising the power of the state under the law of that country. On that basis, their actions would not appear to directly give rise to international responsibility of the state in which they are incorporated or in which they have their principal seat of business.[32] Indeed, their rules and proceedings would not at first sight appear to be subject to public international law obligations at all.

Nonetheless, the obligations of the state may still be engaged, not just the State's own positive obligation to ensure access to a court but also its obligations to protect persons against infringement of their rights by others (assuming that waivable rights have not been validly waived). The right to a fair hearing before an independent and impartial tribunal in the determination of one's 'civil rights and obligations' (as Article 6(1) of the European Convention for the Protection of Human Rights and Fundamental Freedoms (ECHR)[33] puts it) or 'rights and

[30] Lorenzo Casini, 'Global Hybrid Public-Private Bodies: The World Anti-Doping Agency (WADA)' (2009) 6 *International Organizations Law Review* 421.

[31] Rosmarijn van Kleef, 'The Legal Status of Disciplinary Regulations in Sport' (2013) 14(2) *International Sports Law Journal* 24.

[32] Though there may arguably be an issue so far as the participation of states in the policy and rule-making activities of WADA lead to the adoption of rules that violate human rights.

[33] Opened for signature 4 November 1950, 213 UNTS 221 (entered into force 3 September 1953).

obligations in suit at law' (as Article 14 of the International Covenant on Civil and Political Rights (ICCPR)[34] has it) is also clearly engaged by proceedings to determine liability for an alleged anti-doping rule violation, as it limits that right. However, a 'voluntary' waiver[35] of this right through an acceptance of binding arbitration of disputes will normally be enforced by state courts, which will require arbitration and will refuse to review arbitral awards except on the most limited of grounds; this is widely accepted as a permissible limitation on the enjoyment of that right.

The Private International Law and Arbitration Framework: Restrictions on the Challenges to Review

A lynchpin of the international anti-doping regime is its use of the framework of international arbitration to direct the traffic of anti-doping investigations and proceedings through national federation proceedings with an appeal to CAS.[36]

At the risk of oversimplifying a variety of complex legal and practical arrangements, the basic structure of legal regimes relating to anti-doping rules violations generally consists of an agreement between an athlete and a sporting organisation that the athlete will observe particular rules relating to doping (either the Code or rules based on it), will submit to the investigative procedures of the sporting association where an allegation is made that the athlete has failed to comply with these, and will respect any penalty imposed following a finding that the athlete has committed a violation. The 'choice' offered to the individual athlete is generally the lowest level of a cascading series of obligations and incentives to ensure adherence to the Code and its incorporation into association rules.[37]

A central objective of the international anti-doping regime has been to ensure a harmonious and uniform application of rules to athletes and others affected by the rules, and to maintain the adjudication of disputes within the framework of the rules governing the sport. This goal is in the first place advanced by the domestic incorporation of the international norms contained in the Code and related instruments into the rules of the relevant sporting association. As noted above, this is achieved through a system of sticks and carrots: pressure from states

[34] Opened for signature 19 December 1966, 999 UNTS 171 (entered into force 23 March 1976).

[35] See Jérôme de Montmollin and Dmitry A Pentsov, 'Do Athletes Really Have the Right to a Fair Trial in "Non-analytical Positive" Doping Cases?' (2011) 22(2) *American Review of International Arbitration* 187, 206–08.

[36] See generally Paul David, *A Guide to the World Anti-Doping Code: The Fight for the Spirit of Sport* 2nd edn (Cambridge, Cambridge University Press, 2013) 14–51.

[37] See, eg, the relationships between the various actors in *International Paralympic Committee (IPC) v I* (Award, Court of Arbitration for Sport, Case No CAS 2012/A/2789, 17 December 2012) [6.1]–[6.7].

in implementation of their obligations under the UNESCO Convention (often linked to government funding of sporting associations).[38] National sporting organisations will need to agree to this to belong to international federations; competitors in particular events must agree to this in order to participate in those events.

A second strategy for achieving universality and uniformity is pursued by directing disputes to CAS, which is in fact an arbitral tribunal established under Swiss law and based in Lausanne, Switzerland.[39] While there are variants, it is common for the rules of sporting associations to provide for a hearing into any allegation of a violation before a disciplinary tribunal of the association itself, with an 'appeal' to CAS.[40] In fact, the mandate of CAS is to hear cases on the factual and legal merits, and it is not restricted to exercising only a more limited appellate jurisdiction. In some cases, the applicable rules may provide for CAS to be the first (and only) instance to hear a case on the merits.[41]

The decisions of CAS are treated as arbitral awards under both Swiss law and the international law relating to the recognition and enforcement of foreign arbitral awards. Challenges to proceedings before CAS or to awards of CAS are limited by Swiss and other national law relating to the enforcement of agreements to arbitrate, and the recognition and enforcement of arbitral awards. These tend overall to favour enforcing the parties' expressed intention to refer disputes to arbitration. Courts will permit proceedings to be brought in violation of arbitration agreements only in very restricted circumstances, and national laws significantly limit the grounds on which a court may refuse to recognise or otherwise give effect to an arbitral award.[42] The problematic assumption of the truly voluntary nature of the consent of athletes has frequently been highlighted.[43] Indeed, it has been argued and recognised (including by courts)[44] that a simple acceptance of such 'consent' as genuine and valid fails to recognise the power imbalances that exist in most relations between athletes and governing organisations. However, in those

[38] See David (n 36) 52–60; Anderson (n 4) 120–22. For an example of links to funding, see Paul Horvath, 'Anti-doping and Human Rights in Sport: The Case of the AFL and the WADA Code' (2002) 32 *Monash University Law Review*, 357, 357–58.

[39] See Anderson (n 4) 89–92.

[40] Code art 8.

[41] ibid art 8.5.

[42] See Loi fédérale sur le droit international privé 1987 (Private International Law Act) (Switzerland), which permits an arbitral award to be set aside if the arbitral tribunal was not properly constituted (art 190(2)(a)), if the arbitral tribunal wrongfully accepted or declined jurisdiction (art 190(2)(b)), if the principle of equal treatment of the parties or the right to be heard is violated (art 190(2)(d)) or if it is incompatible with public policy (art 190(2)(e)). See David (n 36) 337–46; Antonio Rigozzi, 'Challenging Awards of the Court of Arbitration for Sport' (2010) 1 *Journal of International Dispute Settlement* 217, 235–54. The direct application of the ECHR or of the human rights guarantees under the Swiss Constitution is not possible in such cases: *Pechstein v International Skating Union*, Tribunal fédéral (Swiss Federal Supreme Court), Case No 4A_621/2009, 10 February 2010 [2.2].

[43] See, eg, Jan Łukomski, 'Arbitration Clauses in Sport Governing Bodies' Statutes: Consent or Constraint? Analysis from the Perspective of Article 6(1) of the European Convention on Human Rights' (2013) 13 *International Sports Law Journal* 60, 68.

[44] See *Cañas v ATP Tour*, Tribunal fédéral (Swiss Federal Supreme Court), Case No 4P.172/2006, 22 March 2007 reported in (2007) BGE 133 III 235, cited in Rigozzi (n 42) 227–28.

legal systems in which a finding of legally valid consent is necessary to produce the requisite legal obligations, it is rare that courts displace an express contractual agreement to refer disputes to arbitration.

Thus, the effect of compulsory referral of any appeals to CAS (which has the power to hear each appeal as a dispute de novo) is that there is very limited opportunity to seek a wide-ranging review before a court which can assess the validity of some of the Code provisions against directly applicable substantive human rights norms. The exclusive jurisdiction of the Swiss courts (the Federal Supreme Court) to review awards of CAS also brings into play the provisions of Swiss law on the recognition and enforcement of domestic and foreign arbitral awards. This provides very limited scope for challenging awards on 'human rights' grounds.

Arbitral awards, whether under Swiss law or under the international regime of the Convention on the Recognition and Enforcement of Foreign Arbitral Awards,[45] can be challenged on only a very limited number of grounds. This reflects the policy position that, as the parties to the arbitration have voluntarily consented to the process, they may therefore be considered to have waived their right to a full hearing before a court in the state system.

Notwithstanding the public international law policy framework set out in the UNESCO Convention and other international instruments, the conceptual, legal and practical underpinning of the anti-doping regulatory regime has been primarily that of private law.[46] The law of contract/associations, backed by private international law rules relating to the enforceability of arbitral awards and the limited review by national courts of such awards (the imposition of sanctions for doping violations being characterised as such), has been the primary source of individual obligation and regulatory power. They have operated to produce a legal exclusion zone in which there is relatively little formal scope for the direct intrusion and application of human rights standards and the scrutiny that goes with them.

Thus, the opportunity for the direct application of (international) human rights norms in anti-doping proceedings has been limited, both as regards the substantive norms and procedural review. This reflects the primary orientation of international human rights law, which imposes obligations on the state not to violate human rights. Nonetheless, as outlined above, the scope of states' international obligations in relation to human rights goes beyond merely ensuring that the organs of the state do not directly violate a person's rights, but also includes positive obligations, in particular taking reasonable steps to protect a person against violations of the person's rights by other, non-state actors.[47] This has implications for the extent to which states may permit individuals to contract out of certain substantive and procedural rights.

[45] Opened for signature 18 June 1958, 330 UNTS 3 (entered into force 7 June 1959).
[46] See generally David (n 36).
[47] Łukomski (n 43) 67.

The Infusion of the Anti-Doping Regime by Human Rights Norms and Values

Human rights norms have nevertheless influenced the international rules and procedures relating to anti-doping investigations in a number of other ways, leading to opportunities for the evaluation of those arrangements against human rights norms. First of all, the drafters of the later versions of the Code have taken into account some of the human rights criticisms made of earlier versions, and some amendments to the Code have not only included general references to underlying human rights principles, but have also strengthened specific human rights protections. On the other hand, other criticisms have not led to amendments, and the latest version of the Code contains 'strengthened' provisions that give rise to increased concern about their human rights compatibility.[48] While one would not wish to deprecate the changes that have been made in response to human rights concerns, the interpretation of human rights standards that has been adopted is generally a narrow one that serves the goals of the anti-doping regime and is sometimes at odds with the assessments by external commentators of the human rights compatibility of the provisions in question.

Second, the possibility of review of arbitral awards of CAS has a human rights dimension. In the first instance, CAS awards are subject to review (not appeal) before the Swiss Federal Supreme Court under the provisions of the Swiss private international law statute. The grounds of challenge, while limited, do include a number that would encompass a failure to ensure that a party has enjoyed the right to a fair hearing before an independent and impartial tribunal (Article 6(1) ECHR and Article 14(1) ICCPR) and other serious violations of human rights.[49] These include the principle of equal treatment of the parties, the right to be heard in adversarial proceedings, and a general power of the courts to refuse to enforce an award on public policy grounds (which includes human rights norms). The Swiss Federal Supreme Court has considered a significant number of challenges to arbitral awards, including CAS awards. Its general stance has been internationalist and supportive of a pro-arbitration approach.[50] This involves a reluctance to overturn awards unless there is a clear and significant breach of a right falling within one of the exceptions, and a narrow reading of exceptions such as public policy.

[48] For a detailed discussion of the changes made to the 2009 Code in the 2015 Code, see Antonio Rigozzi, Marjolaine Viret and Emily Wisnosky, 'Does the World Anti-Doping Code Revision Live up to its Promises? A Preliminary Survey of the Main Changes in the Final Draft of the 2015 Code' *Jusletter* (11 November 2013).

[49] See Rigozzi (n 42) 247.

[50] See the discussion in Claude Rouiller, 'Legal Opinion' (25 October 2005) www.wada-ama.org/en/what-we-do/legal/legal-opinions-and-articles-on-the-code.

An award made by CAS might also be challenged before the courts of a state other than Switzerland—for example, if an athlete wishes to challenge an exclusion from participation in a competition that is the result of an adverse CAS award, the recognition of the award may be challenged on grounds set out in either the relevant treaty requiring recognition or the applicable domestic legislation regulating the recognition or enforcement of foreign arbitral awards. These generally include grounds similar to those in the Swiss statute. While some national courts have been prepared not to enforce such awards on grounds such as a lack of real consent or human rights or proportionality grounds, there have been relatively few anti-doping sanctions overturned through such challenges.[51]

These possibilities have no doubt contributed to the express reference to human rights norms in both the text of and comments in the Code. Equally, they have presumably encouraged CAS to explicitly refer to the substance of human rights norms and to apply them in their procedures and decisions.[52] Apart from its own commitment to the values of human rights and a fair procedure, CAS also has hanging over it the prospect that a court might refuse to recognise the effect of one of its awards if the process which it employs does not comply with an appropriate standard of fair hearing.

A further dimension of this is that, absent a different decision by the parties, the law of the place of the arbitration is generally applied by an arbitral tribunal. In the case of CAS, this means Swiss law for the most part, and this would include Swiss principles of procedural public policy, which include human rights public policy.[53]

The Right to a Fair Hearing and the Anti-Doping Regime

The issue that has attracted a great deal of attention in the literature has been whether and how international human rights guarantees of the right to a fair hearing apply to the investigation of and hearings into allegations of anti-doping rules violations before national bodies and CAS.[54] The discussion has taken place

[51] Other bodies of national law, such as competition law, have occasionally led to the invalidation of sanctions, especially those involving lengthy suspensions.

[52] CAS panels 'have always endeavoured to ensure that fundamental principles of procedural fairness are respected in sports disciplinary proceedings': *Adamu v FIFA* (n 29) [67].

[53] See the discussion in *Union Cycliste International (UCI) v Contador Velasco* (Award, Court of Arbitration for Sport, Case Nos CAS 2001/A/2384 and 2386, 6 February 2012) [172]–[177]; *Fenerbahçe Spor Kulübü v Union of European Football Associations (UEFA)* (Award, Court of Arbitration for Sport, Case No CAS 2013/A/3139, 5 December 2013) [93]–[95].

[54] See, eg, Ulrich Haas, 'Role and Application of Article 6 of the European Convention on Human Rights in CAS Procedures' (2012) *International Sports Law Review* 43; Łukomski (n 43); Jernej Letnar Černič, 'Emerging Fair Trial Guarantees before the Court of Arbitration for Sport (Paper presented at

with reference primarily to Article 6(1) of the ECHR, reflecting the Eurocentric structure of the regime. This is in particular the result of the location of CAS in Switzerland and its consequent subjection in certain respects to Swiss law (under which the ECHR is both directly applicable and a part of the fundamental *ordre public* of the Swiss legal order, which acts as a constraint on the recognition of arbitral awards made by CAS). As Switzerland is subject to the jurisdiction of the European Court of Human Rights, there is also the possibility of challenging a failure to respect Article 6 rights (or other rights under the ECHR) before the European Court of Human Rights if an attempt to seek review of an award before the Swiss Federal Supreme Court has not been successful.

Similar situations might also arise under other systems of human rights law. For example, an athlete might seek to challenge the recognition by a country such as Brazil or Australia of a CAS award, on the ground that it was the result of a process that did not provide the due process guarantees required under Article 2 and Article 14(1) of the ICCPR, or under Article 25 of the American Convention on Human Rights.[55] The responsibility of the states in question would be engaged insofar as their legislation or general law would view as valid a contractual agreement to accept CAS arbitration and the law requiring the recognition or enforcement of CAS awards as foreign arbitral awards, but without conditioning that on observance of the rights guaranteed by the relevant human rights treaties. While such challenges would not be as direct as launching a challenge before the Swiss courts, there would appear to be no reason why the issue could not arise in this way. The matter could also arise collaterally before the courts of another country, where that court is asked to recognise or enforce an award, and recognition or enforcement is opposed on the ground that there has been a failure to afford the right to a fair hearing before an independent and impartial tribunal.

The nature of any such 'violation' of the right to a fair hearing is slightly complicated. Because most disciplinary sporting bodies at the national level are not agencies of the state, they are not as such bound by Article 6(1) or its equivalent in other treaties (or by similar constitutional guarantees). Nor is CAS an agency of a state; rather, it is a private association which carries out an arbitral function agreed to by the parties involved.

The potential violation by a state of its obligations in such cases arises from the fact that a state is obliged to ensure a person's access to a fair hearing by an independent and impartial court or tribunal established by law in the determination

the 10th Annual Conference of the European Society of International Law, Vienna, 4 September 2014) http://ssrn.com/abstract=2546183; Juan Carlos Landrove, 'European Convention on Human Rights' Impact on Consensual Arbitration: An *État des Lieux* of Strasbourg Case-Law and of a Problematic Swiss Law Feature' in Samantha Besson, Michel Hottellier and Franz Werro (eds), *Human Rights at the Center* (Zurich, Schulthess Verlag, 2006) 73.

[55] Opened for signature 22 November 1969, 1144 UNTS 1978 (entered into force 18 July 1978).

of that person's civil rights and obligations (or 'rights and obligations in a suit at law' in the English version of the ICCPR). A person must thus have access to at least one instance of justice (court or tribunal) that satisfies the institutional criteria of independence and impartiality, observes the requirements of a fair hearing, and has the power to adjudicate on all disputed questions of fact and law. It is generally accepted that issues of suspension and other penalties arising from adjudication of anti-doping rules fall within the category of a dispute over a person's 'civil rights and obligations'—although some have argued that their seriousness is such that they should be viewed as 'quasi-criminal' or 'criminal' for the purposes of human rights law, thus attracting a higher level of substantive and procedural protection.

A disciplinary tribunal of a national sporting association is not usually 'established by law' and nor is it generally independent of the parties.[56] The fact that it satisfies the requirement of Article 8.1 of the Code to 'provide, at a minimum, a fair hearing within a reasonable time by a fair and impartial hearing panel' and a timely reasoned explanation of an adverse decision (principles 'also found in Article 6.1 of the [ECHR]')[57] would in most cases not be enough to satisfy the independence requirement.

There is some debate over whether CAS satisfies the requirement of being a tribunal established by law:[58] it probably does. However, there is more significant disagreement about whether CAS satisfies the requirements of independence.[59] This last issue was brought to a head by the successful challenge by the German speed skater Claudia Pechstein before the German courts to an award made by CAS which Pechstein had previously challenged without success before the Swiss

[56] See, eg, the comments in *Glaesner v Fédération Internationale de Natation (FINA)* (Award, Court of Arbitration for Sport, Case No CAS 2013/A/3274, 31 January 2014) [65].

[57] Code art 8.1 comment.

[58] See, eg, Łukomski (n 43) 65 (CAS not an art 6 tribunal). Haas argues that, by adopting a functional analysis, CAS could be characterised as such a tribunal: Haas (n 54) 43–45.

[59] See *Mutu v Switzerland* (European Court of Human Rights, Application No 40575/10, 13 July 2010); *Pechstein v Switzerland* (European Court of Human Rights, Application No 67474/10, 11 November 2010) (questions communicated to the parties in each case include ones relating to the application of art 6(1) to CAS and the independence and impartiality of CAS). Similar issues were raised in an earlier case before the European Court of Human Rights, but the applicants indicated their intention not to proceed with the case and the Court removed the case from its list: *Lzutina v Switzerland* (European Court of Human Rights, Application No 3825/03, 3 July 2008). See also the decision of the Oberlandesgericht München in the case of *Pechstein v International Skating Union*, Oberlandesgericht München, U 1110/14 Kart, 15 January 2015, holding, inter alia, that the method of appointment of members of CAS afforded the international sporting federations and the national and international Olympic committees undue influence in the selection of the CAS panels and placed the independence of CAS in doubt: Oberlandesgericht München, Press Release, Zivilsachen 1/15, 15 January 2015. An English version of extracts of the judgment is available at Antoine Duval, 'The Pechstein Ruling of the OLG München (English Translation)', 6 February 2015, http://ssrn.com/abstract=2561297. See also Sergei Gorbylev, 'A Short Story of an Athlete: Does He Question Independence and Impartiality of the Court of Arbitration for Sport?' (2013) 13 *International Sports Law Journal* 294; and Anderson (n 4) 79–87.

Federal Court. The Oberlandesgericht München accepted an argument that CAS as constituted at the time of the original decision against Pechstein did not satisfy the requirements of institutional independence because of the structural influence of sporting federations over the membership of the arbitral panels.[60] CAS strongly contested this finding in a public statement, noting that in any event, recent changes to the structure of the regime made the finding moot for the future.[61]

Under human rights law, states may limit the enjoyment of the right of access to court, provided that any limitation is for a legitimate purpose, is a reasonable and proportionate measure for pursuing the goal, and does not affect the very essence of the right. Providing for the recognition and enforcement of arbitral awards and limiting the power of state courts to review such awards is such a limitation on the enjoyment of the right because the state gives effect to the determination of a non-qualifying tribunal, without providing for a review by a complying tribunal of all disputed issues of fact and law. The issue then becomes whether the limitation is for a legitimate purpose and what must be shown to demonstrate that it is a reasonable and proportionate limitation.[62]

In this context, it has been generally accepted that allowing parties to go to arbitration has its advantages and that it is not unreasonable to give effect to the agreement of parties to abide by the results of the arbitration and to limit their ability to challenge an award. Challenges to arbitral awards are normally limited to cases in which there has been an egregious error or a fundamental failure to observe due process, or where to enforce or recognise an award would be inconsistent with an international *ordre public* or fundamental national *ordre public*. There is nothing in principle which stands in the way of an agreed voluntary referral of a dispute to arbitration and it is consistent with the right to a court if the agreement is 'free, lawful and unequivocal'.[63]

The question arising in the case of anti-doping proceedings, where there is generally an asymmetrical power relationship between the parties 'agreeing' to arbitration[64] (and more generally), is whether an agreed procedure which departs too far from the type of proceedings that might be expected before a state tribunal is a reasonable limitation on the right. Part of the reasonableness equation may also be affected by the seriousness of the consequences, the evidentiary and procedural rules that will be applied, and the potential penalties.

[60] As a response, the German Government introduced a new anti-doping law which makes explicit that arbitration clauses of this sort are lawful, though this law will be subject to constitutional review in any event: *Gesetz zur Bekämpfung von Doping im Sport* [Law to Combat Doping in Sport] (Germany) 10 December 2015, *Bundesgesetzblatt*, Teil I, 2015, Nr 51, 2210 (17 December 2015) § 11.

[61] Court of Arbitration for Sport, 'Statement of the Court of Arbitration for Sport (CAS) on the Decision Made by the Oberlandesgericht München in the Case between Claudia Pechstein and the International Skating Union (ISU)' (27 February 2015) www.tas-cas.org/fileadmin/user_upload/CAS_statement_ENGLISH.pdf.

[62] Łukomski (n 43) 69.

[63] ibid 65.

[64] See ibid 68.

WADA's Proactive and Pre-emptive Moves on Issues of Human Rights Compatibility: Embracing Human Rights Standards and Scrutiny or Attempts to Limit Scrutiny?

Although the largely private law character of the anti-doping regime would appear to be inhospitable to the direct application of international human rights norms, explicit consideration of human rights standards has nonetheless been a feature of WADA's development and promotion of the various versions of the Code and its implementation.[65] In addition to criticism by many athletes of the structures and some of the specific rules contained in the Code, WADA has also had to engage with other external critics raising human rights concerns about proposed provisions of the Code, most notably a robust and rather rancorous exchange with the European Union's Article 29 Data Protection Working Party around the issue of data protection and athletes' privacy.[66]

Since 2003, in the process of the development of successive editions of the Code, WADA has commissioned a number of legal opinions from Swiss and French lawyers with expertise in human rights law and/or arbitration and sports law on various drafts of the Code.[67] WADA has also commissioned advice on the implications of Swiss fundamental rights guarantees for certain provisions of the Code and the possibility of challenges to decisions rendered by CAS when proceedings are brought before the Swiss Federal Supreme Court, the court with exclusive jurisdiction to review such judgments.[68]

A striking feature of these opinions[69] is the starting point of the analysis. Rather than contesting the applicability of human rights obligations to the actions of

[65] This does not seem to have extended to an examination of the relationship between the obligations of states under the UNESCO Convention and human rights treaties insofar as the states party to the UNESCO Convention are obliged to have the Code or its equivalent implemented that may give rise to human rights compatibility issues.

[66] For examples of the exchanges between the two camps, see European Union Article 29 Data Protection Working Group, *Second Opinion 4/2009 on the World Anti-Doping Agency (WADA) International Standard for the Protection of Privacy and Personal Information, on Related Provisions of the WADA Code and on Other Privacy Issues in the Context of the Fight against Doping in Sport by WADA and (National) Anti-doping Organizations* (6 April 2009); and WADA, 'WADA Statement about the Opinion of European Working Party on Data Protection' (15 April 2009).

[67] See WADA, 'Advisory and Legal Opinions on the Code' (2015) www.wada-ama.org/en/what-we-do/legal/legal-opinions-and-articles-on-the-code.

[68] Rouiller (n 50).

[69] See Gabrielle Kaufmann-Kohler, Antonio Rigozzi and Giorgio Malinverni, 'Legal Opinion on the Conformity of Certain Provisions of the Draft World Anti-Doping Code with Commonly Accepted Principles of International Law' (26 February 2003); Gabrielle Kaufmann-Kohler and Antonio Rigozzi, 'Legal Opinion on the Conformity of Article 10.6 of the 2007 World Anti-Doping Code with the Fundamental Rights of Athletes' (13 November 2007); Jean-Paul Costa, 'Legal Opinion Regarding the Draft 3.0 Revision of the World Anti-Doping Code' (25 June 2013) (original version in French, with an English translation for information). All the opinions are available at www.wada-ama.org/en/World-Anti-Doping-Program/Legal-articles-case-law-and-national-laws/Advisory-and-Legal-Opinions-on-the-Code.

private entities, the authors of these opinions approach the task as if the bodies in question were in fact exercising state power and were subject to the human rights obligations directly applicable to states under international law in the exercise of those powers. The upshot of this is that a substantive analysis is undertaken of the human rights compatibility of the nature of the liability imposed, the reasonableness of burdens of proof, the fairness of the procedure and the proportionality of any sanction imposed.

Why was this approach taken? One might surmise that in view of the criticism that some aspects of the Code had received, it was important to engage directly with the substance of the criticism; avoiding the substantive issues simply by involving the state-based paradigm of human rights would have been seen as a technical and unpersuasive response by critics, both those within sporting communities and those external to them. A substantive engagement with the issues in a transparent way and the adoption of amendments where significant problems were identified would be more likely to legitimate the stringent provisions of the Code and strengthen the position of those advocating its implementation at the national level.

Quite apart from any such strategic reason, there appear to be good legal and policy grounds for such an approach. An approach to human rights which sees fundamental rights as objective rights enforceable against any person who infringes them, whether state official or non-state actor, would support such an approach. The hybrid nature of the anti-doping regime and its potential application in national systems where the investigation and disciplinary proceedings are conducted as the exercise of or with the support of state power are likely to engage the human rights obligations of the state under national and international law. Finally, the trend in human rights law over the last few decades has been to extend the reach of human rights obligations by expanding the obligation of the state to protect persons against encroachments by non-state actors, as well as to impose responsibilities on certain categories of non-state actors themselves (corporations being the prominent example).

As the authors of one of the WADA-commissioned opinions put it:

> Like we did in the First Opinion, for the purpose of the present opinion, we will assume that the current approach of the courts might evolve in the future towards enforcement of human rights in sports matters. Indeed, mainly because sports governing bodies hold a monopolistic 'quasi-public' position in their relation with the athletes, there is a growing understanding among legal commentators that sports governing bodies can no longer ignore fundamental right issues in their activities, at least if they intend to avoid governmental intervention. After all, the *UNESCO Convention* itself was adopted with a specific 'refer[ence] to existing international instruments relating to human rights' (see Preamble, first ground).[70]

[70] Kaufmann-Kohler and Rigozzi (n 69) 14 [27] (citations omitted). For discussion of these issues in their earlier opinion, see Kaufmann-Kohler, Rigozzi and Malinverni (n 69) [62]–[73].

The opinions consider in detail most of the human rights issues raised in the critiques of the Code in its various forms, with an emphasis on European jurisprudence but also drawing on case law from elsewhere. There are a number of minor issues about which concerns were raised, and most of these appear to have been taken up in amendments to the Code. The opinions conclude that in most other respects, the concerns raised do not on closer examination give rise to the real possibility of inconsistencies with human rights standards. It is not my purpose to examine in detail the individual issues. Suffice it to say that the analysis offered tends to be plausible, though it shows an overall tendency to support the human rights compatibility of stringent provisions and to defer to WADA's policy choices in this regard. Nonetheless, there are some issues (such as the true nature of consent and the proportionality of certain penalties)[71] that continue to be contentious and about which other conclusions might have been reached (and indeed have been in certain national courts). Thus, while these opinions advance the debate and have had some impact on the provisions of the Code, they do not necessarily settle the debate over the human rights compatibility of some provisions.[72]

The significance of this approach presumably reflects a recognition by WADA that the legitimacy and thereby the effectiveness of its Code depended in part on its being certified as involving no more than necessary infringements on fundamental human rights. This approach is also reflected in the terms of the Code itself, which contains express assertions of its compliance with human rights. These include the opening statement of the 2015 Code that the 'The Code has been drafted giving consideration to the principles of proportionality and human rights'[73] and that the Code's anti-doping rules:

> [A]re not intended to be subject to or limited by any national requirements and legal standards applicable to such proceedings, although they are intended to be applied in a manner which respects the principles of proportionality and human rights.[74]

The strategic prudence of such an approach to defending the legitimacy and human rights consistency of the Code's provisions can be seen in the use made by the Australian Government in its response to concerns expressed about the human rights compatibility of legislation to give effect to changes to Australian law required under the 2015 version of the Code. For example, in his response to

[71] See, eg Matthew Hard, 'Caught in the Net: Athletes' Rights and the World Anti-Doping Agency' (2010) 19 *Southern California Interdisciplinary Law Journal* 533, 551–61.

[72] See, eg, the comments of the three-arbitrator panel of CAS in *H v Association of Tennis Professionals (ATP)* (Award, Court of Arbitration for Sport, Case No CAS 2004/A/690, 24 March 2005) [54]–[55], noting 'some doubt within the Panel' as to the conclusion in the 2003 opinion of Kaufmann-Kohler, Rigozzi and Malinverni (n 69) that a system of fixed sanctions without an examination of proportionality of the sanction in an individual case was compatible with human rights and general legal principles.

[73] Code (n 1) 11.

[74] ibid 17.

concerns raised by the Parliamentary Joint Committee on Human Rights about certain aspects of the Bill introduced to amend Australian law to bring it into conformity with the 2015 Code, the then Minister for Health and Minister for Sport, Mr Peter Dutton, responded:

> I note that one of the key themes throughout the Code Review process was the need to protect the rights of athletes and ensure procedural fairness is observed. The World Anti-Doping Agency engaged Mr Jean-Paul Costa, a former President of the European Court of Human Rights, to provide advice on the international human rights aspects of the proposed revisions throughout the review process. Mr Costa's final opinion on the revised *Code* was tabled at the World Conference in November 2013.
>
> Advice provided by Mr Costa in early 2013 prompted the World Anti-Doping Agency to re-work both the article covering the Prohibited Association anti-doping rule violation (ADRV) and the limitation period for commencing the ADRV process to better align the revised wording with international human rights laws. At the conference, Mr Costa supported the final specification of these provisions.[75]

The Australian Olympic Committee similarly invoked the Costa opinion in its submission to the Australian Senate Committee on Community Affairs as part of that committee's inquiry into the 2014 amendments to the Australian legislation which were intended to implement the detailed provisions of the 2015 Code.[76] This was despite concerns about the changes on human rights grounds expressed by the minority in the Senate Committee[77] and athletes' organisations,[78] as well as by the Parliamentary Joint Committee on Human Rights. The invocation of the Costa opinion was an effective political riposte to these concerns.[79]

[75] Letter from Peter Dutton, Minister for Sport, to Senator Dean Smith, Chair of the Parliamentary Joint Committee on Human Rights (24 September 2014), published in Parliamentary Joint Committee on Human Rights, Parliament of Australia, *Examination of Legislation in Accordance with the Human Rights (Parliamentary Scrutiny) Act 2011: Thirteenth Report of the 44th Parliament* (2014) app 1.

[76] Australian Olympic Committee, Submissions No 2 to Senate Standing Committees on Community Affairs, *Inquiry into the Australian Sports Anti-Doping Authority Amendment Bill 2014* (2 October 2014) 7–8 [41] www.aph.gov.au/DocumentStore.ashx?id=88c653f1-cdc0-480e-a1a7-0191d4e83e12&subId=300640.

[77] Senate Community Affairs Legislation Committee, Parliament of Australia, *Australian Sports Anti-Doping Authority Amendment Bill 2014 [Provisions]* (2014). The Greens Senators' dissenting report sets out a range of human rights and other concerns about the Bill and the Code—including the high level of athlete opposition to many provisions, and the inappropriate application to domestic non-professional sports of sanctions that are in effect designed to apply to high-level elite professional athletes.

[78] Australian Athletes' Alliance, Submission No 6 to the Senate Committee on Community Affairs, *Inquiry into the Australian Sports Anti-Doping Authority Amendment Bill 2014* (3 October 2014) www.aph.gov.au/DocumentStore.ashx?id=4f2efdd7-1971-4793-8314-af2129b87c00&subId=300721.

[79] Parliamentary Joint Committee on Human Rights, Parliament of Australia, *Examination of Legislation in Accordance with the Human Rights (Parliamentary Scrutiny) Act 2011: Tenth Report of the 44th Parliament* (2014) 1–6 [1.1]–[1.23]; Parliamentary Joint Committee on Human Rights, *Thirteenth Report* (n 75) 19–23 [2.1]–[2.8].

Conclusion

It is something of a paradox that, although the international anti-doping regime has been structured in a way to avoid the direct application of the principles and norms of public law (including human rights), WADA has devoted so much effort to undertaking that examination in an informal way through the commissioning of detailed legal analyses as if the system did involve the exercise of state power. While this has not resolved all the disputed issues, its transparency has been important to advancing the debate and it has plainly led to some improvements in the provisions of the Code, as well as advancing WADA's strategic goals in relation to establishing the legitimacy of the Code. The debate about the specific human rights issues to which the Code and its enforcement give rise will continue.

With the framework of the Code and CAS jurisprudence, there has been a (partial) internalisation of human rights standards—both substantively and strategically on the part of WADA in reformulating the various editions of the Code and commissioning opinions on the consistency of contentious provisions of the Code with human rights norms (primarily by reference to the ECHR). Strategic considerations as well as considerations of fairness and concern that Code provisions that were considered unfair might fall foul of general laws (eg competition laws or constitutional rights guarantees) or of laws limiting recognition of arbitral awards on public policy or human rights grounds, appear to have been part of the motivations for these moves.

The efforts to construct an area of industry regulation largely off-limits from the application of public law values and review by national courts have had considerable success.[80] At the same time, human rights values have migrated into and have also been actively imported into the regulatory sphere. This has been the result of the role played by private international boundary controllers in relation to the recognition and enforcement of arbitral awards, external criticism leading to the explicit and implicit adoption of human rights standards in the Code, international human rights law scrutiny by international tribunals, and internal human rights norm entrepreneurs working within CAS.

Even so, while there is, as a result, significant regard for human rights values, it is second-order in important respects and is largely focused on procedural rights, with little attempt made to address concerns about alleged substantive infringements of human rights, such as the right to be presumed innocent, the right to proportionality in penalty, and privacy.

[80] As Scott Jedlicka puts it: 'Not only does the Code entrench WADA's control over anti-doping policy, but it also separates WADA from the purview of mainstream jurisprudence. This discursive device effectively creates a separate world where athletes, while perhaps not subject to the same punishments of traditional legal systems, are also unable to take advantage of the rights and protections afforded by those systems.' Scott Jedlicka, 'The Normative Discourse of Anti-doping Policy' (2014) 6(3) *International Journal of Sport Policy and Politics* 429, 436.

More broadly, the way in which human rights analysis has been applied to this hybrid (though intensely private) regime can be viewed as one example of a long-term trend to increase human rights scrutiny and the accountability of non-state actors on the basis of objective human rights. This gives effect to the notion that a person is entitled to protection against an infringement of basic human rights, whether that is at the hands of a state actor or a private actor—human rights function as a protection against the arbitrary exercise of power, whatever its source.

The body of anti-doping law also protects itself against the intrusion of state law by taking into account the fundamental norms of human rights and claiming that its standards and procedures have been formulated and are applied consistently with them. These are not conclusions that would necessarily follow if an external assessment were undertaken. The objective of eradicating doping in sport is the pre-eminent policy purpose that underpins the anti-doping institutions and will dominate any assessment by them of the human rights compatibility of impugned measures.

A court located outside this value system might well give greater weight to other values and goals, and give less weight than WADA and others do to the anti-doping objectives when deciding whether the extent of incursions on the rights of athletes are a proportionate response to a pressing social need.[81] While thus far the legal structures that have been adopted have limited the extent of direct human rights evaluation, the increasing intertwining of state institutions and powers with 'private' bodies in the sports anti-doping campaign and a growing trend to bring quasi-public private bodies within the framework of human rights may lead to the erosion of the barriers that currently exist to such scrutiny.

[81] See Houlihan (n 12) 424; and Verner Møller 'Who Guards the Guardians?' (2014) 31(8) *International Journal of the History of Sport* 934.

Part III

The World Anti-Doping Code: Procedural Questions

6

Issues in the Gathering and Use of Non-analytical Evidence to Prove Anti-Doping Rule Violations

SUDARSHAN KANAGARATNAM*

The focus of anti-doping organisations the world over is increasingly on the use of non-analytical evidence, being evidence obtained through intelligence and investigation as a means of establishing anti-doping rule violations (ADRVs). Such evidence will usually take the form of witness testimony, documents (typically email communications, recorded telephone conversations and text messages) and things.

The 2015 World Anti-Doping Code (hereinafter the Code),[1] in recognition of the importance of non-analytical evidence, places a greater emphasis than its predecessor on facilitating the gathering and use of non-analytical evidence.

In Australia, Parliament has introduced legislation which gives the Chief Executive Officer (CEO) of the Australian Sports Anti-Doping Authority (ASADA) significant powers aimed at facilitating the gathering of non-analytical evidence and information sharing. Such legislative power, allied with contractual obligations which bind athletes[2] to cooperate with investigations, form the principal means by which ASADA obtains non-analytical evidence.

This chapter examines the powers pursuant to which non-analytical evidence is gathered, the scope of those powers, and some issues that arise from the way in which non-analytical evidence is gathered and used to establish ADRVs. While the chapter addresses the Australian context, the principles discussed have wider applicability as Code signatories worldwide respond to the ever-increasing recognition of the importance of such evidence by adopting policies that enhance the ability to obtain non-analytical evidence.

* Barrister, Sydney.

[1] World Anti-Doping Agency (WADA), World Anti-Doping Code (1 January 2015).

[2] This chapter adopts the definitions used in the 2015 Code: ibid app 1.

Background

The traditional importance of adverse analytical findings,[3] while still crucial in the quest to eradicate doping in sport, is increasingly supplemented by non-analytical evidence as a means of establishing ADRVs.

Such high-profile matters as the Major League Baseball prosecution of Alex Rodriguez,[4] the International Olympic Committee's ultimate sanction of Marion Jones, the ASADA investigation of the Essendon Football Club and the Independent Commission Report into doping and corrupt practices around sample collection and results management by, inter alia, Russia, the International Association of Athletics Federation and the Russian Anti-Doping Agency[5] have all largely proceeded on the basis of non-analytical evidence.

Perhaps the most high profile of all such prosecution was that by the United States Anti-Doping Agency (USADA) of Lance Armstrong.[6] In August 2012, USADA imposed a lifetime sanction on Armstrong and disqualified all the competitive results he had achieved since August 1998. This sanction was imposed after an extensive investigation which resulted in sworn witness statements from over two dozen voluntary witnesses,[7] including 15 professional cyclists and 12 members of Armstrong's cycling teams, bank records showing significant payments by Armstrong to his doctor, Dr Michele Ferrari, voluminous email correspondence and other documentary data. USADA did not rely on a positive analytical result and Armstrong was not charged with the presence of a prohibited substance under Article 2.1 of the Code. Instead, all of the evidence against Armstrong was non-analytical evidence, principally the sworn testimony of his former teammates and employees. Ultimately, Armstrong refused to participate in a hearing and did not contest the evidence against him.[8]

The WADA 2013 Anti-Doping Rule Violations Report,[9] a statistical compilation of all results management outcomes in 2013 and the first such report to be published by WADA, reported that the total number of adverse analytical findings resulting in ADRVs in 2013 was 1,678,[10] while the total number of

[3] ibid art 2.1.

[4] See *Major League Baseball Players Association v Office of the Commissioner of Baseball* (Award, Major League Baseball Arbitration Panel, Case No 2013-02, 11 January 2014).

[5] Independent Commission, 'The Independent Commission Report #1—Final Report' (Report, World Anti-Doping Agency, 9 November 2015).

[6] See *United States Anti-Doping Agency v Armstrong* (Decision, United States Anti-Doping Agency, 24 August 2012).

[7] USADA was unable to issue subpoenas to appear on members of Armstrong's 'inner circle' or those who were unwilling to give evidence absent a subpoena as Armstrong refused to participate in the hearing.

[8] See *United States Anti-Doping Agency v Armstrong* (n 6) 1.

[9] WADA, '2013 Anti-Doping Rule Violations (ADRVs) Report' (Report, 15 May 2015).

[10] A total of 207,513 samples were received and analysed in 2013, with 2,540 samples resulting in an adverse analytical finding, of which 1,678 samples (equating to 66 per cent) were confirmed as an ADRV: see ibid 4, 5–11, 19–29.

non-analytical[11] ADRVs was 266. It is anticipated that the 2014 results management statistics will show an increase in non-analytical ADRVs, a trend that is likely to continue.

Evidence and the 2015 Code

The current Code came into effect on 1 January 2015. It, like its predecessor, provides in Article 3.2 that 'facts related to anti-doping rule violations may be established by any reliable means, including admissions'.[12] The comment to Article 3.2[13] lists, inter alia, admissions, credible testimony of third parties and reliable documentary evidence as specific examples of 'reliable means'. Each of these examples is clearly non-analytical in nature and each has a significant role to play in establishing a range of ADRVs where analytical findings have little, or no, part to play. For instance, non-analytical evidence is likely to be the primary means of establishing breaches of use or attempted use by an athlete of a prohibited substance or a prohibited method (Article 2.2),[14] trafficking or attempted trafficking in any prohibited substance or a prohibited method (Article 2.7), complicity (Article 2.9) or prohibited association (Article 2.10). The importance of non-analytical evidence is highlighted where ADRVs are sought to be established against athlete support personnel or athletes, such as Armstrong or Jones,[15] who have never tested positive.

In recognition of the increased role of non-analytical evidence, the Code introduces a series of amendments to strengthen and facilitate the investigative aspects of establishing ADRVs by non-analytical evidence. Indeed, one of the themes of the 2015 Code is to make 'amendments [that] support the increasing importance of investigations and the use of intelligence in the fight against doping'.[16]

[11] Defined as violations by Athletes and Athlete Support Personnel. For an analysis of the type of violations according to Code articles, see Table 3: ibid 24.

[12] WADA (n 1) art 3.2. See also the comment to art 3.2 which, along with art 2.2 and the comment to art 2.2, distinguishes the proof required to establish an ADRV under art 2.1.

[13] The comments that annotate various articles are to be used to interpret the Code: ibid art 24.2.

[14] The comment to art 2.2 expressly provides that: 'Use or Attempted Use may also be established by other reliable means such as admissions by the Athlete, witness statements, documentary evidence, conclusions drawn from longitudinal profiling, including data collected as part of the Athlete Biological Passport, or other analytical information which does not otherwise satisfy all of the requirements to establish "Presence" of a Prohibited Substance under Article 2.1.'

[15] Marion Jones did have one positive A sample, but the B sample was negative: see Tom Fordyce, 'How Jones was Cleared' *BBC Sport* (7 September 2006) http://news.bbc.co.uk/sport2/hi/athletics/5325262.stm; Juliet Macur, 'In Wake of Jones's Result, Testing Will Be Analyzed' *New York Times* (8 September 2006) www.nytimes.com/2006/09/08/sports/othersports/08track.html.

[16] WADA, 'Significant Changes between the 2009 Code and 2015 Code, Version 4' (1 September 2013) 3, https://wada-main-prod.s3.amazonaws.com/wadc-2015-draft-version-4.0-significant-changes-to-2009-en.pdf.

Keeping with this theme, a new Article 5.1.2, under the subheading the 'Purpose of Testing and Investigations', mandates that investigations shall be carried out and intelligence or evidence, particularly non-analytical evidence, gathered to determine whether an anti-doping violation has occurred under any of Articles 2.2–2.10. While the Code is silent as to the particular tools that anti-doping organisations are to deploy in conducting investigations and gathering non-analytical evidence, it does seek to impose responsibilities on governments, international federations, anti-doping organisations, athletes and athlete support personnel that facilitate investigations. For instance:

— Article 5.8, 'Investigations and Intelligence Gathering', requires anti-doping organisations to ensure that they are able to 'obtain, assess and process anti-doping intelligence from all available sources to … form the basis of an investigation into a possible [ADRV]'[17] and '[i]nvestigate any other analytical or non-analytical information or intelligence that indicates a possible [ADRV] … in order to either rule out the possible violation or to develop evidence that would support the initiation of an [ADRV] … proceeding';[18]
— Article 20.3, 'Roles and Responsibilities of International Federations', requires member 'National Federations to report any information suggesting or relating to an … [ADRV] to their National Anti-Doping Organisation and International Federation and to cooperate with investigations conducted by any Anti-Doping Organisation with authority to conduct the investigation';[19]
— Article 20.5, 'Roles and Responsibilities of National Anti-Doping Organizations', requires cooperation with other relevant national organisations, the vigorous pursuit of all potential ADRVs, the commencement of automatic investigations in certain circumstances involving athlete support persons, and full cooperation with WADA investigations;[20]
— Articles 21.1 and 21.2, 'Roles and Responsibilities of *Athletes*' and 'Roles and Responsibilities of *Athlete Support Personnel*', require athletes and athlete support personnel to cooperate with anti-doping organisations investigating ADRVs;[21]
— Article 22, 'Involvement of Governments', requires governments to 'put in place legislation, regulation, policies or administrative practices for cooperation and sharing of information' and data with, and among, anti-doping organisations,[22] 'encourage cooperation between all … public services or agencies and Anti-Doping Organisations' to facilitate the timely sharing of information[23] and respect of the autonomy of the national anti-doping

[17] WADA (n 1) art 5.8.1.
[18] ibid art 5.8.3.
[19] ibid art 20.3.6.
[20] ibid arts 20.5.3, 20.5.7, 20.5.9, 20.5.10.
[21] ibid arts 21.1.6, 21.2.5.
[22] ibid art 22.2. See also art 22.7, which requires that governments should meet the expectations in art 22.2 by no later than 1 January 2016.
[23] ibid art 22.3.

organisations, and not to interfere with its operational decisions and activities;[24] and

— Article 17, 'Statute of Limitations', extends the limitation period for commencement of an ADRV proceeding to 10 years, which seems to, at least in part, be a recognition of the time which may need to be taken to gather non-analytical evidence and complete complex investigations.

Accordingly, the 2015 Code introduces significant amendments to the 2009 Code to enhance the investigative aspects of gathering non-analytical evidence to establish ADRVs. While these enhancements were made to the Code, it still remained for individual national anti-doping organisations to adopt and adapt those amendments into the anti-doping framework within which each operated.

Application of the Code in the Australian Context

The means by which the Code is given effect in Australia is through a complicated web of legislation and contractual obligations.

Legislation

ASADA was established and operates under the Australian Sports Anti-Doping Act 2006 (Cth) (hereinafter the ASADA Act) and the Australian Sports Anti-Doping Authority Regulations 2006 (Cth) (hereinafter the ASADA Regulations).[25] Section 9 of the ASADA Act requires the establishment of the National Anti-Doping Scheme (hereinafter the NAD Scheme), which is prescribed in Schedule 1 to the ASADA Regulations. The NAD Scheme implements the Anti-Doping Convention 1994[26] and the International Convention against Doping in Sport,[27] and in substance adopts the ADRVs mandated by the Code.[28] The ASADA Act, the ASADA Regulations and the NAD Scheme form the legislative framework for the operation of the Code in Australia. The complex way in which this statutory

[24] But see *Essendon Football Club v Chief Executive Officer of the Australian Sports Anti-Doping Authority* (2014) 227 FCR 1, 19 [79], where Middleton J declined to consider or comment on the propriety of the much-publicised intervention by the then Federal Government during the course of the ASADA investigation into Essendon.

[25] The ASADA Act was amended by the Australian Sports Anti-Doping Authority Amendment Act 2014 (Cth), which received royal assent on 26 November 2014, to incorporate the revised Code and International Standards that came into force on 1 January 2015.

[26] Opened for signature 16 November 1989, CETS No 135 (entered into force 1 March 1990).

[27] Opened for signature 19 October 2005, 2419 UNTS 43649 (entered into force 1 February 2007).

[28] NAD Scheme pt 2, div 2.1 sets out the anti-doping rules. Relevantly, the CEO is required to carry out investigations and manage the results of investigations: pts 3–4.

scheme imports the various international conventions and instruments which underpin the adoption of the Code was considered by the Full Federal Court in *Anti-Doping Rule Violation Panel v XZTT*.[29]

Contract

Despite its fundamental importance, this legislative framework does not confer upon the CEO of ASADA the ability to impose a sanction upon an athlete or athlete support person who, it has been established, committed an ADRV. The imposition of a sanction and the hearing that precedes the imposition of a sanction requires the existence of a contractual relationship between the athlete or athlete support person in question and a national sporting organisation or sporting administration body.[30] It is only via this contractual relationship that ADRVs proscribed by the Code can be tried, sanctioned and enforced.[31] Therefore, enforcement of the Code is achieved by requiring athletes or athlete support persons to enter into contracts that contain express terms requiring them to abide by a particular sport's anti-doping policy (ADP), which in turn incorporates the Code.[32] Typically, this occurs by the sporting administration body having an ADP that is WADA compliant and a registration process by which all participants in the sport agree, as a matter of contract, to be bound by the rules of the sport, which include the Code.[33]

By way of example, the National Anti-Doping Policy of Football Federation of Australia contractually binds all participants, defined as athletes and athlete support personnel, in the sport and relevantly includes the following rules:

> 127. We, ASADA or another Drug Testing Authority may carry out investigations in relation to whether *Participants* have committed an ADRV.
>
> 128. All Persons bound by this ADP and the *sporting administration body* must assist, cooperate, and liaise with *us*, *ASADA* or another *Drug Testing Authority* in relation to any investigation into a potential *anti-doping rule violation*. Specifically, all Persons must cooperate with and assist *us*, *ASADA* or another *Drug Testing Authority*, including by:
>
> (a) attending an interview to fully and truthfully answer questions;
> (b) giving information; and
> (c) producing documents,

[29] *Anti-Doping Rule Violation Panel v XZTT* (2013) 214 FCR 40.

[30] See Alan Sullivan, 'The Role of Contract in Sports Law' The Australian and New Zealand Sports Law Journal (2010) Volume 5 No 1p3

[31] See ibid for a discussion of the fundamental role of contract in sport.

[32] See, eg, Football Federation of Australia, *The National Anti-Doping Policy of the Football Federation of Australia Ltd and Our Member & Sub-Member Organisations* (14 September 2015).

[33] Participants will typically include athletes, athlete support personnel (coaches, trainers, and medical staff), managers and agents.

in an investigation being conducted by *us*, *ASADA* or another *Drug Testing Authority* (where relevant), even if to do so might tend to incriminate them or expose them to a penalty, sanction or other disciplinary measure. For the avoidance of doubt, the common law privileges against self-incrimination and self-exposure to a penalty are abrogated by this Rule 128.[34]

…

183. Hearings shall be conducted with as little formality and technicality as proper consideration of the matter before the Tribunal permits. The Tribunal shall not be bound by judicial rules governing the admissibility of evidence. Instead, facts relating to an alleged ADRV (or other breach) may be established (or defended) by any reliable means, including admissions.[35]

Each of the anti-doping policies of Australia's main codes—the Australian Football League (AFL) Anti-Doping Policy, the Cricket Australia Anti-Doping Policy and the National Rugby League (NRL) Anti-Doping Policy—contains contractual obligations to cooperate with investigations.[36]

These similar obligations provide sporting administration bodies with powerful and enforceable means of gathering non-analytical evidence from those athletes and athlete support personnel who are contractually bound to their anti-doping policies. Such compulsory contractual powers were not historically available to ASADA in conducting investigations and seeking to collect non-analytical evidence as a 'reliable means' by which to establish ADRVs. Rather, ASADA had to rely on either its statutory powers, which until recently did not extend to compulsive powers, or delegated authority from sporting administrative bodies in conducting investigations and gathering evidence. The delegation of a sporting administration bodies' powers to ASADA forms an important means by which ASADA is able to gather non-analytical evidence. Typically, this occurs where an individual sport enters into an agreement with ASADA for ASADA to, relevantly, conduct investigations. That agreement is then reflected in that sports' anti-doping policy.[37]

The extent to which these twin means are at times interwoven, as well as the difficulties such interweaving presents, has been illustrated in Australia by the

[34] This is a clear contractual abrogation of the common law privilege against self-incrimination. Whether such an abrogation is valid has not yet been tested in relation to anti-doping policies. Certainly, the clear and precise language of the draftsperson of the National Anti-Doping Policy of Football Federation of Australia removes any potential ambiguity that may have existed under the provision of previous ADPs in football and other sports as to whether the words 'cooperate' and 'fully and truthfully answer question' implicitly seek to abrogate the privilege. *Participants* can be under no illusion as to their contractual obligations.

[35] Football Federation of Australia (n 32) rr 127–28, 183.

[36] AFL, Australian Football Anti-Doping Code (1 January 2015) cls 7(a), (e)(ix), 13; Cricket Australia, Cricket Australia Anti-Doping Policy (1 January 2015) arts 3.2(l), 3.3(g), 3.5; NRL, Leagues Anti-Doping Policy (1 January 2015) cls 50(2), 107, 126, 128.

[37] See, eg, Bowls Australia Limited, Bowls Australia Limited (BAL) Anti-Doping Policy (at 1 January 2015) r 6A.2.

recent cases of *Essendon Football Club*[38] and *Hird v Chief Executive Officer of the Australian Sports Anti-Doping Authority*.[39]

Essendon Football Club was a case which had its antecedents in an investigation by the Australian Crime Commission, known as 'Project Aperio', into the involvement of organised crime in sport. Part of this investigation concerned the use and source of performance enhancement drugs in Australian sports. Following that investigation, the Australian Crime Commission provided ASADA with certain information concerning two of Australia's major sports: the NRL and the AFL. Having received that information, ASADA, relevantly, determined that it would conduct an investigation into Essendon. Specifically, ASADA investigated a supplements programme implemented by Essendon in the 2011 and 2012 seasons. Ultimately, it was alleged that 34 Essendon players were administered substances that were prohibited by the Code and AFL anti-doping policy. It was also alleged that the senior coach of Essendon, Mr Hird, engaged in conduct—in substance, a failure to take adequate action to ensure that players were not exposed to significant health and safety risks, and the use of prohibited substances—which, inter alia, brought the game of football into disrepute.[40]

Essendon Football Club involved a challenge to the lawfulness of the way in which the CEO of ASADA had conducted the investigation into the involvement of the 34 Essendon players and personnel in that supplements programme. Relevantly at issue was the lawfulness of the CEO's use of the AFL's compulsory contractual powers to obtain non-analytical evidence.[41] This issue arose because the CEO, at the time of the investigation, did not have the legislative power to compel athletes or athlete support personnel to attend interviews, answer questions or produce documents or things.[42] On the other hand, Essendon players and personnel had voluntarily agreed to be bound by a contractual regime which required their 'full cooperation' with any investigation, the provision of 'full and truthful answers' to any question asked for the purposes of such an investigation, and the provision of any relevant document in their possession or control.[43]

Given this contractual regime, the CEO of ASADA and the AFL, in carrying out a cooperative investigation, were able to agree to the AFL's use of its contractual power to compel Essendon players and personnel to attend and answer questions at interviews conducted by ASADA when the AFL was also present.[44] The AFL's compulsory contractual powers were also used to issue a demand to AFL clubs for

[38] *Essendon Football Club* (n 24).

[39] *Hird v Chief Executive Officer of the Australian Sports Anti-Doping Authority* (2015) 227 FCR 95.

[40] The AFL imposed a 12-month sentence on Mr Hird, which he accepted and served: see 'List of Sanctions against Essendon and its Officials' *AFL* (27 August 2013) www.afl.com.au/news/2013-08-27/list-of-charges-against-essendon-and-its-officials.

[41] Thus non-analytical evidence was used to issue non-presence ADRV notices under cl 4.07A of the NAD Scheme.

[42] ASADA had the power to request the voluntary provision of information and attendance at interviews, but lacked the express or implied power to compel provision of information: see *Essendon Football Club* (n 24) 55 [273]–[274] (Middleton J).

[43] AFL, AFL Code cl 12.7; AFL, AFL Player Rules r 1.8. See also ibid 15–18 [51]–[68] (Middleton J).

[44] *Essendon Football Club* (n 24) 9–10 [10]–[12], 25 [126]–[127] (Middleton J).

any investigative information they may have collected on their own initiative,[45] to require the production of physical evidence, documents, computers and phones,[46] personnel records[47] and medical information, and to obtain an analysis of the Essendon accounts system conducted by Deloitte (a third party contracted by the AFL).[48]

The lawfulness of the CEO's agreement with the AFL to use its compulsory contractual powers to obtain non-analytical evidence which, in turn, formed the substantial basis on which the non-presence ADRV notices were issued, turned, as Middleton J formulated it, on the essential question of whether ASADA had 'complied with the rule of law in conducting, in the manner and for the purposes it did, the investigation'.[49] In answering this question in favour of ASADA, Middleton J held that:

— ASADA did have the power to enter into an investigation calling on the cooperation of a sporting administration body (depending on the way in which it occurred). This was because the CEO had the power under section 22 of the ASADA Act to do all things 'convenient' to be done 'in connection' with the performance of her functions, including doing anything incidental to, or conducive to, the performance of the functions in section 21 of the Act;[50]
— ASADA's purpose was to conduct an investigation into possible anti-doping violations, and the procedural steps taken by ASADA and the AFL in working together did not detract from ASADA's lawful purpose;[51]
— 'ASADA acted within the confines of the Act and the NAD Scheme because ASADA's purpose of the investigation was to investigate anti-doping matters';[52]
— ASADA was not using any power of compulsion under the ASADA Act or the NAD Scheme—that is, Essendon players and personnel did not answer questions or provide any information arising from any requirement to do so under, or pursuant to, the ASADA Act or NAD Scheme;[53] and
— the compulsory powers used to gather the non-analytical evidence were the AFL's and were used by the AFL. Those powers were a product of a voluntary acceptance by the Essendon players and personnel of a contractual regime, and their failure to adhere to this agreement would result in a breach of contractual obligations with Essendon and the AFL.[54]

[45] ibid 24 [122] (Middleton J).
[46] ibid 24–25 [124] (Middleton J).
[47] ibid 28 [145] (Middleton J).
[48] ibid 25 [127] (Middleton J).
[49] See ibid 6 [3]–[5], 80 [400]. The investigation was sought to be characterised and impugned as a 'joint investigation': 7 [9(b)], 84 [419].
[50] ibid 82 [407] (Middleton J).
[51] ibid 80 [400], 85 [427] (Middleton J).
[52] ibid 87 [439] (Middleton J).
[53] ibid 87 [440] (Middleton J).
[54] ibid 85 [427] (Middleton J).

The reasoning of Middleton J[55] reinforces the proposition that the ASADA Act envisages that sporting administration bodies should cooperate with, assist and provide information to ASADA in the conduct of its lawful investigations into possible anti-doping violations. The *Essendon Football Club* judgment demonstrates that assistance expected from sporting administrative bodies extends to the use of contractual power to compel athletes and athlete support personnel to the extent that they are contractually bound to cooperate with lawful ASADA investigations. Interestingly, some ADPs now contain an express clause that if ASADA agrees to a sporting administration body commencing its own investigation, the sporting administration body must conduct that investigation in cooperation with any investigation being undertaken by ASADA and must seek ASADA's input into such an investigation.[56]

Such cooperation will result in the production of such important non-analytical evidence as transcripts of interview (which may contain admissions), documents and data contained on computers, phones and other electronic devices—all of which are considered by the Code to be 'reliable means' by which relevant ADRVs can be established. *Essendon Football Club* did not expressly explore the boundaries of what is required by 'cooperation', but to the extent that it did so implicitly, it would seem that contractual powers are sufficient to obtain an extensive range of non-analytical evidence.

Despite the outcome, this case exposed two clear deficiencies in the interwoven legislative and contractual structures used to investigate, establish and impose sanctions. First, there was a clear statutory deficiency in ASADA's lack of any compulsory powers. Second, it became clear that the inability of either ASADA (by legislation) or the sporting administrative bodies (by contract) to impose sanctions on 'consultants' or other third parties who, while not contractually bound to sporting administrative bodies and consequently to its ADPs and the Code, nevertheless perform the functions of an athlete support person or have some material part to play in an asserted ADRV posed a significant problem.

While it may have been said that ASADA's statutory deficiencies in this regard could, in practice, be overcome by its ability to use or request the use of a sporting administrative body's contractual powers, those powers also had their limitations, as identified above. That is to say, ASADA was limited in the scope of the

[55] The Full Federal Court in *Hird* (n 39) dismissed an appeal by Hird. The Full Court, relevantly, found that Hird failed to show that the investigation conducted by ASADA in cooperation with the AFL was not authorised by the ASADA Act and the NAD Scheme. Rather, the Court of Appeal held that the investigation was conducted by ASADA for the lawful purpose of investigating the involvement of Essendon players and personnel in possible violations of anti-doping rules. Further, the challenge to the validity of the disclosure notices issued to the players failed because the Court found that the players entered into a contractual arrangement with the AFL, which, it was accepted, required them to cooperate not only with the AFL but also with ASADA, including by attending interviews and answering questions: 99, 101 [8] (the Court).

[56] See, eg, Bowls Australia Limited (n 37) r 6A.2.2.

non-analytical evidence that it could collect, and important evidence that was in the possession of a person who was not contractually bound could not be compulsorily obtained, for example, documentary records in the possession of a compounding pharmacist or sports scientist.

In an attempt to overcome the first of these deficiencies and strengthen ASADA's investigative powers, Parliament enacted the Australian Sports Anti-Doping Authority Amendment Act 2013 (Cth) (hereinafter the 2013 Amendment Act). The second deficiency may not truly be a matter for legislation, but rather of good governance by sporting administrative bodies in ensuring that each person in a position to perform the role of an athlete support person is contractually bound to adhere to that sport's ADP.

Enhanced Legislative Power of ASADA to Investigate ADRVs

The CEO of ASADA has the power, conferred by section 22 of the ASADA Act, 'to do all things necessary or convenient to be done for or in connection with the performance of his or her functions'. The CEO's functions are broadly described by section 21 of the ASADA Act and include such functions as are conferred on the CEO by the ASADA Act and the NAD Scheme. ASADA's role 'is to assist the CEO in the performance of his or her functions'.[57]

The CEO is, relevantly, authorised by section 13(1)(f) of the ASADA Act and clause 3.27(1) of the NAD Scheme to 'investigate possible anti-doping rule violations' as defined in the NAD Scheme. Section 13(1)(h)–(m) of the ASADA Act and clause 1.02A of the NAD Scheme specify what use the CEO can make of the 'assertions relating to investigations'. Interestingly, while clause 3.27(2) of the NAD Scheme requires an investigation to comply, or substantially comply, with the procedures of the Code and International Standards, non-compliance with those procedures will not invalidate an investigation.[58] This excuse from compliance with International Standards and Code procedures raises a potential tension between the Code requirement of 'reliable evidence', say, credible witness testimony, and testimony that may be gathered by ASADA outside of Code procedures.[59]

[57] ASADA Act s 20B.

[58] NAD Scheme cl 3.27(3).

[59] See the discussion of the ability to use illegally obtained non-analytical evidence in the *Kennedy and Anti-Doping Rule Violation Panel* [2014] AATA 967 and *Earl and Anti-Doping Rule Violation* [2014] AATA 968 cases below.

The CEO's power to investigate and gather evidence has been augmented by the 2013 Amendment Act. Of particular importance and relevance to this discussion is the compulsory investigative power, exercised by the provision of a written disclosure notice pursuant to section 13A of the ASADA Act and division 3.4B of the NAD Scheme, requiring a person to attend and answer questions at interviews conducted by ASADA and to give information or produce documents to ASADA.

Section 13(1)(ea) of the ASADA Act provides and that the NAD Scheme must:

> (ea) authorise the CEO to request a specified person to do one or more of the following within a specified period:
>
> (i) attend an interview to answer questions;
> (ii) give information of a specified kind;
> (iii) produce documents or things of a specified kind;
>
> if the CEO reasonably believes that the person has information, documents or things that may be relevant to the administration of the NAD scheme.

Clause 3.26A of the NAD Scheme provides the statutory basis for the CEO to make such a *request*, while section 13A of the ASADA Act, together with clause 3.26B of the NAD Scheme, authorises the CEO to give a person a written disclosure notice *requiring* the person to, within the period specified in the notice, attend an interview to answer questions, give information of the kind specified in the notice and produce documents or things of the kind specified in the notice.

A failure to comply with the notice within the specified time by not producing the information, document or things specified, not attending at the interview or attending at the interview, or refusing to answer question results in liability for a civil penalty pursuant to section 13C of the ASADA Act. This liability is enforceable by the issue of an infringement notice pursuant to Part 5, division 2 of the ASADA Regulations.

Accordingly, the amendments to the ASADA Act and the NAD Scheme confer upon the CEO the compulsory powers that were lacking at the commencement of the ASADA investigation into Essendon. The conferral of these compulsory powers raises a number of questions, including the mechanism by which a decision to issue a disclosure notice is made and the scope of production pursuant to a notice.

There is also a significant issue as to the application of the privilege against self-incrimination in this context[60] as opposed to an interview conducted pursuant to contractual obligations.[61] Section 13D(1) of the ASADA Act preserves the privilege against self-incrimination in relation to a disclosure notice which requires attendance at an interview to answer questions, but does not afford the same protection with respect to a notice requiring the production of documents,

[60] See Anthony Crocker, 'The Integrity of Sport and the Privilege against Self-incrimination—Is ASADA Playing Fair?' (2014) 9 *Australian New Zealand and Sports Law Journal* 27.

[61] See, eg, Football Federation of Australia (n 35) r 128.

including communication and things.[62] The consideration of this complex matter is beyond the scope this chapter, but see the discussion in *Essendon Football Club*.[63]

Issuing a Disclosure Notice

In order to issue a disclosure notice, the CEO of ASADA must, in writing, declare a reasonable belief that a person has information, documents or things that may be relevant to the administration of the NAD Scheme. In addition, three members of the Anti-Doping Rule Violation Panel (ADRVP) must also agree in writing that the CEO's belief is reasonable.[64]

The formation and written declaration of such a belief must self-evidently require the satisfaction of a number of anterior matters: first, the identification of a 'specific person'; second, the identification of information, documents or things that that specific person 'has'; third, that the information, documents or things the specific person has 'may be relevant' to 'the administration of the NAD Scheme'; and, finally, a reasonable belief as to each of the preceding three matters.

Meeting these anterior matters does not appear to be particularly challenging. The identification of a specific person or entity is generally not problematic. Whether the identified person has the document or thing is a matter that can reasonably be inferred, for instance, email communications with the identified person. The test for relevance is regarded as a low threshold,[65] with the broadness of the 'administration of the NAD Scheme' as the object of relevance serving to lower the threshold even further. The final criterion of 'reasonableness' imports imponderable contextual matters that must be considered in attempting to divine what may constitute a 'reasonable belief'.[66] In this regard, the High Court in *George v Rockett*[67] considered the apposite issue of a statute which prescribes that there must be 'reasonable grounds' for a state of mind, including suspicion and belief. The Court found that it requires the existence of facts which are sufficient to induce that state of mind in a reasonable person. Given the likely factual ease

[62] See ASADA Act s 13D(1A), though a limited process akin to a certificate is put in place by s 13D(2).

[63] *Essendon Football Club* (n 24) 56–58 [279]–[294].

[64] ASADA Act 13A(1A); NAD Scheme cl 3.26B(2). See cl 3.26B(2)(b) of the NAD Scheme as to the requirements if the person is a registered medical practitioner.

[65] In the context of civil litigation in Australia, a document is sufficiently relevant if its production is 'reasonably likely to add, in the end, in some way or the other, to the relevant evidence in the case': *Spencer Motors Pty Ltd v LNC Industries Ltd* [1982] 2 NSWLR 921, 927 (Waddell J). It need only have 'apparent relevance' to the issue in dispute: *Portal Software International Ltd v Bodsworth* [2005] NSWSC 1115 [23]–[24] (Brereton J).

[66] *George v Rockett* (1990) 170 CLR 104, 114.

[67] ibid.

with which the first three criteria can be met, the existence of the requisite factual basis necessary to form a view as to 'reasonableness' is also unlikely to be taxing. As such, any challenge by a recipient to the validity of a disclosure notice at this level is likely to prove difficult.

This difficulty is compounded because it is not clear whether compliance with section 13A(1A) of the ASADA Act and clause 3.26B(2) of the NAD Scheme requires the exposure of the CEO's reasons and the basis on which the CEO's reasonable belief was formed. Given that by section 13(1)(c) of the ASADA Act, three members of the ADRVP must agree in writing that the CEO's belief is reasonable, it would seem that the legislation contemplates the disclosure of the CEO's reasons for forming the requisite belief to members of the ADRVP. If this disclosure were not made, then on what basis would the members of the ADRVP meaningfully and properly determine for themselves whether the belief formed by the CEO was reasonable?

It is possible that the provision by the CEO to the members of the ADRVP of the materials and or information on which the CEO formed the belief, as opposed to express communication of the CEO's reasons, might be sufficient to satisfy the members of the ADRVP that arriving at the CEO's belief was reasonable. However, this is problematic, as minds may well differ as to the conclusions to be drawn from those materials or information, and ultimately what the members of the ADRVP are tasked with is to determine if the *CEO's belief* was reasonably formed and not whether *a* belief may reasonably be formed. In these circumstances, the provision to the members of the ADRVP of the CEO's reasons for forming the requisite belief, together with the underlying documents, is likely to be the more transparent course to follow.

A further question arises as to whether the disclosure of the CEO's reasons and the materials underpinning those reasons to the ADRVP, if that indeed be the case, extends to the disclosure of those reasons to the specified person, the recipient of the disclosure notice.

Clause 3.26B(5) of the NAD Scheme sets out the required contents of a disclosure notice. Nowhere in that section, or indeed in division 3.4B, which governs the particulars of giving disclosure notices and the form and content of interviews, is there a requirement that the CEO should inform the specified person, the recipient of the notice, of the reasons or basis for forming the requisite belief that triggered the issue of the notice.

Such disclosure or non-disclosure becomes relevant if the recipient of the notice wishes to resist it. There is no express provision in the NAD Scheme for an appeal against the issue of a notice.[68] Despite an assertion to the contrary,[69] it seems that

[68] NAD Scheme cl 14(4) provides an express right to appeal to the Administrative Appeals Tribunal (AAT) from the decision of the ADRVP to enter a name on the Register. This perhaps supports the view that no right of appeal is intended with respect to disclosure notices.

[69] The former CEO, Ms Aurora Andruska, indicated in an informal but public setting of an Australia and New Zealand Sport Law Conference that in her view, the issue of a disclosure notice cannot be challenged.

there is no reason why a disclosure notice issued pursuant to Commonwealth legislation involving a decision by a Commonwealth officer could not be reviewed in the AAT or indeed challenged in the Federal Court. Doing so would necessarily require an examination of the reasons and the basis on which the reasonable belief that a person has information, documents or things which may be relevant to the administration of the NAD Scheme was formed by the CEO initially and then by three members of the ADRVP. It is likely that a specified person wishing to challenge the validity of a notice would seek the production of such reasons and underlying materials during the course of such a proceeding. If, as advanced in this chapter, a right of review to the AAT does exist, then a request for a statement setting out the findings on material questions of fact, referring to the evidence or other material on which those findings were based and giving the reasons for the decision, and the person who made the decision, can be made pursuant to section 28 of the Administrative Appeals Tribunal Act 1975 (Cth).

Two potentially relevant cases have recently come before the AAT in the context of decisions by the ADRVP to make entries on the Register of Findings.[70] These cases have also involved the consideration of whether the ADRVP should have had regard to non-analytical evidence which was asserted to be illegally obtained.

In the matter of *Kennedy*,[71] the ADRVP made multiple entries on the Register of Findings on the basis of a finding that there had been possible non-presence anti-doping rule violations by a registered NRL player, specifically, attempted use and possession of various banned substances in August and September 2012.[72] Kennedy argued that the ADRVP should not have had regard to materials downloaded from a mobile phone obtained by the Australian Customs and Border Protection Service and disseminated to the Australian Crime Commission, and from there to the CEO of ASADA and eventually to the ADRVP.[73]

Like the AFL Code and Player Rules, the NRL Anti-Doping Policy, to which players as participants are contractually bound by signing a registered player contract, provided that the NRL or ASADA may carry out investigations in relation to whether participants have committed an ADRV. The NRL Anti-Doping Policy also required participants to cooperate with any such investigation.[74] Kennedy was interviewed by ASADA in the presence of an NRL officer on two occasions in October 2013, pursuant to his contractual obligations to the NRL. While it appears that he participated in the interview and answered questions asked by ASADA, he declined to give ASADA access to his mobile phone. Had the request for the phone

[70] See *Anti-Doping Rule Violation Panel v XZTT* (n 29) as to the operation of the Register of Findings and the powers and purpose of the ADRVP.

[71] *Kennedy and Anti-Doping Rule Violation Panel* [2014] AATA 967. An appeal to this decision was discontinued by consent: *Kennedy v Anti-Doping Rule Violation Panel* [2015] FCA 411.

[72] *Kennedy* (n 59) [4] (Deputy President Frost).

[73] For the detail of how customs obtained copies of the SMS messages on Kennedy's phone and disseminated them, see ibid [22]–[33].

[74] See n 36; ibid [34].

been made by the NRL under its compulsory contractual powers, it is difficult to see how Kennedy could have refused production of the phone without breaching his contractual obligations. ASADA, however, did not have that compulsive power in the absence of a disclosure notice. This dichotomy is interesting, since ASADA must continually be conscious of precisely what powers it can legitimately exercise and the source of those powers, or else it risks acting outside its statutory power and potentially invalidating intelligence collected as a 'reliable means' of establishing facts related to ADRVs.

In December 2013, ASADA issued Kennedy with a disclosure notice which required, inter alia, the production of his mobile phone. Kennedy complied with the notice without challenge.[75] Before the AAT, he challenged the lawfulness of the use of the downloaded materials on the basis that the power to copy the downloaded contents of the phone was not properly engaged.[76] However, the Tribunal held that the power was lawfully engaged, so the dissemination of the information contained on the phone (ultimately to the ADRVP) was not invalid.[77]

Interestingly, Deputy President Frost proceeded to consider how he would have dealt with the downloaded materials if, in copying it, customs had not complied with statutory requirements. The Deputy President resolved this hypothetical question by weighing the competing public interest considerations. In doing so, he held that neither the CEO of ASADA nor the ADRVP, as passive recipients of the information, was responsible for customs' non-compliance with statutory requirements and was, accordingly, free to take the downloaded material into account in reaching its decision as to *possible* non-presence anti-doping rule violations.[78]

This 'hypothetical' result is quite extraordinary as it effectively endorses the 'downstream' use by ASADA and the ADRPV of materials obtained by governmental actions that are beyond statutory power based on a public interest in ensuring that the CEO can fulfil his functions under the ASADA Act and the NAD Scheme. On this analysis, such public interest necessarily outweighs the identified[79] competing public interest in the government complying with statutory requirements designed to protect citizens' rights. If the logic of this reasoning is followed through, then as long at ASADA itself was not complicit in obtaining non-analytical evidence illegally, that material is free from any such taint and can form the 'reliable means' by which facts relating to an ADRV can be established.

Similar issues arose and the same result followed with respect to the use of materials downloaded from a phone in *Earl*.[80] Sandor Earl, also a registered NRL player,

[75] *Kennedy* (n 59) [38].
[76] ibid [55]–[59].
[77] ibid [68]–[70].
[78] ibid [72]–[82].
[79] ibid [81].
[80] *Kennedy* (n 59)

attended and answered questions at interviews pursuant to NRL's compulsory contractual powers[81] and made various admissions on national television.[82] Earl does not appear to have been the recipient of a disclosure notice. Deputy President Frost, in making findings that it was *possible* that Earl had committed a number of the alleged non-presence ADRVs, relied on the admissions made by Earl,[83] thereby reinforcing that admissions are 'reliable means' by which the facts giving rise to the possibility of non-presence ADRVs could be established.

On 14 October 2015, the NRL Anti-Doping Tribunal suspended Earl for a period of four years for use (eight ADRVs) of the peptide CJC-1295, possession of CJC-1295, trafficking in somatropin and clenbuterol, and attempted trafficking in selective androgen receptor modulators and testosterone.[84] Kennedy was issued with an infraction notice by the NRL, but the matter is yet to be heard and determined by the NRL Anti-Doping Tribunal.[85]

These two cases explore in a limited way the use of non-analytical evidence in establishing possible non-presence anti-doping rules violations, but do not provide any insight into the boundaries of a disclosure notice.

The Scope of a Disclosure Notice

What is the scope of disclosure that can be compelled by a disclosure notice? That is to say, is a notice analogous to a subpoena to produce or to attend to give evidence, or is it more akin to discovery, which is much broader in its ambit?

If the power to seek production of documents and things under a notice is to be interpreted as if it were seeking discovery, the scope of the notice would be broad indeed. The only touchstone provided by section 13A of the ASADA Act is relevance to the administration of the NAD Scheme.[86] However, such a touchstone is in itself problematic given the inherent width of the words 'may be relevant' and 'to the administration of the NAD Scheme'. It is not clear what the 'administration of the NAD Scheme' encompasses, but whatever it does, it is further expanded by the use of the word 'may', which gives a wide ambit to the already low threshold of relevance. Given that a central function of the NAD Scheme is the facilitation of

[81] ibid [22]–[39].

[82] ibid [42].

[83] ibid [84]–[108].

[84] NRL, 'Sandor Earl Suspended until 2017' (Press Release, 14 October 2015) www.nrl.com/sandor-earl-suspended-until-2017/tabid/10874/newsid/90545/default.aspx. The NRL Anti-Doping Tribunal's reasons for the decision are not publicly available and the decision has not been appealed to the Court of Arbitration for Sport.

[85] NRL, 'Martin Kennedy Suspended by NRL' (Press Release, 20 March 2015) www.nrl.com/martin-kennedy-suspended-by-nrl/tabid/10874/newsid/84689/default.asp; 'Kennedy's NRL Doping Hearing Postponed' *Triple M* (11 November 2015) www.triplem.com.au/sydney/sport/nrl/news/2015/11/martin-kennedy-nrl-doping-hearing-postponed.

[86] See ASADA Act s 13A(1A)(a).

the investigation of possible anti-doping violations, the potential remit of a notice is extremely wide, both in terms of the material sought and the time period over which those materials can be sought.[87]

Perhaps analogously, courts in Australia are increasingly recognising the problems associated with lengthy and expensive discovery procedures. The civil procedure in relation to discovery, assuming discovery is given at all,[88] is increasingly designed to confine and control discovery to identified topics or classes of documents. While the analogy may not be perfect, given the investigative function of ASADA, the same potential to become mired in voluminous documentary requests is present, particularly if the investigation is not of a single athlete or athlete support person, but extends to a team or a sporting administrative body and associated entities potentially involved in possible anti-doping violations.

The alternative view of the scope of the power is that the notice is more analogous to a subpoena to produce. Such an interpretation is supported by the use of the words 'of the kind specified' in section 13(1)(b) and (c) of the ASADA Act, and could then import the controlling mechanisms found in authorities limiting the scope of a subpoena.[89]

The scope of a disclosure notice may remain *sui generis* or could ultimately find equilibrium between the characteristics of a subpoena to produce and discovery by category. However, challenges to a notice will need to be made before the scope of a notice can be meaningfully ascertained.

Compelling Attendance at ADRV Hearings

Ordinarily, ASADA and sporting administrative bodies will have little difficulty in compelling athletes and athlete support persons to attend ADRV hearings. However, the same cannot be said for those persons somehow involved in asserted ADRVs, but not contractually bound to appear and give evidence at hearings. ASADA faced just this situation in attempting to compel Mr Shane Charter and Mr Nima Alavi-Moghadam's attendance for examination before the AFL Anti-Doping Tribunal hearing into whether 34 current and former players and one former support person at Essendon violated the AFL Anti-Doping Code.[90]

[87] Observing that the limitation period for the commencement of investigation is now 10 years, there is no reason why the timeframe over which documents can be sought should not be similar: NAD Scheme cl 4.23.

[88] Supreme Court of New South Wales, *Practice Note SC Eq 11—Disclosure in the Equity Division* (22 March 2012).

[89] *Commissioner for Railways v Small* (1938) 38 SR (NSW) 564; *Southern Pacific Hotel Services Inc v Southern Pacific Hotel Corp Ltd* [1984] 1 NSWLR 710; *Portal Software International Ltd v Bodsworth* [2005] NSWSC 1115.

[90] *ASADA v 34 Players and One Support Person* [2014] VSC 635.

Faced with a refusal to attend and no contractual means of compelling attendance, ASADA, supported by the AFL, sought to have the Victorian Supreme Court issue subpoenas pursuant to section 27A of the Commercial Arbitration Act 2011 (Vic). Justice Croft refused to issue the subpoenas, holding that proceedings before the AFL Anti-Doping Tribunal are not properly characterised as 'arbitration proceedings' or 'commercial arbitration proceedings' to which the Commercial Arbitration Act 2011 (Vic) applies.[91]

This decision further emphasises the need for sports administrative bodies to think carefully as to those persons that it wishes to and can contractually bind to its ADP, and for ASADA to consider whether the non-analytical evidence that it gathers pursuant to its statutory powers can actually be used in hearings to establish ADRVs.

Conclusion

It is clear that the Code incorporates an increased focus on obtaining non-analytical evidence by investigative means. Non-analytical evidence gathered by investigation forms a 'reliable means' by which facts related to anti-doping rule violations may be established. In Australia, ASADA has been given significant cohesive statutory powers to enhance its investigative abilities. The ambit of these statutory powers is still largely untested. ASADA's use of such statutory power is intertwined with the substantial contractual powers of sporting administrative bodies. The lawful use of these twin sources of power allows ASADA to gather a wide range of non-analytical evidence.

Authorities that have so far considered the interaction between statute and contract in the area of investigations into possible anti-doping violations suggest that ASADA will be granted considerable latitude and 'the adoption of innovative processes and methods of investigation is to be strongly supported' in the performance of 'very important national and international functions'.[92] However, the exercise of these powers by ASADA and sporting administrative bodies are far from straightforward or without their difficulties. As increased importance is placed on non-analytical evidence, these issues will continue to be a fertile area of debate.

[91] ibid [71].

[92] *Essendon Football Club* (n 24) 6 [4] (Middleton J).

7

Hearing Anti-Doping Cases in New Zealand

PAUL DAVID*

Introduction

This chapter outlines the way in which New Zealand provides for the hearing of anti-doping rule violations in accordance with the requirements of Article 8 of the World Anti-Doping Code (hereinafter the Code) and comments on the operation of the New Zealand system. It is written from the perspective of counsel representing the national anti-doping organisation responsible for bringing forward anti-doping allegations for hearing. The Code, of course, operates worldwide across sport at many levels and seeks to create a harmonised approach to the substantive and procedural aspects of anti-doping rules in sport. A vital part of the effective operation of the Code is the creation of an effective system for the hearing of allegations at the national and international levels. National-level hearing systems should operate procedurally and substantively in a manner which provides reasoned decisions that are consistent with those made by other tribunals under the Code. Common subject matter in the form of the substantive anti-doping rules under the Code provides a sound foundation, but a measure of consistency in procedural approaches is also essential. While different approaches to hearing systems will be adopted at the national level to achieve the aims of the Code (and this is expressly recognised in the Code[1]), there is much to be learned from the experiences of other national anti-doping organisations. Observations on the operation of one national anti-doping system will often provide insight and assistance for those who have to establish and run the hearing processes under the Code in other jurisdictions.

* QC BA (Hons), LLM (Cantab), Eldon Chambers Auckland. He is the author of *A Guide to the World Anti-Doping Code* 2nd edn (Cambridge, Cambridge University Press, 2012 – 3rd edn to be published 2016). He has been independent counsel to Drug Free Sport New Zealand for over 15 years. He is an arbitrator with the Court of Arbitration for Sport.

[1] See the note to Article 8 of the Code.

The New Zealand system which has developed to afford hearings for alleged anti-doping violations provides an effective means of producing the timely reasoned decisions required and this chapter seeks to identify the key components of the system.

Article 8 of the 2015 Code sets out the mandatory requirements for fair hearings in terms which are readily understandable in all legal jurisdictions whether civil or common law-based. While the current version of Article 8 expresses the requirements more concisely than earlier versions of the Code,[2] its earlier formulations in the 2003 and 2009 Codes expressed the same fundamental principles—timely fair and impartial hearings, and timely reasoned decisions on allegations of breaches of the Code. While the manner in which the requirements for hearings under Article 8 are met is a matter for national anti-doping organisations, the provision of a hearing system which does meet these requirements at the national and international levels is mandatory and fundamental to the effective operation of the Code worldwide. Article 8.1 of the 2015 Code provides as follows:

> **8.1 Fair Hearings**
>
> For any *Person* who is asserted to have committed an anti-doping rule violation, each *Anti-Doping Organization* with responsibility for results management shall provide, at a minimum, a fair hearing within a reasonable time by a fair and impartial hearing panel. A timely reasoned decision specifically including an explanation of the reason(s) for any period of *Ineligibility* shall be *Publicly Disclosed* as provided in Article 14.3.

National- and international-level anti-doping organisations have to put in place systems for the hearing of alleged violations under the Code. This covers first instance and appeal tribunals. At the national level, appeals from first instance decisions will be to national appeal bodies or the Court of Arbitration for Sport (CAS), if the anti-doping organisation adopts that course where national-level athletes are involved. Where international-level athletes are concerned, appeals will be made to CAS. While CAS plays an important role as the final appeal tribunal, subject to limited rights of appeal to the Swiss Federal Tribunal, the majority of anti-doping rule violations will be heard by tribunals at the national level.

This decision-making system (like the Code overall) functions by agreement, with the result that first instance tribunal or CAS determinations may well be considered a form of arbitration by many legal systems. However, unlike arbitration, where proceedings and decisions are usually confidential to the parties, decisions under the Code have an important public aspect for all those bound by the Code and, accordingly, the Code requires the publication of decisions.[3] As a

[2] In terms which reflect the provisions of art 6 of the European Convention on Human Rights (ECHR).

[3] See Article 14.3 2015 Code for the provisions on public disclosure. Article 14.3.2 makes mandatory public reporting of the disposition of anti-doping proceedings where a violation has been found to have been committed. Earlier disclosure of the identity of athletes facing allegations under the Code is a matter for national systems. This Article of the Code is implemented under the Sports Anti-Doping Rules 2016 ("SADR") under the New Zealand system which implements the Code.

result, decisions under the Code cannot properly be regarded as entirely private adjudications of rights reached in a consensual process between those subject to the Code. Rather, they form a body of law interpreting and applying the Code which is publicly available to all those affected by the Code. This broader public role of decisions under the Code highlights the importance of the decision-making process and the need for reasoned decisions by tribunals or CAS, which are accessible and capable of providing the required certainty for all those affected by the Code. These needs place strong emphasis on having appropriate hearing systems in place.

In order to identify the key features of the New Zealand system and assess how effectively it operates in terms of meeting the requirements of the Code, and to determine whether elements of the system may provide assistance for those responsible for hearing systems under the Code in other jurisdictions, some history is required to explain how and why the current system for hearing doping violations under the Code in New Zealand has developed.

New Zealand—Anti-Doping Regime Before the Code

New Zealand has had a national anti-doping agency for over 20 years. Well before the adoption and international implementation of the Code in 2004 and the establishment of the New Zealand Sports Disputes Tribunal in 2003,[4] drug testing was carried out by the statutory predecessor of Drug Free Sport New Zealand (DFSNZ), the New Zealand Drug Agency (the Agency). The New Zealand Sports Drug Agency Act 1994 (NZ) created the Agency, a crown entity with the responsibility of running a drug testing programme.[5] Statutory regulations provided for the sampling and testing process, and also contained the list of prohibited substances, which was taken from the International Olympic Committee list before the advent of the World Anti-Doping Agency (WADA).

A national anti-doping programme had, in fact, been in existence in New Zealand for some time before the creation of this statutory process. After the Ben Johnson scandal at the 1988 Seoul Olympics,[6] the New Zealand Olympic and Commonwealth Games Association introduced an anti-doping testing programme in the lead-up to the 1990 Commonwealth Games in Auckland. After the Games, the

[4] Sports Tribunal of New Zealand, 'History' (2015) www.sportstribunal.org.nz/about-us/history.

[5] New Zealand Sports Drug Agency Act 1994 (NZ) ss 4, 6.

[6] In Canada, the scandal prompted a Royal Commission. The finding of the Commission led to significant changes in the organisation of testing for prohibited substances in Canada and other countries. See Canada, Commission of Inquiry into the Use of Drugs and Banned Practices Intended to Increase Athletic Performance, *Report* (1990).

programme continued and expanded with financial support from the Hillary Commission for Sport, Fitness, and Leisure, the crown agency then responsible for sport and recreation in New Zealand. A task force then recommended that an agency independent of sport be established by the government to combat the misuse of drugs in sport. An interim agency commenced operations in 1993 in Auckland and operated under the terms of the draft legislation before the Agency took up the functions under the 1994 Act when it became law.[7]

This initial New Zealand legislative scheme in the anti-doping area was based on legislation which had been operating in Australia since 1990—the Australian Sports Drug Agency Act 1990 (Cth). However, as discussed below, the adoption of the Code and the need to implement it led to significant changes in the New Zealand system and the repeal of the 1994 Act.[8] It is interesting to note that the Australian legislative system has not evolved in the same way and still maintains the same general procedural approach to the hearing and determination of anti-doping rule violations under the Code.[9]

Early Statutory Process Under the New Zealand Sports Drug Agency Act 1994 (NZ)

Under the 1994 Act, as noted above, the Agency was responsible for maintaining a schedule of banned substances, and for testing competitors and determining whether a doping infraction had occurred.[10] Where the Board of the Agency determined that an infraction had occurred, it had to enter the name of the athlete who had committed the infraction on a statutory register kept by the Agency and had to notify the national sporting organisation to which the athlete belonged of the infraction.[11] The regime focused on testing—the only available infractions were doping and refusal to comply with a request to provide a sample without reasonable cause. If the athlete wanted to challenge a decision by the Agency to enter a finding on the register, he or she had a right of appeal to the District Court, with further rights of appeal to the High Court and Court of Appeal on points of

[7] See generally New Zealand, *Parliamentary Debates*, House of Representatives, 29 March 1994 (John Banks, Minister for Sport, Fitness and Leisure).

[8] The Australian statutory system still provides for a process which involves both statutory determinations by the national anti-doping organisation that can be challenged in the court system, and hearings in domestic tribunals and CAS. This has considerable disadvantages in providing an efficient hearing system.

[9] See generally Australian Sports Anti-Doping Authority, 'Rule Violation Management Process' (2005) www.asada.gov.au/rules-and-violations/rule-violation-management-process.

[10] New Zealand Sports Drug Agency Act 1994 (NZ) s 6.

[11] ibid ss 17–18.

law.[12] When notified of the determination made against the athlete by the Agency, the relevant national sporting organisation was responsible for determining the sanction under the applicable sporting rules.[13]

With the establishment of the New Zealand Sports Disputes Tribunal in 2003, sporting organisations could agree under their own rules to refer anti-doping violation findings made by the Agency under the Act to the Tribunal. When the Code was introduced in 2004 and adopted by many international sporting organisations, national sporting organisations were encouraged to adopt model anti-doping policies which implemented the Code. The Agency began to operate under the Code and used the WADA Prohibited List, but the system of findings being made by the Agency under the 1994 Act and referred to national sporting organisations for further action was initially maintained, while the work was carried out to change the legislative framework.

Both before and after the establishment of the New Zealand Sports Disputes Tribunal, the process under the 1994 Act produced somewhat uneven results. This was caused by the split nature of the system. Appeals to the courts were available under the Act to challenge determinations by the Agency that a doping infraction had been committed and an entry on the statutory register should be made, while tribunal hearings determined sanctions under the rules of the relevant sporting organisation. This system meant that proceedings might be drawn out by a court challenge and also that it was possible to have one outcome for a doping infraction under the legislative process and another when the same evidence was examined by a sporting tribunal under the sports' rules.[14] In addition, even with a great deal of encouragement to implement up-to-date model anti-doping policies, the rules of national sporting organisations often proved inadequate and out-of-date when the sport sought to rely on them to impose a sanction on the athlete. Before the advent of the Tribunal and the Code, this meant that sports domestic tribunals sometimes imposed inadequate sanctions or, worse still, were found to have no jurisdiction under the applicable rules or policy. The same problems were encountered in the early years of the Tribunal, although, perhaps to a lesser degree, as sporting organisations became more aware of their obligations in the area. Indeed, the first decision by the Tribunal in 2003[15] was that it did not have jurisdiction to hear an anti-doping matter referred to it by a national sporting organisation because of deficiencies in the sport's rules and that no purposive reading of the rules could remedy the situation. The result was that the allegation had to be dealt with by an internal tribunal.

[12] ibid ss 20, 24.

[13] See ibid s 19.

[14] For an historic example of this, see CAS 2001/A/337 *B v Fédération Internationale de Natation*, where the statutory regime applicable at the time in New Zealand and the sporting arbitration process produced different results after lengthy hearing processes.

[15] *New Zealand Powerlifting Federation v Doyle* SDT 01/03, 30 October 2003.

One major inefficiency and burden of the system under the 1994 Act was that the national sporting organisation had to bring the proceedings against the athlete, who was the subject of the determination and entry on the statutory register under the Act. In practice, where cases were more complicated, the Agency had to carry the primary responsibility for the preparation and presentation of the case. This was particularly the case where there were difficulties in the interpretation and application of the applicable rules of the sport in relation to such matters as sanctions.[16] The central role of the Agency was emphasised by the fact that, after the establishment of the Tribunal, the Agency would be designated an interested party under the Tribunal's rules.

Legislative Change to the System

This early regulatory framework and procedure changed with the passing of the Sports Anti-Doping Act 2006 (NZ). This Act continued the existing Sports Disputes Tribunal of New Zealand under the new name of the Sports Tribunal of New Zealand,[17] and continued and renamed the Crown entity responsible for the implementation of the Code as DFSNZ.[18] The Act repealed the 1994 Act[19] with appropriate transitional provisions[20] and replaced the system for handling breaches of anti-doping rules under the 1994 Act with a simpler system, which made the Sports Tribunal the body responsible for hearing and determining allegations and imposing sanctions.[21] This was achieved by the making of regulations—the Sports Anti-Doping Rules (SADR)[22]—under the Act which contained the core provisions of the Code and provided for the investigation and bringing of alleged violations by DFSNZ. The implementation of the SADR was achieved by national sporting organisations agreeing to apply the SADR under their rules in a manner which bound their members. DFSNZ was responsible for doing all things necessary to implement the Code in New Zealand, but it no

[16] See, eg, *New Zealand Wrestling Union Inc v Mark Hogarth* SDT 06/04, 30 August 2004 (on retroactive application for therapeutic use exemption and application of sanction provisions in a manner consistent with the Code); *New Zealand Federation of Body Builders Inc v Tony Ligaliga* SDT 11/05, 8 December 2015) (on the interpretation and application of Article 10.5.2 of the Code).

[17] Sports Anti-Doping Act 2006 (NZ) s 29.

[18] ibid ss 6–7.

[19] ibid s 59.

[20] ibid ss 55–58.

[21] ibid s 38.

[22] At the time of writing, the most current version of the SADR are the Sports Anti-Doping Rules 2016 which came into effect on 1 January 2016 and references throughout the chapter are made to that version, unless otherwise stated. The SADR 2015 implemented the significant changes made by the 2015 Code. The SADR 2016 made only minor changes to the SADR 2015. While the SADR have to change each year to incorporate by reference the annual changes to the Prohibited List and each year minor changes are made to the SADR, the major changes to the SADR have taken place after the Code has been reviewed and changed—2009 and 2015.

longer had any statutory role in making determinations in relation to anti-doping rule violations.[23] Its functions essentially involved doing everything to implement the Code, which included investigating and bringing forward allegations to the Sports Tribunal for determination. While the bodies responsible under the system remained creatures of statute, the important result of this change was to replace a system which involved statutory determinations (and possible court process in respect of those determinations) as well as decisions by private sporting tribunals with one which would only involve the referral of allegations to a specialised independent tribunal.

The Current Legislative Scheme

Under the Sports Anti-Doping Act 2006 (NZ), DFSNZ has the function of making regulations—the SADR—in order to implement the Code.[24] The Sports Tribunal has the statutory function to take all necessary steps to implement the SADR made by DFSNZ. The process of making the SADR annually includes an obligation to consult with national sporting organisations and others.[25] When the SADR were first made in 2007, national sports organisations agreed to them as their anti-doping policies binding their members. Under the SADR, national sports organisations recognise the role of DFSNZ in investigating possible anti-doping rule violations and bringing such allegations before the Sports Tribunal.[26] This rule-making process produces a uniform set of rules that sports are in effect obliged to adopt and bind their members to. DFSNZ is no longer responsible for making determinations as to doping infractions, but rather has become responsible for investigating, bringing and proving anti-doping allegations under the SADR before the Sports Tribunal. While national sporting organisations remained interested parties in doping matters before the Tribunal and were responsible for bringing provisional suspension applications until 2012 (when DFSNZ was also given this role), they no longer carried the primary responsibility of bringing the anti-doping rule violation against their members. Their main responsibility became and remains that of considering and implementing the SADR and amendments so as to bind their members and athletes who compete in events organised by them.[27]

[23] Sports Anti-Doping Act 2006 (NZ) ss 12–13.

[24] ibid ss 12, 13, 16.

[25] ibid s 16(4) requires consultation with 'national sporting organisations, athletes and the Privacy Commissioner'.

[26] SADR 1.2 for the application of the SADR to national sporting organisations.

[27] Agreement to the SADR will be required if a national sporting organisation is to be recognised by the government entity responsible for sport: see Sport New Zealand, 'Eligibility Criteria' (2015) www.sportnz.org.nz/about-us/who-we-are/how-we-invest/investment-framework.

Sports Tribunal Hearings Under the Sports Anti-Doping Act 2006 (NZ)

The observations which follow primarily relate to the operation of the Sports Tribunal in the period since the passing of the Sports Anti-Doping Act 2006 (NZ) which marked the advent of the current system under which national sporting organisations agree to the application of the SADR and, by this agreement, that the Sports Tribunal is to be responsible for hearing and determining anti-doping rule violations referred to it by DFSNZ.[28] However, the earlier statutory history shows that the first significant change in the New Zealand system was the move to bring all aspects of anti-doping proceedings before the Sports Tribunal under a common set of rules—the SADR—which implemented the Code, with the national anti-doping organisation having the role of investigating, bringing forward and proving allegations. This change was made when DFSNZ had to consider the best way to implement the Code in New Zealand and provide for hearings of anti-doping rule violations. The change was important because it provided a simpler process for hearing anti-doping violations and provided a platform upon which the Tribunal could develop a consistent approach to the determination of anti-doping rule violations. The changed structure immediately appeared to provide a better opportunity for speedy efficient decisions which were consistent with the SADR (and, because of the nature of the SADR, the Code) because a single tribunal was responsible for determining whether there had been a violation and imposing the applicable sanction, and there was no separate avenue for challenge before the courts. DFSNZ was also given a clearer simplified role. It no longer made determinations as part of its statutory functions, but rather was the party responsible for bringing and proving allegations before the Tribunal under the SADR.

In order to make some observations on the operation of the Tribunal in practice in this period and its effectiveness, it is necessary to outline its composition and statutory powers, the work which it does and the procedural rules which it has made to regulate proceedings. These features all contribute to the performance of the Tribunal and are important in any assessment of its work in the hearing of anti-doping proceedings (and, of course, generally).

[28] Under the SADR national sporting organisations are permitted to set up their own anti-doping tribunals and refer allegations under the SADR to an NSO Anti-Doping Tribunal as opposed to the Sports Tribunal. If they choose to do this, the NSO Anti-Doping Tribunal will apply the SADR in anti-doping proceedings and has to follow the requirements of the SADR relating to the conduct of hearings by the Sports Tribunal in hearing anti-doping allegations (SADR 8.6.2). Only two significant sports—cricket and rugby—do not refer allegations under the SADR to the Sports Tribunal. Both sports recognise the role of DFSNZ in bringing forward allegations under the SADR before their National Sporting Organisation Anti-Doping Tribunals.

The Sports Tribunal: Composition and Statutory Powers

The Tribunal was the result of a 2001 report and a 2002 review concerning the needs of the sports sector for dispute resolution.[29] The Tribunal was established in 2003 by the Board of Sport and Recreation New Zealand under section 8(i) of the Sport and Recreation Act 2002 (NZ).[30] The ministerial task force which recommended its establishment stated that it should be set up to:

> [H]ave a primary focus on national sport to assist National Sporting Organisations to avoid lengthy and costly legal battles; ensure quality and consistent decision making for athletes in New Zealand sport; add credibility to the operation of elite sport in New Zealand and provide for appeals to the Court of Arbitration for Sport.[31]

A subsequent report following consultation with sporting organisations called for the establishment of an independent body to hear and resolve sports disputes in a fair, consistent, timely and affordable way.[32]

Composition of the Tribunal

The Sports Anti-Doping Act 2006 (NZ) sets out the composition and jurisdiction of the Sports Tribunal. The Tribunal must be made up of no less than five and no more than nine members.[33] Members are appointed by the Governor General on the recommendation of the Minister after consultation with the Board of Sport and Recreation New Zealand.[34] All members have to have a significant interest in, and understanding of, sport. The chairperson and at least two other members have to be lawyers.[35] The chair must be either a retired judicial officer, or a senior barrister or solicitor of repute of over seven years' standing.[36] The other lawyer members may be appointed deputy chairpersons.[37] Members are appointed for terms not exceeding five years and can be reappointed.[38] The current convention

[29] Ministerial Taskforce on Sport, Fitness & Leisure, *Getting Set for an Active Nation*, Report (2001). See also Nick David, Marinka Teague and Sonia Ogier, 'Dispute Resolution in the Sport and Recreation Sector and the Role of the Sports Tribunal' (Report, MartinJenkins, May 2009) 22.

[30] See also 'Sports Disputes Tribunal on the Way' *New Zealand Herald* (10 October 2002) www.nzherald.co.nz/sport/news/article.cfm?c_id=4&objectid=2998510.

[31] Ministerial Taskforce on Sport (n 29) 108.

[32] David, Teague and Ogier (n 29) 22.

[33] Sports Anti-Doping Act 2006 (NZ) s 30(1).

[34] ibid s 30(2).

[35] ibid ss 31(2), 33(1).

[36] ibid s 31(2).

[37] ibid s 32.

[38] Ibid s 34(1).

appears to be that members will not be appointed for more than two terms. The current chairperson is Sir Bruce Robertson KNZM VGSM, a former judge of the Court of Appeal. He took up his position in 2013 and succeeded Barry Paterson CNZM OBE QC, a former High Court judge who had been the chair for 10 years. The other current members of the Sports Tribunal are Alan Galbraith QC (Deputy Chair), Dr James Farmer QC (Deputy Chair), Ron Cheatley MBE, Dr Lynn Coleman MNZM, Chantal Brunner, Robert Hart, Georgina Earl ONZM and Paula Tesoriero MNZM.[39] In addition to the chair and deputy chairs, 3 of the 6 general members have legal backgrounds.

The Act provides that the Tribunal has the function of doing all things necessary to implement the SADR in New Zealand.[40] Its jurisdiction involves hearing anti-doping allegations under the SADR, hearing appeals from the decisions of national sporting organisations and the New Zealand Olympic Committee (NZOC) where the rules of the organisations provide for that, and hearing other sports-related disputes where the parties have agreed to the jurisdiction of the Tribunal and the Tribunal agrees to hear the dispute. The Tribunal has the power to determine its own procedures in carrying out its functions, although it must ensure that it complies with and implements the SADR made by DFSNZ in determining those procedures.[41] Under the Act, the Tribunal is given the power to receive material into evidence which would not admissible in a court of law.[42] It has the power to issue summons to persons to appear and/or produce documents.[43] It can make costs orders which are enforceable through the District Court.[44]

Sports Tribunal Procedural Rules

General Rules

The Tribunal makes procedural rules under section 39 of the Act. The rules are divided into four parts, with specific parts for anti-doping matters, appeals and sports-related disputes following general rules that are applicable to all proceedings which come before the Tribunal.[45] The appendices to the rules contain forms for the applications which can be made to the Tribunal. The forms provide

[39] Sports Tribunal of New Zealand, 'Members of the Tribunal' (2015) www.sportstribunal.org.nz/about-us/members-of-the-tribunal.

[40] Sports Anti-Doping Act 2006 (NZ) s 38.

[41] ibid s 39.

[42] ibid s 40.

[43] ibid s 41.

[44] ibid s 47.

[45] Sports Tribunal of New Zealand, 'Rules of the Sports Tribunal of New Zealand 2012' (6 March 2012) r 4.

simplified pleadings for the cases in each area of the Tribunal's jurisdiction. The rules and forms are available on the Tribunal's website is an interactive format.[46] They are short and clear, and several provisions underline the overall approach which the Tribunal adopts to disputes.

The rules are to be construed to 'secure the just, speedy and inexpensive determination of any proceeding' and provide that '[w]here any matter is not provided for in the rules, the Tribunal has the jurisdiction to make orders or give directions as it considers to be consistent with the just, speedy and inexpensive determination of the Proceeding'.[47] The general rules provide for panels to be established from the members of the Tribunal by the Chair or Deputy Chair. Disputes as to jurisdiction can be determined as the Tribunal sees fit and the panel deciding on jurisdiction may not necessarily be the panel which decides the substantive dispute if it goes forward. There is specific provision for decisions on preliminary matters to be made by the Chair or Deputy Chair by holding a pre-hearing telephone conference at which the directions that are considered appropriate for the 'just speedy and inexpensive determination of the Proceeding' will be given.[48] The Tribunal has the power to appoint an expert to advise and assist it, whether on its own motion or on the application of the parties.[49] The Tribunal can also appoint counsel to assist it in any proceeding by advising on matters of law, procedure and evidence.[50] A party which is not a party to the proceedings may be added to the proceeding as an interested party where the Tribunal determines that it has sufficient interest in the proceeding to be considered as an interested party.[51] Where an interested party files the relevant form electing to become such a party, it becomes a party to the proceeding with all the rights of a party.[52] The Tribunal has inquisitorial powers as to the production and inspection of documents by parties or persons bound by the rules,[53] in addition to the formal power to issue a summons under the Act. Where the Tribunal makes orders under these powers, it can draw such inferences and conclusions as it considers appropriate from a failure to comply.[54] In addition to the power of receiving evidence under the Act, the rules provide that facts relating to any proceedings may be established by any reliable means.[55] The Tribunal has to observe the principles of natural justice in all matters.[56]

[46] Sports Tribunal of New Zealand, 'Rules of the Sports Tribunal' (2015) www.sportstribunal.org.nz/rules-and-procedures/rules-of-the-sports-tribunal.
[47] Sports Tribunal of New Zealand (n 45) r 30.
[48] ibid r 11.
[49] ibid r 12(a).
[50] ibid r 12(b). These powers to appoint experts or counsel to assist the Tribunal have not been used to the writer's knowledge.
[51] ibid r 13.
[52] ibid r 14.
[53] ibid r 15.
[54] ibid r 15(c).
[55] ibid r 16.
[56] ibid r 17.

As would be anticipated, the rules cover in concise terms such other matters as language, the registry, service of documents (email is one of the modes of service) and representation.[57] The rules make general provision for proceedings to be private and confidential.[58] While this is the usual position with other proceedings which are within the Tribunal's jurisdiction, the rules stipulate that anti-doping proceedings will be private and confidential, save where the parties otherwise agree, and that decisions in those proceedings will be published as required by the SADR.[59] The Tribunal hears and determines matters in accordance with the laws of New Zealand.[60] Decisions, which can be by majority,[61] may be given orally, but in every proceeding the Tribunal has to give a written decision with reasons as soon as it is expedient. In addition, the Tribunal has the power to make non-binding recommendations to a national sporting organisation or other party arising out of the proceeding.[62] Decisions are enforceable under the law of contract in the courts of New Zealand. Decisions are expressed to be final and binding and are not to be questioned in a court of law.[63] Appeals to CAS will, however, be available if the rules or policies of the relevant national sporting organisation or international federation so provide.[64] The Tribunal may make costs orders, including filing fees or witness expenses, as it thinks fit and these are enforceable through the District Court if they are not paid.[65]

Specific Tribunal Rules in Anti-Doping Proceedings

The procedural rules specific to anti-doping proceedings are set out in Part B of the Rules of the Sports Tribunal. The substantive content in anti-doping proceedings and some procedural elements are set out in the SADR. Forms are attached to the rules for the bringing of anti-doping proceedings, applying for a provisional suspension and for the filing of a defence to the application.[66]

[57] ibid rr 20–23.

[58] ibid r 25.

[59] SADR 8.8 for Confidentiality and public reporting of Tribunal decisions.

[60] Sports Tribunal of New Zealand (n 45) r 26.

[61] ibid r 27. This is very rare, but has occurred in the context of the interpretation of Article 10.4 of the 2009 Code: see *DFSNZ v Takerei* ST 01/12, 5 December 2014. The point has, of course, caused division between CAS Panels. A decision by a majority of the Sports Tribunal was also given in the context of a selection appeal, see *Henderson v NZWP* ST 12/15, 29 July 2015.

[62] Sports Tribunal of New Zealand (n 45) r 27(c). The Tribunal also has a power to make orders for an issue before it to be mediated before a Tribunal member or an independent person: at r 31. This power has never been applied in anti-doping cases and, it is submitted, that it cannot be because of the essentially adjudicative nature of such cases.

[63] Ibid r 28(a). The enforceability of this provision has not been considered by the New Zealand courts. The proceedings before the Sports Tribunal would seem to be arbitrations and be potentially subject to the Arbitration Act 1996 (NZ).

[64] ibid r 28(b).

[65] ibid r 29.

[66] ibid app (forms 1, 2, 5, 6).

If a party wishes to either defend the application for an anti-doping rule violation or admit the violation and take part in the hearing on sanctions only, it must file and serve the specified form within seven working days of the service of the application.[67] Under the SADR, all applications, including applications for provisional suspension, are brought by DFSNZ. The national sporting organisation of the athlete will be joined as an interested party and DFSNZ is obliged to send a copy of the application and all relevant documents to the head office of the national sporting organisation.[68]

The rules provide for a pre-hearing conference to be held within five working days of the filing of the defence or notice of participation form.[69] That conference will normally be by way of telephone hearing. At the conference, the date of the hearing, its nature and appropriate procedural directions will be given, along with any other order required to 'facilitate the prompt and just expedition of the matter'. The pre-hearing conference can become the final hearing. The rule also provides that the final hearing may, in appropriate cases, be by way of telephone conference. The hearing will determine the application in accordance with the SADR, with the Tribunal receiving evidence in accordance with the Act and imposing a sanction as provided for by the SADR if the violation is proved. Decisions are published as provided for by the SADR. The Tribunal rules record that anti-doping violation proceedings have to be completed in a timely manner and shall normally be completed within three months of the notification of the violation to the athlete. The Tribunal will take all necessary steps to expedite the proceeding, provided the steps are consistent with natural justice. The Tribunal is obliged to endeavour to make and issue its decision within seven working days of the conclusion of the hearing.[70] Applications for provisional suspensions are considered in accordance with the requirements of the SADR. Such applications have to be considered urgently in accordance with the requirements of SADR and will invariably be dealt with by a telephone hearing if opposed.[71]

Anti-Doping Cases Before the Sports Tribunal

Over the 11 years in which it has been operating, the work of the Tribunal has come from two main areas—anti-doping allegations and appeals against decisions made by national sporting organisations or the NZOC. While many tribunal decisions have involved positive tests or refusals, in more recent times, proceedings involving violations of the SADR arising from the importation and supply

[67] ibid app (form 2).
[68] ibid r 36.
[69] ibid r 37.
[70] ibid r 39.
[71] The Sports Tribunal Rules refer to r 12 of the 2012 SADR. This is now r 7.9 of the SADR 2016.

of prohibited substances and other conduct established by evidence not coming from the testing process have become more common.[72] This development reflects the changing emphasis in anti-doping investigation under the Code and International Standards.[73] However, as with anti-doping tribunals worldwide, the Tribunal has had to deal with many cases which result from the testing of athletes. The Tribunal has considered the appropriate sanction under the SADR where an athlete has tested positive as a result of taking a recreational substance such as cannabis without considering his or her obligations under the SADR,[74] or has mistakenly ingested a prohibited substance in a supplement, or, more rarely, has been prescribed a prohibited substance by his or her doctor after not taking the proper steps to inform the doctor of his or her status as an elite athlete. In many cases, the Tribunal has been concerned with the interpretation and application of the requirements in the SADR for a reduction in sanction. Among the cases, some athletes who have cheated or sought to cheat have been caught by targeted testing, or as a result of investigations. Some investigations involved the use of information provided by other government agencies such as Customs or Medsafe concerning the importation of substances on the Prohibited List.

Consistent with the approach adopted in the Tribunal's procedural rules, cases have generally proceeded rapidly to hearing and decision. Rare delays in the Tribunal hearing and determining an allegation within its jurisdiction have occurred where the athlete faces other proceedings, generally proceedings in the criminal courts, but also, on occasion, anti-doping allegations in another jurisdiction. In those circumstances, the Tribunal has decided that those proceedings should be determined before the proceedings before the Tribunal.[75]

As with all proceedings falling within its jurisdiction, the Tribunal has, consistently with its rules, adopted a relatively relaxed approach to the formalities of procedure and has sought to tailor its processes to meet the overall aims under the SADR/Code and its rules.

Over time, the use of telephone hearings for procedural conferences has extended and a practice has developed in anti-doping proceedings of conducting substantive hearings, in particular those which concern the applicable sanction for doping violations, by telephone. There is no requirement under the Code that a hearing should take place in person and the use of technology to provide

[72] See, for some examples, *Drug Free Sport New Zealand v Rodney Newman* ST 17/10 31 January 2012 (participation in breach, refusal, use and attempted use, possession); *Drug Free Sport New Zealand v Daniel Milne* ST 11/14, 25 November 2014 (possession, attempted trafficking); *Drug Free Sport New Zealand v Andrew Ciancio* ST 03/14, 24 June 2015 (whereabouts, tampering with doping control); *Drug Free Sport New Zealand v Kris Gemmell* ST 08/13, 12 February 2014 and on appeal CAS 2014/A/2, 1 December 2014 (whereabouts breaches).

[73] The 2015 Code and WADA International Standard for Testing and Investigations 2015 places greater emphasis on intelligence led testing and investigations into conduct which breaches the Code.

[74] The occurrence of anti-doping rule violations involving cannabis has reduced very significantly with the change in decision limits for the reporting of an adverse analytical finding.

[75] In these rare cases, the athlete was under provisional suspension over the period of the delay.

for a hearing is accepted practice.[76] The use of this form of hearing can make it more difficult to determine credibility issues which arise where a tribunal is considering the requirements for a reduction of the standard period of ineligibility.[77] The choice of this method of hearing proceedings has been driven primarily by the logistical difficulties in arranging urgent hearings involving parties from around New Zealand and the considerable cost savings for all parties and, in particular, athletes. Generally, the process has worked well. Where an athlete requests a hearing in person, the Tribunal will make procedural directions to allow for that and DFSNZ will agree to that course of action.

In violations involving cannabis, the Tribunal produced a Minute, setting out its approach to sanctions which served to notify national sporting organisations and athletes of its approach and to abbreviate sanctions hearings.[78] While this kind of approach can be seen to make a hearing unnecessary, it has remained important for the Tribunal to hold a hearing process where the athlete is able to explain in person why he or she has fallen short of the standards required by the Code. Where DFSNZ is able to reach an agreement with an athlete and his or her advisers on the applicable sanction under the SADR on the basis of agreed facts, as is contemplated by the Code,[79] it will refer that agreement to the Tribunal which will produced a reasoned decision as required by the Code. Generally, where a reduction in sanction requires an athlete to prove that a particular set of circumstances applies to the violation which may bring about a reduction in the standard period of ineligibility, DFSNZ considers that the better course of action remains to have a short hearing process before the Tribunal, after which the Tribunal will decide on the applicable period of ineligibility and will produce a written reasoned decision. This approach follows from the role of DFSNZ as a body which presents allegations for determination and does not adjudicate on them. It reflects the principle that all decisions which result in sanctions being imposed should ultimately be the responsibility of a tribunal which is independent of the anti-doping organisation responsible for the investigation and proving violations. Such a process protects the integrity of the decision-making system.

[76] Article 8 2009 Code made express reference to telephone hearings. While the shortened Article 8 2015 does not contain this reference, the WADA Guidelines on Results Management Hearings and Decisions (at paragraph 5.1.2) make it clear that hearings using technology and indeed on written materials can be used to meet the requirements under Article 8.

[77] The provisions for sanctions are in SADR 10, which implement Article 10 of the 2015 Code. Issues of credibility are particularly likely to arise in considering questions under SADR 10.2–10.4 (the same Articles in the Code).

[78] Sports Disputes Tribunal of New Zealand, *Minutes of Sports Disputes Tribunal—Re Cannabis Sanctions*, 15 December 2006. The Minute does not have continuing relevance for sanctions under the SADR given the changes on sanctions as a result of the 2015 Code and the changes in relation to the decision limits for adverse analytical findings for cannabis.

[79] Article 8.3 Waiver of hearing.

The product of the hearing process before the Sports Tribunal in anti-doping proceedings[80] and in other proceedings within its jurisdiction has to be a speedy reasoned decision. In anti-doping proceedings, the Tribunal is the body which DFSNZ has agreed will fulfil the task of meeting the requirements for a hearing under Article 8 of the Code. A national anti-doping organisation in the position of DFSNZ, and those who represent it, has to do all it can to ensure that the Tribunal produces decisions by a process which meets the requirements of Article 8 and which are Code compliant. This process has both procedural and substantive aspects. The substantive rules in the SADR implement the Code and the rules of the Sports Tribunal clearly prescribe processes which should produce a reasoned decision in good time. As far as substantive Code compliance is concerned, a national anti-doping organisation like DFSNZ has to ensure that the Tribunal is properly directed on the substantive law relevant to a particular case, especially on any relevant CAS awards. While the outcome under the SADR/Code in a particular set of circumstances may be straightforward, understanding and explaining how the rules operate to produce that outcome may not be. As with the operation of any set of legal rules, the production of written reasoned decisions will inevitably, from time to time, require considered legal analysis. In addition, the sporting context requires that hearings take place and written reasoned decisions are produced in a timeframe which meets the requirements of sporting competition and are in a form which is readily understood and accessible to those who are affected by the rules. It is one thing to understand a complex set of rules, but quite another to give prompt advice and make legal submissions in a digestible form explaining those rules, and yet another to provide a timely written decision on the application of the rules which can be readily understood by those who do not know the regulatory framework, but are bound by it.

Counsel for an anti-doping organisation like DFSNZ has, from time to time, to play a role in proceedings which may be broader than the role of counsel in normal proceedings. On occasion, the role requires that assistance be given to athletes, lawyers and others representing athletes on the operation and interpretation of the SADR. More conventionally, although in all cases the focus has to be on interpreting the provisions of the SADR in a straightforward way and applying them to the particular case, counsel also has to ensure that the Tribunal is referred to any relevant CAS awards (or indeed other tribunal decisions) for the case in hand[81] which may assist in interpreting and applying the SADR.

It has been beneficial for the Tribunal decision-making process to have had one chairperson for a period of 10 years (followed in 2012 by another experienced

[80] The Sports Tribunal procedural rules provide that a decision will usually be made within three months of the proceedings being filed with the Tribunal: Sports Tribunal of New Zealand (n 45) r 39.

[81] It must be observed that the determination of questions relating to sanctions essentially involves applying the words of the Code read as a free-standing document (as required by Article 24 of the Code) to a particular factual situation—an exercise which will generally not be assisted by reference to a multitude of CAS awards on different facts.

lawyer chairperson) and a significant degree of consistency in the Tribunal membership. While many cases might ultimately be seen as involving a straightforward application of the SADR, the demands of the decision-making process mean that the lawyers on the Tribunal have had a central role in producing a body of decisions applying the SADR written in a style which can guide athletes and others bound by the rules.

In most cases, anti-doping decisions have been produced in final written form and published on the Tribunal's website within days of the hearing.[82] The Tribunal has been able to deal quickly with a wide range of legal issues under the SADR/Code—such as the proper approach to the now repealed Article 10.4 of the 2009 Code (then SADR 14.4), issues arising from the changed status of prohibited substances and the application of the doctrine of *lex mitior*, and the imposition of sanctions for multiple violations. This kind of work can require significant legal input, and the composition of the Tribunal and the experience of its members has meant that it has been able to provide this.

Review of the Tribunal's Work

An independent report was commissioned into the performance of the Tribunal and was produced in 2009 after a number of users were surveyed.[83] It contains a summary of anti-doping proceedings brought before the Tribunal. The summary, while containing several examples of athletes deliberately taking prohibited substances in order to cheat in sporting performance, shows that most of the violations coming before the Tribunal involved negligent mistakes by athletes rather than deliberate attempts to cheat. The report records general satisfaction from sporting organisations and athletes with the performance of the Tribunal, particularly with the change in the operation of the rules which has seen DFSNZ replace national sporting organisations as the body responsible for bringing forward anti-doping proceedings. The Tribunal is generally found to have delivered on its aim of producing written reasoned decisions in a timely and cost-effective manner, and to have been highly responsive in carrying out its functions. The main factors in this effectiveness are found to be the high-calibre membership of the Tribunal, the leadership of the chairperson, and an ability to tailor the Tribunal processes without compromising the integrity of decision-making and efficient administration.[84]

[82] All the Tribunal's decisions can be searched for on the Tribunal's website: www.sportstribunal.org.nz. See SADR 8.8 for reporting of decisions.

[83] David, Teague and Ogier (n 29). A further review into the work of the Tribunal in late 2015 has been conducted and a report is likely to be published in March 2016.

[84] ibid 3, 44–46.

Since this report, DFSNZ has also assumed responsibility for bringing applications for provisional suspension before the Tribunal. The general trend in anti-doping proceedings has continued, with many cases concerned with the negligent consumption of supplements and/or performance boosters which contained prohibited substances, with hearings concerning the requirements under the SADR for the imposition of a reduced sanction. In the more recent period, DFSNZ has, like other anti-doping organisations operating under the Code and in particular with the recent amendments to the Code in its 2015 version and the related International Standards, increased its focus on the investigation of deliberate efforts to cheat. This has gradually begun to produce cases which are the product of intelligence-led investigations and this trend seems likely to continue.

Some Key Elements

It is difficult to look back over this history in which the Tribunal has developed and responded to the various changing anti-doping rules, and to identify the key factors in its performance. However, some important general features are:

— a separation between the body investigating and making allegations under the SADR and the body deciding on allegations;
— one process for handling violations with no statutory process of appeals to courts operating alongside the tribunal system;
— a tribunal which is independent of the national sporting organisations and the national anti-doping organisation;
— tribunal members who are experienced in sport, but appointed externally by government and who serve for periods of time which allow expertise to be acquired;
— a tribunal with a significant number of experienced lawyer members who can identify key issues quickly, can tailor procedure to meet the needs of cases and produce written decisions quickly;
— procedural rules which are simple, have clearly stated aims and can be flexibly applied; and
— a commitment on the part of the Tribunal to producing short reasoned decisions as quickly as possible, which focus on the issues for decision and are expressed in straightforward language.

Nonetheless, this kind of agreement-based system has weaknesses. First, it depends on agreement and it is possible that national sporting organisations may not do what is required to implement the rules. There have, however, been no instances of this in recent times because a sporting organisation has to agree to the SADR in order to be recognised as a sporting organisation by the New Zealand government for the receipt of public funds. More importantly an agreement-based arbitral system cannot have the freedom from challenge enjoyed by a court system which operates as part of the general national court structure. Sport has, however, chosen this kind of arbitral/tribunal system under the Code and in other areas to provide the decision-making process and decisions which best fit the sporting context. It has to be accepted that where national tribunals and CAS are not true courts it will always be possible to challenge their decisions on national legal principles. Such challenges may come from disappointed parties who challenge decisions of national tribunals or CAS on the basis that they contravene fundamental principles of national or international law, whether in private or public law proceedings. In New Zealand, the statutory origin of the Sports Tribunal means that disappointed parties may seek to bring judicial review proceedings in relation to Tribunal decisions. While the Tribunal rules seek to close off this avenue of court challenge, and it can be contended that the arbitral nature of the proceedings with a CAS appeal would effectively exclude national courts, the 'weakness' cannot be removed. Indeed, it must be an accepted feature of private agreement-based hearing procedures that they may be subject to challenge in national courts or supranational tribunals on the basis that their operation in some way contravenes the fundamental legal principles that any private hearing body must obey under the law of the land. No system of the kind established under the SADR or under the Code can truly remove this risk.

Accordingly, the aim of those creating and maintaining such a hearing system should not be to bring about immunity from challenge, but rather to operate a system which generally satisfies users. The possibility of challenge cannot be removed, but if the system provides a fair hearing and timely accessible decisions, challenge is much less likely.

Each of the features of the Tribunal set out above has been a valuable ingredient in the New Zealand system. In combination, they have operated to produce the fair hearing and decision-making process required under Article 8 of the Code. In particular, the product of the process—the decisions of the Tribunal—is readily and quickly available, and accessible to those who are bound by the SADR/Code.

This last feature is particularly important. Perhaps the greatest challenge facing tribunals and CAS in rendering decisions under the Code is to produce decisions in good time which are truly accessible to those who are affected by the rules. In the anti-doping area this can be difficult to achieve. In one CAS recent award concerning the vexed question of the proper interpretation and application of Article 10.4 of the Code, the CAS Panel felt obliged to remark in relation to its analysis and application of the rule: 'The Panel will endeavour to do so in a straightforward fashion, avoiding elaborate distinctions or the gloss of abstractions which it does not believe are conducive to a useful understanding of the rules on the part of those it affects the most.'[85]

[85] CAS 2012/A/3029 *WADA v Anthony West*.

However, the hardest task for lawyers and others who have to communicate difficult ideas to a wider audience is to express the complex in simple terms. The challenge only seems likely to get harder in the current environment where the anti-doping regime has seen further significant change under the 2015 Code.

Challenges Ahead

The 2015 Code and the amended International Standards—in particular, the International Standard for Testing and Investigations—reflect a greater focus on investigating, prosecuting and imposing penalties on those who intentionally take prohibited substances in order to 'cheat' in sporting competition, and those who assist them to do this. Inevitably, as this system continues to develop, DFSNZ and other anti-doping organisations will become more involved in bringing anti-doping proceedings which involve the proof of anti-doping allegations by evidence obtained by investigation rather than by positive tests. Such cases tend to be more complex and involve more evidence and the forensic analysis of that evidence against the applicable standard of proof. In addition, in the 2015 Code itself, there are provisions which seem destined to produce the same kind of challenge as Article 10.4 under the 2009 Code.[86]

These features will present a challenge for DFSNZ, the Sports Tribunal and those representing athletes. The challenges will be the same for all anti-doping organisations which have to apply the Code and/or provide hearings under it. It will be more difficult to produce the required speedy reasoned decisions. However, given the needs of sporting competition, the aim in the anti-doping area will remain the same whether the allegations and evidence are straightforward or not. The New Zealand Sports Tribunal has to date established a sound foundation of procedural rules which provide appropriate flexibility and a body of available decisions applying the SADR. The Tribunal should with the assistance of DFSNZ be able to continue to build on this foundation and maintain its reputation for fair efficient process and rapidly available clear decisions in the changing and more complex anti-doping environment. The early establishment of the Tribunal with the identified features and clearly stated aims that reflect the obligations relating to hearings under the Code has put New Zealand in a good position to meet the challenges ahead. A system with the same general features seems likely to be successful in providing fair hearings for other anti-doping organisations given the aims shared by all organisations which have to implement and apply the Code.

[86] By way of example, the provisions relating to 'intentional' anti-doping rule violations justifying the imposition of a four-year period of ineligibility under Article 10.2 of the Code/SADR 10.2 seem likely to produce difficult cases.

8

Doping in Sport: What Role for Administrative Law?

NARELLE BEDFORD* AND GREG WEEKS **

Administrative law is the legal field which is concerned with challenges to both the merits and legality of decisions made by governments and other administrative decision-makers. It includes institutions such as courts and tribunals, which this chapter will discuss in detail. It also includes bodies and mechanisms such as ombudsmen, human rights commissions and the freedom of information regime,[1] which may have a peripheral impact in doping-related matters and decisions made by administrators. However, these will not be considered in this chapter. Administrative law is relevant to those accused of doping infringements. These people might seek to use general administrative law principles, such as the right to a fair hearing and an unbiased decision-maker, to challenge decisions by official bodies. This may be possible even where a person cannot obtain administrative law's remedies, available only where the decision-maker is a government entity, because the body at issue is a private association.

As a matter of domestic Australian law, it is possible to challenge certain doping-related determinations either through merits review in the Administrative Appeals Tribunal (AAT) or by way of an application for judicial review made to a court. Judicial review determines the highly technical point of whether a decision was made within jurisdiction, which is to say the limits of the decision-maker's lawful authority. By contrast, merits review is conducted by a tribunal and assesses the merits of the case afresh to determine whether a challenged decision is the 'correct or preferable' decision.[2] It is available only where provided for by statute because it authorises the tribunal to 'stand in the shoes' of the original decision-maker and perform his or her statutory task. The separation of judicial power doctrine prevents federal courts from reviewing decisions on this basis.

* Lecturer, Faculty of Law, Bond University.

** Senior Lecturer, UNSW Law.

1 See, eg, *Re Clews and Australian Sports Commission* [2006] AATA 373.

2 *Drake v Minister for Immigration and Ethnic Affairs* (1979) 2 ALD 60, 70 (Bowen CJ and Deane J).

At an international level, doping sanctions are generally challenged in the Court of Arbitration for Sport (CAS).[3] Consideration will be given to the nature of CAS, its governing rules and the possible development of a global principle concerning fair process.

Challenging Doping Decisions in Australia

In Australia, the body responsible for policing anti-doping violations and sanctions is the Australian Sports Anti-Doping Authority (ASADA). ASADA is governed under the ASADA Act and the Australian Sports Anti-Doping Authority Regulations 2006 (Cth) (hereinafter the ASADA Regulations). An athlete who wishes to challenge a decision of ASADA may apply to the AAT for review of the merits of the decision and, thereafter, to a court for judicial review.

First Option: Merits Review by a Tribunal

The benefits of merits review compared to review by a court are that it is designed to be 'accessible', 'fair, just, economical, informal and quick' and 'proportionate to the importance and complexity of the matter'.[4] It can be beneficial to have the facts of a case reconsidered in circumstances where the decision to impose sanctions is discretionary, as it can be possible to persuade the tribunal to adopt a different factual conclusion. Additionally, merits review tribunals are generally able to consider new evidence that was not available at the time of the original decision.[5] Thus, if an athlete is able to provide new evidence, either scientific or from witnesses, merits review can be an effective and fast mechanism to have this material taken into consideration. Finally, Australian tribunals offer a considerable advantage over courts in that they are able to substitute their decision for the original. This means that if the tribunal is persuaded to a different outcome, either by factual reconsideration or new evidence, the decision will be changed and the athlete will benefit from the new decision immediately. Such a result can be immensely important for an athlete prevented from competing or training for a period by a doping sanction. By contrast, courts can do no more than require that a decision be remade according to law. They have no constitutional power to do the job assigned by statute to the decision-maker.

Under the ASADA Regulations, the National Anti-Doping Scheme (hereinafter the NAD Scheme) implements Australia's obligations under the relevant

[3] This is despite s 8 of the Australian Sports Anti-Doping Authority Act 2006 (Cth) stating that the Act has extra-territorial application.

[4] Administrative Appeals Tribunal Act 1975 (Cth) s 2A.

[5] *Shi v Migration Agents' Registration Authority* (2008) 235 CLR 286, 299–300 [40]–[41] (Kirby J), 315 [99]–[100] (Hayne and Heydon JJ).

international conventions.[6] The NAD Scheme authorises the Chief Executive Officer (CEO) of ASADA 'to investigate possible violations of the anti-doping rules' and the Anti-Doping Rule Violation Panel (ADRVP) 'to make assertions relating to' such investigations.[7] ASADA must establish and maintain a register of the findings made in the course of such investigations,[8] which the CEO may then present 'at hearings of the Court of Arbitration for Sport and other sporting tribunals' and otherwise publish.[9] In the course of investigations and prior to hearings by the ADRVP, the CEO of ASADA has broad powers to gather information and compel disclosure.[10]

An athlete who is the subject of an investigation has limited rights under the ASADA Act. In accordance with the principles of natural justice, the athlete must be notified of the possible consequences of failing to cooperate with the investigation and is entitled, prior to the ADRVP entering the athlete's name on its register of findings, to:

— be notified of the ADRVP's proposed course of action;
— have his or her submissions on the matter heard; and
— be notified of the ADRVP's final decision.[11]

If the ADRVP decides to enter the athlete's name and particulars on the register, the athlete has a right to apply to the AAT for merits review of that decision.[12] This is a desirable course of action for athletes facing the possibility of sanctions in a private tribunal run by their sporting association. For example, Sandor Earl, a rugby league player, was alleged to have committed over 30 anti-doping violations between 2011 and 2013, including the use of peptide CJC-1295 while recovering from shoulder surgery. In June 2014, he obtained an interlocutory injunction to prevent his name being added to the ADRVP register unless and until his case was heard in full by the AAT. This had the effect of preventing the National Rugby League (NRL) Tribunal from hearing his case, based upon his alleged doping offences constituting a contractual breach of his player registration, until after the AAT had determined his case on the merits.[13] This was a significant outcome

[6] ASADA Regulations sch 1. Specifically, the Anti-Doping Convention 1994, opened for signature 16 November 1989, CETS No 135 (entered into force 1 March 1990); and the International Convention against Doping in Sport 2005, opened for signature 19 October 2015, 2419 UNTS 43649 (entered into force 1 February 2007): ASADA Act s 9. See *Anti-Doping Rule Violation Panel v XZTT* (2013) 214 FCR 40, 42 [2] (the Court).

[7] ASADA Act s 13(1)(f), (h).

[8] ASADA Act s 13(1)(i); ASADA Regulations cl 4.08.

[9] ASADA Act s 13(1)(k), (m).

[10] ASADA Act ss 13A, 13B, 13C, 13D.

[11] ASADA Act s 14(2)–(3); ASADA Regulations cl 4.09.

[12] ASADA Act s 14(4). Alone amongst the rights stipulated in s 14, the right to seek review in a tribunal or court cannot be waived: s 14(5).

[13] See Chris Barrett, 'Sandor Earl Wins Injunction against ASADA' *Sydney Morning Herald* (20 June 2014) www.smh.com.au/rugby-league/league-news/sandor-earl-wins-injunction-against-asada-20140620-zsg9g.html.

for Earl,[14] since some sporting bodies and particularly the NRL have for many years exercised 'police-style functions' over their registered athletes, notably with regard to the athletes' use of prohibited drugs.[15] Police-style functions include the power to require compulsory tests for prohibited drugs, and the ability to investigate possible infringements and to prosecute and/or sanction contraventions.

Merits review is exclusively a creature of statute: there is no general right to seek review of a decision on its merits unless such a right is provided by legislation.[16] Here, the right of an athlete to seek review in the AAT is provided only in respect of decisions made by the ADRVP to enter that athlete's details on the register and does not extend, for example, to challenges to the manner in which the CEO exercises the power to conduct investigations.

The Register of Findings and the AAT

The AAT has developed a small body of jurisprudence on the merits review of decisions related to the register of findings. Most recently, in 2012, the AAT affirmed the decision of the ADRVP to enter the name of an athlete on the Register in *Re Toskas and Anti-Doping Rule Violation Panel*.[17] Mr Toskas was registered with the Victorian Athletic League and was found by the ADRVP to have refused to comply with a valid request made by a person authorised by ASADA to submit a blood and urine sample, and to have evaded sample collection in breach of the ASADA Act. The Tribunal rejected submissions in which Mr Toskas denied he was present on the collection day and preferred the evidence of two ASADA officials, as well as a coach and another athlete who confirmed the applicant was present.

In 2011, *Re Peters and Anti-Doping Rule Violation Panel*[18] affirmed the decision of the ADRVP to make two entries relating to the applicant on the Register—the first that a banned substance had been detected and the second that the applicant had used the banned substance. The applicant was a player in the Queensland Rugby League (QRL) and tested positive to a banned substance, a stimulant called 1,3-dimethylpentylamine, which he consumed in a product known as 'Jack3d'. The banned substance was not included on Jack3d's ingredient list, but 'geranium root' was included. The banned substance is extracted from geranium root. The AAT held that 'if the applicant had made more searching inquiries, he would have realised that [the banned substance] is extracted from geranium plants. That

[14] Although he was ultimately banned in 2015 for four years by an Anti-Doping Tribunal chaired by former High Court judge Ian Callinan for using performance-enhancing drugs, including eight violations relating to the use of peptide CJC-1295; see Michael Carrayannis, 'Former NRL winger Sandor Earl given four-year ban for drug use' *Sydney Morning Herald* (15 October 2015) www.smh.com.au/rugby-league/league-news/former-nrl-winger-sandor-earl-given-four-year-ban-for-drug-use-20151014-gk8xdd.html.

[15] JRS Forbes, *Justice in Tribunals* 4th edn (Sydney, Federation Press, 2014) 48.

[16] Administrative Appeals Tribunal Act 1975 (Cth) s 25.

[17] *Re Toskas and Anti-Doping Rule Violation Panel* [2012] AATA 662.

[18] *Re Peters and Anti-Doping Rule Violation Panel* [2011] AATA 333.

substance is on the list of banned substances for the purpose of [the NAD Scheme] because it is a stimulant'.[19]

The AAT rejected the applicant's arguments that he was not subject to the drug testing rules. He had contended that his contractual arrangements with his club did not effectively incorporate the anti-doping rules to which the Australian Rugby League (ARL) and the NRL were parties.[20] The AAT held that the applicant's contract with his club expressly required him to observe the QRL's rules and the QRL rules expressly referred to and incorporated the ARL's anti-doping policy, and that policy in turn conformed to and incorporated the NAD Scheme arrangements.[21]

The AAT also noted the applicant's claim that he was denied procedural fairness, which was based on alleged process failures centred on the applicant's assertion that the testing process was required to comply strictly with the provisions regarding the presence of an independent witness. The independent witness was present for the opening of the B sample, but not for the entirety of the testing process. The AAT dealt with the substance of this claim without using the expression 'procedural fairness', which is a ground of judicial review and is therefore irrelevant to the merits of a case. It noted that the NAD Scheme in clause 3.24 contained the express words that the testing process 'comply or substantially comply'[22] with the World Anti-Doping Agency Code (hereinafter the Code) and the relevant international standards. The AAT was satisfied that there had been substantial compliance.

A distinction must be drawn between according procedural fairness by providing fairness to the accused and complying with procedures mandated by the Code. The athlete's characterisation of this issue as one of 'procedural fairness' was ill-founded, since a party owing procedural fairness is generally required to comply completely with the requirements of procedural fairness unless failure to do so would cause no 'practical injustice'.[23] The law on purely 'technical' or 'inconsequential' breaches of procedural fairness is heavily fact-based and revolves around the question of whether there is a reason why the court ought not to issue relief.[24]

There have been two examples where ASADA appealed to the Federal Court after an athlete was successful in having a decision overturned by the tribunal.[25] The potential for ASADA to exercise appeal rights should therefore always be

[19] ibid [7] (Deputy President Hack and Senior Member McCabe).

[20] ibid [29] (Deputy President Hack and Senior Member McCabe).

[21] ibid [30] (Deputy President Hack and Senior Member McCabe).

[22] ibid [25] (Deputy President Hack and Senior Member McCabe).

[23] *Re Minister for Immigration and Multicultural Affairs ex p Lam* (2003) 214 CLR 1, 14 [37] (Gleeson CJ).

[24] Mark Aronson and Matthew Groves, *Judicial Review of Administrative Action* 5th edn (Sydney, Thomson Reuters, 2013) 477–81.

[25] *Re MTYG and Australian Sports Anti-Doping Authority* [2008] AATA 448, subsequently appealed to the Federal Court of Australia as *Australian Sports Anti-Doping Authority v Muhlhan* (2009) 174 FCR 330; *Re XZTT and Australian Sports Anti-Doping Authority* [2012] AATA 728, subsequently appealed to the Federal Court as *Anti-Doping Rule Violation Panel v XZTT* (n 6). Appeals from decisions of the AAT lie on 'a question of law' to the Federal Court: Administrative Appeals Tribunal Act 1975 (Cth) s 44.

taken into account and athletes should be advised that success in the tribunal does not automatically mean the end of the matter. Athletes should also be aware that the AAT has powers to dismiss applications for review should any requirements not be complied with or deadlines not met.[26]

There are many sections of the ASADA Act that contain the possibility of decisions being made against athletes that may not be reviewed on the merits. An example is if a person is given a notice which requires him or her to attend an interview to answer questions and he or she fails to comply with the notice, he or she has contravened the Act and may be fined 30 penalty units.[27] No circumstances are provided for in which a failure to attend an interview might not require or deserve the penalty stipulated. The AAT has warned about the risk of injustice where decision-makers apply inflexible, blanket policies which fail to recognise, for example, that letters do 'go astray in the post'.[28] The principle is no different where legislation treats every failure to attend an interview as being qualitatively the same. There might be many reasons why a person does not attend an interview, which range from a simple refusal to having been involved in an accident en route to the interview. It is unlikely that the legislation's drafters intended to treat each circumstance in the same way, but the subsection leaves little scope for inquiry into *why* a person has failed to attend an interview. This is compounded by the fact that a person with a perfectly good reason for not attending is subject to a $5,400 fine and is not entitled to challenge the imposition of that fine before the AAT.[29]

Second Option: Judicial Review by a Court

In Australia, there are two mechanisms under which an athlete may make an application for judicial review. The first is under the Administrative Decisions (Judicial Review) Act 1977 (Cth) (hereinafter the ADJR Act) to the Federal Court of Australia,[30] while the second involves an application for judicial review made under section 75(v) of the Constitution to the High Court of Australia or, using the identical jurisdiction provided by section 39B of the Judiciary Act 1903 (Cth), to make an application to the Federal Court of Australia. The latter is often termed common law judicial review, as it has developed through cases.

[26] See Administrative Appeals Tribunal Act 1975 (Cth) s 42A(5)(b); *Re Al Shaick and ASADA* [2007] AATA 1076.

[27] ASADA Act s 13C(3). Thirty penalty units currently amounts to $5,400: Crimes Act 1914 (Cth) s 4AA(1).

[28] *Re Goodson and Secretary, Department of Employment, Education, Training and Youth Affairs* (1996) 42 ALD 651, 654–55 (Deputy President Barnett).

[29] A person in these circumstances could seek judicial review of the decision made under the ASADA Act, although where the statutory scheme is so clear, it can be difficult to find an appropriate ground of review to attack its application.

[30] ADJR Act s 8(1).

Judicial Review Using the ADJR Act

The ADJR Act was enacted to codify the state of common law judicial review,[31] but the course of time has left it significantly different from the common law, since the ADJR Act has rarely been amended, while the common law has done as its nature demands and has marched on. The ADJR Act has threshold requirements that: (1) there must be a decision, or conduct related to a decision,[32] (2) which is of administrative character,[33] (3) made under an enactment.[34] The third element, requiring the decision to have been made under an enactment, has in practice been the most restrictive aspect of the legislative threshold for jurisdiction under the ADJR Act and the one furthest removed from the common law, which allows judicial review of decisions that do not have a statutory basis.[35] Notably, ADJR Act jurisprudence has excluded judicial review of decisions made in consensual relationships,[36] which are reviewable using common law judicial review.[37]

In relation to the ASADA Act, an applicant for judicial review under the ADJR Act needs to demonstrate that the relevant decision was either required or authorised by the ASADA Act or the ASADA Regulations, and that the decision derives, either expressly or impliedly, from the ASADA Act on the basis that it conferred, altered or otherwise affected legal rights or obligations. In other words, the relevant legislation must be the driving force behind the decision, which is not the case where the decision is made under a contract or another mutual, voluntary agreement. It is doubtful whether an athlete would succeed in establishing that the Federal Court has jurisdiction under the ADJR Act where the dispute is essentially for breaching the terms of a contract that requires compliance with the ASADA Act and related instruments.

Judicial Review at Common Law

In order to apply for judicial review at common law in Commonwealth jurisdiction, it is necessary to establish that the decision to be reviewed has been made by

[31] Administrative Review Council, *Federal Judicial Review in Australia*, Report No 50 (2012) 57 [3.47].

[32] *Australian Broadcasting Tribunal v Bond* (1990) 170 CLR 321, 337 (Mason CJ).

[33] *cf* Legislative Instruments Act 2003 (Cth) s 5(2). See also *Federal Airports Corporation v Aerolineas Argentinas* (1997) 76 FCR 582.

[34] *Griffith University v Tang* (2005) 221 CLR 99, 130–31 (Gummow, Callinan and Heydon JJ).

[35] See, eg, in the UK: *Council of Civil Service Unions v Minister for the Civil Service* [1985] AC 374; and in Australia: *Minister for Arts, Heritage and Environment v Peko-Wallsend Ltd* (1987) 15 FCR 274.

[36] As distinct from contractual relationships, which neither the common law nor the ADJR Act will review: *R v Disciplinary Committee of the Jockey Club ex p Aga Khan* [1993] 1 WLR 909; *General Newspapers Pty Ltd v Telstra Corporation* (1993) 45 FCR 164.

[37] *Griffith University v Tang* (n 34) 128–29 [81]–[82] (Gummow, Callinan and Heydon JJ). *cf* Mark Aronson, 'Private Bodies, Public Power and Soft Law in the High Court' (2007) 35 *Federal Law Review* 1.

an 'officer of the Commonwealth'.[38] The High Court has been reluctant to explore the possible scope of that term,[39] and significant uncertainty remains about whether and when it might extend to people or bodies not in an employment relationship with the Commonwealth.[40] Both ASADA and the ADRVP are established under Commonwealth legislation, but there are many examples of institutions created under Commonwealth legislation which were nonetheless found not to be 'officers of the Commonwealth'.[41]

Regardless of whether ASADA or the ADRVP may be characterised as an officer of the Commonwealth, which remains unsettled, the CEO of ASADA, at least, is an officer of the Commonwealth. As a result, in *Essendon Football Club v Chief Executive Officer of the Australian Sports Anti-Doping Authority*,[42] Middleton J of the Federal Court was prepared to hear and decide judicial review proceedings brought against the CEO by the Essendon Football Club and James Hird under section 39B of the Judiciary Act 1903 (Cth). Essendon and its coach, Mr Hird, had come to the notice of ASADA as a result of its systematic injection of its players with supplements, a practice with a long history.[43] Both the club and Mr Hird sought judicial review of the joint investigation into possible anti-doping rule violations conducted by ASADA and the Australian Football League (AFL), arguing that such a joint investigation was beyond the scope of the investigatory powers under the ASADA Act, the ASADA Regulations and the NAD Scheme. Justice Middleton rejected this argument. Essendon and Mr Hird also argued that ASADA had breached the confidentiality obligations imposed on it under the ASADA Act and the NAD Scheme. Justice Middleton noted that:

> [W]hatever label is given to the investigation is of little relevance. The important enquiry is to consider the nature, purpose and conduct of the investigation itself. The investigation, from ASADA's point of view, was part of a wider investigation by ASADA under the [ASADA Act] and [the NAD Scheme] of the [ASADA Regulations].[44]

[38] With regard to seeking review in the original jurisdiction of the High Court of Australia, this phrase can be found in s 75(v) of the Constitution. The phrase also appears in the Judiciary Act 1903 (Cth) s 39B with reference to seeking review in the Federal Court of Australia.

[39] See *Plaintiff M61/2010E v Commonwealth of Australia* (2010) 243 CLR 319, 345 [51] (the Court).

[40] See *R v Murray and Cormie ex p the Commonwealth* (1916) 22 CLR 437, 452 (Isaacs J); Janina Boughey and Greg Weeks, '"Officers of the Commonwealth" in the Private Sector: Can the High Court Review Outsourced Exercises of Power?' (2013) 36 *University of New South Wales Law Journal* 316, 325–26.

[41] Aronson and Groves (n 24) [2.160].

[42] *Essendon Football Club v Chief Executive Officer of the Australian Sports Anti-Doping Authority* (2014) 227 FCR 1.

[43] In the 1930s, Wolverhampton Wanderers and other English football clubs injected their players with 'monkey glands', extracts from monkey testicles, to improve player performance. The practice had mixed results and, while decreed permissible by the FA, was also seen as 'immoral' by some players: see Neil Carter, 'Monkey Glands and the Major: Frank Buckley and Modern Football Management' in Dave Day (ed), *Sporting Lives* (Manchester, Manchester Metropolitan University Institute for Performance Research, 2011) 179.

[44] *Essendon* (n 42) 6.

Justice Middleton concluded that the investigation was in accord with the ASADA Act and dismissed the judicial review application. Following the conclusion of the matter, the World Anti-Doping Agency (WADA) issued a statement welcoming the decision of Middleton J and noting that 'Collaborations between different organizations are an important aspect of any anti-doping investigation, provided rules and laws permit such sharing', but declined to comment any further.[45]

It is significant that neither Essendon nor Mr Hird sought judicial review remedies against the AFL itself, although this is also unsurprising inasmuch as the AFL is a private body and is not an 'officer of the Commonwealth' under the existing case law.[46] While judicial review's *principles* have long been able to extend beyond strictly public bodies,[47] its *remedies* do not. The remedies available under section 75(v), in particular, were intended to have an accountability purpose that is properly directed to public bodies or, at the highest that one could argue the point, to bodies performing public functions.[48] Other countries have adopted a different approach on this complex modern issue of privatisation/contracting-out. In particular, in *R v Panel on Takeovers and Mergers ex p Datafin plc*, the UK focused on the nature of the power being exercised and not the identity or source of power of the decision-maker.[49] The Australian High Court has so far seemed unconvinced by this reasoning, although the issues considered in *Datafin* have never arisen squarely for argument before it.[50] Indeed, they have seldom arisen in the UK since *Datafin*.

Subsequently, Mr Hird, but not Essendon, appealed to the Full Court of the Federal Court.[51] A unanimous Full Court dismissed the appeal and agreed with the reasoning of Middleton J that the investigation was authorised by the ASADA Act; there was no improper purpose, no unlawful disclosure and no practical unfairness.

What Do You Need to Show a Court to Succeed in a Judicial Review Application?

Judicial review actions require the applicant to identify a 'ground' of review, which is an established basis on which an error might be identified in the original decision. This requirement applies regardless of whether the action is commenced in the Federal Court under the ADJR Act, in the Federal Court under section 39B

[45] WADA, 'WADA Statement on Joint ASADA/AFL Investigation' (19 September 2014) www.wada-ama.org/en/media/news/2014-09/wada-statement-on-joint-asadaafl-investigation.
[46] *R v Murray and Cormie ex p the Commonwealth* (n 40) 452 (Isaacs J).
[47] Aronson and Groves (n 24) [7.410].
[48] Boughey and Weeks (n 40) 320–23.
[49] *R v Panel on Takeovers and Mergers ex p Datafin plc* [1987] 1 QB 815, 847 (Lloyd LJ).
[50] *NEAT Domestic Trading Pty Ltd v AWB Ltd* (2003) 216 CLR 277.
[51] *Hird v Chief Executive Officer of the Australian Sports Anti-Doping Authority* (2015) 227 FCR 95.

of the Judiciary Act 1903 (Cth) or in the High Court under section 75(v) of the Constitution.[52]

Breach of procedural fairness is the ground of judicial review, which will be most commonly pleaded in doping-related challenges, either under legislation or at common law.

Procedural Fairness

Procedural fairness is a core concept of administrative law, which encapsulates the right to a fair hearing and the right to an unbiased decision.[53] The principles of procedural fairness, which have a long history,[54] are widely applied across all common law jurisdictions,[55] and continue to evolve and attract regular judicial consideration.

The threshold question which must be first asked in any case is whether the decision-making body owes a duty to accord procedural fairness to the applicant. In Australia, the rule that procedural fairness requires a fair hearing has, since *Kioa v West*,[56] been applied so broadly to decisions by public authorities that the true issue becomes not whether it applies, but what it requires in any given set of circumstances.[57] As explained above, the AAT has held that ASADA must 'substantially comply' with the statutory procedures in the ASADA Act, but this is not truly a procedural fairness obligation, nor is it the full extent of what is required of ASADA with regard to procedural fairness. There has been a sequence of cases at the state level which have confirmed that 'statutory tribunals, being creatures of parliament (and therefore not founded on private consensus or contract) are required as a matter of public law to apply the principles of natural justice to any disciplinary hearing'.[58]

ASADA owes a general duty to accord the *principles* of procedural fairness and, as a 'creature of Parliament', is also likely to be subject to judicial review's *remedies* for any failure to do so. By contrast, private disciplinary bodies which impose sanctions as a matter of contract, such as the NRL Judiciary and comparable bodies, owe a duty to accord procedural fairness largely as part of an obligation not to

[52] The ASADA Act additionally provides some avenues of review that go beyond common law judicial review principles, such as the capacity to challenge a civil penalty order on the basis of a mistaken but reasonable belief about certain facts: s 73Q. At common law, there is almost no scope for an error of fact to form the basis of a successful claim for judicial review.

[53] See Aronson and Groves (n 24) [7.20].

[54] See, eg, *Bonaker v Evans* (1850) 16 QB 162; *Cooper v Wandsworth Board of Works* (1863) 14 CB NS 180; *Ridge v Baldwin* [1964] AC 40.

[55] See, eg, *Baker v Canada (Minister of Citizenship & Immigration)* [1999] 2 SCR 817; *Khalon v Attorney General* [1996] 1 NZLR 458.

[56] *Kioa v West* (1985) 159 CLR 550.

[57] ibid 585 (Mason J); Aronson and Groves (n 24) [8.10].

[58] David Thorpe et al, *Sports Law* 2nd edn (Oxford, Oxford University Press, 2013) 49. See *Freedman v Petty and Greyhound Racing Authority* [1981] VR 1001; *Gleeson v New South Wales Harness Racing Authority* [1990] 21 ALD 515; *Carter v NSW Netball Association* [2004] NSWSC 737.

unduly harm livelihoods or reputations,[59] but are not subject to judicial review's remedies for breach of that duty. In these contexts, the application of the administrative law principle of procedural fairness is by analogy rather than as an application of administrative law per se, since any failure to apply procedural fairness is a breach of a private law obligation and is not remediable by administrative law.

Information Obtained by Informants

Doping sanctions may conceivably take into account circumstantial evidence, including information provided by persons other than those against whom the doping allegations have been made. It has become more common for sanctions to be based on non-analytical findings, which is to say other than by a positive drug test result.[60] It has been noted that 'while analytical evidence will usually be the most significant evidence in a sport drug test, testimonial evidence given either orally, by written statement, or by a phone link up, can also be highly significant in some cases'.[61]

For example, in three CAS cases from 2008,[62] testimonial evidence was relied on to determine whether or not a doping infringement had occurred in the circumstances. The importance of evidence from informants, and also non-analytical sources, was also central in the high-profile instances involving Lance Armstrong and Marion Jones.[63]

Information prejudicial to the accused may sometimes be provided on an anonymous basis. In Australia, the hearing rule of procedural fairness requires that a person be given the opportunity to know and respond to the case against him or her, and in particular to any material adverse to his or her interests.[64] The High Court of Australia considered the issue of sensitive, anonymous information in *Applicant VEAL of 2002 v Minister for Immigration and Multicultural and Indigenous Affairs*.[65] The context of *VEAL* was different: it concerned an applicant for a protection visa who was anonymously accused of assassinating a prominent

[59] See Aronson and Groves (n 24) [7.410].

[60] See, eg, *French v Australian Sports Commission and Cycling Australia* (Award, Court of Arbitration for Sport, Case No CAS 2004/A/651, 11 July 2005); *Marinov v Australian Sports Anti-Doping Authority* (Award, Court of Arbitration for Sport, Case No CAS 2007/A/1311, 9 June 2007).

[61] Chris Davies, 'The "Comfortable Satisfaction" Standard of Proof: Applied by the Court of Arbitration for Sport in Drug-Related Cases' (2012) 14 *University of Notre Dame Australia Law Review* 1, 21.

[62] *World Anti-Doping Agency v International Ice Hockey Federation* (Award, Court of Arbitration for Sport, Case No CAS 2008/A/1564, 23 June 2009); *Fedrazione Italiana Giuoco Calcio v World Anti-Doping Agency* (Award, Court of Arbitration for Sport, Case No CAS 2008/A/1557, 27 July 2009); *World Anti-Doping Agency v Comitato Olimpico Nazionale Italiano* (Award, Court of Arbitration for Sport, Case No CAS 2008/A/1551, 18 March 2009).

[63] See generally Richard H McLaren, 'Is Sport Losing its Integrity?' (2011) 21 *Marquette Sports Law Review* 551.

[64] *Kioa v West* (n 56) 582 (Mason J).

[65] *Applicant VEAL of 2002 v Minister for Immigration and Multicultural and Indigenous Affairs* (2005) 225 CLR 88.

political figure in his country of origin. Nonetheless, *VEAL*'s reasoning can be applied by analogy to the situation of adverse material provided by an anonymous informant in a doping matter. In a unanimous judgment, the High Court held that:

> [B]ecause principles of procedural fairness focus upon procedures rather than outcomes, it is evident that they are principles that govern what a decision-maker must do *in the course* of deciding how the particular power given to the decision-maker is to be exercised. They are applied to the process by which a decision will be reached.[66]

The test which governs when information must be disclosed is that the information must be 'credible, relevant and significant',[67] such that the decision-maker could not dismiss it from further consideration. The High Court said that whether the information is credible, relevant and significant 'must be determined by [the] decision-maker before the final decision is reached'.[68] In *VEAL*, procedural fairness required that the information be drawn to the attention of the party, but the High Court balanced this against public interest immunity considerations that required the identity of the informant not to be disclosed to the affected party in circumstances where the informant had asked for anonymity. The Court said:

> That public interest, and the need to accord procedural fairness to the appellant, could be accommodated. They were to be accommodated, in this case, by the Tribunal telling the appellant what was the substance of the allegations made … and asking him to respond to those allegations.[69]

Thus, were a doping sanction or related decision to be made on the basis of information or material provided by an informant, anonymous or otherwise, the affected party would need to be apprised of the substance of the allegations, without necessarily revealing the identity of the informant if he or she had requested anonymity, and be provided with an opportunity to comment in response, assuming that the information provided met the standard of being 'credible, relevant and significant'. Failure to do so could place the ultimate decision at risk of challenge by way of judicial review on the ground that the decision-maker had failed to provide a fair hearing.

Breach of Statutory Limits on Power

An exercise of a statutory power may be invalidated if the decision-maker acts in breach of the statute.[70] This is not automatic; ultimately it is a question of statutory interpretation which is determined by giving 'the words of a statutory

66 ibid 96 [16] (the Court) (emphasis in original).
67 *Kioa v West* (n 56) 629 (Brennan J).
68 *VEAL* (2005) 225 CLR 88, 96 [17] (the Court).
69 ibid [29] 100 (the Court).
70 See, eg, *Australian Broadcasting Corporation v Redmore Pty Ltd* (1989) 166 CLR 454.

provision the meaning that the legislature is taken to have intended them to have'.[71] Sometimes, it is irresistibly clear that the legislature intends a decision to be valid regardless of breach. For example, section 11 of the ASADA Act requires that:

> (1) Before making an instrument … amending the NAD scheme, the CEO must:
> (a) publish a draft of the instrument and invite people to make submissions to the ASADA on the draft; and
> (b) consider any submissions that are received within the time limit specified by the CEO when he or she published the draft.

However, section 11(3) then says expressly that a 'failure to comply with this section does not affect the validity of the instrument'.[72]

Other sections of the ASADA Act include requirements of which a breach is more likely to result in invalidity. The requirement in section 13A that 'the NAD scheme must authorise the CEO to give a person a written notice (a *disclosure notice*)' before that person can be required to attend an interview or produce documents is one example. Australian courts have shown a tendency to view such language as indicating a 'mandatory' requirement.[73] Statutory requirements to provide written notice have in particular been strictly construed by the High Court.[74]

Unreasonableness

The *Wednesbury* unreasonableness ground of review, where a decision is so unreasonable that no reasonable person could have made it, was for many years seen in Australia as the last refuge of desperate counsel when it appeared that other grounds for judicial review would not succeed.[75] Australian courts had not generally applied the *Wednesbury* ground with the abandon of the UK judiciary. Instead, they have stuck closer to the reasoning behind the now much-maligned speech of Lord Greene MR in *Wednesbury* that courts only have jurisdiction to interfere in the most extreme circumstances, which is widely held to amount to little short of lunacy. Brennan J was disquieted even by this modest scope for judicial intervention, reminding his judicial colleagues that courts have no power simply to cure administrative injustice.[76]

[71] *Project Blue Sky v Australian Broadcast Authority* (1998) 194 CLR 355, 384 [78] (McHugh, Gummow, Kirby and Hayne JJ).

[72] See the comparable provisions to the ASADA Act in the Legislative Instruments Act 2003 (Cth) ss 17, 19.

[73] DC Pearce and RS Geddes, *Statutory Interpretation in Australia* 8th edn (Sydney, LexisNexis, 2014) 451–52.

[74] *SAAP v Minister for Immigration and Multicultural and Indigenous Affairs* (2005) 228 CLR 294, 319–22 [72]–[77] (McHugh), 345–46 [173] (Kirby), 353–55 [204]–[208] (Hayne J). This is so even where the requirements of common law procedural fairness would not have been breached. See *SZBYR v Minister for Immigration & Citizenship* (2007) 81 ALJR 1190; Greg Weeks, 'The Expanding Role of Process in Judicial Review' (2008) 15 *Australian Journal of Administrative Law* 100, 104–05.

[75] See *Associated Provincial Picture Houses Ltd v Wednesbury Corporation* [1948] 1 KB 223, 228 (Lord Greene MR).

[76] *Attorney General (NSW) v Quin* (1990) 170 CLR 1, 36 (Brennan J).

This state of affairs had seemed utterly fixed in Australian law. It was therefore a surprise when the High Court handed down its decision in *Minister for Immigration and Citizenship v Li*,[77] the finer points of which are still a matter of debate.[78] What seems clear, however, is that in unanimously holding that the Migration Review Tribunal (MRT) acted unreasonably in refusing to grant Ms Li a further adjournment, the High Court primarily took issue with the manner of the MRT's refusal rather than the fact of it. The MRT's failure to articulate its reasons for refusing the requested adjournment was the basis on which the High Court held that it had made a jurisdictional error; nothing in the High Court's judgments indicates that the MRT might not validly have refused the adjournment had it given adequate reasons. However, the High Court relied on a series of authorities which hold, in essence, that if a decision-maker fails to provide reasons for a decision, and a good reason is not obvious to a reviewing court, then that court is entitled to conclude that no good reason exists and may therefore hold that the decision is invalid on the *Wednesbury* ground.[79] This reasoning makes it imperative that people making decisions under the ASADA Act and related legislation provide appropriate reasons. This is not generally a demanding standard, so it is critical that some effort is made to explain the reasoning behind any doping sanction.

Irrationality Grounds

A decision-maker may also commit jurisdictional error by failing to take into account considerations which he or she was bound by statute to consider, or conversely by taking into account matters which he or she was forbidden by statute to take into account. This can include matters that can be inferred from the legislation. Consequently, for example, a Minister who was under no obligation on the face of the statute to consider matters that arose after a formal inquiry, was nonetheless held to be obliged to consider new factual material, since it could be inferred from the statutory scheme that the Minister was required to make his determination based on the most current material.[80] If an athlete submits that the exercise of a statutory power will affect him or her adversely, such a submission will generally be a mandatory consideration.[81]

A related ground is acting for an improper purpose. It is difficult on an evidentiary level to prove that a decision-maker has acted for a purpose not authorised by the statute. An unauthorised purpose will generally not be inferred unless the evidence *cannot* be reconciled with the proper exercise of the power.[82] In practice,

[77] *Minister for Immigration and Citizenship v Li* (2013) 249 CLR 332.

[78] See the Hon John Basten, 'Judicial Review of Executive Action: Tiers of Scrutiny or Tears of Frustration?' in Neil Williams (ed), *Key Issues in Judicial Review* (Sydney, Federation Press, 2014) 35.

[79] *Minister for Immigration and Citizenship v Li* (n 77) 364 [68], 367 [76] (Hayne, Kiefel and Bell JJ).

[80] *Minister for Aboriginal Affairs v Peko-Wallsend Ltd* (1986) 162 CLR 24, 30 (Gibbs CJ). See Aronson and Groves (n 24) 274–75.

[81] Mark Robinson (ed), *Judicial Review: The Laws of Australia* (Sydney, Thomson Reuters, 2014) 155.

[82] *Industrial Equity Ltd v Deputy Commissioner of Taxation* (1990) 170 CLR 649, 672 (Gaudron J).

it is difficult for an applicant to find evidence to support such a claim. The CEO of ASADA may perform his or her functions only for the purposes set out in section 21(2) of the ASADA Act and is at risk of committing a jurisdictional error if he or she acts for any other purpose. However, the purposes for which the CEO may validly act are broadly drafted and it seems unlikely that an athlete could establish that the CEO had acted for another purpose, given the high evidentiary hurdle.

Third Option: Appeal from Tribunal to a Court

Rather than seeking judicial review, a person may choose to appeal to the Federal Court on the basis that the tribunal found incorrectly on a question of law.[83] In practice, there does not seem to be any distinction or advantage between an appeal from the AAT to the Federal Court compared to a judicial review application to the court. Both of the matters that have been litigated under the ASADA Act following an AAT hearing and determination, *Muhlhan*[84] and *Re XZTT and Anti-Doping Rule Violation Panel*,[85] were brought as appeals against decisions of the AAT, but might also have been run as judicial review matters challenging the decision of the AAT member as an officer of the Commonwealth. One noteworthy aspect of the appeals to the Federal Court in *Muhlhan* and *XZTT* is that ASADA and the ADRVP respectively were active participants in both the merits review and appellate processes.

In *Muhlhan*, Jessup J heard an appeal by ASADA against the decision of the AAT to set aside ASADA's decision to enter Mr Muhlhan's name on the Register of Findings on the ground that 'before requesting [Mr Muhlhan] to provide a [urine] sample, [ASADA] had not complied with clause 4.6.2 of the International Standard for Testing ("the Standard") made by the World Anti-Doping Agency under the World Anti-Doping Code'.[86]

The AAT had held that clause 4.6.2 set out a number of considerations which ASADA 'shall' take into account 'as a minimum' before selecting an athlete for target testing.[87] The AAT found as a fact that ASADA had not considered the items listed (a)–(j) in clause 4.6.2 and that the test was therefore invalid.

Justice Jessup took a different view of the meaning of clause 4.6.2 of the Standard. His Honour reasoned that the Standard noted in several places that certain minimum steps must be taken before ASADA could act in a nominated manner, but that: 'There is no suggestion that the precise format or content of the testing regimes established pursuant to the Standard will be identical

[83] Administrative Appeals Tribunal Act 1975 (Cth) s 44(1).
[84] *Australian Sports Anti-Doping Authority v Muhlhan* (2009) 174 FCR 330 (n 25).
[85] *Re XZTT and Anti-Doping Rule Violation Panel* (2012) 131 ALD 169.
[86] *Muhlhan* (n 25) 331 [4].
[87] *Re MTYG and Australian Sports Anti-Doping Authority* [2008] AATA 448 [48] (Deputy President Donald, Member Breen).

in all places.'[88] Justice Jessup did not read clause 4.6.2 restrictively, as permitting target testing only in the circumstances listed, but as setting out the *minimum* matters which should be 'included in a particular target testing regime as justifying tests'.[89] The regime specifies certain circumstances in which non-random testing *must* be considered, but does not prohibit non-random testing in other circumstances, as determined by ASADA in its discretion. His Honour held that the AAT had erred in law by finding otherwise and set aside its decision, effectively meaning that Mr Muhlhan's name remained on the Register.

The second matter litigated under the ASADA Act was *Anti-Doping Rule Violation Panel v XZTT*, which was heard on appeal by a Full Court of the Federal Court in 2013.[90] The matter concerned the ADRVP deciding to place the athlete in question on the Register for having tested positive to a small amount of the principal metabolite of cocaine after competing in an international competition in China. The AAT held that the ADRVP and ASADA had each misconceived their respective responsibilities under the ASADA Act, the ASADA Regulations and the NAD Scheme, and set aside the ADRVP's decisions.[91] In a unanimous judgment, the Full Court allowed the ADRVP's appeal against the AAT's findings.[92]

The meaning of the ADRVP's statutory role to 'establish and maintain a Register of Findings for the purpose of *recording findings*' of the ADRVP was an issue of fundamental dispute between the parties.[93] The AAT had held that 'a "possible" finding is not a finding for the purposes of the NAD Scheme', which required '*evidence* of a violation' in the form of the presence of a prohibited substance having been identified in the athlete's sample by an accredited laboratory.[94] Consequently, the AAT ordered that an entry be made in the Register recording a violation based upon the 'presence' of a prohibited substance in the athlete's system, but held that the entry in the Register recording the athlete's 'use' of that substance could not be supported and ordered that it be removed.

The Full Court came to a different conclusion, based heavily upon its view that references to 'findings' in the NAD Scheme were 'unfortunate',[95] inasmuch as they really recorded what were nothing more than 'assertions'.[96] It summarised the true operation of the statutory scheme in this way:

> The duty of the [ADRVP] is to consider any submissions made by an athlete and to decide whether or not an entry will be made on the Register … There is no question in this case that the Athlete received the requisite notifications, made submissions and

[88] *Muhlhan* (n 25) 335 [13].
[89] ibid 335 [14].
[90] *Anti-Doping Rule Violation Panel v XZTT* (n 6).
[91] *Re XZTT and Anti-Doping Rule Violation Panel* (n 85) 172 [3] (Kerr J, Member Nicoletti).
[92] It also dismissed the athlete's cross-appeal, which was based on 'egregious' delays in handling the matter which were the fault neither of the athlete nor of the ADRVP or ASADA: ibid 188 [123] (Kerr J, Member Nicoletti); *Anti-Doping Rule Violation Panel v XZTT* (n 6) 43 [9] (the Court).
[93] ASADA Regulations cl 4.08 (emphasis added); *Anti-Doping Rule Violation Panel v XZTT* (n 6) 42 [6] (the Court).
[94] *Re XZTT and Anti-Doping Rule Violation Panel* (n 85) [66] (emphasis added).
[95] *Anti-Doping Rule Violation Panel v XZTT* (n 6) 62 [88] (the Court).
[96] Ibid. See *NAD Scheme* cl 2.04(m).

> the response period had expired. As a consequence, the Panel was empowered to decide whether or not to make an entry.[97]

The AAT's error, therefore, was 'that it treated the [ADRVP] as if it was to make *actual* findings of violations and that it records such *actual* breaches on a Register'.[98] The ADRVP's processes are internal only and contain no provision for hearings.

Anti-Doping Rule Violation Panel v XZTT was decided essentially on the principle that the NAD Scheme contained sufficient 'contrary intention'[99] for the Court to conclude that a 'finding' should not be given its usual or literal meaning.[100] The statutory definition of 'finding' was later changed in the NAD Scheme to reflect the result in *Anti-Doping Rule Violation Panel v XZTT*, although the 'unfortunate' use of the defined term was retained. Whereas the term 'finding' had been defined as 'a finding by the Panel that an athlete or support person *has committed*'[101] an anti-doping rule violation, it has now been altered to:

> [A] finding by the ADRVP that:
>
> (a) there is an adverse analytical finding; or
> (b) it *is possible* that an athlete or support person has committed a non-presence anti-doping rule violation.[102]

This change is consistent with ASADA's contention in *XZTT* that, following analysis of the athlete's A and B samples, there was then enough evidence for the ADRVP to be '*prima facie satisfied* that [the Athlete] has *possibly* used cocaine in-competition'[103] and that this would suffice for the ADRVP to make a 'finding' under the terms of the NAD Scheme.

Challenging Doping Decisions at an International Level

As the international regulatory body responsible for doping, WADA is a unique body described as 'emblematic of the emergence of new forms of hybrid

[97] *Anti-Doping Rule Violation Panel v XZTT* (n 6) 65 [94]–[96] (the Court).

[98] ibid 65 [99] (the Court) (emphasis added). The AAT was held not to have understood, as it ought, that such an interpretation would invalidly bypass certain essential matters, such as the contractual operation of the Code, the procedural fairness rights of athletes in relation to possible sanctions, and the proper functions of CAS. Details as to hearings are contained in the Code, and the NAD Scheme ought not to be interpreted such that it would deny 'the athlete all the processes set out in the WADA Code for a hearing': at 66 [99] (the Court).

[99] ibid 66 [101]–[102] (the Court).

[100] Pearce and Geddes (n 73) 317–19.

[101] *Anti-Doping Rule Violation Panel v XZTT* (n 6) 43 [10] (the Court) (emphasis in original).

[102] *Australian Sports Anti-Doping Authority Amendment Regulation 2012 (No 1)* (Cth) sch 1 cl 6 (emphasis added).

[103] *Anti-Doping Rule Violation Panel v XZTT* (n 6) [26] (the Court) (emphasis in original).

public-private governance mechanisms in the global sphere'.[104] The power of WADA in respect of decisions and actions taken in individual sports remains strong. In fact, WADA takes an active role in overseeing individual domestic anti-doping authorities. This power was publicly demonstrated in September 2014, when WADA issued a statement on the sanction imposed by ASADA on 12 NRL players from the Cronulla Rugby League Club.[105] The statement is notable for the fact that it is critical of the delays it found to be directly the result of a 'lack of activity or decision by either ASADA or the Australian Government'.[106] It concluded by stating that 'WADA is not entirely satisfied with the outcome of this case and the practical period of the 12 month suspensions that will be actually served by the players', but decided against lodging an appeal as it 'would not advance the fight against doping in any meaningful way'.[107]

The Code is the core document that provides the framework for harmonised anti-doping policies, rules and regulations within sport organisations and among public authorities around the globe.[108] The new version of the Code commenced operation on 1 January 2015. Article 8.1 contains some general guidance on procedural fairness principles to be applied by doping decision-makers in the following terms:

> For any *Person* who is asserted to have committed an anti-doping rule violation, each *Anti-Doping Organization* with responsibility for results management shall provide, at a minimum, a fair hearing within a reasonable time by a fair and impartial hearing panel. A timely reasoned decision specifically including an explanation of the reason(s) for any period of *Ineligibility* shall be *Publicly Disclosed* as provided in Article 14.3.[109]

The commentary to Article 8.1 also explains that the principles of a fair hearing are 'also found in Article 6.1 of the Convention for the Protection of Human Rights and Fundamental Freedoms and are principles generally accepted in international law'.

This provision must, of course, be read and applied with regard to Australia's common law and statutory provisions regarding the application of the hearing rule of procedural fairness. To the extent that the Code and Australian domestic law differ in this regard, precedence must be given to Australian law, under which initial challenges to decisions by anti-doping bodies will be made. The comment to Article 8.1 in the 2015 Code state that the article is 'not intended to supplant each Anti-Doping Organization's own rules for hearings but rather to ensure that

[104] Lorenzo Casini, 'Global Hybrid Public-Private Bodies: The World Anti-Doping Agency (WADA)' (2009) 6 *International Organization Law Review* 421, 424.

[105] WADA, 'WADA Statement on NRL Sanctions' (29 September 2014) www.wada-ama.org/en/media/news/2014-09/wada-statement-on-nrl-sanctions.

[106] ibid.

[107] ibid.

[108] The first iteration of the Code was adopted on 1 January 2004.

[109] World-Anti-Doping Agency, World Anti-Doping Code (1 January 2015) art 8.1 (emphasis in original).

each Anti-Doping Organization at least provides a hearing process consistent with these [underlying] principles'.

Challenges to doping sanctions in the international context are made to CAS. CAS has been referred to as a 'kangaroo court' by Marion Jones and also by contrast as 'an innovative and efficient way to settle the sports world's disputes'.[110] It is governed by its Statutes and Rules, which together are informally referred to as the 'the CAS Code'.[111] The Statutes establish CAS and its governing body, the International Council of Arbitration for Sport (ICAS), whilst the Rules prescribe procedural matters. The CAS operates in a manner similar to the AAT, in that it conducts a de novo review and has 'full powers to review both the facts and law and to either issue a new decision or refer the case back to the original sports body for reconsideration'.[112]

Once an application to CAS has been lodged, the CAS Code directs that a panel be formed to hear and determine the matter. Under rule 40.1, the panel is composed of one or three arbitrators. Parallels exist between the common law procedural fairness rule against bias[113] and rule 33, which provides for the independence and qualifications of arbitrators as follows:

> Every arbitrator shall be and remain impartial and independent of the parties and shall immediately disclose any circumstances which may affect his independence with respect to any of the parties.
>
> Every arbitrator shall appear on the list drawn up by the ICAS in accordance with the Statutes which are part of this Code, shall have a good command of the language of arbitration and shall be available as required to the complete the arbitration expeditiously.

The CAS Code also contains a provision allowing a challenge to be made against the chosen arbitrator where 'the circumstances give rise to a legitimate doubt over his independence or over his impartiality'.[114] Two motives for the establishment of CAS have been expounded, the first being dissatisfaction with internal mechanisms, and the second being the avoidance of the courts. On this first motive, it has been explained that 'where the sports body itself convenes the tribunal and appoints its members, there is a potential for perceived, if not actual, lack of independence on the part of the tribunal'.[115]

In respect of the general right to a fair hearing, the CAS Code contains detailed provisions in rule 44 concerning the procedure to be adopted before the Panel. These procedures cover written submissions and hearings and specific provisions

[110] Michael Straubel, 'Enhancing the Performance of the Doping Court: How the Court of Arbitration for Sport Can Do its Job Better' (2005) 36 *Loyola University Chicago Law Journal* 1203, 1203.

[111] The Statutes and Rules are contained together in one document: CAS, Statutes of the Bodies Working for the Settlement of Sports-Related Disputes (1 March 2013).

[112] Straubel (n 110) 1217.

[113] Aronson and Groves (n 24) ch 9.

[114] CAS Code r 34.

[115] Andrew Vaitiekunas, *The Court of Arbitration for Sport: Law-Making and the Question of Independence* (Bern, Stämpfli Verlag, 2014).

relating to appeals, although it is possible for CAS to make a decision on the papers alone. Nonetheless, 'doping allegations, regardless of whether they are quasi-criminal in nature or breach of contract in nature, are accusatory and therefore require a heightened level of fairness, apparent to all parties'.[116]

Although CAS does not formally apply a doctrine of binding precedent in its own decisions, and the CAS Code is silent on the issue of precedent as it is understood in common law countries, CAS aims to be consistent in its decision-making, and matters previously decided by the CAS are persuasive.[117] It has been explained that: 'This sparse use of precedent could be due to the civil law traditions of the majority of the early and active CAS arbitrators. Nevertheless, panels over the past three to four years have demonstrated and created a willingness to cite and rely on CAS precedent.'[118]

Therefore, the decision by CAS in 2011 in a judgment between the Croatian Golf Federation and the European Golf Association (EGA) is significant, as it explained that:

> The right to be heard is a fundamental and general principle which derives from the elementary rules of natural justice and due process … CAS has always protected the principle *audiatue et altera pars* in connection with any proceedings, measures or disciplinary actions taken by an international federation *vis-à-vis* a national federation, a club or an athlete.[119]

In that case, the CAS ruled in favour of the applicant, the Croatian Golf Federation, and set aside the decision of the EGA to expel the Croatian Golf Federation from its organisation. Whilst not finally determining the issue of whether the EGA decision was set aside on the basis of non-current information being relied upon by the EGA or a breach of the fair hearing rule by the EGA, CAS did indicate that either would form a sufficient basis for the decision to be overturned.

More than 20 years ago, it was contended that it is in the area of procedural concerns that 'most of the recent challenges to drug testing have been made'.[120] We believe that this point remains accurate. Procedural concerns may relate to a failure to follow appropriate testing protocols, as well as a lack of procedural fairness or defects with evidence-handling. As a general rule, 'disciplinary tribunals are not generally required to apply the rules of evidence as strictly as trial courts'.[121]

[116] Straubel (n 110) 1223.
[117] ibid 1255.
[118] ibid 1256.
[119] *Croatian Golf Federation v European Golf Association* (Award, Court of Arbitration for Sport, Case No CAS 2010/A/2275, 20 June 2011) 11 [29].
[120] Tony Buti and Saul Fridman, 'Drug Testing in Sport: Legal Challenges and Issues' (1999) 20(2) *University of Queensland Law Journal* 153, 159.
[121] ibid 161.

Other commentators have posited a potential application of international law, such as the European Convention on Human Rights,[122] to international sports arbitration, particularly in respect of protections of a fair trial. However, at this time, these commentators have concluded that it appears questionable.[123] Given the points made in this chapter, we have reached the same conclusion. Similarly, a detailed analysis of the 2015 Code concluded that: 'The application of human rights principles is a debated topic in anti-doping.'[124] While welcoming the alignment to human rights, it was also noted that the references 'remain either purely aspirational or too vague to provide concrete guidance to [anti-doping organisations] to design their disciplinary process'.[125] We need do no more than note that Australia has no human rights protection of either a constitutional or a statutory nature at the Commonwealth level, or in most States,[126] and conclude that, as a result, the application of international human rights principles in Australian domestic proceedings is at present likely to be no more than nugatory.

In a similar vein, initial consideration has been devoted to the emergence of a global administrative law regime[127] and its application, particularly to global hybrid public-private bodies such as WADA.[128] Global administrative law gives recognition to the idea that there are basic requirements in the process of adjudication that exist regardless of the 'economic or social sector in which global administrative activity is being conducted'.[129] The elements of procedural fairness contained in both the Code and the CAS Rules could be considered as fulfilling this basic principle of global administrative law.

Conclusions

The role of administrative law in the context of doping is in its infancy, but this chapter has explored some areas on both the domestic and international stage

[122] Convention for the Protection of Human Rights and Fundamental Freedoms, opened for signature 4 November 1950, 213 UNTS 222 (entered into force 3 September 1953), as amended by Protocol No 14 to the Convention for the Protection of Human Rights and Fundamental Freedoms, opened for signature 13 May 2009, CETS No 194 (entered into force 1 June 2010).

[123] See Ulrich Haas, 'The European Convention on Human Rights (ECHR) in the Jurisprudence of the Court of Arbitration for Sport' (Speech delivered at the Staff Seminar Series, University of New South Wales, 27 May 2014).

[124] Antonio Rigozzi, Marjolaine Viret and Emily Wisnosky, 'Does the World Anti-Doping Code Revision Live up to its Promises?' (2013) 11 *Jusletter* 1, 37.

[125] ibid.

[126] Both the Victorian and the Australian Capital Territory Parliaments have passed legislation recognising and protecting human rights: Human Rights Act 2004 (ACT); Charter of Human Rights and Responsibilities Act 2006 (Vic).

[127] Sérvulo Correia, 'Administrative Due or Fair Process: Different Paths in the Evolutionary Formation of a Global Principle and of a Global Right' in Gordon Anthony et al (eds), *Values in Global Administrative Law* (Oxford, Hart Publishing, 2011) 313.

[128] Casini (n 104).

[129] Correia (n 127) 314–15.

where it may possibly assist in understanding the obligations that investigatory bodies have to athletes. This assistance has been framed negatively, ie, in terms of those seeking to challenge doping-related sanctions, but it is equally relevant when seen from the perspective of those exercising powers. Such decision-makers must be aware of the potential for administrative law to be used to challenge their decisions and take measures to ensure that procedural fairness is accorded to the athletes at each stage of the doping-related decision-making process. Given the serious nature of doping infringements and the monumental impact this can have on an athlete's career, it is essential for those against whom doping allegations are made to be accorded procedural fairness by those who investigate and determine infringements and the imposition of penalties. Furthermore, each decision must also be accompanied by a full statement of reasons. In Australia, ASADA is subject to administrative law review mechanisms as a government agency. To the extent that this is true of testing authorities in other countries, administrative law should be viewed as central to the legal accountability processes which apply to decision-making about doping allegations.

Part IV

The World Anti-Doping Code: Obligations and Liability

9

Modern-Day Gladiators: The Professional Athlete Employment Relationship Under the World Anti-Doping Code

JOELLEN RILEY* AND DAVID WEILER**

Sport as Employment

When Australian Sports Anti-Doping Agency (ASADA) was investigating Australian Football League (AFL) and National Rugby League (NRL) teams for breaches of the World Anti-Doping Code (hereinafter the Code), it appears that several individual players sought to bring their own private law suits against clubs. For example, according to news reports at the time, a former Cronulla Sharks player, Broderick Wright, joined two other former players in a lawsuit against the club, claiming negligence, breach of contract and intentional tort as a consequence of receiving prohibited supplements from a sports scientist engaged by the club.[1] On 26 November 2015, Hal Hunter (who played for Essendon in 2011–12) was granted an order for discovery of documents pertaining to the AFL, Essendon and Mr Stephen Dank, with a view to bringing proceedings against each of those parties for breaches of duty towards him in respect of supplements use during the 2011–12 AFL season.[2]

This chapter does not seek to investigate specific cases like this. Many of these matters are settled out of court and provide no public record for interrogation. Nevertheless, cases like this raise important general questions about the respective

* Dean and Professor of Labour Law, Sydney Law School.

** Legal Practitioner.

1 Michael Chammas, 'Broderick Right to Sue Cronulla over Supplements' *Sydney Morning Herald* (6 February 2014) www.smh.com.au/rugby-league/league-news/broderick-wright-to-sue-cronulla-over-supplements-20140205-321sp.html.

2 *Hunter v Australian Football League and another* [2015] VSC 666.

rights and responsibilities of sportspeople and sporting organisations under the general law regulating working relationships when doping scandals arise.[3]

Sportspeople are workers after all and, like regular employees, owe and are owed certain common law duties in respect of their work.[4] The employment status of sportspeople has been the subject of some debate, and some professional athletes will be properly characterised as 'independent contractors' whose contracts of engagement are governed by the general commercial law,[5] but it is generally accepted that professional football players engaged by clubs are appropriately characterised as employees. See *Buckley v Tutty*,[6] where the Court said:

> The fact that football is a sport does not mean that a man paid to play football is not engaged in employment. 'It may be sport to the amateur, but to a man who is paid for it and makes his living thereby it is his work': *Walker v Crystal Palace Football Club Ltd* [1910] 1 KB 87, at p 93. The position of a professional footballer vis-a-vis his club is that of employer and employee: *Commissioner of Taxation (Cth) v Maddalena* (1971) 45 ALJR 426, at p 427.[7]

The typical rugby league player contract explicitly describes the relationship between the player and the club as 'employment'.[8]

In the US as well, team sports players have been held to be employees for the purposes of accessing collective bargaining rights under national labour relations legislation. Even college players have won the right to collective bargaining as a consequence of a National Labor Relations Board ruling that football scholars at Northwestern University were in fact employees for the purposes of labour rights.[9] If sportspeople are employees, then the sporting organisations engaging

[3] This chapter will not consider any special regulatory scheme established and administered by the sporting bodies themselves, although clearly many of the legal actions arising, and likely to arise, as a consequence of the doping scandals will involve fines and penalties under sporting codes, and challenges to those sanctions.

[4] See Emma Bicknell Goodwin, 'Rules, Referees and Retribution: Disciplining Employee Athletes in Professional Team Sports' (2005) 18 *Australian Journal of Labour Law* 240, 248.

[5] In Australia, this includes the Competition and Consumer Act 2010 (Cth). See, eg, *Magro v Freemantle Football Club Ltd* (2005) 142 IR 445, which concerned a club breaching an obligation not to engage in 'misleading and deceptive conduct' in respect of its recruitment negotiations with a team coach.

[6] *Buckley v Tutty* (1971) 125 CLR 353. For a note on this case, see Braham Dabscheck, 'Righting a Wrong: Dennis Tutty and His Struggle against the New South Wales Rugby League' (2009) 4 *Australian and New Zealand Sports Law Journal* 145.

[7] *Buckley v Tutty* (n 6) 372.

[8] See, eg, Newcastle Rugby League, 'Senior Rugby League Players Contract for Season 20' (18 April 2012) www.newcastlerugbyleague.com.au/wp-content/uploads/2012/05/2012-PLAYERS-CONTRACT-18.04.12.doc.

[9] See *Northwestern University and College Athletes Players Association* (Decision, National Labor Relations Board, Case No 13-RC-121359, 26 March 2014). However, when the players petitioned to form a union following this decision, the National Labor Relations Board dismissed their application. The five-member panel did not base its decision on whether or not the players were employees. It refused to exert its jurisdiction altogether, stating: 'In such a situation, asserting jurisdiction in this case would not promote stability in labor relations.' (*Northwestern University and College Athletes Players Association (CAPA), Petitioner, p 5*). (www.nytimes.com/2015/08/18/sports/ncaafootball/nlrb-says-northwestern-football-players-cannot-unionize.html?_r=0).

their labour are employers and owe all the usual employment law obligations in respect of their players.

Doping scandals raise particularly difficult employment law problems. It is not always easy to identify who owes whom which duties when many parties to the work relationship have engaged in questionable behaviour. Does the worker who has taken a prohibited substance bear all blame for his or her conduct? Can the worker cast responsibility on managers or, in this kind of case, coaches and advisers? How far up the chain of command will responsibility rise when a pattern of misconduct is revealed? And what are the consequences of ascribing blame for misconduct? For example, if a player is given a lifelong ban from the sport as a consequence of breaching the drug code, can he or she claim damages from a club that encouraged the conduct? This chapter considers those questions, principally from the perspective of the common law governing employment relationships, but also includes some brief reflections on the applicability of statutory work health and safety laws.[10]

Focus on the Australian Experience

Doping in sport occurs throughout professional and amateur leagues around the world, and is a matter of international concern. Different countries and regions take different approaches to regulation.

This chapter focuses on Australia because Australian employment law principles are largely congruent with those in other common law jurisdictions, and so provide a useful study of the likely responsibilities of clubs as employers, and because in Australia the major sporting leagues are governed by the rules of the World Anti-Doping Authority (WADA).[11] Breaching the Code can have career-destroying consequences for players, so arguments about the relative

[10] Many jurisdictions impose special work safety obligations on employers, breach of which attracts regulatory penalties. As one example, this chapter briefly considers the statutory work health and safety obligations of all 'persons in control of a business undertaking' under the Work Health and Safety Act 2011 (NSW) ss 18–22.

[11] On 12 January 2016, WADA successfully appealed a decision by the AFL Anti-Doping Tribunal to clear 34 past and present Essendon Bombers charged with using a prohibited substance (Thymosin Beta 4 or TB-4). The AFL determined that based on the evidence presented it could not be 'comfortably satisfied' that the players had been administered the banned substances. The Court of Arbitration for Sport allowed WADA's appeal by applying a different standard required for the governing body to be comfortably satisfied when examining the same evidence that was before the AFL Anti-Doping Tribunal. This evidence included abnormally high amounts of TB-4 found in frozen urine samples of two players from 2012, along with "*text messages about sourcing Thymosin Beta 4, for the purpose of doping the Essendon team, testimonies from players and officials, and a scientific analysis of substances sourced for the team.*" The players received two-year bans which were then backdated taking into account provisional suspensions served in 2013 and delays to the proceedings outside their control. The majority of the bans are set to expire at the end of 2016. (https://www.asada.gov.au/news/court-arbitration-sport-decision-essendon-players).

responsibility of the players and the clubs for aberrant conduct are likely to raise employment law issues. This is not necessarily the case in North American organisations, because North American sports are not subject to compulsory control by the Code.

The rules concerning doping, or the use of performance-enhancing drugs, in North American sports are negotiated through collective bargaining between the players' unions and the leagues.[12] The substances that are banned and the methods for testing vary from sport to sport and, more importantly, the sanctions for any violations lie within the collective bargaining agreements. While all Australian clubs are required by the government to comply with the principles enshrined in the Code, North American professional athletes are able to negotiate through their unions the drug-testing regimes that govern their respective sport.

This does not mean that the leagues and the players' unions necessarily take a more lax stance against doping; it means only that they have more control of the processes around testing and the outcomes of violations. Players have limited grounds for an appeal against a positive test, so liability is 'strict' as under the Code, but there tend to be more safeguards and protections with regard to due process than under the Code.[13] The flexibility of the American labour relations approach to regulation can be seen in the penalties given for drug violations.

For example, an Australian AFL player testing positive for a prohibited substance is likely to be suspended from *all* WADA-governed competition for no less than two years.[14] There are exceptions for 'no-fault' or 'no significant-fault' findings and where the player has assisted in investigations. The exceptions are nearly impossible to establish for 'no-fault' findings, but more likely for 'no significant fault findings'.[15] Such a long suspension will generally be devastating for a player's career. The four major sports in North America are baseball, basketball, football and hockey, with the respective professional leagues: Major League Baseball (MLB), the National Basketball Association (NBA), the National Football League (NFL) and the National Hockey League (NHL). They have varying anti-doping policies, but the NFL is the most analogous to the AFL. The NFL player, for his first violation, receives a mandatory four-game suspension.[16] This equates to one-quarter of the regular season in the NFL. Therefore, a player in a league governed by WADA is liable to penalties that are eight times as harsh for the first offence of doping. This severity is multiplied for second-time offenders. In the NFL, if a player tests positive twice, he will receive a minimum eight-game suspension.

[12] Matthew J Mitten, 'Drug Testing of Athletes—An Internal, Not External, Matter' (2005) 40 *New England Law Review* 797, 803.

[13] Maureen A Weston, 'Doping Control, Mandatory Arbitration, and Process Dangers for Accused Athletes in International Sports' (2009) 10 *Pepperdine Dispute Resolution Law Journal* 5, 31–32.

[14] AFL, National Anti-Doping Code (June 2013) cl 14.1.

[15] ibid cl 14.4.

[16] National Football League, Policy on Performance-Enhancing Substances 2015 (2015) s 6, https://nflpaweb.blob.core.windows.net/media/Default/PDFs/Player%20Development/2015%20Policy%20on%20Performance-Enhancing%20Substances.pdf.

In the AFL, a second-time offender can receive anywhere from eight years to a life ban.[17] The NFL player can actually test positive three times and only receive a 12-month ban, but will only be allowed back to play at the Commissioner's discretion. Moreover, a player banned, either indefinitely or permanently, from the NFL could play another sport and not be restricted by the previous employer's sanctions.

The Australian Government's commitment to implementing the Code in its privately organised national leagues places a heavy onus on players and clubs to abide by the strict and arguably harsh governance of doping in sport. These terms cannot be altered through private contract or collective bargaining, so athletes are subject to the rules of an international, quasi-governmental body during their employment. This means that questions of ultimate responsibility for the consequences of breaches of the Code are particularly acute.

Team Sport as Special Employment

Although many of the cases discussed in this chapter do not involve sportspeople, the principles articulated in these cases apply equally to professional footballers engaged by clubs. If anything, sporting clubs seek to assert tighter controls over the lives of their players than any ordinary employer can claim over employees, especially when it comes to their freedom to change clubs[18] and controls over their private lives.[19] Indeed, the way in which players are commonly treated by their clubs, their fans and the broader community suggests they enjoy very little in the way of a completely private life.[20]

[17] AFL (n 15) cl 14.6.

[18] See Maeve McDonagh, 'Restrictive Provisions in Player Agreements' (1991) 4 *Australian Journal of Labour Law* 126; Braham Dabscheck and Hayden Opie, 'Legal Regulation of Sporting Labour Markets' (2003) 16 *Australian Journal of Labour Law* 259; James Johnson, 'Restraint of Trade Law in Sport' [2009] *Bond University Sports Law eJournal*, http://epublications.bond.edu.au/slej/10; David Thorpe, 'The Use of Multiple Restraints of Trade in Sport and the Question of Reasonableness' (2012) 7 *Australian and New Zealand Sports Law Journal* 63.

[19] See Casinova O Henderson, 'How Much Discretion is Too Much for the NFL Commission to Have over the Players' Off-the-Field Conduct?' (2010) 17 *Sports Lawyers Journal* 167; Annette Greenhow, 'Anti-doping Suspensions and Restraint of Trade in Sport' [2008] *Bond University Sports Law eJournal*, http://epublications.bond.edu.au/slej/7; James J Paterson, 'Disciplining Athletes for Off-Field Indiscretions: A Comparative Review of the Australian Football League and the National Football League's Personal Conduct Policies' (2009) 4 *Australian and New Zealand Sports Law Journal* 105; Glen Bartlett and Regan Sterry, 'Regulating the Private Conduct of Employees' (2012) 7 *Australian and New Zealand Sports Law Journal* 91; Saul Fridman, Chris Davies and Anne Amos, 'Should Athletes Be Tested for Recreational Drugs? Three Sporting Federations Kick around the Proverbial Football' (2007) 2 *Australian and New Zealand Sports Law Journal* 59.

[20] Players also face weak privacy protection under general law: see David Rolph, 'Playing away from Home: Sportspeople, Privacy and the Law' (2011) 6 *Australian and New Zealand Sports Law Journal* 35.

Today's football stars are like the gladiators of ancient Rome.[21] Matches between local teams, states and even countries occupy a great deal of contemporary society's time, effort and money. Lang Park in Brisbane, a host stadium for the annual State of Origin matches, holds approximately the same number of spectators as the Roman Colosseum did hundreds of years ago.[22] Like today's grand stadiums with their private corporate boxes, the Colosseum also fashioned artificial lighting and comfortable members' seating for society's elites.[23] Roman families kept terracotta lamps in the shape of a gladiator's helmet, like modern-day memorabilia. The popularity of contests created a major economic incentive to train and own gladiators.[24] The greater the potential profits, the greater the control exerted by the owners over the gladiators. The extent of this control was virtually limitless and amounted to supervision of *every aspect* of the gladiator's life: training, diet, accommodation and exclusive ownership of services. Although many gladiators were slaves or criminals, there were free men who took the gladiatorial oath, hence relinquishing nearly all of their legal rights as Roman citizens for the opportunity of fame, glory[25] and sometimes even fortune.[26]

The price modern-day gladiators pay for public acclaim is servitude not only to their club, but also to an insatiable public who claim an interest in their private lives. The special level of control asserted over sporting star employees was apparent when the Canterbury Bulldogs Club was successful in obtaining an injunction to prevent a famously talented footballer, Sonny Bill Williams, from breaking his contract to go and play another football code in the South of France.[27] A person less familiar with Australians' and perhaps the world's obsession with sport might have found it shocking that such a young person could have been so constrained in his life choices. An ordinary worker who wanted to change jobs and travel abroad would be unlikely to have been subjected to a five-year global restraint.[28] But Sonny Bill was important public property. The grounds given for the injunction included that his participation in the team contributed to 'the goodwill, patronage, membership subscriptions, pride, prestige and standing' of the Canterbury Bulldogs.[29]

[21] For a picture of the life of the gladiator, see Roland Auguet, *Cruelty and Civilization: The Roman Games* (London, Routledge, 1994); Alison Futrell, *Historical Sources in Translation: The Roman Games* (Oxford, Blackwell, 2006); Thomas Wiedemann, *Emperors and Gladiators* (London, Routledge, 1992).

[22] Wiedemann (n 22) 14, 21.

[23] Auguet (n 22) 35.

[24] Futrell (n 22) 141.

[25] ibid 135.

[26] Auguet (n 22) 164–65.

[27] *Bulldogs Rugby League Club Ltd v Williams* [2008] NSWSC 822. Sonny Bill played Rugby League in Australia, but Rugby Union in France.

[28] The doctrine making certain unreasonable restraints of trade illegal would normally limit the duration and scope of a contractual restraint. See generally JD Heydon, *The Restraint of Trade Doctrine* 3rd edn (London, LexisNexis Butterworths, 2008). For a general discussion of injunctions enforcing restrictive covenants in employment contracts, see Joellen Riley, 'Sterilising Talent: A Critical Assessment of Injunctions Enforcing Negative Covenants' (2012) 34 *Sydney Law Review* 617.

[29] *Bulldogs Rugby League Club Ltd v Williams* (n 28) [45] (Austin J). For a discussion of the particular pressures on the restraint doctrine in the context of the 'mythological importance attached to club loyalty' in team sports, see Neil Bieker and Paul von Nessen, 'Sports and Restraint of Trade: Playing the Game the Court's Way' [1985] 13 *Australian Business Law Review* 180.

According to the court in *Patrick Stevedores (No 1) Pty Ltd v Vaughan*,[30] the employer's duty to take reasonable care to avoid exposing employees to unnecessary risk of injury 'arises from the degree of control that the employer exercises over the lives of the employees'.[31] Clubs—purporting to protect the public interest in well-managed and competitive sporting contests—certainly exert a jealous control over the on- and off-field activities of their player employees, so they can expect to be held to a high standard of care in their dealings with players. Reputational harm potentially influences clubs' ability to attract sponsorship dollars, a fact that was recognised when another celebrity footballer, Andrew Ettingshausen, brought a defamation suit after he was photographed without his permission in the shower. He successfully sued for substantial damages to his reputation on the basis that publication of the photograph imputed that he was a person unfit to be a role model for young players.[32] The significant risk of reputational harm means that sporting clubs can arguably claim a legitimate prerogative to control illegal out-of-hours conduct in ways that other employers may not be able to do.

In considering the employment rights and responsibilities of sports players and organisations, this chapter is framed around two essential questions:

— To what extent do employment law principles require players to take responsibility for their own actions in using illicit substances?
— In what circumstances will clubs bear responsibility for the actions of their coaches and sports clinicians?

These questions will be applied to two hypothetical sets of facts, each assuming that the players are paid professional athletes of a major club within a league (such as the NRL or the AFL) which is governed by ASADA and would be deemed to be employees for the purposes of employment law.

Hypothetical 1—Arthur: Arthur is a player who knowingly ingests a banned substance and/or commissions a third party, without the consent or knowledge of the club, to administer and/or supply banned substances. Arthur tests positive for the banned substance, is issued a 'show-cause' notice by ASADA and is ultimately suspended by the league for two years.

Hypothetical 2—Barry: Barry participates in training programmes that have been either explicitly or implicitly mandated by the club and under the supervision

[30] *Patrick Stevedores (No 1) Pty Ltd v Vaughan* [2002] NSWCA 275. This case concerned a supervisor on the docks during the Waterfront dispute.

[31] ibid [16] (Davies AJA). See also *Crimmins v Stevedoring Industry Finance Committee* (1999) 200 CLR 1, 98 [276] (Hayne J): 'The common law imposes a duty on the employer because the employer is in a position to direct another to go in harm's way and to do so in circumstances over which that employer can exercise control. The duty is, of course, not absolute; it is the duty "of a reasonably prudent employer and it is a duty to take reasonable care to avoid exposing the employees to unnecessary risks of injury".' See also *Goldman Sachs JB Were Services Pty Ltd v Nikolich* [2007] FCAFC 120 [324] (Jessup J) for confirmation of the employer's common law duty of care.

[32] *Ettingshausen v Australian Consolidated Press* (1991) 23 NSWLR 443, 445 (Hunt J). For commentary on this case, see David Rolph, *Reputation, Celebrity and Defamation Law* (Aldershot, Ashgate, 2008) 148–53.

of experts employed by the club. These include conditioning specialists, coaches, who may themselves be former stars and therefore have valuable knowledge and advice for current athletes, and the increasingly popular 'sports scientists'. Barry tests positive for a banned substance, is given a 'show-cause' notice by ASADA and is suspended by the league for two years.

Arthur: Player Misconduct

Arthur is what judges sometimes describe as the 'author of his own misfortune' and is likely to bear the full burden of his misconduct alone. His conduct is very likely to be a breach of his employment contract as well as a breach of ASADA's anti-doping rules,[33] and leaves him vulnerable to the potential termination of his contract.

Players are invariably subject to detailed player contracts, which stipulate obligations to refrain from any form of misconduct, in both general and specific terms. Players generally agree to refrain from any activity that would bring the club or the sport into disrepute, and particularly agree not to commit any drug-related offences and to submit to drug tests at the request of the club.[34] Debates occasionally arise when a player is found to have taken an illicit recreational drug, which the player contends neither unfairly enhances nor is detrimental to his or her sporting performance, and so falls outside of the scope of his or her contractual obligations to the club. Both effects of a drug are problematic: the first may signal cheating and break the rules of the competition, while the second may signal disregard of his or her obligation to maintain peak physical fitness. Each of these would be a breach of the player's obligations under his or her contract.

A player's contention that he or she used drugs recreationally in his or her own private time appeals to the argument that employees do have a right to a private life and should be free from scrutiny when they are relaxing on their own time.[35] This assertion has been relied upon to limit the extent to which employers in other industries can insist on drug testing. In industries where drug testing is tolerated

[33] Australian Sports Anti-Doping Authority Regulations 2006 (Cth) sch 1, cl 2.01A–B. For a discussion of issues arising from the application of the Code to team sports, see Victoria Wark, 'All for One and One for All … For How Much Longer? How WADA Could Tackle Doping in Professional Team Sport' (2014) 9(1) *Australian and New Zealand Sports Law Journal* 1.

[34] See, eg, the standard form Rugby League Player Contract posted by Fox Sports for recommended use by clubs: Rugby League Playing Contract cl 8.2, www.sportingpulse.com/get_file.cgi?id=99639.

[35] See generally Ronald McCallum, *Employer Controls over Private Life* (Sydney, UNSW Press, 2000). For sports writers' views on this debate, see Fridman, Davies and Amos (n 20); James Halt, 'Where is the Privacy in WADA's "Whereabouts" Rule?' (2009) 20 *Marquette Sports Law Review* 267; Paul Horvath, 'Anti-doping and Human Rights in Sport: The Case of the AFL and the WADA Code' (2006) 32 *Monash University Law Review* 357.

because drug use would raise serious safety concerns, employee representatives have often succeeded in arguing for some constraints. For example, urine testing has been successfully resisted by some unions in the mining sector on the basis that it is an unnecessarily invasive form of testing and will pick up earlier, pre-shift drug use. Oral swabs, which test for more immediate use, are permitted.[36]

Footballers, however, are likely to find that recreational drug use is a breach of contract whenever it occurs and is discovered because it brings into question the player's broad obligation not to bring the sport into disrepute.[37] Finding that a player's illicit drug use is a breach of his contract is not the end of the matter—the question of what sanctions will be applied arises. Not every breach of contract will justify termination of an employment contract and not every breach that justifies termination will result in termination, because these gladiators are often extraordinarily valuable talent. So long as they remain capable of winning competitions, clubs will want to keep them on teams. Even sponsors may be forgiving in time.[38]

Some contracts do not prohibit doping absolutely, but provide for sanctions if the athlete is convicted of doping or returns a positive sample.[39] Others by their terms prohibit doping absolutely. Typically, the fines for misconduct stipulated in player contracts operate as liquidated damages clauses, by which the players agree to be subject to a financial penalty for a breach of contract, even if they will keep their places on the team after their infringement of the rules. Of course, keeping a place on the team will be impossible where the illicit drug use also breaches the Code and attracts a compulsory ban, or if it attracts a custodial sentence under criminal laws.

Barry: Victim of Experimentation by Coaches and Medical Advisers

Barry's scenario is considerably more complex. One of the aspects of recent doping scandals is the allegation that players have been encouraged to take illicit substances by sports medicine professionals engaged by clubs. If the coaches and medical advisers concerned are also employees of the club, the club is likely to be vicariously, or possibly directly, responsible for their actions. Although one would

[36] See, eg, *Endeavour Energy* [2014] FWC 198; *Maritime Union of Australia v DP World Brisbane Pty Ltd* [2014] FWC 1523.

[37] Likewise, drug testing of police officers is defensible because they bear the burden of public trust that law enforcement officers are law-abiding themselves: see *Anderson v Sullivan* (1997) 78 FCR 380, 398 (Finn J).

[38] Note the observations by Fridman, Davies and Amos (n 20) 72 on the differential treatment of 'fringe' and 'star' players.

[39] One might infer from such clauses that the employer is happy with doping as long as the athlete is not caught, because the activity of taking a prohibited substance as such is not prohibited.

hope that club officials would never authorise medical advisers to prescribe illicit substances, the fact that such conduct occurred in the course of the adviser performing his or her duties would be sufficient to raise the risk of the club's vicarious liability for that conduct. An employer will still be liable for the misdeeds of employees who use unauthorised methods to perform their designated duties, so long as those unauthorised methods can still be seen to be modes, albeit improper modes, of performing authorised duties.[40] Harm inflicted by one employee on another will become the responsibility of the employer if the harm was caused by the employee in the course of employment.[41]

However, what if Barry's medical advisers are not employees of the club, but are independent professionals who provide services to the club? This raises more complex questions about the potential vicarious liability of a club for the tortious actions of third parties. If the club expressly authorised sports medical professionals to administer performance-enhancing drugs, then it would be responsible as the principal for the acts of authorised agents, but that is an unlikely scenario. More difficult questions arise if the coaches and sports scientists acted on their own initiative, but under pressure from the club to push the boundaries of permissible supplement use. Additionally, there is also a question about whether the club, as the employer of the players, will be responsible for harm suffered by players who have been subjected, even unknowingly, to harm at the hands of people engaged by the club to provide these services.

In *New South Wales v Napier*,[42] an employee working as a supervisor in a prison factory suffered extreme mental distress from being attacked by prisoners assigned to work in the factory. The employee worked for a contractor of the prison, so was not a direct employee of the Department of Corrective Services and could not claim on the basis of any contractual duty owed to him by the Department. Nevertheless, he was able to establish that the Department owed him a duty of care in tort on the basis that the plaintiff worker could establish three necessary and interrelated elements:

— the tort victim's vulnerability;
— the alleged tortfeasor's right and capacity to exert control over the situation; and
— the tortfeasor's assumption of responsibility, in this case, for security in the prison.[43]

If we consider these elements in relation to the hypothetical situation of a young football player who submits to dangerous, or at least foolhardy, experimentation with performance-enhancing drugs at the hands of a person paid by his club to

[40] See *New South Wales v Lepore* (2003) 212 CLR 511, 536 [42] (Gleeson CJ). See also *Starks v RSM Security Pty Ltd* (2004) Aust Torts Reports 81-763, 65,991–93 [12]–[24] (Beazley JA).

[41] See *Klesteel Pty Ltd v Mantzouranis* (2008) 49 MVR 460.

[42] *New South Wales v Napier* [2002] NSWCA 402.

[43] See ibid [13]–[21] (Spigelman CJ).

assist him, it is certainly arguable that the player is vulnerable to harm, that the club has a right and capacity to direct those whom it engages to provide services to its players, and that the club—through its extensive and detailed contracts with players—has assumed responsibility for controlling this aspect of the players' lives.

These principles continue to apply even where medical advisers have obtained consent from players who were prescribed experimental supplements. Consent needs to be fully informed if it is to sterilise the responsibility of a medical adviser. Arguably, unless players were clearly warned of the potential illegality and potential harmfulness of supplements—even of uncertain possibilities of harm—those prescribing the substances could be responsible in tort.[44]

Given the high level of control over players' lives asserted by clubs through their contracts, it seems unreasonable to assume that a signature on a consent form would be sufficient to dispense with the medical advisers' and the club's responsibility. An anecdote reported in the newspapers at the time when Sonny Bill Williams was experiencing difficulties with his contract with the Bulldogs provides an illustration of how questionable players' consent may be when they are acting under guidance from their coaches and managers. In *Bulldogs Rugby League Club Ltd v Williams*,[45] it was argued that Sonny Bill had signed a contract asserting, in one clause, that he had taken independent legal advice on its terms. If we can believe a newspaper report,[46] Sonny Bill's approach to seeking advice was somewhat less thorough than his contract asserted. The following exchange of 'advice' was taken on his French contract:

> Sonny Bill: 'Bro, are you sure this is legit?'
>
> Coach Tana Umaga: 'Yeah.'[47]

After that comprehensive legal briefing, Sonny Bill said it only took 'about five or ten minutes' to complete the documentation for his new contract, and 'straight away I knew I had made the right decision'.[48] This is a picture of a person who is particularly susceptible to taking advice from others and is consequently vulnerable to any harm flowing from taking their advice.

Remedies?

In Barry's scenario, the player has suffered potentially compensable physical harm, but also a substantial economic loss because of the ban imposed on him. If Barry

[44] See *Rogers v Whitaker* (1992) 175 CLR 479, 490 (Mason CJ, Brennan, Dawson, Toohey and McHugh JJ).

[45] *Bulldogs Rugby League Club Ltd v Williams* (n 28).

[46] See Brad Walter, 'French Leave: How Sonny Bill Found Freedom in Toulon' *Sydney Morning Herald* (6–7 June 2009) 3.

[47] ibid.

[48] ibid.

can establish that the club's conduct constitutes a breach of its duty of care to him under the player contract, he may also claim damages calculated on the basis of his loss of an opportunity to earn during his period of suspension.[49] If he was entitled to bring a claim under English employment law principles, he may also be able to argue that the club had acted in a manner calculated or likely to destroy trust and confidence in the employment relationship by running a non-ASADA-compliant training programme. This is much in the same way as the plaintiffs in *Malik v Bank of Credit and Commerce International SA (in Liquidation)*[50] argued that they had suffered loss as a consequence of the employer bank running a corrupt business. This kind of argument has more uncertain prospects in Australian law, where an employee's right to sue for damages for breach of the employer's duty of mutual trust and confidence cannot be implied by law into the employment contract.[51]

What Should Clubs Have Done?

In cases like Barry's, clubs are vulnerable to carrying the blame for the conduct of coaches and medical advisors. If an employer club does put its player employees into the hands of others for medical supervision, what steps should clubs take to satisfy their responsibilities under general employment law for the health and safety of those employees? In *Naidu v Group 4 Securitas Pty Ltd*,[52] Adams J was faced with a complaint of extreme bullying from the employee of a labour hire security firm who had been placed with a host employer, News Ltd. The bullying took place at the hands of an employee of News Ltd in News Ltd's premises, so the labour hire employer sought to avoid any responsibility to the employee. In finding the employer liable for a proportion of the damages awarded to the employee, Adams J identified a number of actions that the employer ought to have taken to fulfil its non-delegable contractual obligation[53] to provide a safe system of work to its staff, notwithstanding that they were employed to work at other premises and under the control of a host employer's supervisors.

These actions include:

— establishing clear policies prohibiting harmful conduct—in *Naidu v Group 4 Securitas Pty Ltd*, this was harassment and racial vilification;

[49] For the acceptance of 'loss of chance' damages in Australian contract law in the employment context, see *Guthrie v News Ltd* (2010) 27 VR 196; *Silverbrook Research Pty Ltd v Lindley* [2010] NSWCA 357.

[50] *Malik v Bank of Credit and Commerce International SA (in Liquidation)* [1998] AC 20, 34 (Lord Nicholls of Birkenhead).

[51] *Commonwealth Bank of Australia v Barker* (2014) 253 CLR 169, 195 [40]–[41] (French CJ, Bell and Keane JJ), 214 [109]–[110] (Kiefel J), 216 [115] (Gageler J).

[52] *Naidu v Group 4 Securitas Pty Ltd* [2005] NSWSC 618.

[53] ibid [188], citing *TNT Australia Pty Ltd v Christie* (2003) 65 NSWLR 1.

— educating staff about policies;
— establishing clear channels for staff to make complaints and providing training in how to manage complaints; and
— taking complaints seriously and investigating them properly.[54]

At first instance, the labour hire employer, Group 4, was held liable for not enforcing its own policies effectively.[55] Most interesting was the fact that the employer was taken to have the knowledge of its own employees who were aware of the misconduct at the News Ltd site. Their failure to report was attributed to the company.

On appeal, the New South Wales Court of Appeal overturned this aspect of the decision[56] and by majority also overturned the award of damages against the labour hire employer. Chief Justice Spigelman and Basten JA determined that sufficiently senior management at Group 4 did not know of the bullying, and so Group 4 was in no position to foresee the harm caused to the employee. All members of the court decided that liability in this case should not be decided on the basis of 'systems failure'.[57] This was too artificial an analysis of a fact situation that was really a case of intentional and not merely negligent harm inflicted deliberately by an employee of the host employer, News Ltd. Nevertheless, the Court of Appeal did pass harsh judgment on News Ltd, and some of the aspects of the appeal decision are also of interest for the hypothetical we are considering here. It was held that News Ltd was directly, and not merely vicariously, responsible for the conduct of the perpetrator of the bullying because he was a senior supervisor. His deliberately tortious conduct was held to be the conduct of News Ltd.[58] This is a sobering finding for any large organisation. On this reasoning, clubs would be directly responsible for the torts of their senior staff, including coaches and managers, even if club directors were not themselves actually aware of what was going on in the locker rooms.

'Systems Failure'

Although Adams J's first instance decision was overturned on the facts, employers do need to be mindful of their obligations to put in place appropriate systems for supporting the health and safety of their employees at work. The risks created by doping are arguably very different kinds of risks from the ordinary risks inherent in playing physically strenuous sports. The principle established in *Agar v Hyde*[59]

[54] *Naidu v Group 4 Securitas Pty Ltd* (n 53) [193].
[55] ibid [195].
[56] See *Nationwide News Pty Ltd v Naidu* (2007) 71 NSWLR 471, 480 [39] (Spigelman CJ).
[57] ibid 483 [48] (Spigelman CJ), 516–17 [324] (Beazley JA).
[58] ibid 488 [84] (Spigelman CJ). For Justice Beazley's reasoning on this point, see *Nationwide News Pty Ltd v Naidu* [2007] NSWCA 377 [276].
[59] *Agar v Hyde* (2000) 201 CLR 552.

that an international rule-making body did not owe a duty to amend the rules of the game to reduce the risk of physical injury to players would not, we argue, limit the responsibility of clubs to manage their own practices in compliance with the Code dealing with the abuse of drugs.

The Code defines 'athlete support personnel' as 'any coach, trainer, manager, agent, team staff, official, medical, paramedical personnel, parent or any other *Person* working with, treating or assisting an *Athlete* participating in or preparing for sports *Competition*',[60] and section 21.2.1 requires athlete support personnel to be knowledgeable of and comply with all anti-doping policies and rules adopted pursuant to the Code and which are applicable to them or the athletes whom they support. So the rules of the game already impose obligations on clubs, and indeed on all participants, to be vigilant to manage the risk of drug abuse in the sport.

An interesting section of the AFL Anti-Doping Code states that:

> Each Club must … educate its Players, Officers and Officials in respect of: the *dangers and consequences* of the use of performance enhancing substances and to this end will ensure that all such persons attend all drug awareness or education lectures given by the AFL in conjunction with ASADA.[61]

This section, beyond any common law duties of employers, arguably places a specific duty on club officers to arrange appropriate drug awareness education programmes for players and coaches, and to ensure that they attend and absorb the message. They should also establish and clearly disseminate policies and procedures for making enquiries and complaints, and reporting breaches. They should ensure that they take any complaints seriously, investigate them thoroughly and sanction breaches consistently.

Workplace Health and Safety Legislation

In addition to common law duties of care, employers in most jurisdictions owe statutory duties to regard the health and safety of their employees, and indeed of any other worker who comes within their control in the course of conducting their business undertaking. The dangers associated with experimental or 'cutting-edge' sport science programmes may not necessarily cause grievous bodily harm or death, but it is not inconceivable that serious health implications could arise from such practices.

The Work Health and Safety Act 2011 (NSW) is based on the national model legislative framework recently rolled out across the states of Australia. The

[60] WADA, World Anti-Doping Code (1 January 2015) app 1 (definition of 'athlete support personnel') (emphasis in original).

[61] AFL (n 15) cl 7.7 (emphasis added).

introduction of this legislation has wide-reaching implications and there is no reason to believe it would not apply to sporting clubs.[62]

The Act requires any person conducting a business or undertaking (PCBU) to ensure, so far as reasonably practicable, the health and safety of workers engaged, or caused to be engaged by that person and workers whose activities in carrying out work are influenced or directed by that person.[63]

The relevant matters for determining whether something was reasonably practicable are found in section 18 of the Act and include:

(a) the likelihood of the hazard or the risk concerned occurring, and
(b) the degree of harm that might result from the hazard or the risk, and
(c) what the person concerned knows, or ought reasonably to know, about:
  (i) the hazard or the risk, and
  (ii) ways of eliminating or minimising the risk, and
(d) the availability and suitability of ways to eliminate or minimise the risk, and
(e) … whether the cost is grossly disproportionate to the risk.

It would be very difficult to argue that exposing players to either explicitly prohibited substances or substances not approved for human use was not a breach of the obligation to take all practicable steps to guard against health risks.

These obligations fall not only on the PCBU, but also on all workers within the organisation. The meaning of 'worker' is found in section 7 of the Act, and section 28 demands that a worker, while at work, takes reasonable care for his or her own health and safety,[64] that he or she complies with any reasonable instruction given by the PCBU to allow the person to comply with the Act,[65] and finally the duty to cooperate with any reasonable *policy or procedure* of the PCBU relating to health or safety at the workplace that has been notified to workers.[66] Therefore all players, coaches and others involved in managing the sport share this responsibility.

Part 6 of the Act explicitly prohibits discrimination against workers who raise safety concerns. A list of protected conduct is found in section 106 of the Act.

The Act also places a duty on officers of the PCBU to exercise due diligence to ensure that the PCBU complies with that duty or obligation.[67] The Act defines

[62] On 9 November 2015, this was confirmed when the state regulator, WorkSafe Victoria, announced that it had charged the Essendon Bombers with breaches of the Occupational Health and Safety Act 2004 (Vic) in respect of the club's 2012 supplement programme. The organisation plead guilty to the charges that it had breached s 21(1) and 21(2)(a) of the Occupational Health and Safety Act 2004 by 'failing to provide and maintain for employees' a working environment and a system of work 'that is, so far as reasonably practicable, safe and without risks to health'. On 28 January 2016 the Bombers were fined $200,000 for the breaches. (www.abc.net.au/news/2016-01-28/essendon-fined-for-failing-to-provide-players-safe-workplace/7120044).

[63] Work Health and Safety Act 2011 (NSW) s 19.

[64] ibid s 28(a).

[65] ibid s 28(c).

[66] ibid s 28(d).

[67] ibid s 27(1).

due diligence to include taking reasonable steps: 'to acquire and keep up-to-date knowledge of work health and safety matters'; 'to gain an understanding of the nature of the operations of the business or undertaking of the' PCBU 'and generally of the hazards and risks associated with those operations'; to ensure the PCBU has 'appropriate resources and processes to eliminate or minimise risks to health and safety from work carried out as part of the conduct of the business or undertaking'; to ensure that the PCBU 'has appropriate processes for receiving and considering information regarding incidents, hazards and risks and responding in a timely way to that information'; and finally to ensure that the PCBU 'has, and implements processes for complying with any duty or obligation of the person conducting the business or undertaking'.[68]

The penalties for contravention of the Act are wide-ranging and can include an order to pay a monetary penalty deemed appropriate and to 'make any other order the court considers appropriate, including an injunction'.[69]

What Should Clubs Do to Meet their Employment Law Obligations?

Clearly, clubs bear a significant burden—as a consequence of their potential direct and vicarious liability under their common law duty of care, and of their onerous work health and safety obligations—to take all practicable steps to prevent harm to players from performance-enhancing drug experimentation.

According to the Australian Crime Commission Report on Organised Crime and Drugs in Sport[70] and the Switkowski Report, an internal report commissioned by the Essendon Football Club in the AFL,[71] sports scientists are believed to be the main drivers of supplement programmes. Their increasing influence over training regimes was evident in both of these investigations into doping scandals. So clubs are on notice that there needs to be oversight of sports scientists and their consultations with players.

What should that oversight look like if clubs are to protect themselves from allegations that they have failed in a duty to provide a 'safe system' for players' work? The Switkowski Report made a number of recommendations for the Essendon

[68] ibid s 27(5). The case of *Kumar v Ritchie* [2006] NSWIR Comm 323 is the high-water mark of the personal liability provisions, but was decided during the old occupational health and safety legislative regime. Arguably the new regime is more stringent in its imposition of obligations on officers.

[69] Work Health and Safety Act 2011 (NSW) s 259.

[70] Australian Crime Commission, *Organised Crime and Drugs in Sport: New Generation Performance and Image Enhancing Drugs and Organised Criminal Involvement in Their Use in Professional Sport* (2013).

[71] Ziggy Switkowski, 'Dr Ziggy Switkowski Report' (6 May 2013) Essendon Football Club, www.essendonfc.com.au/news/2013-05-06/dr-ziggy-switskowski-report.

Football Club and the AFL. Arguably, these recommendations provide a useful guide for clubs and their boards of directors. In brief, these recommendations are as follows:

1. Clubs should leave all 'pioneering work' with supplements to the Australian Sports Commission and should show 'zero tolerance' for any drug experimentation.
2. Clubs should establish a clear framework of accountability for all medical, sports and nutrition scientists, and other professionals.
3. Generally, the club doctor should be the signing authority for all medicines, supplements, diagnostic tests and therapeutic treatments.
4. Although clubs may employ full-time medical staff of their own, the advantages of engaging external professionals in private practices, which include keeping them abreast of best practices, should not be ignored.
5. Medical officers must authorise and keep detailed records of any intravenous injections.
6. Ultimate accountability should rest with the Chief Executive Officer (CEO), who should oversee all football operations.
7. The General Manager of Football Operations role should be filled by a strong capable individual who has the respect of the football staff and the support of the CEO.
8. Reporting lines within the organisation must be clear and employees should be held to account in their roles.
9. Bad news must be reported quickly, and senior management and the Board should regularly interrogate operations.
10. The club's policies and procedures, especially those on compliance with codes of conduct, should be reviewed and updated regularly, and should be submitted annually for endorsement by the Board.
11. Clubs should engage in regular risk assessment and mitigation.
12. The Board's regular meeting agenda should include issues of player welfare and the Board should consider occasional attendance of players at its meetings.
13. The executive should regularly report to the Board on the implementation of these practices and these reports should be shared with the competition organisation (in the case of the Switskowski report, the AFL).

The first of these guiding principles deserves elaboration. Clubs should leave all 'pioneering work' with supplements to the Australian Sports Commission and should show 'zero tolerance' for any drug experimentation, notwithstanding the incredible pressure on professional athletes to perform at their absolute peak. The gladiatorial performance culture in professional sport does encourage the most ambitious players to sacrifice their long-term health for immediate performance enhancement, especially as clubs are notorious for dropping players who have been perceived to be underperforming or suffering injury.

Clubs who neglect to take these kinds of steps to establish systems of accountability arguably run a risk of being found to have ignored foreseeable risks to their players if these players do become implicated in doping scandals as a consequence of following advice from club-appointed advisers.

Conclusion

This chapter has reflected on the general employment law implications of doping scandals and has focused particularly on the rights and obligations of the players and clubs as parties to employment contracts. Of course, there are many other forms of regulation that are likely to have more immediate implications for players and clubs—fines and bans under the self-regulatory codes, for example. These are designed to ensure fair competition and the efficient management of this multi-billion dollar industry, in the interests of all its participants, not just clubs and players, but also the fans, and those investors and sponsors who profit from the industry.

It is worth remembering, however, that the players—super-human gladiators that they sometimes seem to be—are also workers, and their relationships with the clubs who engage them are susceptible to regular employment regulation. Clubs do bear significant duties of care as employers, and these duties are engaged when players become embroiled in doping scandals.

10

Doping as Tort: Liability of Sport Supervisors and the Problem of Consent

PRUE VINES*

It is each *Athlete*'s personal duty to ensure that no *Prohibited Substance* enters his or her body. Athletes are responsible for any *Prohibited Substance* or its *Metabolites* or *Markers* found to be present in their *Samples*. Accordingly, it is not necessary that intent, fault, negligence or knowing *Use* on the Athlete's part be demonstrated in order to establish an anti-doping violation under Article 2.1.[1]

Introduction

This chapter considers the position of the athlete who is harmed by doping. In particular, it considers the position where the doping occurs because a coach or supervisor has administered or advised the use of the relevant substance. The tortious liability of such a supervisor may arise well after the actual doping event, because any harm to the athlete which eventuates from the doping event may actually appear quite some time later. It thus could be quite separate from a determination by the World Anti-Doping Agency (WADA) that there has been an anti-doping violation. Because athletes range from children to amateurs to professional elite sportspeople, the breadth of possible athlete/supervisor relationships is extraordinarily wide, and this makes the consideration of legal liability correspondingly complex. Actions in relation to doping have been rare up to the present, the majority of tort cases on sporting matters being concerned

* Professor, Faculty of Law, UNSW Australia.

[1] World Anti-Doping Authority (WADA), World Anti-Doping Code (1 January 2015) art 2.1.1 (hereinafter the Code) (emphasis in original).

with incidents during participation, such as personal injury of one player by another. It has been assumed that those who participate consent to at least some of the dangers of the activity and that it is only where that consent is exceeded that liability will arise.[2]

We have yet to see many actions taken by athletes concerning later harm caused by doping. This chapter considers what such actions would look like and suggests that the best legal analogy is not the earlier sporting cases, but medical malpractice cases—and, indeed, the team doctor may be the relevant supervisor. It also argues that the question of consent or voluntary assumption of risk is more complex in this area than in the other sporting cases because of the increasing level of pressure to perform and the normalisation of performance-enhancing substances amongst the population of athletes.[3]

Tortious Liability for Doping within or Outside WADA

Most of this book concerns doping as defined by WADA. There are issues about what doping is, of course.[4] For example, giving amateur players caffeine drinks such as Red Bull at break time instead of what used to be the ubiquitous orange quarters may or may not be doping depending on one's view. This chapter defines doping as the administration of any substance for the purpose of performance enhancement. This is a very broad definition. That is, doping is allowing any prohibited substance into the athlete's body. This definition is strict and does not require intent, fault or knowledge of the use. This definition is used to determine whether an anti-doping violation has occurred in a sport that is signed up to the Code.

[2] See *McNamara v Duncan* (1971) 26 ALR 584.

[3] A 2014 Australian study suggested that young athletes, who are aware that they themselves are unlikely to be tested, have a perception that about one-third of elite athletes take performance-enhancing drugs and supplements, and found that one in three young athletes take supplements: Natasha Boddy, 'Juniors Using Performance Raising Drugs' *Sydney Morning Herald* (9 July 2014) 3. The study is published in Stephen Moston, E Terry Engelberg and James Skinner, 'Perceived Incidence of Drug Use in Australian Sport: A Survey of Athletes and Coaches' (2015) 18 *Sport in Society* 91. See also J Bojsen-Møller and AV Christiansen, 'Use of Performance- and Image-Enhancing Substances among Recreational Athletes: A Quantitative Analysis of Inquiries Submitted to the Danish Anti-doping Authorities' (2010) 20 *Scandinavian Journal of Medicine & Science in Sports* 861, 863–66, which noted that approximately 15 per cent of enquirers who were young males in their mid-twenties who exercise in gyms were users of anabolic steroids or other banned substances and another 15 per cent had considered it.

[4] See, eg, James AR Nafziger and Stephen F Ross (eds), *Handbook on International Sports Law* (Cheltenham, Edward Elgar, 2011) 139; Doriane Lambelet Coleman and James E Coleman Jr, 'The Problem of Doping' (2008) 57 *Duke Law Journal* 1743, 1751–54; V Lentillon-Kaestner and F Ohl, 'Can We Measure Accurately the Prevalence of Doping?' (2011) 21 *Scandinavian Journal of Medicine & Science in Sports* e132, e132–33.

However, doping, in the sense of the use of any substance which alters the body chemistry,[5] is a tortious issue, whether or not a WADA determination is involved. For the purposes of torts, in most cases, the issue will be whether an athlete who is harmed by such doping can sue the person who has given the substance. This chapter considers the tortious liability of sports supervisors when an athlete they are supervising takes performance-enhancing drugs or prohibited substances. The issue arises when the taking of such substances causes harm to the athlete. 'Sports supervisor' in this chapter means the roles of coach, trainer and sports scientist, including sports medical practitioner. The variety of these roles hints at the complexity of the legal issues involved. The torts which may be used include intentional torts such as trespass to the person—assault and battery, for example,[6] where substances are given to a person without their knowledge or are given to or forced on them without their consent—and negligence. Negligence as a common law tort requires the establishment of three elements: duty of care, the breach of that duty and that the breach caused the harm.[7] Negligence is the most likely cause of action to be used to establish tortious liability of supervisors in relation to doping, and in this chapter I will concentrate on negligence and its equivalents outside the common law world.

This chapter argues that the most problematic issue in the context of the tortious liability of supervisors is the question of consent or voluntary assumption of risk. If a cause of action in tort is proved but there is consent, there will be no liability. There is therefore a strong interest by sports supervisors in demonstrating that the athletes concerned consented to the administration of any performance-enhancing drug. However, the context within which this happens raises some interesting issues about the extent to which consent can be regarded as real or, indeed, to the extent to which athletes in some situations can be regarded as *capable* of consent.

The Harm

Consider these two scenarios. First, a US football player is suing his former team and a pharmaceutical company associated with it. He alleges that they gave him

[5] I take 'dope' to be a synonym for 'drug', which is defined as '[a] medicine or other substance which has a physiological effect when ingested or otherwise introduced into the body': Oxford University Press, 'Drug—Definition of Drug in English from the Oxford Dictionary' (2015) *Oxford Dictionaries* www.oxforddictionaries.com/definition/english/drug.

[6] Assault in 'common law private law' is a description of a type of law. The difficulty is distinguishing between civil law within the common law and civil law systems: see *Barton v Armstrong* [1969] 2 NSWR 451, 455 (Taylor J). Battery is the infliction of unwanted or offensive touching: see *Collins v Wilcock* [1984] 1 WLR 1172, 1177–78 (Goff LJ).

[7] See *Tame v New South Wales* (2002) 211 CLR 317, 348–49 [88] (McHugh J).

painkilling injections that led to a heart attack that jeopardised his potential National Football League (NFL) career.

Second, Australian fullback Isaac Gordon suffered a 'bizarre injury' when he was 'corked' during a rugby league game.[8] The bizarre injury was severe bruising from groin to ankle—'My leg was black'—which appeared the next day. This led to blood tests being taken and, apparently, the sports scientist involved being dismissed from the club. The suspicion was that some kind of drug had been given to Gordon, which caused him to bleed more than normal.

These are both examples of physical harm that might arise from doping. Harm must be established in order to bring an action for negligence.[9] The harm that might arise from doping includes physical injury at the time or in later life, or it could be pure economic loss caused by a loss of reputation with a consequential loss of sponsorships or career prospects in sport. The reputation loss might be caused by publicity about a WADA determination that a prohibited substance has been taken and led to a positive drug test.[10] The case of Lance Armstrong is a salient example of economic loss arising out of doping becoming known.[11] The harm could be caused by a prohibited substance which is in a supplement of some kind; it could be caused by a prescription drug which has been taken in much higher amounts than would normally be prescribed; it could involve the taking of a drug which is experimental and has not yet been accepted by the drug administration of the relevant country; or it could occur through black market usage of drugs which could be contaminated or whose dosage might not be what it should be. There could also be problems where a supervisor has failed to warn the athlete that a particular supplement or drug could contain a prohibited or dangerous substance.[12]

[8] Michael Chammas, 'I Was Told it was Bruising You'd Only See on a 90-Year-Old Lady' *Sydney Morning Herald* (22 March 2013) www.smh.com.au/rugby-league/league-news/i-was-told-it-was-bruising-youd-only-see-on-a-90yearold-lady-20130321-2gitt.html.

[9] See *Williams v Milotin* (1957) 97 CLR 465, 474 (the Court); *Tabet v Gett* (2010) 240 CLR 537, 577 [109] (Kiefel J).

[10] Note that where there is a breach of the Code, this may arise where the particular drug is not illegal or necessarily dangerous outside the Code. For example, caffeine may lead to an athlete being regarded as breaching the Code, which in turn might lead to banning and some kind of economic loss because the athlete is regarded as breaking the rules; however, some performance-enhancing drugs are also dangerous. See WADA, The World Anti-Doping Code—The 2015 Prohibited List (at 1 January 2015).

[11] Lance Armstrong admitted and apologised for his doping in an interview with Oprah Winfrey on 13 January 2013. He subsequently lost his sponsorships and was stripped of sporting medals and Tour de France titles: see, eg, William Fotheringham, 'Timeline: Lance Armstrong's Journey from Deity to Disgrace' *The Guardian* (9 March 2015) www.theguardian.com/sport/2015/mar/09/lance-armstrong-cycling-doping-scandal.

[12] There is evidence that many medical sports supervisors are not as aware as they should be of the list of WADA-prohibited substances: Peter Greenway and Mary Greenway, 'General Practitioner Knowledge of Prohibited Substances in Sport (1997) 31 *British Journal of Sports Medicine* 129; H Kuipers and G Ruijisch van Dugteren, 'Letters to the Editors—The Prohibited List and Cheating in Sport' (2006) 27 *International Journal of Sports Medicine* 80.

Negligence

Liability in negligence will arise in common law systems if the plaintiff can show that the defendant owed to the plaintiff a duty of care, that the duty was breached by the defendant and that the breach caused the harm suffered by the plaintiff. If the defendant can prove a defence, then the liability may be reduced or negated. In civil law systems, the equivalent would be, for example, section 823 of the Bürgerlichen Gesetzbuch (Civil Code) (Germany), which states:

> A person who, intentionally or negligently, unlawfully injures the life, body, health, freedom, property or another right of another person is liable to make compensation to the other party for the damage arising from this.[13]

This creates the equivalent obligation to the common law duty in negligence or intentional torts such as assault or battery, although the definition of negligence may be stricter than the common law definition:[14] a person acts negligently if he or she fails to exercise 'the socially required level of care'.[15]

Most of this chapter focuses on common law negligence for reasons including the familiarity of the author with this area and because the differences are not great.

The issue of the duty of care when personal injury is the harm is fairly easily established, so the duty is owed in most sporting cases.[16] Where there is a closer connection between the plaintiff and the defendant's actions, a duty to take reasonable care to avoid harm will generally arise.[17]

When will a duty of care arise in relation to doping? A duty of care is likely to be clear if it is reasonably foreseeable that physical harm might come to the plaintiff if the defendant supervisor gives or advises the taking of the substance. The analogy with medical care is the most useful as 'doping' is the giving of medication, which is normally the prerogative of the medical profession. The question is whether it is foreseeable for the medical professional or the sports supervisor that if he or she administers a particular drug, physical harm might come to the athlete. For example, there may be well-known side-effects as with anabolic

[13] Bürgerlichen Gesetzbuch (Civil Code) (Germany) § 823(1).

[14] ibid § 276; Marc Stauch, *The Law of Medical Negligence in England and Germany: A Comparative Analysis* (Oxford, Hart Publishing, 2008) 35.

[15] Stauch (n 14) 35, intepreting Bürgerlichen Gesetzbuch (Civil Code) (Germany) § 276(2).

[16] The standard test for duty is that it is reasonably foreseeable that harm might come to a person in the class of the plaintiff if the defendant carried out the contemplated act or omission: *Donoghue v Stevenson* [1932] AC 562, 582 (Lord Atkin). Other factors may be needed to establish a duty where matters other than ordinary personal injury are at issue. The duty has been held not to be owed in a situation where members of the International Rugby Football League were sued on the basis that their ability to change the rules of the game gave rise to a duty of care to players in relation to the risk of injury. The High Court rejected this proposition on the basis that if such a duty existed, it would be owed to hundreds of thousands of players across the world, which would be absurd: *Agar v Hyde* (2000) 201 CLR 552, 578 [67] (Gaudron, McHugh, Gummow and Hayne JJ).

[17] See *Wyong Shire Council v Shirt* (1980) 146 CLR 40, 44 (Mason J).

steroids; there may be both known and yet unknown side-effects or harms from prescription drugs when used in unusual doses; and there may be unknown side-effects where drugs are experimental or illegally produced so that they might also be contaminated or dosages may be unclear. All these could be regarded as foreseeable harms.

Where doping has occurred but the athlete has not been physically injured and the damaged career or lost economic opportunity is the harm that has been suffered, the test in Australia will be whether the athlete was a specifically foreseeable plaintiff whose economic loss was also foreseeable.[18] As the supervisor is in a direct relationship with the athlete, this test is likely to be easily met. In the UK, the test may be whether there was a relationship of reliance and an assumption of responsibility between the parties.[19] Again, this is clearly met by a sports supervisor/athlete relationship. In Canada and New Zealand, there has been less willingness to accept a bright-line distinction between personal injury, property damage and pure economic loss.[20] Where there was a close relationship between the adviser who gave or advised the use of the relevant substance, this might not be a difficult hurdle to get over.[21] So in most cases, it seems likely that a duty of care in relation to both personal injury and pure economic loss would be easy enough to establish. Further, it seems likely that this position would apply in both common law and civil law countries.

The Standard of Care

The more critical issue in this context is the question of the standard of care to be reached. If the defendant has not met the standard of care, he or she has breached his or her duty. It has been convincingly argued that when personal injury arises within games, participants must be seen to have accepted some level of inherent risk and that this affects the standard of care they themselves have to reach in relation to their liability towards each other.[22] However, this version of the standard of care is unlikely to be applicable in the context of doping.

[18] *Perre v Apand* (1999) 198 CLR 180, 220 (McHugh J); *Caltex Oil Pty Ltd v The Dredge 'Willemstadt'* (1976) 136 CLR 529, 555 (Gibbs J), 572–78 (Stephen J), 590–93 (Mason J).

[19] See cases concerning misleading advice: *Hedley Byrne & Co Ltd v Heller & Partners Ltd* [1964] AC 465, 502–04 (Lord Morris of Borth-y-Gest); *White v Jones* [1995] 2 AC 207, 268–69 (Lord Goff of Chieveley), 273–74 (Lord Browne-Wilkinson).

[20] See *Invercargill City Council v Hamlin* [1994] 3 NZLR 513; *Riddell v Porteous* [1999] 1 NZLR 1; *Rolls-Royce New Zealand Ltd v Carter Holt Harvey Ltd* [2005] 1 NZLR 324. Note that in New Zealand, the Accidents Compensation Commission will manage personal injury compensation unless it involves negligence serious enough to justify punitive damages. Pure economic loss, however, is dealt with as a matter of tort law.

[21] *cf West Bromwich Albion Football Club Ltd v El-Safty* [2007] PIQR P7 [80]–[84] (Royce J).

[22] Stanley Yeo, 'Accepted Inherent Risks among Sporting Participants' (2001) 9 *Torts Law Review* 114.

To establish whether the duty has been breached, the plaintiff must show that the defendant did not act like a reasonable person in the circumstances.[23] This means, where the defendant is a professional or a person with a special skill, the question is what a reasonable professional would have done in the circumstances.[24] In Australia, England and Canada, we ask whether what the defendant did was something other professionals of the same class would consider reasonable,[25] subject to the court thinking that the action taken was not irrational.[26]

The English test is 'the standard of the ordinary skilled man exercising and professing to have that special skill'.[27] In the US, the standard is that of the person having the 'knowledge, training and skill (or ability and competence) of an ordinary member of the profession in good standing'.[28] In Germany, the test for medical practitioners has been the need to meet the standard of the 'respectable and conscientious medical professional of average expertise in the relevant field'.[29] The law across these jurisdictions is fairly similar and many aspects of them can be considered together.

First, who is a professional in these circumstances? The term 'professional' seems to have no special meaning in the context of tortious liability. The question is what did the defendant hold out his or her level of skill as being? In the US, skill is regarded as that which is developed through training and experience.[30] Where a coach holds himself or herself out as a coach, the question will be what a reasonable coach would do in the circumstances—if the circumstances include that the coach was employed to be a coach, that will be considered, while if the coach was doing it in his spare time as an amateur, that will also be taken into account in establishing the standard of care. However, the fact that a role is being carried out without pay will not necessarily reduce the standard of care required.

[23] *Vaughan v Menlove* (1837) 3 Bing NC 468, 475; 132 ER 490, 493 (The Court); American Law Institute, *Restatement (Third) of Torts: Liability for Physical and Emotional Harms* (2005) § 3; *Wyong Shire Council v Shirt* (n 17) 47–48 (Mason J).

[24] American Law Institute (n 23) § 12, cmt (a).

[25] *Rogers v Whitaker* (1992) 175 CLR 479, 483 (Mason CJ, Brennan, Dawson, Toohey and McHugh JJ): 'The standard of reasonable care and skill required is that of the ordinary skilled person exercising and professing to have that special skill.' See also American Law Institute (n 23) § 3. *Bolitho v City and Hackney Health Authority* [1998] AC 232, 241–42 (Lord Browne-Wilkinson); Civil Liability Act 2002 (NSW) s 5O.

[26] See, eg, *Edward Wong Finance Co Ltd v Johnston Stokes and Masters* [1984] AC 296, where the solicitor was found negligent despite following the universal conveyancing practice of Hong Kong in Hong Kong.

[27] *Bolam v Friern Hospital Management Committee* [1957] 1 WLR 582, 586 (McNair J).

[28] Victor E Schwartz, Kathryn Kelly and David F Partlett, *Prosser, Wade and Schwartz's Torts: Cases and Materials* 10th edn (Sydney, Foundation Press, 2000) 168. Note this is explicitly not modified in the US where pro bono work is being done (*Becker v Janiski* 15 NYS 675, 677 (Pryor J) (NY Sup Ct, 1891)) and implicitly not modified elsewhere (*Prosser* at 70).

[29] Bundesgerichtshof (German Federal Court of Justice), III ZR 54/59, 13 June 1960, reported in (1961) NJW 600, 600. Similarly, a medical specialist is required to show the expertise of that particular speciality: Bundesgerichtshof (German Federal Court of Justice), VI ZR 34/00, 13 February 2001, reported in (2001) NJW 1786. Both decisions are cited in Stauch (n 14) 36.

[30] American Law Institute (n 23) § 12 cmt (a).

Similarly, the fact that a person is a learner driver or a doctor on his or her first day at work does not absolve him or her from acting like a reasonably experienced practitioner.[31]

A sports scientist would be expected to have the knowledge and training of a reasonably experienced sports scientist, a coach would be expected to have the knowledge and training of a reasonably experienced coach and so on. In determining what the defendant supervisor should have done, the courts have considered how to balance the factors that the defendant should have considered. Thus, the reasonable supervisor would have considered the likelihood of harm to the athlete, the gravity of the harm should it come to pass, what could have been done to avoid the harm and how easy was it, whether there were other justifications for carrying out the particular act and so on.[32] For this purpose, let us take two scenarios at the point in time before any drugs have been taken or harm has been done. In Scenario 1, we have Steve, a professional coach/sports scientist in a professional football club. The players he deals with are professionals for whom playing sport is their livelihood. Some of the younger ones are on the cusp of being signed up to first grade and embarking on a professional career. One of these is Arthur. Others have been playing professionally for some years. One of these is Ahmed.

In Scenario 2, we have Sam, a newly graduated sports trainer training a 17-year-old athlete, Alex, who wishes to become a professional basketball player and is not quite there in terms of strength and speed, but is clearly very close.

Suppose the question for the supervisors is whether to advise the athlete to take a steroid. The risks of anabolic steroid use are now known to include immediate and later physical problems, including heart attack, loss of testosterone, fertility damage and many others. They are performance enhancing because they allow muscles to repair themselves faster, among other things. They are also prohibited under the Code, so there is the added risk that if they are taken, the athletes may be caught in a breach of the Code. If Arthur is caught, he may lose his possible job; if Ahmed is caught, he may also lose his job or possible future sponsorship deals. If Alex is caught before he becomes a professional, he may lose the opportunity to become a professional; if he is caught after he becomes a professional, he may lose his place or future earnings based on competing in sport. But if they are not caught, they may win more games or get into the various positions in sport that they wish to. No reasonable supervisor would advise this now, and the answer if such a case came to trial would be almost certainly that this advice breached their duty of care.

[31] See, eg, cases involving learner drivers: *Imbree v McNielly* (2008) 236 CLR 510: *Nettleship v Weston* [1971] 2 QB 691, 699–700 (Lord Denning MR). For cases involving inexperienced doctors, see *Wilsher v Essex Area Health Authority* [1987] QB 730; *Aldana v March* (1999) 44 CCLT (2d) 164 [32].

[32] Sometimes this is called the 'calculus of negligence': *United States v Carroll Towing Co* 159 F 2d 169, 173 (Learned Hand J) (2d Cir, 1947); *Wyong Shire Council v Shirt* (n 17) 47–48 (Mason J). In most jurisdictions outside the US, the decision of whether the standard has been met is no longer made by a jury.

Suppose Sam and Steve had just heard of a new supplement not on the WADA Prohibited List, which was said to enhance muscle growth as fast as steroids, but not carry the heart attack risks. Let us call it 'Wondermuscle'. Both have read literature on it on Google Scholar, which reports on a trial carried out in South America by a doctor over six months with 30 subjects. It is new and is available on the internet, but does not have Australian pharmaceutical approval, which can take a considerable time. Suppose they persuaded their athletes to take it and 10 years later it became clear that it was carcinogenic? Or suppose a standard antibiotic, such as erythromycin, was thought to be performance enhancing if it was given for five days before a sporting event in doses 20 times higher than normal. There was a period when this was done for many footballers playing for clubs until it lost its status, but 10 years later, it became apparent that it caused serious osteoporosis. Note that because the usage of quite legal drugs in the high doses that may be used for performance enhancement is unethical, there may be no way to predict its effect on athletes, because empirical studies using such high doses are not carried out. These two situations are not quite as clear. Weighing up the factors does not necessarily lead to an obvious conclusion that there is a breach of duty; it will have to be weighed up in each case, relative to the knowledge at the time and the likelihood of harm eventuating.

In the jurisdictions using the reasonable person standard modified for the profession of the defendant, the plaintiff will bring evidence to show that the supervisor had not been doing what the profession usually did or that what the profession was doing was quite irrational.

It is arguable that if it did become evident that coaches habitually advised footballers to take banned substances or substances with known severe side-effects, the court might well regard that as irrational. A small number of medical cases have taken the view that certain defendants have been acting like 'rogue experts'. For example in *Hucks v Cole*,[33] a doctor had failed to prescribe penicillin in a situation where the patient had symptoms likely to lead to puerperal fever. Although there was evidence from experts that they would not have prescribed penicillin, the court took the view that this was negligent because it was irrational. Recently it was reported that a group of experienced sports physicians argued that an unproven and unapproved therapy made from a combination of drugs to be injected into the athlete for acute muscle strain should be considered 'an important part of the landscape of management options'.[34] This may well be an example of behaviour by a group of medical practitioners that would be struck down by the courts as irrational because it involved the use of a drug combination which had not been tested and had not been through the drug regulatory agencies.

Further examples include the use of black market drugs and supplements, which include prohibited substances that are sometimes prohibited and at other

[33] *Hucks v Cole* [1993] 4 Med LR 393.

[34] A Franklyn-Miller, J Etherington and P McCrory, 'Sports and Exercise Medicine—Specialists or Snake Oil Salesmen?' (2011) 45(2) *British Journal of Sports Medicine* 83, 83.

times not prohibited (eg, pseudoephedrine and caffeine). If the supervisor administers this substance or advises that it should be used, he or she may be in breach of his or her duty if a reasonable sports supervisor would not do so. It might be, for example, that a reasonable sports coach would not advise about any drug, but would refer to a sports scientist or sports physician in relation to such substances. The sports scientist or sports physician would be expected to act like a reasonable sports scientist or sports physician. This would mean that he or she would be expected to know about drugs and their chemistry, and to understand the processes by which such drugs are tested and when they become available. Similarly, he or she should understand dosages. This would be a matter of expert evidence at the time that the drug was administered. The level of trust and reliance on a team sports scientist or a team physician would be very high, and in relation to advice about doping, the expectation that the athlete would follow a team sports scientist or team doctor's advice would be very high, probably higher than the advice of a coach.

The example of the gymnast Andrea Raducan is illustrative. Raducan was stripped of her Sydney Olympic Games gold medal after she tested positive for pseudoephedrine, now taken off the Prohibited List, which had been prescribed for her by her team doctor. She had complained of a headache, a running nose and congestion, and was given Nurofen by the doctor during the Games. The team doctor was banned for two Olympic cycles.[35] Suppose the publicity about this led to her losing sponsorships that she was about to sign contracts for. There would be little doubt that the doctor would be held liable in negligence for prescribing and giving the Nurofen as he would either have known or should have known that Nurofen contained pseudoephedrine, which was then a prohibited substance under the Code. Because of the relationship between team doctor and athlete, which is a relationship of trust and confidence, she would be expected to rely on his advice and, indeed, could probably be censured for not following his advice in some cases, so no defence of consent or voluntary assumption of risk would apply here.

Supplements are particularly problematic because their ingredients may not be known and because there is often an assumption that they must be harmless—they are generally able to be purchased over the counter and do not require a prescription. Athletes are sometimes warned that: 'ASADA cautions athletes to take extreme care when it comes to supplements … Read the ingredients label, does it say "proprietary blend"? If it does, there is no telling what has been added in the manufacturing process and this is the risk you take.'[36]

In the medical context, where a procedure or course of treatment is being considered, a duty to warn of the risks arises. The failure to warn is a breach of the duty

[35] See Nenad Dikic et al, 'Sports Physicians, Ethics and Antidoping Governance: Between Assistance and Negligence' (2013) 47 *British Journal of Sports Medicine* 701.

[36] Rowing Australia, 'Athlete Advisory—Supplements and Prohibited Stimulants' (27 June 2014) www.rowingaustralia.com.au/athlete-advisory-supplements-and-prohibited-stimulants.

of care of medical practitioners in most jurisdictions.[37] The patient is required to be warned of the risks he or she would consider material in Australia and England (a more subjective test),[38] while in the US and Canada, the warning should be what a reasonable person in the patient's position would require, which is a more objective test.[39] In Germany, the test is also quite subjective.[40] This means that what should be warned of may be quite different in jurisdictions where the warning requirement is subjective compared with the jurisdictions where the warning requirement is objective. Then the causation test becomes whether the patient would have gone ahead with taking the substance or doing the operation if the proper warning had been given.

Defences to Negligence and Consent

Defences to negligence include contributory negligence, where the plaintiff has not taken sufficient care of himself or herself. Another defence is the defence of illegality.[41] In this context, it is important to note that many of the prohibited substances are not illegal,[42] and the Code's application is a matter of contract rather than criminal law.[43]

For our purposes, the most interesting defence is the voluntary assumption of risk and, in relation to this, the most problematic issue is the question of consent. Voluntary assumption of risk will arise as a defence where the plaintiff has, with full knowledge, voluntarily and freely accepted the risk.[44]

Consent may be implied or express, but it must be real and freely given. For consent to be real, the plaintiff must have enough knowledge to understand what

[37] *Canterbury v Spence* 464 F 2d 772, 790 (Robinson J) (DC Cir, 1972); *Reibl v Hughes* [1980] 2 SCR 880; *Sidaway v Governors of Bethlem Royal Hospital* [1985] AC 871, 895 (Lord Diplock), 900 (Lord Bridge of Harwich); *Chester v Afshar* [2005] 1 AC 142 [11] (Lord Steyn); *Rogers v Whitaker* (n 25) 490 (Mason CJ, Brennan, Dawson, Toohey and McHugh JJ); *Chappel v Hart* (1998) 195 CLR 232, 247 [34] (McHugh J). In Germany, there is a very strict disclosure rule; see Marc S Stauch, 'Malpractice and Compensation in Germany' (2011) 86 *Chicago-Kent Law Review* 1139, 1157–58.

[38] *Chester v Afshar* (n 37); *Rogers v Whitaker* (n 25) 490 (Mason CJ, Brennan, Dawson, Toohey and McHugh JJ); *Chappel v Hart* (n 37) 246 [32] (McHugh J), 272 [93], 276–77 [96] (Kirby J).

[39] *Reibl v Hughes* [1980] 2 SCR 880; *Arndt v Smith* [1997] 2 SCR 539; *Canterbury v Spence* (n 37) 784 (Robinson J) (DC Cir, 1972),

[40] Bundesgerichtshof (German Federal Court of Justice), VI ZR 7/79, 24 June 1980, reported in (1980) NJW 2751, 2752–53, cited in Stauch (n 14) 108.

[41] See *Gray v Thames Trains Ltd* [2009] 1 AC 1339; *Gala v Preston* (1991) 172 CLR 243; *Miller v Miller* (2011) 242 CLR 446.

[42] Note, however, that there is a black market in drugs and substances prohibited under the Code, including peptides and hormones and anabolic steroids: Australian Crime Commission, *Organised Crime and Drugs in Sport: New Generation Performance and Image Enhancing Drugs and Organised Criminal Involvement in their Use in Professional Sport* (2013) 12.

[43] See Paul David, *A Guide to the World Anti-Doping Code: A Fight for the Spirit of Sport* 2nd edn (Cambridge, Cambridge University Press, 2013) 123.

[44] *Osborne v London and North Western Railway Co* (1888) 21 QBD 220, 223–24 (Wills J).

he or she is consenting to. Traditionally, where the action was for trespass, consent was generally regarded as sufficient if the individual understood the nature of a procedure, such as in an operation where:

> Once the patient is informed in broad terms of the nature of the procedure which is intended, and gives her consent, that consent is real, and the cause of action on which to base a claim for failure to go into risks and implications is negligence, not trespass. Of course if information is withheld in bad faith, the consent will be vitiated by fraud. Of course if by some accident, as in a case in the 1940s in the Salford Hundred Court where a boy was admitted to hospital for tonsillectomy and due to administrative error was circumcised instead, trespass would be the appropriate cause of action against the doctor.[45]

There is a common law presumption in favour of the capacity to decide. In England and Wales, the Mental Capacity Act 2005 (UK) ch 9, s 2 defines capacity.[46] The position of the statute is reasonably consistent with other jurisdictions' view of capacity. At common law, capacity is a transaction-based concept—the question is whether the person is capable of understanding whatever the transaction is.[47] This means that a person can have capacity to enter into some transactions, but not others. However, the common law presumption is that there is capacity, as stated above. We need to ask whether this presumption should apply in the case of elite athletes in team sports.

When a professional gives advice to a person about the taking of a drug or the use of some procedure or system, there is a question about the information or warning that is given to the plaintiff. As discussed above, in the context of medical practice, the courts have held that an ordinary skilled medical practitioner has a duty to warn a patient of the material risks inherent in the medical treatment.

This view is common across the jurisdictions.[48] A psychiatrist who failed to warn a patient about the side-effects of a drug and prescribed the drug for a period in excess of the limits in practice guidelines was held liable to the patient in *B v Marinovich*.[49] This is analogous to a sports physician prescribing higher dosages of a prescription drug for the purpose of enhancing performance. In Germany, the importance of the patient's consent is even more important than elsewhere because of the protection of dignity, self-development and bodily integrity in the constitution,[50] and there is a sense in which the lack or failure of consent is seen

[45] *Chatterton v Gerson* [1981] QB 432, 443 (Bristow J), confirmed by *Rogers v Whitaker* (n 25) 490 (Mason CJ, Brennan, Dawson, Toohey and McHugh JJ), followed in the US in *Scott v Bradford* 606 P 2d 554 (Okla, 1979).

[46] Mental Capacity Act 2005 (UK) ch 9, s 2.

[47] *Gibbons v Wright* (1954) 91 CLR 423, 438 (The Court).

[48] *Reibl v Hughes* [1980] 2 SCR 880; *Rogers v Whitaker* (n 25); *Canterbury v Spence* (n 37) 784 (Robinson J) (DC Cir, 1972). However, some US states prefer to use existing medical practice as the criterion rather than the reasonable patient test, which is applied in *Pearce v United Bristol Healthcare NHS Trust* [1999] PIQR P53, 59 (Lord Woolf MR), cited in *Chester v Afshar* (n 37) 143 [15] (Lord Steyn).

[49] *B v Marinovich* [1999] NTSC 127.

[50] Grundgesetz für die Bundesrepublik Deutschland (Basic Law of the Federal Republic of Germany) arts 1(1), 2.

as amounting to harm in itself.[51] However, the failure to warn is similarly seen as a serious issue; the German Court has held that the need for information of the particular patient is the yardstick for what should be disclosed.[52]

There is reason to think that this would also apply to supervisors of athletes. Thus, where a supervisor advises an athlete to take a substance of some kind, he or she must advise about the risks which the athlete would think were material, at least in Australia, England and Germany, while in the US and Canada, the test would be what the reasonable athlete would think was material. So, if Sam and Steve have read about 'Wondermuscle' and they themselves think there is little risk of later side-effects and that it will enhance Arthur, Ahmed and Alex's performance, what should they tell them about 'Wondermuscle'? The answer depends on the jurisdictional requirements and how the athletes are likely to respond. Suppose they are in Germany. They need to tell the athletes what the particular athlete would think was material. This is not simple, because, for example, Alex, who is 17 and wants to become a professional basketball player, might not want to know anything and might be happy to go ahead.[53] Similarly, Arthur, who is on the cusp of first grade, might also be not very interested in being told all the possible risks, while Ahmed, who is an experienced player, might wish to know about all the possible risks to him, both physically and professionally, before he goes ahead.

On the other hand, if the test is, as it is in the US, based on the reasonable athlete, what needs to be told to the athlete may be the same for Alex, Ahmed and Arthur. All three run the risk that the drug is untested by the pharmaceutical regulatory authority of their own country; they should probably be informed of the fact that the risks are unknown and might be serious, and that there is a possibility that it might cause physical harm, including cancer, in the future.

In the absence of detailed warnings can the defendant argue that the plaintiff consented to the risk? To what extent can the plaintiff be treated as if he or she has no idea about the risks of drug taking? Most of us are aware that some performance-enhancing drugs can cause later problems, eg, heart problems caused by steroids. Side-effects of drugs are always an issue—consider the connections between growth hormones given in the 1960s and 1970s and the later Creutzfeld-Jakob Syndrome (similar to bovine spongiform encephalopathy, more commonly known as mad cow disease). However, professional athletes are often held very closely by their clubs, are very closely controlled and are often in the habit of doing what they are told. Can consent be regarded as real in such a situation?

[51] Stauch (n 14) 101.

[52] Bundesgerichtshof (German Federal Court of Justice), VI ZR 188/82, 7 February 1984, reported in (1984) NJW 1395, cited in Stauch (n 14) 118.

[53] Alex is technically a minor, so it may be that his parents might have to be informed, which might alter the response or likelihood of consent considerably. If Alex had just turned 18, there would be no need to involve his parents, but the likelihood of him having developed a greater level of risk averseness is not high.

Consent cannot be real where a procedure or drug is experimental and the patient has not been told of its experimental status. Similarly, where there is some form of duress, consent will not be valid. Actions where consent has been regarded as vitiated have included those where there is pressure from family members to agree to or refuse medical treatment.[54] In order to have voluntarily assumed the risk, the decision should be the free and independent decision of the athlete. Could an athlete whose coach is advising him to take some treatment be considered to be taking an independent decision? To what extent can an elite athlete such as Alex, Ahmed or Arthur be regarded as capable of saying no to a drug, even after a warning, if his or her sports physician or sports scientist is urging him or her to take it?

There is a significant amount of evidence, at least anecdotally, that athletes will simply follow the instructions of coaches:

> Elite athletes are a vulnerable group often happy to accept at face value a treatment purported to expedite their return to play for a variety of factors. In the dependent relationship that may exist between the team doctor and athlete, particular attention has to be given to whether the doctor's ethical responsibility to fully inform has been discharged.[55]

In considering how athletes might respond to risk warnings, it is important to consider the extreme motivation to win amongst elite athletes. Elite athletes or those seeking to enter elite levels may not be very risk averse. There is the interesting evidence of a well-known survey of elite athletes who were asked if they would take a drug that would guarantee that they won every competition for five years, but that after five years they would die. Fifty-two per cent of the athletes stated that they would take the drug.[56]

Conclusion

This chapter has considered how liability of sports supervisors might arise in the context of harm caused by doping, and I have sought to explain the situation of athletes and supervisors in such a way as to put the spotlight on the notion of consent or the voluntary assumption of risk. Where a sports supervisor has offered or suggested that a drug be taken and the athlete has done so, there is strict liability in the WADA regime; and in the civil liability regime, a presumption or implication of consent where a person is regarded as of full capacity.

[54] *Re T (Adult: Refusal of Treatment)* [1992] 4 All ER 649, 662–63 (Lord Donaldson MR), 668 (Butler-Sloss LJ), 669 (Staughton LJ).

[55] Franklyn-Miller, Etherington and McCrory (n 34) 84.

[56] Bob Goldman, Patricia J Bush and Ronald Klatz, *Death in the Locker Room: Steroids & Sports* (South Bend, IN, Icarus Press, 1984), cited in AJ Bloodworth et al, 'Doping and Supplementation: The Attitudes of Talented Young Athletes' (2012) 22 *Scandinavian Journal of Medicine & Science in Sports* 293, 299.

Where an athlete has sourced his or her own drugs, he or she is clearly entirely responsible. Although his or her level of knowledge may not be adequate to really understand the risks being run, any damages awarded might be significantly reduced depending on the level of knowledge of the athlete. Similarly, when a sports trainer in a gym tells an athlete to take a particular supplement or drug and the athlete is not tied to the trainer in any way, there may well be a voluntary assumption of risk by the athlete and little reason to think that the sports trainer should be held wholly responsible.

But consent in many circumstances where athletes are at the elite level or close to it may not be as real as it seems. The capacity of athletes, both minors and the technically adult,[57] to be able to withstand the pressures of elite sport so as to say no is doubtful. This, twinned with their reliance on their supervisors, suggests that consent or the voluntariness of the taking of the doping substance may be more shadow than substance in many instances. Justice requires the law to take account of this.

[57] And indeed older adults as well.

Part V

The World Anti-Doping Code as Regulation: Governance and Compliance

11

Governance and Anti-Doping: Beyond the Fox and the Hen House

MARINA NEHME* AND CATHERINE ORDWAY**

Introduction

Sport plays a key role in our society. In fact, it may be viewed as an engine of economic growth[1] and social change.[2] Since its humble beginnings, a form of social contract has developed between sport organisations and governments, resulting in the establishment of voluntary sport associations which create their own rules and regulations.[3] The state plays a limited role in the imposition of rules and obligations arising from the growth of the sport sector.[4] This social contract is embedded in the foundation of the sporting entities. For example, after the establishment of the International Olympic Committee (IOC), the key authority on all issues relating to the Olympic Movement, its founder, Pierre de Coubertin, noted that 'the beam formed by the goodwill of all members of an autonomous sport, relaxes when the giant figure of this dangerous and imprecise figure called state appears'.[5] Similarly, the Fédération Internationale de Football Association

* Senior Lecturer, Faculty of Law, UNSW Australia.
** Anti-doping consultant and Professor of Practice (Sport Management), La Trobe University.

1 See, eg, Wladimir Andreff and Stefan Szymanski (eds), *Handbook on the Economics of Sport* (Cheltenham, Edward Elgar, 2006); SportsEconAustria et al, 'Study on the Contribution of Sport to Economic Growth and Employment in the EU' (Final Report, 2012) http://ec.europa.eu/sport/library/studies/study-contribution-spors-economic-growth-final-rpt.pdf.

2 Roger Levermore and Aaron Beacon, 'Sport and Development: Mapping the Field' in Roger Levermore and Aaron Beacon (eds), *Sport and International Development: Global Culture and Sport* (Basingstoke, Palgrave Macmillan, 2009) 1.

3 Michaeël Mrkonjic and Arnout Geeraert, 'Sports Organisations, Autonomy and Good Governance' in Jens Alm (ed), *Action for Good Governance in International Sports Organisations* (Copenhagen, Danish Institute for Sports Studies, 2013) 133, 134.

4 John Locke, *Two Treatises of Government* (New York, Hafner Publishing Co, first published in 1690, 1947 edn) 184–86. While not specifically addressing sport as an institution, Locke's work discussed the development of rules and sanctions before the creation of the state. Sport has had a comparable development history.

5 Jean-Loup Chappelet, *Autonomy of Sport in Europe* (Strasbourg, Council of Europe Publishing, 2010), 14, cited in Mrkonjic and Geeraert (n 3) 133, 134.

(FIFA) was established in 1904 by men who also believed in the separation of sport from the state.[6] Arguably, this has led to what Hans Buyninckx, the Executive Director of the European Environment Agency, calls the concept of 'exceptionalism' of sport: the general 'rules' required of all other institutions and corporations within society do not apply to sporting organisations.[7]

The double-edged sword of elite sport is that the same positive drivers needed to achieve perfection in human athletic pursuits can also lead to greed, selfishness, egotism and cheating in both athletes and support staff. These drivers, combined with the explosion in the commercialisation of sport, have led to the regular occurrence of sport scandals ranging from doping by athletes to bribery of officials.[8] When combined, these factors have shaken the foundation of the existing social contract and the concept of 'exceptionalism' of sport is no longer acceptable: the community's expectation has shifted towards greater accountability of sporting organisations, athletes and sport officials.[9]

In response, state representative organisations such as the European Commission have indicated that if the sports sector wishes to remain self-regulated and autonomous, then a key condition is good governance in sport.[10] Governance of an organisation has many definitions and interpretations.[11] Corporate governance, for instance, has been defined as 'the system by which companies are directed and controlled'.[12] This simple definition may be applied in the context of sport organisations and may additionally include 'the development and maintenance of practical and ethical self-regulation to achieve diverse objectives such as enforcing the rules of the game, implementing anti-doping policies and disciplining athletes'.[13]

[6] Mrkonjic and Geeraert (n 3) 134.

[7] Hans Bruyninckx, 'Global Sports: Time for a Changing Climate, in Times of Climate Change' (Paper presented at the Play the Game Conference, Denmark, 27 October 2015). See also Hans Bruyninckx, 'Sports Governance: Between the Obsession with Rules and Regulation and the Aversion to Being Ruled and Regulated' in Barbara Segaert et al (eds), *Sports Governance, Development and Corporate Responsibility* (Abingdon, Routledge, 2012) 107.

[8] See, eg, David Rowe, 'Sport: Scandal, Gender and the Nation' (Institute for Culture and Society Occasional Paper 4.3, 2013) 4–8 http://uws.edu.au/__data/assets/pdf_file/0005/539123/ICS_Occasional_Paper_Series_4_3.pdf.

[9] Arnout Geeraert, 'The Governance Agenda and its Relevance for Sport: Introducing the Four Dimensions of the AGGIS Sports Governance Observer' in Alm (n 3) 9, 10.

[10] European Commission, 'Communication from the Commission to the European Parliament, the Council, the European Economic and Social Committee and the Committee of the Regions: Developing the European Dimension of Sport' (Report No COM(2011) 12 final, 18 January 2011) para 4.1, 10, http://eur-lex.europa.eu/LexUriServ/LexUriServ.do?uri=COM:2011:0012:FIN:en:PDF.

[11] Kees van Kersbergen and Frans van Waarden, 'Governance' as a Bridge between Disciplines: Cross-Disciplinary Inspiration Regarding Shifts in Governance and Problems of Governability, Accountability and Legitimacy' (2004) 43 *European Journal of Political Research* 143, 147.

[12] Committee on the Financial Aspects of Corporate Governance, 'The Financial Aspects of Corporate Governance' (Report, 1 December 1992) [2.5], www.icaew.com/~/media/corporate/files/library/subjects/corporate%20governance/financial%20aspects%20of%20corporate%20governance.ashx.

[13] Deborah Healey, 'Governance in Sport: Outside the Box' (2012) 23(3) *Economic and Labour Relations Review* 39, 39.

In adopting this interpretation of governance, a range of questions arises. What is good governance in sports? Are the principles of good governance in sport similar to those that apply generally to corporate governance or do the principles of good corporate governance need to be adjusted and adapted to the sport sector? From the perspective of contingency theory,[14] these questions may be answered by noting that there is not one best design for an institution's governance. Context and actors need to be taken into account when designing the governance of an organisation.[15] Despite this, broad generalisations about governance may still be made in the sport sector and corporate governance may be adapted to suit the needs of these organisations, as all entities are dependent on systems that have to be carefully managed to balance the internal needs and external demands that an organisation may face.

Doping remains the primary threat to sport.[16] Cheating to win through doping has led to extensive and varying legislative, education, testing and research responses from sport and governments alike for more than 50 years. However, these reforms have been ineffective as recent evidence highlights that long-term, systematic and extensive doping has continued to thrive, with the World Anti-Doping Agency (WADA) failing to make a change in the '[d]eeply [r]ooted [c]ulture of [c]heating' in sport.[17] These disturbing findings were the result of an investigation conducted by the Independent Commission (IC) at the behest of WADA in December 2014. The IC was tasked with investigating the following allegations made against Russian athletics. There seems to have been:

> [N]ot only complete compliance failures, but also institutional failures to deal with doping or suspected doping in a timely manner. Some of those institutions had both operational and monitoring responsibilities pursuant to the Code. They include, for purposes of this [IC] Report, the All-Russian Athletics Federation (ARAF), the Russian Anti-Doping Agency (RUSADA), the International Association of Athletics Federations (IAAF) and WADA itself.[18]

Governments, Olympic committees and sport federations seek to benefit from the success of their athletes, whether directly through increased sponsorships, broadcasting, memberships and other financial support, or through a sense of shared national success, assertions of superiority, and projected business confidence. In a system where the 'fox is put in charge of guarding the hen house',[19] the foxes

[14] Gareth Morgan, *Images of Organization* (London, Sage Publications, 1997).

[15] Paul R Lawrence and Jay W Lorsch, *Organization and Environment: Managing Differentiation and Integration* (Homewood, IL, Richard D Irwin, 1969) 185–86.

[16] Ethics Commission, 'Sports Movement Agrees on Unified Strategy to Tackle Irregular Betting', *Olympics.org* (24 June 2010) www.olympic.org/news/sports-movement-agrees-on-unified-strategy-to-tackle-irregular-betting/92584.

[17] Independent Commission, 'The Independent Commission Report #1' (Final Report, 9 November 2015) 10, www.wada-ama.org/en/resources/world-anti-doping-program/independent-commission-report-1.

[18] ibid 275.

[19] Former US President Harry S Truman is credited with stating that 'You don't set a fox to watch the chickens, just because he has a lot of experience in the hen house': see, eg, Robert H Ferrell, *Harry S Truman: A Life* (Columbia, MO, University of Missouri Press, 1996) 392.

that profit from maximising sporting achievements could be tempted to subvert their oversight role and instead use unfair means to maximise these profits. In the case of Russian athletics, both the vertical level of oversight through the ARAF, RUSADA and the Moscow WADA-accredited laboratory failed to fulfil their obligations, as did the horizontal oversight role of the IAAF and WADA, leading to the 'perfect storm' environment for what may end up being hundreds of athletes and complicit officials doping over 'many years'.[20]

Unless strong compliance and governance systems are both established and then enforced by all parties entrusted with oversight roles, the 'foxes' will continue to encourage and perhaps mandate the cheating practices in the 'hen house'. The 'hen house' analogy can be seen as sport industry generally, and the elite athlete programmes particularly. Therefore, this chapter explores the governance structures and composition mechanisms that have been used to reduce the risk of doping in sport. As the international anti-doping watchdog, this chapter focuses on WADA's own governance system. WADA is a hybrid public-private entity and good governance is crucial for its existence as governance plays a key role in maintaining WADA's reputation and image, as well as confidence in the sport sector. Through the World Anti-Doping Program, including the World Anti-Doping Code (hereinafter the Code)[21] and the International Convention against Doping in Sport 2005 (hereinafter the UNESCO Convention),[22] WADA can use either mandatory requirements or otherwise include in its guidelines proposals to enhance the governance of anti-doping organisations. Accordingly, this chapter first considers the birth of WADA and the role it plays in the sport sector, and then focuses on the governance of WADA in order to provide recommendations on how to enhance this organisation's internal accountability processes.

WADA

WADA was created in 1999 and plays a key role in ensuring the consistency of anti-doping policies and regulation around the world.[23] In order to fully appreciate the types of accountability required of WADA, it is important to understand the circumstances giving rise to its establishment and the means by which its success is measured.

[20] Independent Commission (n 17) 23. The second IC report will be released in 2016.

[21] Unless otherwise specified, the 2015 version of the Code is referred to throughout this chapter.

[22] Opened for signature 19 October 2015, 2419 UNTS 43649 (entered into force 1 February 2007).

[23] Dag Vidar Hanstad, Andy Smith and Ivan Waddington, 'The Establishment of the World Anti-Doping Agency: A Study of the Management of Organizational Change and Unplanned Outcomes' (2008) 43 *International Review for the Sociology of Sport* 227.

The Birth of WADA: Why and How?

The Legitimacy of the IOC in Doubt

WADA's birth was the direct result of a crisis in the legitimacy of the IOC due to the failure of the organisation to curb the doping culture within Olympic sport.

The IOC may be perceived as the 'leader of international sporting regulation'.[24] However, a number of high-profile and well-televised sport scandals[25]—most embarrassing for the IOC being Ben Johnson's failed drug test following his world record in the men's 100-metre athletics final at the 1988 Seoul Olympic Games[26] and culminating in what has been termed the 1998 French cycling 'Tour de Doping'[27]—challenged the legitimacy of the organisation.[28] The IOC's credibility on matters of integrity was further called into question when details relating to the IOC awarding the rights to host the 2002 Olympic Winter Games to Salt Lake City led to widespread condemnation. In exchange for their votes, IOC members were found to have been variously bribed through the provision of medical care for relatives, workplace internships or scholarships at major universities for their children, expensive guns and majorly reduced land deals.[29]

The passive approach taken by the IOC when faced with persistent doping problems highlighted that its value system no longer reflected the values and expectations of the wider community.[30] The IOC's ineffectiveness led national governments to assert their ownership of the doping problem. The international sport sector viewed such involvement as a hijacking of the powers and rights of the civic sports bodies.[31] However, the intervention of the police in the 1998 Tour de France illustrated that governing sport bodies were not properly monitoring the use of performance-enhancing drugs.[32] This weakened the social contract that

[24] Christopher S Groleau, 'Weird Science: A Look at the World Anti-Doping Agency's Questionable Testing Methods and the Need for Change to Protect International Athletes' (2009) 13 *Quinnipiac Health Law Journal* 85, 86.

[25] Christopher McKenzie, 'The Use of Criminal Justice Mechanisms to Combat Doping in Sport' (2007) *Bond University Sports Law e-Journal*, http://epublications.bond.edu.au/cgi/viewcontent.cgi?article=1003&context=slej.

[26] Charlie Francis and Jeff Coplon, *Speed Trap: Inside the Biggest Scandal in Olympic History* (New York, St Martin's Press, 1991); Canada, Commission of Inquiry into the Use of Drugs and Banned Practices Intended to Increase Athletic Performance, *Report* (1990) xviii; John Hoberman, 'A Pharmacy on Wheels—The Tour de France Doping Scandal' on Meso-RX Steroids (15 November 1998) https://thinksteroids.com/articles/festina-tour-de-france-doping-scandal.

[27] See, eg, 'About Us' TourDeDoping.com (15 July 2015) http://tourdedoping.com/about.php.

[28] Hanstad, Smith and Waddington (n 23) 229–31; Vanessa McDermott, *The War on Drugs in Sport: Moral Panics and Organizational Legitimacy*. (New York, Routledge, 2015) V57.

[29] Bill Mallon, 'The Olympic Bribery Scandal', *Journal Of Olympic History*, May 2000, http://library.la84.org/SportsLibrary/JOH/JOHv8n2/johv8n2f.pdf.

[30] See generally Craig Deegan, 'The Legitimacy Effect of Social and Environmental Disclosures—A Theoretical Foundation' (2002) 15 *Accounting, Auditing and Accountability Journal* 282, 293.

[31] John J MacAloon, 'Steroids and the State: Dubin, Melodrama and the Accomplishment of Innocence' (1990) 2(2) *Public Culture* 41, 50.

[32] Hanstad, Smith and Waddington (n 23) 230.

existed at that time between the states and sporting organisations. The IOC, for instance, was heavily criticised for 'a lack of internal democracy, accountability and honesty',[33] and its position as the 'leader of international sporting regulation' was at stake.

In an effort to restore its image, the IOC brought together representatives of governments, intergovernmental and non-governmental organisations, international sports federations (IFs), National Olympic Committees (NOCs) and many elite athletes for the First World Conference on Doping in Sport in 1999.[34] Such a move was reactive and was aimed at counteracting the threat to the legitimacy of the organisation.[35] For example, the IOC controlled the conference agenda, while the IOC's president chaired the conference and had the discretion to invite who would speak at the conference. However, although the first two hours of the conference glorified the role of the IOC, the organisation underestimated the threat to its legitimacy.[36] From Elias' figurational perspective of the situation, one may say that the existing interdependency between players in a particular field results in the application of different game models:[37] a united opposition would have a greater chance in defeating a stronger player than a fractured opposition.[38] In sport, the IOC may be viewed as the strongest player in the field and may defeat people who criticise it if this is done in an uncoordinated way; the IOC could deal with each country that criticises its performance separately and consequently can maintain its dominant position in the arena of doping regulation.

However, the IOC failed to note the formation of a coalition of countries that opposed its mandate; this coalition meant that the IOC was no longer facing individual players. The conference provided a vehicle for this coalition to put forward its criticism of the organisation. This meant that the IOC was now playing simultaneously against several other players. Even though, individually, the countries were weaker opponents, the fact that they had a united purpose severely weakened the IOC's position. The unified and harmonious criticism they directed towards the organisation meant that the IOC ultimately had to bow to the pressure on it to support the establishment of an independent international new anti-doping watchdog: WADA.[39] It was the only way for the IOC to retain its legitimacy.

[33] Ivan Waddington and Andy Smith, *An Introduction to Drugs in Sport: Addicted to Winning* (Abingdon, Routledge, 2009) 190.

[34] ibid 187.

[35] Vanessa McDermott, *The War on Drugs in Sport: Moral Panics and Organizational Legitimacy.* (New York, Routledge, 2015) V57.

[36] Hanstad, Smith and Waddington (n 23) 237–38.

[37] Norbert Elias, *What is Sociology?* (Stephen Mennell and Grace Morrissey (trans), New York, Columbia University Press, 1978) (translation of *Was ist Soziologie?* (1970)) 81–84.

[38] See Ben Avison, 'IOC President Bach Ripostes to SportAccord President Vizer', *Host City* (20 April 2015) www.hostcity.com/event-management-news/ioc-president-bach-ripostes-sportaccord-president-vizer.

[39] Hanstad, Smith and Waddington (n 23) 243.

The Establishment of WADA

WADA was registered as a Swiss private law foundation in November 1999.[40] WADA's President, Sir Craig Reedie, has noted that the organisation 'has evolved into a global leader tasked with harmonizing, coordinating and promoting an effective fight against doping in sport'.[41] However, doubt remains regarding whether WADA has truly achieved such leadership.[42]

Partly to avoid any perception of control and influence by the IOC, its headquarters moved from Lausanne, Switzerland, where the IOC and many international sport federations are based, to Montreal, Canada. To ensure greater geopolitical representation and reach, WADA also operates out of its regional offices in Cape Town, South Africa; Tokyo, Japan; Montevideo, Uruguay; and Lausanne.[43]

WADA is equally funded by the sport movement and the governments of the world, and accordingly considers itself to be a hybrid public-private entity.[44] While the IOC and WADA may share a 'common moral vision for sport and society',[45] the hybrid nature of WADA means there is not one player in control of the organisation and this is said to entrench the independence of the organisation. Instead, an intertwining network of stakeholders is created. However, this also means that WADA's role is more opaque to individual stakeholders as they do not have the ability to directly control the organisation.[46] Further, disagreements between the stakeholders and WADA create difficulties in the management of the organisation, causing WADA to shift its focus from the anti-doping regulatory regime to solving the stakeholders' struggles and disagreements.[47] All these considerations highlight the importance of governance in WADA, where 'accounting for and appealing to multiple political and public interests is a core part of WADA's mission'.[48]

Additionally, while WADA is accountable to a range of stakeholders that have different agendas, half of its budget comes from the sport movement that has a united objective: ensuring the independence of sport. The sport movement once again becomes the stronger player between the different stakeholders. This raises the possibility of WADA being captured. Simply put, capture is the process through which regulated entities end up manipulating the regulators that are supposed to

[40] WADA, Constitutive Instrument of Foundation of the World Anti-Doping Agency (4 July 2014).

[41] Craig Reddie, 'President's Welcome Message' (2015) www.wada-ama.org/en/who-we-are/presidents-welcome-message.

[42] This position will be discussed later on in this chapter; see Independent Commission (n 17) 10.

[43] WADA, 'Regional Offices' (2015) www.wada-ama.org/en/contact-us/regional-offices.

[44] WADA, 'Annual Report 2013', 32, https://wada-main-prod.s3.amazonaws.com/resources/files/wada-2013-annual-report-en.pdf.

[45] Kathryn Henne, 'WADA, the Promises of Law and the Landscapes of Antidoping Regulation' (2010) 33 *Political and Legal Anthropology Review* 306, 312.

[46] Elias (n 37) 88.

[47] Ulrik Wagner, 'The World Anti-Doping Agency: Constructing a Hybrid Organisation in Permanent Stress (Dis)Order?' (2009) 1 *International Journal of Sport Policy and Politics* 183, 196.

[48] Henne (n 45) 311.

control and monitor them.[49] Therefore, there is a risk that WADA's decisions may be influenced by the needs and the desire of the sport movement, and, consequently, it will fail to detect instances of doping such as those that took place in the case of Russian athletics. This means that the foxes rather than an independent watchdog supervise the hens.

The Code and its Limits

WADA implemented the Code, a key document founding an international anti-doping policy. It aims to harmonise the different anti-doping regimes of various nations and various sports.[50]

Tensions between the Stakeholders Regarding the Terms of the Code

The Code aims to achieve a balance between three systems:

— sport: Part 1 of the Code specifically deals with doping control, including banned substances, testing, investigation and sanctions;
— politics: Part 3 of the Code outlines the responsibility of the states and Part 4 outlines the way in which the law of each country is to complement this process; and
— science and education: Part 2 of the Code highlights key principles regarding science and education initiatives which WADA supports.[51]

These three systems can sometimes be at odds with each other and a loss of confidence in one system may negatively impact the support of the different stakeholders to the Code. Such losses of confidence are a blow to WADA's authority and legitimacy, particularly as WADA is dependent on its members to harmonise the anti-doping regime and to monitor anti-doping in sport.

The history of the adoption of the Code highlights this tension. There were two opposing positions at that time: support for the Code by governments, and less support from some sporting organisations. The Code was drafted over several years, beginning in 2001. In 2003, the first version of the Code was finalised and this document was tabled at The Second World Conference on Doping in Sport. At the conference, the Copenhagen Declaration on Anti-Doping and Sport[52] was

[49] For more on capture, see, eg, Paul Sabatier, 'Social Movements and Regulatory Agencies: Toward a More Adequate—and Less Pessimistic—Theory of "Clientele Capture"' (1975) 6 *Policy Sciences* 301; Michael E Levine and Jennifer L Forrence, 'Regulatory Capture, Public Interest, and the Public Agenda: Toward a Synthesis' (1990) 6 *Journal of Law, Economics & Organization* 167.

[50] Barrie Houlihan, 'Civil Rights, Doping Control and the World Anti-Doping Code' (2004) 7 *Sport in Society* 420, 425.

[51] Wagner (n 47) 195.

[52] Paul Marriott-Lloyd, 'International Convention against Doping in Sport' (UNESCO Doc No SHS/2010/PI/H/2, 2010) 3, http://unesdoc.unesco.org/images/0018/001884/188405e.pdf: 'While a large number of sporting organisations signed the Code and ensure its global application through a

adopted. The Declaration was an official contract between the IOC and different governments. It allowed these governments to declare their recognition and support for WADA, accept the Code and endorse a process which would lead to the UNESCO Convention. The Convention itself stated that 'to coordinate the implementation … State Parties commit themselves to the principles of the Code'.[53] To achieve state support, a range of measures are adopted, including 'legislation, regulation, policies or administrative practices' by the signatories to the Convention.[54] The UNESCO Convention was the most successful international convention in the history of United Nations Educational, Scientific and Cultural Organization (UNESCO) in terms of the speed of its development and entry into force.[55] It came into effect in 2007.[56]

However, some sporting organisations such as FIFA, and athletes generally, resisted the adoption of certain parts of the original Code, especially the introduction of a general two-year ban on athletes involved in doping for a first violation and a lifetime ban if there is a second violation by the same athlete. This resulted in the amendment of the Code in 2009, which led to the removal of the lifetime ban.[57] The 2003 and 2009 versions of the Code both highlight the difficulty in harmonising sanctions in the sporting arena as it is argued that different sports should attract different considerations when a ban is being considered.[58]

This history reflects the challenges that WADA faces in finding a balance between competing interests. Further, WADA's stakeholders range from large politically and financially powerful sports and nations to those that have very small populations or membership bases and challenges to their basic humanitarian needs. Among the Code signatories,[59] there are vastly different cultures, attitudes and approaches to issues such as nationalism and patriotism on one side, and corruption, fraud, nepotism, cronyism and bribery on the other, which directly impact

series of cascading relationships, it is not legally binding for governments. In fact, governments cannot be direct parties to the Code because of its legal status and that of WADA under whose authority it was elaborated. The Code is a non-governmental document that operates in the realm of private or contractual law and WADA, despite equal governmental involvement in its funding and management, was established as a private foundation.'

[53] UNESCO Convention, opened for signature 19 October 2015, 2419 UNTS 43649 (entered into force 1 February 2007) art 4.

[54] ibid art 5.

[55] UNESCO, International Convention against Doping in Sport (2015) www.unesco.org/new/en/social-and-human-sciences/themes/anti-doping/international-convention-against-doping-in-sport.

[56] Marriott-Lloyd (n 52) 1–3: 'The Convention was developed after extensive drafting and consultation meetings involving representatives from over 95 countries. It was the product of three meetings of an experts group and three intergovernmental meetings between 2004 and 2005. Further, the *Fourth International Conference of Ministers and Senior Officials Responsible for Physical Education and Sport* (MINEPS IV) considered the draft Convention and helped to resolve a number of outstanding issues.'

[57] Wagner (n 47) 196.

[58] WADA, World Anti-Doping Code (March 2003) 1, art 10.2 (comment); WADA, World Anti-Doping Code (1 January 2009) 11, art 10.2 (comment).

[59] WADA, 'Code Signatories' (2015) www.wada-ama.org/en/what-we-do/the-code/code-signatories.

on WADA's work targeting cheating in sport.[60] These issues reflect the tensions within the philosophy and ethics of elite sport: sport promotes positive attributes of excellence, joy and health, while encouraging negative traits such as cheating, superiority and bribery.

As Schneider observed, the challenges faced by WADA are:

> [E]normous. The agreements required to harmonize the practices of myriad International Federations and National Government testing programs are very complex. There we [sic] still overlapping jurisdictions, and the consequent turf battles with the IOC Medical Commission. Finally, and most importantly, there is the task of building a genuine relationship of trust with athletes.[61]

Weak Deterrence and No Governance

In its current version, the Code seems to have reached a new position regarding deterrence. It appears to have struck a compromise between the different stakeholders to raise the ban on athletes who are involved in doping from two to four years.[62] A similar ban will also apply if an athlete fails to provide a sample for doping control to the relevant authority.[63] The Code further creates an 'aggravated doping' offence for those found to be directly involved or covering up doping violations: these parties are subjected to more severe sanctions than the athletes who test positive for doping.[64] For instance, stakeholders can be declared Code non-compliant in order to motivate them to enhance integrity in sport.[65] WADA may impose internal measures against Code-non-compliant stakeholders such as forfeiture of representation on WADA's committees.[66] In addition, for a laboratory to maintain its accreditation, its National Anti-Doping Organisation and/or NOC must be declared Code compliant by WADA.[67]

Further, the Code states that certain stakeholders from the international sport movement have jurisdiction to impose consequences on those who are declared

[60] See, eg, Transparency International, 'Corruption, Perception Index 2014' (2015) www.transparency.org/cpi2014.

[61] Angela J Schneider, 'Olympic Reform, Are We There Yet?' (Paper presented at *Bridging Three Centuries: Fifth International Symposium for Olympic Research*, International Centre for Olympic Studies, University of Western Ontario, Canada, September 2000) 225, 230, http://library.la84.org/SportsLibrary/ISOR/ISOR2000zb.pdf.

[62] WADA, World Anti-Doping Code (1 January 2015) art 10.2.

[63] ibid art 10.3. This regime would apply together with any other sanctions that may be imposed as a result of anti-doping regulation regimes that exist in different countries that are signatories to the Code. Each of the anti-doping rule violations (ADRVs) attracted the same two-year ban under previous versions of the Code, unless no fault or no significant fault was established, or the substance is a specified substance. That is, a refusal to provide a sample is treated the same as testing positive.

[64] WADA, World Anti-Doping Code (1 January 2015) art 10.3.3 (comment).

[65] ibid art 23.5.4.

[66] ibid art 23.6.

[67] WADA, World Anti-Doping Code: International Standard for Laboratories (January 2015) art 4.4.

non-compliant by WADA's Foundation Board. For example, the IOC has mandated that only Code-compliant sports can be part of the Olympic programme.[68] On 18 November 2015, WADA declared six countries Code non-compliant.[69] A further seven countries have been put on the watchlist and have been given until 18 March 2016 to become fully compliant with the Code.[70]

But even with such serious consequences, the deterrence regime has its limits. Assuming that all athletes are rational maximisers of their own welfare, it may be said that the disqualification regime has a low deterrence impact, even though disqualification has serious punitive effects, such as the loss of a person's livelihood and reputation.[71] The same may be said of being declared Code non-compliant. After weighing up the costs against the benefits of doping, a rational actor might reach the conclusion that doping was not likely to lead to any action by WADA given the low likelihood of conduct being exposed due to the dominant cheating culture in professional sport.[72] A rational actor may therefore choose the action that maximises his or her personal advantage even though that action may breach the regulation.[73] For example, the most recent scandal regarding Russian athletics was not exposed by WADA, but by a German television channel documentary *Top Secret Doping: How Russia Makes its Winners*.[74] In fact, this scandal highlights a failure in monitoring and supervision on multiple levels.

Arguably, the Code should not only consider sanctions that may be imposed on different parties and ways to investigate non-compliance with the Code, but should also put in place measures to enhance WADA's monitoring and supervision powers, and focus on introducing changes to modify the cheating culture that is prevalent in sport. This may be achieved through a focus on governance, as governance may lead to a change in the sport culture. Despite this reality, the Code itself outlines the key responsibilities of its members and does not address issues of governance in any way. Further, compliance with the Code has been interpreted very narrowly by WADA.[75] The primary focus of WADA has been ensuring that signatories conduct Code-compliant anti-doping education and testing programmes. Therefore, aside from reflecting basic natural justice requirements

[68] WADA, World Anti-Doping Code (1 January 2015) art 23.6.

[69] WADA, 'Code Compliance' (2015) www.wada-ama.org/en/what-we-do/the-code/code-compliance. *cf* Independent Commission (n 17) 273.

[70] WADA, 'Code Compliance' (2015) www.wada-ama.org/en/what-we-do/the-code/code-compliance.

[71] Marina Nehme, 'Latest Changes to the Banning Order Regime: Were the Amendments Really Needed?' (2013) 31 *Company and Securities Law Journal* 341.

[72] Gennaro F Vito, Jeffrey A Maahs and Ronald M Holmes, *Criminology: Theory, Research and Policy* 2nd edn (Burlington, MA, Jones & Bartlett Publishers, 2007) 15.

[73] Milton Friedman, *Essays in Positive Economics* (Chicago, University of Chicago Press, 1953) 15, 22, 31.

[74] *Geheimsache Doping—Wie Russland seine Sieger macht* (*Top-Secret Doping: How Russia Makes its Winners*) (directed by Hajo Seppelt, ARD Sportchau, 2014). Note that WADA was also not responsible for exposing confessed dopers, Lance Armstrong, Marion Jones or the BALCO case (see www.usada.org)

[75] McKenzie (n 25).

stipulating the independence of hearing bodies,[76] the Code does not generally set good governance standards. It only refers to the importance of the independence of sporting organisations, and promotes values of integrity and accountability without further guidance.[77] The lack of consideration of governance issues arguably means that the Code is more reactive than proactive in dealing with doping violation.

The Governance of WADA

Prior to the establishment of WADA, doubt surrounded the efficiency of the IOC Medical Committee, the committee created by the IOC body to deal with anti-doping issues. For example, following the doping scandal in cross-country skiing during the 2001 Nordic World Ski Championship in Lahti, Finland, the International Ski Federation (FIS) perceived the IOC Medical Committee as a passive organisation in its fight and reporting on doping. Some members of the FIS Council even suspected that the Medical Committee was not reporting findings of doping to the relevant sporting organisation.[78]

Trust and legitimacy are key to ensuring the success of WADA. Without it, WADA will arguably cease to exist and state intervention in areas of sport anti-doping will be more pronounced. The UK provides an example of a system where courts take active steps to monitor the sport sector.[79] Justice Richards noted that the court's role is to:

> [E]nsure that the primary decision-maker has operated within lawful limits … In each case the essential concern should be with the lawfulness of the decision taken [by sporting organisations and others]: whether the procedure was fair, whether there was any error of law, whether any exercise of judgement or discretion fell within the limits open to the decision-maker, and so forth.[80]

Accordingly, to avoid further intrusion of the state in sporting affairs, WADA's governance must be beyond reproach. Schneider noted that a 'credible anti-doping agency needs to be independent, open to public scrutiny, and accountable'.[81] Therefore, the next section will consider WADA's structure and accountability mechanisms.

[76] WADA, World Anti-Doping Code (1 January 2015) art 3.
[77] ibid art 20.5.
[78] Dag Vidar Hanstad, 'Drug Scandal and Organizational Change within the International Ski Federation: A Figurational Approach' (2008) 8 *European Sport Management Quarterly* 379, 388.
[79] James Lewis, 'The Insider Track: Interview with Mark Beloff' [2015] (February/March) *IBA Global Insight* 12, 15.
[80] *Bradley v Jockey Club* [2004] EWHC 2164 (QB) [37]; *Chambers v British Olympic Association* [2008] EWHC 2028 (QB) [33] (Mackay J).
[81] Schneider (n 62) 228.

Requirements under Swiss Law and WADA's Initiatives to Enhance Accountability

As noted previously, WADA is registered as a foundation under Swiss law. Consequently, it must comply with Swiss regulation. However, the Swiss Civil Code, which regulates foundations, is not prescriptive in its regulation towards these organisations. It only sets minimum external accountability requirements that have to be met.[82] The regime is thus appealing for organisations which do not particularly want to be monitored or controlled, providing them with a favourable environment free of economic and political state intervention.[83] The flexibility of the Swiss regime has attracted many global sporting organisations to Switzerland.[84] These organisations view the Swiss approach to regulation in a positive light as most consider that accountability is irrelevant to them because they are cultural, global, not-for-profit and an 'apolitical guardian' of the sport sector.[85]

Swiss Law: A Light-Handed Regulatory Approach

Accountability is a cornerstone of good governance in both public and private organisations. It minimises the abuse and misuse of public authority, provides assurance that the organisational resources are being used properly in accordance with the values of the organisation, and encourages as well as promotes learning to continuously improve the management of the entity.[86]

Bovens narrowly defines accountability by noting that it is 'a relationship between an actor and a forum, in which the actor has an obligation to explain and to justify his or her conduct, the forum can pose questions and pose judgement, and the actor may face consequences'.[87] However, the Swiss Civil Code provides an even narrower definition of accountability. This definition is focused on the Anglo-Norman origin of the term: accounting and bookkeeping.[88] In fact, the legislation requires WADA to maintain its business ledgers[89] and to appoint external auditors.[90] After conducting an audit, the external auditors are required to provide

[82] Schweizerisches Zivilgesetzbuch (Swiss Civil Code) (Switzerland) 10 December 1907, SR 210, ch 3.

[83] John Forster and Nigel KL Pope, *The Political Economy of Global Sporting Organisations* (Abingdon, Routledge, 2004) 9.

[84] ibid 112.

[85] ibid 9.

[86] Peter Aucoin and Ralf Heintzman, 'The Dialectics of an Accountability for Performance in Public Management Reform' (2000) 66 *International Review of Administrative Sciences* 45, 45.

[87] Mark Bovens, 'Analysing and Assessing Accountability: A Conceptual Framework' (2007) 13 *European Law Journal* 447, 467.

[88] ibid 448.

[89] Schweizerisches Zivilgesetzbuch (Swiss Civil Code) (Switzerland) 10 December 1907, SR 210, art 83a.

[90] ibid art 83b(1).

a copy of their report and all important communications with the foundation to the supervisory authority.[91] Organisations registered as foundations then have the freedom to decide on other aspects of accountability, including the structure of the organisation and issues of transparency.

Towards More Accountability

WADA has adopted the minimal requirements regarding accountability set out by the Swiss legislation. However, more needs to be done to enhance the governance of the organisation.

The Threat to the Social Contract

A social contract arguably exists between Switzerland and the sporting entities registered under its laws from the minimal regulation imposed under Swiss law on sport organisations. De Coubertin noted that: 'Olympism will find in the independent and proud atmosphere that we breathe in Lausanne, the guarantee of freedom that it needs to progress.'[92] However, the existence of this social contract is currently frayed and is in danger of unravelling quickly due to the sports scandals that have occurred over the last two decades. The reality is that suspicion and threat now exists between sporting organisations and the Swiss Government, with sporting organisations expressing a desire to leave Switzerland if the Swiss authorities do not comply with their wishes.[93]

Despite these threats, the recent FIFA bribery scandal has once again turned attention to the social contract, as the Swiss Parliament made changes to its money laundering law, allowing additional scrutiny of bank accounts held by sporting bodies and their leaders.[94] In view of this development, the ongoing behaviour of sports entities and their leaders will impact on any future Swiss reforms in the area of governance and accountability.[95] Until this happens, however, Swiss law is confined to the minimal level of accountability for foundations such as WADA. Nevertheless, the threat of more regulation does provide an incentive for these organisations to enhance their governance systems and accountability.

[91] ibid art 83c.

[92] Michaël Mrkonjic, 'The Swiss Regulatory Framework and International Sports Organisations' in Alm (n 3) 128, citing 'History: The Origines [sic] of the Olympic Capital' (2015) City of Lausanne, www.lausanne.ch/en/thematiques/sport-et-olympisme/lausanne-capitale-olympique/cio/historique-origines-capitale-olympique.html.

[93] ibid.

[94] Bundesgesetz über die Bekämpfung der Geldwäscherei und der Terrorismusfinanzierung im Finanzsektor (Federal Act on Combating Money Laundering and Terrorist Financing in the Financial Sector) (Switzerland) 10 October 1997, SR 955.0.

[95] Graham Dunbar, 'Swiss Law Allows More Scrutiny of Sports Finances', *Yahoo! Sports* (12 December 2014) http://sports.yahoo.com/news/swiss-law-allows-more-scrutiny-sports-finances-133729114--sow.html.

Transparency and Communication

Key elements of good governance and accountability are transparency and communication.[96] These elements are not only relevant for sport governance but also corporate governance where a range of corporate scandals are linked to a lack or limited disclosure of the full picture.[97] Transparency can relate to organisational structures as well as reporting requirements.[98] WADA, since its inception, has taken some positive steps towards creating a transparent system in both these areas.

For example, WADA publishes on its website information regarding its vision, its strategic plans, its organisational structure, the minutes of its meetings, the Code and implementation policies, as well as information regarding doping investigations. The majority of information regarding WADA, including its financial situation, is published every year in its annual report.[99] Following the recommendation of the European Union Expert Group on Good Governance,[100] WADA's website is also used for consultation with its stakeholders and members of the public. However, many of submissions and outcomes relating to its previous consultations, such as the submissions leading to the amendments to the Code, are no longer available to the public. This may be viewed as a form of censorship and may cast doubt on the image of transparency and independence that WADA is attempting to send to the public.

More Accountability Needed

All the above initiatives enhance organisational and reporting transparency, and set an example for other entities to achieve such transparency in a cost-effective way through the use of its website. However, WADA's system is not perfect and could be improved. For example, there is minimal information regarding the role of the Foundation Board and the Executive Committee on its website. This is in contrast with one of the key principles of good governance: organisations should clearly state the role of individual directors, their responsibility, organisational expertise and role of the board in general.[101] None of this information

[96] Ngaire Woods, 'Good Governance in International Organizations' (1999) 5 *Global Governance* 39, 44.

[97] Organisation for Economic Co-operation and Development, G20/OECD Principles of Corporate Governance (30 November 2015) 42.

[98] Jean-Loup Chappelet and Michaeël Mrkonjic, 'Basic Indicators for Better Governance in International Sport (BIBGIS): An Assessment Tool for International Sport Governing Bodies' (Working Paper 1/2013, Institut de Hautes Etudes en Administration Publique, January 2013) 9.

[99] WADA, 'Annual Reports' (2015) www.wada-ama.org/en/resources/finance/annual-report.

[100] European Union Expert Group on Good Governance, 'EU Work Plan for Sport 2011–2014: Deliverable 2—Principles of Good Governance in Sport' (September 2013) 13, http://ec.europa.eu/sport/library/policy_documents/xg-gg-201307-dlvrbl2-sept2013.pdf.

[101] Australian Institute of Company Directors, 'Principle 1: Roles and Responsibilities' (2015) www.companydirectors.com.au/director-resource-centre/not-for-profit/good-governance-principles-and-guidance-for-nfp-organisations/principle-1-roles-and-responsibilities.

is available to the public in the case of WADA: while a list of members of the Foundation Board and the Executive Committee is disclosed, the organisation does not publish on its website biographical information and contact information regarding its management; it merely provides the name, position and country of the people on its boards and committees. The provision of additional information in that regard is beneficial to highlight the skills of each of the members of the board. It is time for WADA to adopt a more transparent approach regarding its management structure by disclosing the role of its board and management, and how their performance is monitored and evaluated. All this may start changing the attitude and perception that stakeholders have towards this organisation; they currently perceive WADA as a service provider rather than a regulator.[102] Additionally, more information could be provided regarding the percentages paid by each government. Currently, the information released relates to percentages paid by continents to WADA.[103]

Further, even more concerning is the fact that the organisation has not always been forthcoming with its findings. For instance, as FIFA did recently regarding its bribery scandal,[104] WADA initially withheld from publication research that questioned the regime's effectiveness. The research highlighted that although two per cent of samples taken from athletes yield positive tests for doping, the rate of doping is much higher than this figure.[105] This again highlights the failure of WADA to tackle the doping problem. The 2015 IC's report regarding its investigation of Russian athletics also reflects this reality: it found that WADA had failed to ensure the compliance of countries with the Code.[106]

Setting Clear Guidelines to Enhance Governance

Currently, WADA has issued model rules for different stakeholders in order to assist them in drafting anti-doping rules that are in line with the Code.[107] This is a good attempt to harmonise the regulation of anti-doping. However, these guidelines do not seriously consider any governance issues that may arise from

[102] In the sense that WADA has been established to supervise the integrity of the sports industry insofar as it relates to doping. See also the Independent Commission (n 17) 31.

[103] WADA, 'Funding by Governments' (2015) www.wada-ama.org/en/funding-by-governments.

[104] Lewis (n 80) 15.

[105] Kathryn Henne, 'Reforming Global Sport: Hybridity and the Challenges of Pursuing Transparency' (2015) 37 *Law & Policy* 324, 338. 'Recent survey findings (which WADA initially withheld from publication) indicate much higher rates of doping (29–45 percent), at least among track-and-field athletes (Rohan 2013).' Noting that in 2011 WADA's David Howman was acknowledged that the figure was in the viscinity of 10%, (www.telegraph.co.uk/sport/olympics/london-2012/8710041/London-2012-Olympics-one-in-10-athletes-are-drugs-cheats-says-anti-doping-chief-executive.html) and by 2015 had increased this estimation to 20% (www.heraldscotland.com/sport/13195498.WADA_S_tougher_sentencing_for_drugs_cheats_must_be_applauded_but_it_is_not_enough_simply_to_increase_the_length_of_bans/)

[106] Independent Commission (n 17) 45–48.

[107] WADA, 'Model Rules, Guidelines and Protocols' (2015) www.wada-ama.org/en/model-rules-guidelines-and-protocols.

doping. Further, even though the IC Report on the Russian athletics scandal found that there is a failure at different levels to ensure the integrity of sport, most of its recommendations were reactive rather than proactive in nature. The Report failed to provide solutions to tackle the cheating culture within sport.

Instead, the recommendations were focused towards the smaller rather than the bigger issue attached to the cheating culture. The focus was once again on deterrence and imposing sanctions on offending parties. A few of the recommendations required the contravening organisations to introduce compliance programmes to ensure they become Code compliant. But even then, the recommendations did not provide guidance on how to achieve this and how a compliance programme might lead to a change in the culture of the offending organisation. Further, very little guidance is available in the IC Report on how compliance will be monitored. The only recommendation in the Report regarding this is that WADA's compliance working group should report to the Foundation Board on the way in which WADA protects clean athletes.[108] There is an assumption that this will monitor the conduct of the contraveners and the steps they have put in place to enhance their organisations. For these reasons, it is important for WADA to issue additional guidelines that specifically target the issue of governance. However, before doing that, WADA's own management structure needs to be revamped to enhance its own accountability mechanisms.

The Structure of WADA and the Need for Improvement

The Swiss Civil Code leaves it up to an individual foundation to determine the structure of its governing bodies and constituent document, called its constitutive instrument.[109] The structure of WADA reflects the fact that the organisation is equally funded by governments and the sport movement.[110] For instance, equal numbers of government and Olympic Movement representatives sit on WADA's Foundation Board, its decision-making body, and are responsible for policy-making through WADA's Executive Committee. This structure raises concerns about the internal accountability of the organisation as there are no guidelines regarding the way in which different committees are held accountable.

This is especially problematic as WADA does not have shareholders. In a company, shareholders have an interest in monitoring their investments and, as a group, management owes them a range of duties. In the case of WADA, each stakeholder has a different agenda. The stakeholders may hold management accountable through the appointment of their representatives on the Foundation Board and, more drastically, by withdrawing their funding and support of

108 Independent Commission (n 17) 47, 322 (recommendation 12).

109 Schweizerisches Zivilgesetzbuch (Swiss Civil Code) (Switzerland) 10 December 1907, SR 210, art 83.

110 WADA (n 40) art 7.

WADA. The latter option would mean that WADA would cease to exist, having lost its legitimacy. WADA's management does not owe any particular duty to its stakeholders.

The issue of WADA's internal accountability to date has attracted little attention from commentators and academics. While there is emphasis on the need for the independence of bodies having anti-doping responsibility from organisations responsible for developing elite-level talent, reflected in the wording of the Code, the so-called 'fox guarding the hen house' argument, there has been very little academic analysis or discussion on the compositional or structural governance of WADA, or other organisations responsible for implementing the WADA programme at the highest levels.[111] A look at WADA's structure raises a range of concerns due to the lack of transparency surrounding the way in which the organisation is run. However, a quick review of WADA's decision-making structure also suggests that the organisation may wish to adopt a two-tier board approach to enhance its governance.

The Management Structure of WADA

The Foundation Board is WADA's supreme decision-making body. It can have up to 40 members, up to 18 of whom are appointed by the Olympic Movement, with another maximum of 18 appointed by public authorities, and four appointed jointly by these two groups.[112] To ensure equal partnership between its funders, the position of the chairman alternates between the Olympic Movement and public authorities. Similarly, the position of vice chairman is nominated by a public authority if the chairman is a person nominated by the Olympic Movement and vice versa.[113] WADA is currently composed of a 38-member Foundation Board, which is comprised equally of IOC appointees[114] and appointees from national governments or other public authorities. The Foundation Board is required to meet at least once a year.[115]

The Foundation Board delegates the actual management and running of the agency to the 12-member Executive Committee.[116] The Executive Committee is WADA's ultimate policy-making body. It is also composed equally of representatives from the Olympic Movement and governments.

[111] The focus tends to be on WADA's compliance regime. See, eg, Arnout Geeraert, 'Compliance Systems: WADA' in Alm (n 3); Barrie Houlihan, 'Managing Compliance in International Anti-doping Policy: The World Anti-Doping Code' (2002) 2 *European Sport Management Quarterly* 188. See also Nicolas Eber, 'Credibility and Independence of the World Anti-Doping Agency: A Barro-Gordon-Type Approach to Antidoping Policy' (2002) 3 *Journal of Sports Economics* 90; Lorenzo Casini, 'Global Hybrid Public-Private Bodies: The World Anti-Doping Agency (WADA)' (2009) 6 *International Organizations Law Review* 421.

[112] WADA (n 40) art 6.

[113] ibid art 7.

[114] WADA, 'Governance' (2015) www.wada-ama.org/en/who-we-are/governance.

[115] WADA (n 40) art 8.

[116] WADA, 'Executive Committee' (2015) www.wada-ama.org/en/who-we-are/governance/executive-committee.

WADA has a number of other committees, such as the Athlete, Education, Finance & Administration, and Health, Medical & Research Committees, which have an advisory function and provide guidance to WADA's programmes. However, an issue regarding transparency appears once again at this level as vacancies in WADA's senior management positions, with the exception of the Director-General position, are not advertised and are shrouded in secrecy. Today, such an approach is often regarded as representative of cronyism, which reflects badly on WADA's culture.[117] A more transparent mechanism is needed to make the process of appointment more in line with normal business practices and to ensure the diversity of its board.

Should WADA Implement a Two-Tier Board Approach?

Unlike corporations which have shareholders or members, WADA does not have members because it is a foundation. Accordingly, as noted previously, the organisation has one less decision-making organ than a company, which negatively impacts on the accountability of the organisation. However, even though this is a fundamental difference with the structure of a corporation, parallels can still be drawn regarding the management of these two entities, as both have a hierarchical scheme of control.

In a corporation, the board of directors provides a 'hierarchical scheme of accountability'[118] and plays a key role in ensuring good corporate governance in an organisation.[119] The board of directors is the 'directing mind and will of the corporation'.[120] Within WADA, the Foundation Board and the Executive Committee are the decision-makers, and are in charge of the management of the organisation. The WADA hierarchy is built around a chain of command where a range of responsibilities are delegated to committees, as noted previously.

The Foundation Board and the Executive Committee are the two organs in charge of management of the organisation. This structure is reminiscent of the German two-tier system of corporate governance, which is based on the establishment of two boards in a corporation: the Management Board is in charge of the management of the company and the Supervisory Board, constituted from a range of stakeholders, is responsible for monitoring the Management Board.[121] As with WADA's Foundation Board electing its Executive Committee,[122]

[117] A culture which has in large part been inherited from the IOC, IFs and other international organisations.

[118] Mark Bovens, *The Quest for Responsibility: Accountability and Citizenship in Complex Organisations* (Cambridge, Cambridge University Press, 1998) 74.

[119] Healey (n 13) 48.

[120] *HL Bolton (Engineering) Co Ltd v TJ Graham & Sons Ltd* [1957] 1 QB 159, 172 (Lord Denning); *Lennards' Carrying Co Ltd v Asiatic Petroleum Co Ltd* [1915] AC 705, 713 (Lord Haldane).

[121] See Thomas J Schoenbaum and Joachim Lieser, 'Reform of the Structure of the American Corporation: The "Two-Tier" Board Model' (1973) 62 *Kentucky Law Journal* 91.

[122] WADA (n 40) art 10.

the Supervisory Board elects the Management Board.[123] The two-tier system provides a relationship between management and stakeholders as the stakeholders, through their representatives on the Board, have a say in the strategic management of the organisation.[124] In the case of WADA, this model may be viewed positively as the organisation is dependent on its stakeholders to survive and consequently involving them in the management creates an additional accountability layer for the organisation, and enhances its legitimacy.

The two-tier structure has a number of advantages, including the fact that the smaller size of the Executive Committee and the Management Board, when respectively compared with the current potential size of the Foundation Board or the Supervisory Board, allows quick and efficient decision-making.[125] The division of monitoring and management between two boards also provides a better accountability regime than in instances where the monitoring and management functions are intertwined.

However, the two-tier model also has its detractors. One of the criticisms directed at the two-tier model is the fact that the Supervisory Board is ineffective. It is argued that the Supervisory Board cannot fulfil its role of monitoring and overseeing the Management Board if it only meets a few times a year. This same criticism can be applied to the current Foundation Board, which only needs to meet once a year.[126] A review of the meeting minutes for the Foundation Board highlights that since its inception, the Board has only met a maximum of twice a year.[127] This is of concern as the Foundation Board is not only charged with monitoring its Executive Committee but also of supervising compliance of the stakeholders with the Code. Further, the main source of information about the Foundation Board comes from its Executive Committee, which also limits its monitoring power. For these reasons, the Foundation Board must take a proactive role in monitoring its Executive Committee to ensure that it holds the Executive Committee members accountable for their conduct.

Managing Conflict

Additionally, the involvement of stakeholders in the strategic management of WADA may raise conflict of interest issues, as the stakeholders have different interests and for this reason their views of the organisation may vary.[128] A dominant sport movement, for instance, may push towards more self-regulation

123 Schoenbaum and Lieser (n 122) 96.

124 Jean J du Plessis et al, *German Corporate Governance in International and European Context* (New York, Springer, 2007) 11.

125 Grant T Savage et al, 'Governance of Integrated Delivery Systems/Networks: A Stakeholder Approach' (1997) 22(1) *Health Care Management Review* 7.

126 WADA (n 40) art 8.

127 WADA, 'Foundation Board Meeting Minutes' (2015) www.wada-ama.org/en/resources/governance/foundation-board-meeting-minutes.

128 See, eg, John Carver, 'Remaking Governance: The Creator of "Policy Governance" Challenges School Boards to Change' (2000) 187(3) *American School Board Journal* 26.

of the sporting system, which may diminish the role that WADA plays in the area of doping. Systems need to be established within WADA to manage any conflict that may affect the decision-making process and the ability of the Foundation Board to independently monitor the Executive Committee.[129] Accordingly, WADA must develop guidelines on the management of conflict of interests within the Board. Anything less may result in the capture of its Foundation Board. It is crucial to consider such risk as the Board is already influenced by WADA's stakeholders who are behind the appointment of its members.

The Composition of the Foundation Board and the Executive Committee

WADA plays a key role in ensuring the integrity of sport in the context of anti-doping. Appropriate governance and transparency are paramount to ensure the legitimacy of the organisation, particularly during this period of heightened scrutiny of sporting organisations and their managers.[130] Stakeholders need to be sure that WADA has the necessary resources and skills to achieve its aims and objectives. Despite this, as noted previously, the appointment of the members of its Foundation Board and Executive Committee is an opaque process.

Further, there is no documented requirement that the nominees satisfy a 'good character' test, or even to make a declaration of their commitment to anti-doping.[131] This is surprising, as it is key for the management of WADA to be beyond reproach in its stance against doping, as a scandal associated with members of its management would negatively impact the reputation of the organisation. Additionally, WADA provides no information about the values, skills, experience or attitudes of any of the Foundation Board members. WADA's website and publications do not provide bibliographies of the members of its Foundation Board or members of its Executive Committee. A range of empirical evidence suggests that the strategic capabilities of a sport organisation are linked to the ability of its management.[132] In view of this, it is important for WADA to seriously consider the expectations of the global community. If we consider the Foundation Board as a supervisory board, then best practice would require the Board to be composed of people who have the knowledge, ability and experience needed

[129] Heribert Hirte, 'The Two-Tier System in Italy and Germany' (Paper presented at the Seminar on Comparative Corporate Law, University of Hamburg, 2007) 12.

[130] Lesley Ferkins and David Shilbury, 'Developing Board Strategic Capabilities in Sport Organisations: The National-Regional Governing Relationship' (2010) 13 *Sport Management Review* 235, 235.

[131] Such as required by the Australian Olympic Committee for all Australian Olympic team members and national sport organisations, including board members, staff and athletes: Australian Olympic Committee, 'Anti-doping' (2015) http://corporate.olympics.com.au/athlete-hub/anti-doping; Australian Olympic Committee, 'Notes: Statutory Declaration Regarding Anti-Doping Matters' (February 2013) http://corporate.olympics.com.au/files/dmfile/AOCStatutoryDeclaration-NotesSampleStatDec.pdf.

[132] See, eg, David Shilbury, 'Examining Board Member Roles, Functions and Influence: A Study of Victorian Sporting Organisations' (2001) 2 *International Journal of Sport Management* 253.

to properly complete the task.[133] Transparency is paramount to ensure that the Foundation Board members fulfil these requirements.

Further, one key difference between the two-tier model and the current WADA structure is that the WADA structure does not really have an independent Foundation Board. One of the key strengths of the two-tier model is that the Supervisory Board has an independent view separate from the perspective of management, since there is no overlap between the two boards.[134] In the case of WADA, the majority of the 12 members of the Executive Committee are chosen from the Foundation Board members.[135] To implement a proper monitoring system and enhance the accountability of WADA, the Executive Committee should be formed from a majority of independent managers.

The process of appointing managers should be transparent and based on specific advertised criteria. It is crucial to remember that corporations, which are recognised as good corporate citizens, transparently demonstrate how board members are selected and how their performance is assessed.[136] This is especially important as there appears to be a great cultural shift in modern corporations and society's expectation regarding the management of organisations in general. Sleeping directorship is no longer the standard. It is time for the governance of sporting organisations to match standard business practices: managers in WADA should not have an expectation that they can maintain their position of power and influence without accountability.[137]

Lastly, gender diversity is also now considered an important feature of director selection. Diversity of board members may improve the performance of an organisation as it provides the board with new insights and perspectives.[138] There is mounting evidence in the corporate world[139] and in anti-corruption research[140]

[133] Weil, Gotshal & Manges LLP, 'International Comparison of Selected Corporate Governance Guidelines and Codes of Best Practice: United States, United Kingdom, France, Germany, OECD, Netherlands, Norway, Switzerland, Australia, Brazil, China, Hong Kong, India, Russia, United Arab Emirates' (June 2014) 25, www.lexology.com/library/detail.aspx?g=701a6be8-9c7f-462b-a571-52eb60e0b1f5.

[134] Gregory F Maassen and Frans AJ van den Bosch, 'On the Supposed Independence of Two-Tier Boards: Formal Structure and Reality in the Netherlands' (1999) 7 *Corporate Governance: An International Review* 31, 34; Carsten Jungmann, 'The Effectiveness of Corporate Governance in One-Tier and Two-Tier Board Systems—Evidence from the UK and Germany' (2006) 3 *European Company and Financial Law Review* 426, 452.

[135] WADA (n 40) art 11.

[136] See, eg, BHP Billiton Ltd, 'Annual Report 2011' (21 September 2011) 117–24, www.bhpbilliton.com/~/media/bhp/documents/investors/reports/2011/bhpbillitonannualreport2011.pdf?la=en.

[137] See also Saul Fridman, 'Conflict of Interest, Accountability and Corporate Governance: The Case of the IOC and SOCOG' (1999) 22 *University of New South Wales Law Journal* 781.

[138] Julie I Siciliano, 'The Relationship of Board Member Diversity to Organizational Performance' (1996) 15 *Journal of Business Ethics* 1313.

[139] See, eg, Nicholas van der Walt and Coral Ingley, 'Board Dynamics and the Influence of Professional Background, Gender and Ethnic Diversity of Directors' (2003) 11 *Corporate Governance: An International Review* 218; Winifried Ruigrok, Simon Peck and Sabrina Tacheva, 'National and Gender Diversity on Swiss Corporate Boards' (2007) 15 *Corporate Governance: An International Review* 546.

[140] Transparency International, 'Gender, Equality and Corruption: What are the Linkages?' (Policy Brief No 01/2014, 7 April 2014).

that leadership diversity, and gender equity in particular, is a risk management tool that could positively impact on integrity outcomes in sport.[141] Requiring sporting organisations to report on the gender split of their executive, senior managers and coaching, high-performance and officiating staff also promotes transparency.[142]

However, social psychological studies on hiring practices consistently demonstrate that applicants that come from a similar background to the hirer have a greater chance of receiving a job offer than a person coming from a different background.[143] Given the international position of WADA, this bias is less likely and the board is culturally diverse. However, gender diversity on its Foundation Board and its Executive Committee should be improved as currently the membership of women on these organs is respectively 21 per cent and 25 per cent. Currently, some stakeholders promote gender equality in their appointments, while others are male-dominated. Given the relationship between WADA and UNESCO, and that the key priorities for UNESCO include gender equity,[144] it is important for WADA to reflect these priorities. At a practical level, not only because women make up half the world's population, but it is important because women make up a significant proportion of sports participants. It could, for example, include requirements that governments and members of the Olympic Movement nominate equal numbers of female and male representatives to the Foundation Board.

In summary, the appointment of members to the Foundation Board and the Executive Committee should be transparent, and should meet the governance expectations of the international community. Vacant positions for the Foundation Board and the Executive Committee should be advertised using specific selection criteria. The appointment of board members should be made on merit

[141] The change in Swiss corporate law recommending greater intervention and accountability is timely, given the FIFA scandal. The draft consultation period ended on 15 March 2015. For an overview of the initiatives proposed in the preliminary draft, see, eg, Daniel Daeniker and Daniel Hasler, 'Corporate Law Reform in Switzerland' *Who's Who Legal* (June 2015) http://whoswholegal.com/news/features/article/32338/corporate-law-reform-switzerland. The initiatives included encouraging gender diversity: 'The Draft proposal aims to encourage gender diversity in larger listed companies. After a five-year transition period, each company is expected to have both genders represented by at least 30 per cent in its board and in its executive management. If a company fails to reach these targets, it shall explain the reasons for the underrepresentation and the efforts it takes to further promote gender diversity ("comply or explain").'

[142] At the international level, more detail can be found at Sydney Scorecard, 'Global Scoreboard' (2015) www.sydneyscoreboard.com/global-scoreboard. See also Women on Boards, 'Gender Balance in Global Sport Report: Females Second Class Citizens in Sport' (Press Release, 7 July 2014) www.womenonboards.org.au/news/2014/media140707-sportreport.htm. In Australia, the Australian Sports Commission has a 40 per cent 'quota' for women on national sport organisation boards: Australian Sports Commission, 'Mandatory Sports Governance Principles' (June 2015) 5 [2.6].

[143] James D Westphal and Edward J Zajac, 'Who Shall Govern? CEO/Board Power, Demographic Similarity, and New Director Selection' (1995) 40 *Administrative Science Quarterly* 60, 61.

[144] UNESCO, UNESCO Priority Gender Equality Action Plan—2014–2021 (UNESCO Doc No 37 C/$-C/5-Compl. 1, 2014) http://unesdoc.unesco.org/images/0022/002272/227222e.pdf.

against objective criteria and with due regard to the benefits of cultural and gender diversity.[145]

Duration of Appointment

While Foundation Board members are appointed for three years,[146] the appointment of the members of the Executive Committee is for renewable one-year periods.[147] This coincides with the recommended duration of the Swiss Code of Best Practice for Corporate Governance.[148] This limited duration may be viewed as a way to strengthen the accountability of the Executive Committee to the Foundation Board.[149] However, arguably this is too short a period for a range of reasons.

First, a short term weakens the position of the Executive Committee and may lead to short-term planning rather than a focus on long-term plans for WADA.[150] Second, board continuity may be affected, as the Executive Committee may be at the mercy of political appointments by stakeholders at the level of the Foundation Board. Valuable knowledge may be lost if there is a quick turnover of the Executive Committee.[151] Due to the political motivations that different representatives in the Foundation Board may have, WADA should ensure that any conflict of interest is managed and does not impact on the appointment of the Executive Committee, which, as noted previously, should be independent from the Foundation Board. One way to manage the conflict is for the Executive Committee to have a longer term than one year.

In summary, the Executive Committee should be able to put forward and execute its strategies without its members having to justify their appointment on an annual basis. Currently, the Foundation Board annually reviews the performance of the Executive Committee through its monitoring and supervisory role. A renewable term of three years (or four to reflect the Olympic cycles) up to a maximum of ten years would be desirable as it would allow the Foundation Board

145 See, eg, Financial Reporting Council, 'The UK Corporate Governance Code' (September 2014) 11, www.frc.org.uk/Our-Work/Publications/Corporate-Governance/UK-Corporate-Governance-Code-2014.pdf.

146 WADA (n 40) art 7.

147 ibid art 11.

148 Economiesuisse, Swiss Code of Best Practice for Corporate Governance (28 August 2014) art 13. This is also a mandatory rule for listed corporations in Switzerland: Verordnung gegen uëbermaëssige Verguëtungen bei boërsenkotierten Aktiengesellschaften (Ordinance against Excessive Compensation in Listed Corporations) (Switzerland)J e generally dation' (2002) 15(rganizational Change and Unplanned Outcomes 20 November 2013, SR 221.331, art 3.

149 Economiesuisse, Swiss Code of Best Practice for Corporate Governance (28 August 2014) art 13.

150 Australian Institute of Company Directors, 'Principle 2: Board Composition' (2015) www.companydirectors.com.au/director-resource-centre/not-for-profit/good-governance-principles-and-guidance-for-nfp-organisations/principle-2-board-composition.

151 Urs P Gnos, Jan H Hoffman and Alexander Nikitine, 'Adjustments to the Swiss Corporate Governance Framework' (2014) 36 *Comparative Law Yearbook of International Business* 136, 147.

to develop a medium-term succession plan that allows for a balance of experience and skills in the members of WADA's executive committee.[152]

Conclusion

To ensure its integrity, WADA should not only promote the importance of independence and accountability of sporting organisations but should also lead by example by implementing key changes that ensure that these two values are embedded within the organisation. One way to achieve this is for WADA to focus on its internal governance.

Key areas for enhancement are the transparency of communication and the board structure. Clear communication of WADA's structure and reporting is crucial in view of the fact that WADA is accountable to a range of stakeholders that come from different backgrounds and have different agendas. Transparency and reporting on WADA's operations would solidify the legitimacy of the organisation and highlight the steps that it is taking to improve its governance.

Additionally, changing its management structure is important to improve the organisation's internal governance. Adopting the two-tier board approach, which is common in countries such as Germany, China and Japan, may positively affect its management, as it will create an independent board that can monitor the conduct of the executive management of the organisation. The proposed changes in this chapter may not stop the fox from guarding the hen house, but may lead to a change in the culture of WADA and result in a more proactive regulation of doping. It is a move towards the right direction.

[152] Australian Sports Commission, 'Mandatory Sports Governance Principles', (June 2015), 4 [2.1], www.ausport.gov.au/__data/assets/pdf_file/0003/531165/Mandatory_Sports_Governance_Principles_FINAL.pdf; Mauritius Institute of Directors, 'Best Practice Guidelines for the Appointment of Directors' (Directions Forum, 2012) 6 [2.6.2], www.afcgn.org/wp-content/uploads/2013/11/Best-Practice-Guidelines-for-the-Appointment-of-Directors.pdf.

12

The Chimera of Compliance with the World Anti-Doping Code

JASON MAZANOV*

Introduction

Drug control in sport uses a legalistic prohibitionist policy framework to restrict the use of certain substances in an attempt to regulate the rapidly evolving field of sports science. Significant effort has been expended to develop an elegant legal framework that integrates the World Anti-Doping Code (hereinafter the Code), international treaties, domestic laws and contractual arrangements to regulate both international institutions and individual athletes in a clear and consistent manner. Reports from the World Anti-Doping Agency (WADA) suggest Code compliance has advanced considerably since the introduction of the Code in 2003 and continues to improve. While there appears to be breadth in Code compliance (eg, the volume of Code-compliant countries), this compliance appears to lack depth. Evidence from the social sciences suggests this is because the elegant legal framework is inaccessible to athletes and support personnel[1] and, as a result, is perceived as irrelevant to the practice of sport. This creates a chimera of compliance,[2] where the headline success of international compliance exists next to the failure to achieve compliance with the Code where it matters—the daily practice of athletes and support personnel. In this chapter, the experience of athletes and support

* Senior Lecturer, School of Business, UNSW-Canberra.

[1] The Code defines athlete support personnel as 'any coach, trainer, manager, agent, team staff, official, medical, paramedical personnel, parent or any other Person working with, treating or assisting an Athlete participating in or preparing for sports Competition': WADA, World Anti-Doping Code (1 January 2015) app 1 (definition of 'athlete support personnel').

[2] The chimera is a fire-breathing monster from Greek mythology with the body, head and tail coming from three different animals, usually a lion, goat and snake. In the contemporary context, the chimera is used to describe something that implausibly or unexpectedly combines parts.

personnel are used to inform recommendations for where changes to the legal framework might be made to promote compliance with the Code in the daily practice of sport.

From International Regulation to Individual Compliance

WADA was founded in response to a series of drug crises for sport[3] and a rather bruising international convention in Lausanne that saw sovereign governments regain some control over sport from the growing International Olympic Committee (IOC) hegemony.[4] WADA was therefore funded and controlled equally by both governments and the IOC to develop and administer the Code with the overarching goal of international policy harmonisation.[5] That is, athletes and support personnel should experience anti-doping in the same way independent of sport, event or location, which should then promote the ideology of drug-free sport in a consistent manner.

Having achieved agreement between the controlling interests of WADA, which should be acknowledged as a significant feat in itself, the Code establishes the foundation of practice by setting out the mechanisms governing the system and the responsibilities of governments, sports, athletes and support personnel to protect the integrity of anti-doping. The Code places significant emphasis on institutional responsibility to enact anti-doping. Institutional compliance is achieved through both international treaties, such as the International Convention against Doping in Sport,[6] and the IOC hegemony.[7] There have been some attempts to resist the coercive IOC hegemony by both Olympic and non-Olympic sports, but these have usually resulted in capitulation once political pressure was applied either by governments[8] or by threats to exclude the sport from lucrative Olympic events.[9]

[3] Barrie Houlihan, *Dying to Win: Doping in Sport and the Development of Anti-doping Policy* 2nd edn (Strasbourg, Council of Europe Publishing, 2002), 149–81; Thomas M Hunt, *Drug Games: The International Olympic Committee and the Politics of Doping* (Austin, University of Texas Press, 2011).

[4] Dag Vidar Hanstad, Andy Smith and Ivy Waddington, 'The Establishment of the World Anti-Doping Agency' (2008) 43 *International Review for the Sociology of Sport* 227, 228–49.

[5] Houlihan (n 3) 183–203.

[6] Opened for signature 19 October 2005, 2419 UNTS 43649 (entered into force 1 February 2007).

[7] The IOC relies on nations wanting to be represented at or host an Olympic event, and so Code compliance is part of the criteria for accessing Olympic events. Equally, for a sport to be considered as an Olympic event, it must be Code compliant: see WADA, 'Questions & Answers: World Anti-Doping Code' (2015) www.wada-ama.org/en/questions-answers/world-anti-doping-code.

[8] The Australian Government threatened to take away public funding from the Australian Football League unless it became Code compliant: Bob Stewart, Daryl Adair and Aaron Smith, 'Drivers of Illicit Drug Use Regulation in Australian Sport' (2011) 14 *Sport Management Review* 237, 239–40.

[9] The Federation International de Football Association resisted external drug control, but eventually signed up to the Code: Ulrick Wagner, 'Towards the Construction of the World Anti-Doping Agency: Analyzing the Approaches of FIFA and the IAAF to Doping in Sport' (2011) 11 *European Sport Management Quarterly* 445, 446.

Anti-doping at the national level occurs in terms of government and sporting administrative apparatus. The government interest in anti-doping is evident in legislation created to provide the architecture that enables National Anti-Doping Organisations (NADOs) to support the Code. For example, the Australian Sports Anti-Doping Authority Act 2006 (Cth) sets out the requirements for the National Anti-Doping Scheme, administrative arrangements (eg, Chief Executive Officer powers, requirements to comply with the international treaties, and civil penalties for those who fail to give evidence to investigations when asked) which are yet to be tested on appeal. Anti-doping manifests itself in sport through compliance with the rules set out by the international federation in the domestic context. For example, the national sports governing body requires member organisations (eg, state or provincial organisations) to be Code compliant, which in turn require member clubs to be compliant.

Institutional Code compliance is typically translated into individual Code compliance using membership agreements. Membership agreements form the foundation of the relationship between an athlete (eg, an agreement to abide by the rules of the sport) and a sport (eg, the limit of responsibilities of event organisers), with membership a condition of being able to access events related to that sport (eg, training or competition). Code compliance is addressed in the context of other aspects of membership, such as indemnity and insurance. Membership in junior sport requires parents to sign on behalf of children, which means that both parent and child have agreed to be Code compliant.

The situation is much the same in professional sport, except that employment contracts are used in place of membership agreements, noting that athletes have also usually agreed to Code compliance in order to qualify as a member of various sporting organisations. The difference is that Code compliance is a non-negotiable condition of employment. For example, scholarship holders to the Australian Institute of Sport lose their place, stipend and access to facilities, including accommodation, for an anti-doping rule violation (ADRV).[10]

While this brief summary can only hint at the regulatory elegance of the anti-doping system in striving to achieve international policy harmonisation, it is clear the legal framework has been designed to enable compliance with the Code to occur on the same basis, no matter where sport is practised. In theory, the only deviation from the Code should occur as a function of variation in domestic laws leading to different approaches being used to achieve the desired effects, eg, accounting for variation in privacy laws. Code compliance should therefore be relatively straightforward for both institutions and individuals. The 2013 WADA Annual Report provides a compelling account of activities and investment that demonstrates the overwhelming commitment to anti-doping among the 176 Code-compliant countries, from institutional arrangements with Interpol and the World Customs Agency to attracting over 10,000 followers on Twitter.

[10] Australian Sports Commission, Anti-Doping Policy (1 January 2015) art 10.10; Australian Sports Commission, Anti-Doping Policy (1 March 2010) art 19.4.1.

The Practice of Compliance

Despite the regulatory elegance and apparent success of anti-doping on the international stage, the evidence suggests that Code compliance is difficult for both institutions and individuals. Institutional variation in policy implementation remains a feature of anti-doping across jurisdictions. For example, there is significant variation in practices associated with athletes making themselves available for drug testing.[11] This variation appears to be a function of a focus on breadth, eg, administration to maintain Code compliance status, rather than depth of compliance, eg, providing access to sport specific anti-doping education.[12]

The difference between breadth and depth of compliance has been demonstrated in the *Cycling Australia Review*.[13] The prosecution of Lance Armstrong led to a number of high-profile Australian cyclists admitting to doping, prompting the Australian Government to commission a review that demonstrated, among other things, the depth of Code compliance at Cycling Australia. At the surface level, Cycling Australia met the requirements for Code compliance with one part-time anti-doping manager responding to an organisation of 20,000 members and their events. The manager may well have spent most of his or her time responding to the paperwork required to maintain Code compliance (breadth) rather than administering measures to support Code compliance among athletes and support personnel (depth). For example, members of Cycling Australia had to rely on third-party resources for generic anti-doping education, eg, Australian Sports Anti-Doping Authority online education, rather than education specific to doping across the cycling disciplines in Australia, eg, endurance mountain bike events. The Cycling Australia experience indicates that the regulatory elegance of anti-doping may have difficulty translating breadth of compliance into depth of compliance.

The difficulties translating breadth into depth are explored using evidence from the social sciences that examine how drugs in sport are experienced by the individuals required to be compliant with the Code. For example, at some point, the management team at Cycling Australia made an explicit decision to pursue breadth rather than depth in terms of Code compliance. Developing an insight into such a decision may inform how the legal framework underpinning anti-doping may need to evolve to enable depth. This insight is developed by exploring how athletes and support personnel[14] experience Code compliance in terms of

[11] Dag Vidar Hanstad, Eivind Å Skille and Signmund Loland, 'Harmonization of Anti-doping Work: Myth of Reality?' (2010) 13 *Sport in Society* 418, 419, 421–22.

[12] Barrie Houlihan, 'Achieving Compliance in International Anti-doping Policy: An Analysis of the 2009 World Anti-Doping Code' (2014) 17 *Sport Management Review* 265, 266–76.

[13] James Wood, *Cycling Australia Review* (Report, Department of Regional Australia, Local Government, Arts and Sport, January 2013).

[14] The Cycling Australia management team are considered athlete support personnel under the Code.

their ability to understand what compliance means, and then how they implement anti-doping in their day-to-day sporting practice.

Understanding of and Compliance with the Code

The argument and evidence around the relationship between understanding and compliance is developed around three main themes. The first is drawn from the Code ensuring athletes and support personnel are knowledgeable about their obligations under the Code,[15] negating ignorance as an excuse for non-compliance. The second is drawn from the requirement that athletes adopt the values of the Code and that support personnel use their influence to promote anti-doping;[16] that is, attitudes towards the Code. The third relates to the experience of the Code among support personnel as the people recognised as having the most influence on athlete doping behaviour.[17] These three themes are drawn together to given an insight into how the legal framework around the Code is understood by individuals and then to inform how the legal framework may need to be adapted to promote depth of compliance.

Knowledge

While there seems to be no lack of education offered by anti-doping organisations,[18] the evidence indicates that there is a general lack of knowledge that brings into question the capacity of athletes and support personnel to comply with the Code. Elite, college and school-aged athletes demonstrate a lack of basic awareness about the Code,[19] although there are signs that the level of understanding among athletes is rising.[20] Notably, athletes who use performance-enhancing supplements have a better knowledge of the Code[21] and these athletes

[15] WADA, World Anti-Doping Code (1 January 2015) arts 21.1.1.1, 21.2.1.

[16] ibid art 21.2.3.

[17] Jason Mazanov et al, 'Australian Athlete Support Personnel Lived Experience of Anti-doping' (2015) 18 *Sport Management Review* 218.

[18] eg, UK Anti-Doping has expended significant resources developing publicly accessible online anti-doping education resources called 'The Learning Zone': UK Anti-Doping, 'Learning Zone' (2015) www.ukad.org.uk/learningzone.

[19] Susan Backhouse et al, 'International Literature Review: Attitudes, Behaviours, Knowledge and Education—Drugs in Sport: Past, Present and Future' (Report, Carnegie Research Institute, January 2007).

[20] Jaime Morente-Sánchez and Mikel Zabala, 'Doping in Sport: A Review of Elite Athletes' Attitudes, Beliefs and Knowledge' (2013) 43 *Sports Medicine* 395, 395.

[21] Jason Mazanov et al, 'Towards an Empirical Model of Performance Enhancing Supplement Use: A Pilot Study of High Performance UK Athletes' (2008) 11 *Journal of Science and Medicine in Sport* 185, 189.

are also more likely to dope,[22] with evidence emerging that athletes with the strongest understanding about the Code are also those most likely to dope.[23]

Athlete support personnel are no better informed than athletes. For example, a sample of 292 Australian support personnel were asked to respond to 35 statements drawn from across the Code by indicating whether they thought the statement was true or false.[24] The statements were drawn equally from seven categories: prohibited substances and methods; sample collection rules; ADRVs; athlete rights and responsibilities; nutritional supplements; the substance/method prohibition process; and support personnel rights and responsibilities. For example, respondents were asked to identify the veracity of statements like:

- 'caffeine is a substance on the prohibited list';
- 'ASADA is required to publish a list of safe supplements available on the market'; and
- 'it is the responsibility of athlete support personnel to be knowledgeable about the rules and policies set out in the Code'.

Notably, many support personnel and some peak organisations declined the opportunity to participate, claiming that anti-doping was irrelevant to their practice.[25] This created a bias in the sample that respondents were more likely to perceive anti-doping as an important part of practice and therefore have a greater knowledge of the Code. The results, corrected for the sample bias,[26] showed that respondents were able to correctly identify 63–79 per cent of the items. Conversely, support personnel were unable to identify 21–37 per cent of the basic elements of the Code. This result is consistent with reviews of international data that demonstrates similar gaps in the knowledge about the Code among sports physicians[27] and coaches.[28]

In terms of the administrators and managers that make the critical decisions around depth of compliance, administrators responding to the survey[29] identified 79 per cent of items correctly. They did best on identifying ADRVs (94 per cent) and worst at the obligations of support personnel (66 per cent). Noting that this is by no means a representative sample, both in terms of sample bias and the jobs of

[22] Fotios Papadopoulos et al, 'Doping Use among Tertiary Education Students in Six Developed Countries' (2006) 21 *European Journal of Epidemiology* 307, 310–12.

[23] Anna Loraschi et al, 'Dietary Supplement and Drug Use and Doping Knowledge and Attitudes in Italian Young Elite Cyclists' (2014) 24 *Clinical Journal of Sport Medicine* 238.

[24] Jason Mazanov et al, 'Athlete Support Personnel and Anti-Doping: Knowledge, Attitudes, and Ethical Stance' (2014) *Scandinavian Journal of Medicine and Sciences in Sports* 846.

[25] Despite being clearly identified as an athlete support person under the Code: see (n 1).

[26] One tailed 95 per cent confidence intervals were used to correct for the sample bias; see Mazanov et al (n 24).

[27] Susan Backhouse and Jim McKenna, 'Doping in Sport: A Review of Medical Practitioners' Knowledge, Attitudes and Beliefs' (2011) 22 *International Journal of Drug Policy* 198.

[28] Susan Backhouse and Jim McKenna, 'Reviewing Coaches' Knowledge, Attitudes and Beliefs Regarding Doping in Sport' (2012) 7 *International Journal of Sports Science and Coaching* 167.

[29] A total of 21 administrators responded to the survey.

sports managers, it does suggest that one of the reasons for the failure to translate from breadth to depth was because administrators understand, at best, two-thirds to three-quarters of the legal system. Unfortunately, there has been no research on the knowledge of anti-doping officials or sports scientists about their obligations in relation to Code compliance. Given the importance of these actors, one would hope they are knowledgeable of the Code, although the results from the other aspects of sport suggest that such hopes may be misplaced.

Attitudes

Athlete and support personnel attitudes to doping in sport are variable. According to survey evidence using standardised questionnaires, both the average athlete[30] and the average support person[31] tend to take a slightly negative attitude towards doping in sport. Given the breadth of sampling around athletes, this can be taken as indicative that there is a general disquiet around the role of doping in sport. However, methodological questions have been raised around whether athletes report a negative attitude because of socially desirable responding, such as any other response raising suspicions of doping that threatens the athlete's career.[32] The sample bias problem observed for athlete support personnel knowledge of the Code is repeated for attitudes, meaning that the data is representative of support personnel who are motivated to respond to surveys on anti-doping as they see it as a significant issue in their daily practice. Accounting for this bias means that the slightly negative attitude might change to be neutral or even slightly positive if a broader sample of support personnel were to be taken.[33] Standardised survey evidence suggests that attitudes to anti-doping are at best slightly negative, but are more likely to be closer towards neutral.

Sports organisations confronting a decision about whether to invest in achieving depth of compliance with the Code do so with attitudes ranging from mild concern to ambivalence. Given that sports organisations have to prioritise where to invest resources across a range of issues (eg, talent identification, development programmes and event management), Code compliance could simply be given a lower priority than other activities. In this sense, Cycling Australia's decision to achieve breadth rather than depth of compliance appears to be a rational one given the general attitude towards doping in sport among athletes and support personnel.

[30] Andrea Petróczi and Eugene Aidman, 'Measuring Explicit Attitude Toward Doping: Review of the Psychometric Properties of the Performance Enhancing Attitude Scale' (2008) 10 *Psychology of Sport and Exercise* 390.

[31] Mazanov et al (n 24) 851; Backhouse and McKenna (n 28) 173.

[32] Andrea Petróczi and Declan P Naughton, 'Impact of Multidisciplinary Research on Advancing Anti-doping Efforts' (2011) 3 *International Journal of Sport Policy and Politics* 235, 236–39.

[33] Mazanov et al (n 24) 852.

The Lived Experience

While research on knowledge and attitudes provides an insight into the outcomes of the breadth of compliance, it does little to explain how or why knowledge or attitudes are at these levels. As a result, survey researchers speculate as to why these results emerge. Rather than speculate, other researchers have asked athletes and support personnel about how they experience the Code, in order to develop insights into compliance among individuals in sport that explain how and why knowledge and attitudes are at the observed levels.

Athletes' Experience of the Code

In terms of knowledge, athletes reported that their understanding of the Code, and drugs in sport more generally, is derived from the media and online communities rather than official sources.[34] This emerged from a general distrust of official sources, with athletes more likely to turn to coaches or senior athletes for advice.[35] This is problematic given the evidence that the media and online communities repeat inaccurate information about the performance-enhancing and health consequences of doping,[36] and that coaches appear to be as knowledgeable as the athletes they are advising. The coaches' knowledge is discussed below.

Athletes from non-elite or junior sport appear to experience the Code in the manner in which it was intended. Non-elite and junior athletes typically describe doping in moral terms as threats to performance in terms of authenticity of performance and the level playing field, and health in terms of anxiety of potential unknown effects on longevity.[37] In particular, junior athletes take a particularly hard line against doping, calling for stronger institutional control measures, such as more restrictive out-of competition testing and harsher punishments.

Elite athletes appear to have a more nuanced understanding of the role of drugs in sport and the Code, where drugs are seen as a natural part of sport.[38] For example, drugs are seen as useful to temporarily enhance performance to break through career barriers (eg, scholarships that enable access to sophisticated sports science facilities) or prolong careers.[39] Athletes also cite the role of drugs as an

[34] V Lentillon-Kaestner and C Carstairs, 'Doping Use among Young Elite Cyclists: A Qualitative Psychosociological Approach' (2010) 20 *Scandinavian Journal of Medicine and Science in Sport* 336; Aaron CT Smith et al, 'Contextual Influences on Athlete Attitudes to Drugs in Sport' (2010) 13 *Sport Management Review* 181.

[35] Jason Mazanov and Twan Huybers, 'An Empirical Model of Athlete Decisions to Use Performance Enhancing Drugs: Qualitative Evidence' (2010) 2 *Qualitative Research in Sport and Exercise* 384.

[36] Bernat López, 'Creating Fear: The Social Construction of Human Growth Hormone as a Dangerous Doping Drug' (2013) 48 *International Review for the Sociology of Sport* 220.

[37] Andrew Bloodworth and Michael McNamee, 'Clean Olympians? Doping and Anti-doping: The Views of Talented Young British Athletes' (2010) 21 *International Journal of Drug Policy* 276.

[38] See Lentillon-Kaestner and Carstairs (n 34); Smith et al (n 34).

[39] Jason Mazanov, Twan Huybers and James Connor, 'Qualitative Evidence of a Primary Intervention Point for Elite Athlete Doping' (2011) 14 *Journal of Science and Medicine in Sport* 106, 108.

acceptable method for a range of activities in contemporary society and challenge why their role in sport has been made an exception for sport. Such arguments are consistent with work that demonstrates an increasing acceptance of healthy people using pharmaceutical substances to enhance some aspect of their lives, whether at work (eg, stimulants) or leisure (eg, mood-altering substances).[40] There is also a rejection of the Code for failing to protect and manage athlete health relative to the understanding that failure of performance is the single greatest threat to an athlete.[41]

This pattern of results suggests that attitudes towards doping evolve with experience in sport. One explanation for this can be framed as the 'natural history of drug use in sport'. Younger athletes are unlikely to see much value in using drugs as they are still maturing, which means they see performance improvements and overcome injuries relatively quickly without drugs. Drug use becomes far more functional[42] for older athletes who need to sustain performance[43] and require assistance overcoming injuries, both of which are greatly enhanced by both legitimate and illegitimate drug use. As a result, athlete attitudes towards the role of drugs fundamentally change over the course of their career. In terms of the observed athlete attitude from the survey data, the negative views of the large number of young athletes participating in sport are likely to be averaged out by the more permissive views of more experienced athletes, leading to the slightly negative attitude observed across samples.

Athlete Support Personnel

The only significant study of the lived experience of anti-doping among athlete support personnel[44] reports findings from a series of interviews about experiences implementing the anti-doping system. Consistent with the research on support personnel knowledge and attitudes,[45] support personnel had little experience with athletes who doped and saw the issue as largely irrelevant to their daily practice. While generally aware of the overarching principles of the Code (eg, sanctions and the prohibition of illicit drugs), they were generally unaware of how it worked in practice. For example, the interviewer had to explain the athlete whereabouts

[40] Claus Møldrup, Janine Morgall Traulsen and Anna Birna Almarsdóttir, 'Medically-Enhanced Normality: An Alternative Prescription to the Use of Medicines for Non-medical Purposes' (2003) 11 *International Journal of Pharmacy Practice* 243.

[41] Evdokia Pappa and Eileen Kennedy, '"It was My Thought … He Made it a Reality": Normalization and Responsibility in Athletes' Accounts of Performance Enhancing Drug Use' (2013) 48 *International Review for the Sociology of Sport* 277.

[42] Andrea Petróczi and Eugene Aidman, 'Psychological Drivers of Doping: The Life-Cycle Model of Performance Enhancement' (2008) 3 *Substance Abuse Treatment, Prevention and Policy*, http://link.springer.com/article/10.1186/1747-597X-3-7/fulltext.html.

[43] The effect of anabolic androgenic steroids on Major League Baseball pitchers appears to be sustaining their fastball speed throughout their career rather than making them pitch faster: Vittorio Addona and Jeremy Roth, 'Quantifying the Effect of Performance Enhancing Drug Use on Fastball Velocity in Major League Baseball' (2010) 6(2) *Journal of Quantitative Analysis in Sport.*

[44] See Mazanov et al (n 17).

[45] See Mazanov et al (n 24).

system[46] to several interviewees to elicit their opinions about out-of-competition drug testing. It seemed that anti-doping was perceived as being 'too difficult' among the competing priorities related to preparing athletes for competition. Support personnel assumed they would be able to work out what to do if anything happened through the information available via their professional networks.[47] Thus, the bias in the survey relating to support personnel knowledge and attitudes can be explained by the perceived lack of relevance of the Code to daily practice, and therefore give a corresponding low priority relative to other aspects of sporting practice.

Interviews with athlete support personnel suggest that the slightly negative views can be explained by a conflict between views on the different aspects of drug control for sport. On the one hand, they see the need for drug control in sport while being critical of the methods employed by the Code to achieve drug control. For example, support personnel prefer to give athletes a chance to reform their drug use behaviour rather than immediately report transgressions. The general negative view of doping is softened by the dislike for the methods used by the Code, leading to the slightly negative or neutral attitude.

The combination of an 'in-principle' understanding of the Code and being critical of how it was assumed to work saw support personnel take an intuitive approach, preferring to do what they felt was right. What was felt to be right generally drew on the primary discourses underpinning the anti-doping movement in terms of the warfare discourse integrating disparate health, ethical, legal, educational and political discourses,[48] emphasising health and morality—that is, cultural tropes around threats to the naturalness and authenticity of sporting performances. Support personnel demonstrated their intuitive approach when responding to questions about how they would respond if they found out a hypothetical athlete was doping. They looked to pass on responsibility for reporting or protect the athlete from the negative consequences of an ADRV. For example, if confronted with an athlete who doped, the interviewees preferred to refer the case to their manager or counsel the athlete in an attempt to dissuade further drug use. If the athlete was an adolescent, some interviewees preferred to defer to the young person's parents rather than see his or her career end by reporting to the

[46] The athlete whereabouts system is used to enable out-of-competition testing. In Australia, athletes in the registered testing pool are required to nominate, three months in advance, one hour of every day and a location where they will be available for unannounced drug testing, risking sanction if they are unavailable at the nominated time and place. Some commentators have observed that this level of violation of human rights (eg, autonomy, freedom of movement and right to self-determination) is reserved for registered sex offenders: Barrie Houlihan, 'Civil Rights, Doping Control and the World Anti-Doping Code' (2004) 7 *Sport in Society* 420, 421–33; Ivan Waddington 'Surveillance and Control in Sport: A Sociologist Looks at the WADA Whereabouts System' (2010) 2(3) *International Journal of Sport Policy and Politics* 255.

[47] Support personnel would seek information from managers or colleagues in the first instance about local (organisational) policies and NADOs as a second source.

[48] Ulrik Wagner and Kasper Pederson, 'The IOC and the Doping Issue—An Institutional Discursive Approach to Organizational Identity Construction' (2014) 17 *Sport Management Review* 160.

relevant NADO. From this point of view, support personnel appear to be trying to protect athletes from the harms arising from the Code as much as protecting them from the harms arising from substance misuse and abuse. These examples stand in contrast to the clear requirement to report or be potentially complicit in aiding or abetting an ADRV under Article 2.9 of the Code.

The reasons underlying the reluctance to report instances of doping were clarified by comments from health professionals—eg, physicians and psychologists—about the potential for reporting to undermine both their therapeutic relationship with clients and professional reputation in the community. This is known as the 'disclosure problem'.[49] For example, a sports psychologist may become aware of an ADRV in diagnosing anabolic-androgenic steroid dependence and may elect to prioritise athlete welfare in a manner consistent with the laws and code of conduct for their profession. This may result in an ADRV for being complicit in covering up an ADRV.[50] If an ADRV is recorded against the sports psychologist, Article 2.10 of the Code means that any athlete treated by or any support person working with the psychologist can also be sanctioned. If the psychologist chooses to be Code compliant, they risk losing the trust necessary to conduct therapeutic work and professional accreditation for disclosing information given in confidence. Without professional accreditation, the psychologist is unable to trade. It seems that support personnel who are health professionals risk harm no matter what they do and are probably right to prioritise their professional integrity over that of the Code.[51]

Experience of the Code and Compliance

Accounts of how the Code is experienced by athletes and support personnel suggest that the reason behind the level of knowledge and attitudes emerges from either ignorance or misinformation. Code compliance is given a low priority because it rarely occurs in practice or the consequences of compliance are onerous for the individual, such as taking responsibility for getting an athlete in trouble or implications for professional practice. It is clear that the frameworks around Code compliance create a complex set of practices that cause athletes and support personnel to adopt a strategy of deferring action until there is no other choice—eg, a drug scandal. This creates the reactionary crisis management approach that has characterised drug control in sport for much of its history.[52]

[49] M McNamee and N Phillips, 'Confidentiality, Disclosure and Doping in Sports Medicine' (2011) 45 *British Journal of Sports Medicine* 174, 175–77; Nenad Dikic et al, 'Sports Physicians, Ethics and Anti-doping Governance: Between Assistance and Negligence' (2013) 47 *British Journal of Sports Medicine* 701, 702–04.

[50] WADA, World Anti-Doping Code (1 January 2015) art 2.9.

[51] The definition of support personnel includes legal practitioners. Like the disclosure problem for health professionals, concerns have been raised about whether legal privilege holds in relation to the Code: Rule of Law Institute of Australia, Australian Sports Anti-Doping Authority Act (26 March 2013) www.ruleoflaw.org.au/australian-sports-anti-doping-authority-act.

[52] See Houlihan (n 3) 149–81; Wagner and Pederson (n 48); Hunt (n 3) x, 1–99.

Athletes, Support Personnel and Depth of Compliance

The evidence from the social sciences around knowledge, attitudes and experience of the Code suggests that the decisions taken by the management of Cycling Australia would be replicated across other sporting contexts. Individual decision-makers within a sporting organisation, whether administrators, coaches or athletes, make their decisions around compliance based on an incomplete, 'in-principle' understanding of the Code. There is broad support for some kind of drug control in sport, which is possibly the result of an incomplete understanding of the Code. At some point, each person eventually makes a decision to either follow the Code or substitute it for personal beliefs about how they feel drug control should be handled. These beliefs seem to focus on protecting athletes from the harms of drug misuse and abuse, and also on protecting athletes from the harms arising from the Code.

Drug Decisions

With a background into the attitudes, knowledge and experience of the Code, any attempt to transition from institutional to individual compliance needs a better insight into the decision to use drugs to achieve sporting outcomes. The psychology of athlete drug use has matured significantly, moving well beyond simplistic 'to win' characterisations. By comparison, the psychology of athlete support personnel in doping decisions is less well developed.

Athlete Drug Decisions

Early work on athlete decision-making focused on the motivating impact of winning, citing the seductive lure of celebrity and wealth as the primary drivers for doping. This simplistic description failed to account for the many reasons why athletes use drugs. Drugs have four main effects of interest to sport: (i) therapeutic use in response to illness; (ii) treatment and prevention of injuries; (iii) recreational and social use; and (iv) performance enhancement.[53] Athletes may look to drugs for any of these effects, independently of any desire to win. For example, athletes may turn to drugs to help transition from semi-professional to professional sport or to prolong their careers by preventing and managing injury.[54] Equally, winning to achieve celebrity and wealth is only useful when describing the rarefied atmosphere of high-profile professional sport rather than the

[53] David R Mottram (ed), *Drugs in Sport* 5th edn (Abingdon, Routledge, 2011) 16.
[54] See Mazanov, Huybers and Conner (n 39); Addona and Roth (n 43).

experience of athletes in low-profile elite sports—eg, fencing—or non-elite sport. For example, athletes may feel an obligation to their extended support network—eg, family, friends, trainers, administrators, sponsors and sports organisations—to justify the significant investment made in their sporting career.[55] It is relevant to recognise that athlete decision-making around drug use occurs within a social context that includes commercial pressures for on-field success, nationalism and sport culture.[56]

Athlete decisions around doping appear to be rational in character[57]—that is, athletes evaluate the advantages and disadvantages of taking a drug. The only empirically defined model of athlete decision-making around doping indicates that the expected outcome of use—eg, injury recovery, injury prevention or performance enhancement—is considered relative to the expected effects on health, the likelihood that the drug would be detected and whether he or she would be prosecuted as a result.[58] Given the evidence that drug testing fails to identify the majority of doping,[59] it is the perceived likelihood of being detected and prosecuted that influences behaviour rather than the actual likelihood. As a result, athletes appear to rationalise their decisions relative to a social rather than objective context.

If athletes see drug taking as a rational response to their social context, it suggests that it is the social context that needs resolution rather than an attempt to control individuals through institutional regulation. Elite athletes must find a path between their significantly increased relative risk of injury and the ongoing demands for performance[60] as a contracted employee—eg, appearance fees.[61] Non-elite athletes have to find a similar path between injury and potentially losing their ability to earn their primary income. Drugs then become a rational response to protect their health and welfare by preventing injury or illness, or speeding up recovery.

Support Personnel Drug Decisions

While athletes' drug decisions relate to their own health and welfare, support personnel are making decisions for another person who then either enjoys or

[55] Lev Kreft, 'Elite Sportspersons and Commodity Control: Anti-doping as Quality Assurance' (2011) 3 *International Journal of Sport Policy and Politics* 151.

[56] Bob Stewart and Aaron Smith, *Rethinking Drug Use in Sport: Why the War Will Never Be Won* (Abingdon, Routledge, 2014) 103–20.

[57] Twan Huybers and Jason Mazanov, 'What Would Kim Do: A Choice Study of Projected Athlete Doping Considerations' (2012) 26 *Journal of Sport Management* 322.

[58] See Mazanov and Huybers (n 35).

[59] Donald A Berry, 'The Science of Doping' (2008) 454 *Nature* 692, 693; Werner Pitsch, 'Tacit Premises and Assumptions in Anti-doping Research' (2013) 2 *Performance Enhancement & Health* 144.

[60] Ivan Waddington and Andy Smith, *An Introduction to Drugs in Sport: Addicted to Winning?* (Abingdon, Routledge, 2009), 16–34.

[61] See Kreft (n 55).

suffers the consequences of those decisions. Support personnel may experience a conflict of interest between acting as an agent of their sport and acting as an agent for the athlete. For example, medical practitioners employed by a sports club can easily find themselves in a professional conundrum in terms of acting in the best interests of their patient's health and acting in the best interests of their employer.[62] Equally, administrators can find themselves with a conflict of interest based on their multiple roles within sport.[63] For example, Pat McQuaid was simultaneously the President of the Union Cycliste Internationale (UCI), a member of the IOC and a member of the Executive Board for WADA. At this level, it is unclear whether a decision made in any of these three roles would be made in the best interests of the UCI, the IOC or WADA.[64]

Decisions around doping are particularly difficult when support personnel employment contracts are tied to performance outcomes, such as the number of wins in a season, championships or medals. This puts support personnel in an invidious position. For example, contracts may see support personnel more concerned about getting a key player into a game rather than concern for the well-being of the athlete either in the short term (eg, the rest of the season) or long term (eg, post-career health). These sorts of pressures mean that support personnel looking to preserve athlete rosters may no longer have the luxury of whether to use drugs in their sports programmes, but only which drugs to use.

The interests of individual athletes may also be compromised by support personnel interests in the success of their sports programmes. For example, support personnel need to consider how drugs are used by competitors without actually knowing what drugs are being used.[65] In this instance, strategising a season may involve anticipating competitors' potential performance benefits relative to the perceived likelihood of competitors being sanctioned. From this point of view, the optimal strategy would be to have some athletes who abstain from drug use entirely, some who use uncontaminated supplements, some who use drugs absent from the Prohibited List, some who use drugs on the Prohibited List and some who use experimental drugs likely to appear on the Prohibited List in the future. This strategy ensures that the programme achieves some benefit from drug use while insuring against prosecution and sanction. As a result, the issue again becomes less about whether drugs are used and more about which drugs to use.

[62] Daniela Testoni et al, 'Sports Medicine and Ethics' (2013) 13(10) *American Journal of Bioethics* 4.

[63] Emma Sherry and David Shilbury, 'Board Directors and Conflict of Interest: A Study of a Sport League' (2009) 9 *European Sport Management Quarterly* 47.

[64] See generally Cycling Independent Reform Commission, *Report to the President of the Union Cycliste Internationale* (February 2015).

[65] Game theoretic analysis indicates asymmetric information (eg, whether competitors are doping and the likelihood of their being sanctioned is unknown) is a feature of strategising doping behaviour: Kjetil K Haugen, 'The Performance-Enhancing Drug Game' (2004) 5 *Journal of Sports Economics* 67, 82.

The role of drugs is so entrenched in sport that support personnel have developed a sophisticated incremental normalisation of substance-based performance enhancement that starts in junior sport.[66] Junior athletes are introduced to the idea of using substances to overcome fatigue, boost their immune system, rehydrate more effectively or enhance performance using legitimate supplements as part of their broader introduction to sports science. These may be the first steps towards ensuring that athletes are compliant with the broader scientisation and medicalisation of sport.[67]

Compliance and Decision-Making

Decisions to use drugs in pursuit of sporting outcomes appear to be a rational response to modern sport. Institutionally, employees are readily substitutable commodities;[68] organisations can simply replace athletes who fail in terms performance, injury or Code compliance.[69] Athletes and support personnel are unable to substitute sporting institutions for the same failures, so drugs play an important part in preserving their ability to sustain both performance and health. Achieving depth of compliance could mean redressing the imbalance, such that institutions bear some responsibility for failures to comply with the Code. For example, the Code could require the employer to continue rather than terminate employment in response to an ADRV.[70] Eliminating substitutability this way redresses some imbalance and may promote depth of compliance. Another way to work towards depth of compliance based on the way in which decisions are made is to refocus employment contracts for both athletes and support personnel to prioritise health as a performance measure. For example, coaching contracts could include bonus payments for the proportion of athletes who remain injury-free across a season.

Slaying the Chimera of Code Compliance

The headline compliance reported institutionally indicates that many organisations see advantages in agreeing to be Code compliant. The chimera of compliance emerges in the assumption that breadth of compliance corresponds with depth of compliance. This is explained by the long-standing problem from the

[66] See Mazanov et al (n 17).

[67] Ask Vest Christiansen and John Gleaves, 'What Do the Humanities (Really) Know about Doping? Questions, Answers and Cross-disciplinary Strategies' (2014) 2 *Performance Enhancement and Health* 216. See also Wagner and Pederson (n 48).

[68] See Kreft (n 55).

[69] James Connor, 'The Athlete as Widget: How Exploitation Explains Elite Sport' (2009) 12 *Sport in Society* 1369, 1370–77.

[70] See Australian Sports Commission, Anti-Doping Policy (1 January 2015).

management literature that describes the folly in assuming that rewarding a specific target behaviour compels the adoption of a related desirable behaviour.[71] For example, universities reward research excellence in the hope that it leads to teaching excellence. In the context of the Code, the legal framework has been designed to reward institutional compliance (eg, sporting federation access to Olympic events or public funds) in the hope that it leads to depth of compliance and consequently changes doping behaviour in the daily practice of sport.

Part of the reason for this is that doping only becomes observable at the institutional level. For example, it takes intensive testing in mass participation events before enough doping is detected for it to become of interest to institutions, even at the elite level of sport where the behaviour has its most significant implications (eg, prize money and celebrity). By comparison, doping is an apparently rare experience for individual athletes and support personnel. This raises the question as to which level of regulation should be taking place to achieve depth of compliance. The challenge for those responsible for updating the Code and its supporting legal frameworks is to look more deeply at how to achieve depth of compliance.

Two strategies emerge to achieve depth of compliance at the institutional level. One strategy is to invoke stronger punishments for organisations. For example, depth of compliance would be achieved very quickly if entire nations were disqualified from the Olympics for a single ADRV. The business realities of sport makes such institutional level punishment unfeasible; banning the US Olympic team would see the IOC lose billions of dollars in broadcast, sponsorship and advertising revenues. A more moderate response might be to force organisations to develop depth of compliance with more rigorous reporting and audits, perhaps with penalties for failure to achieve specific activities that are deemed to demonstrate depth of compliance. For example, an accreditation system could be put in place to ensure minimum standards of knowledge of the Code as a condition of practice. This comes with significant costs that may exceed the assumed financial harms of doping.[72] This approach also perpetuates the chimera of compliance; rather than resolving depth, it effectively replicates the folly of rewarding organisational compliance in the hope it leads to individual compliance.

The alternative strategy is to regulate individual behaviour in a way that is sympathetic with daily practice. The legalistic prohibitionist approach might be complemented by a system more consistent with the sentiments of those who implement drug control in their daily practice; support personnel inclinations to protect athletes from drug misuse and abuse appear sympathetic to the health-based harm minimisation approach, where athlete health and well-being

[71] Steven Kerr, 'On the Folly of Rewarding A, While Hoping for B' (1975) 18 *Academy of Management Journal* 769.

[72] Doping is assumed to reduce the commercial value of sport despite the absence of evidence supporting this assumption. For example, the commercial value of the Olympics and the Tour de France has continued to grow despite more than a century of doping in those events.

is prioritised with treatment rather than punishment.[73] A cornerstone of this approach is medically supervised drug use by athletes to ensure they use substances within known safety limits. Harm minimisation has been argued to resolve a number of the barriers to individual compliance by, among other things, making it easier for athletes and support personnel to access advice rather than risk both health and career by doping without support.[74] Athletes and support personnel theoretically volunteer to enter the drug control system rather than disengage from it for fear of sanction or complexity. For example, it remains to be seen whether support personnel would be more inclined to report an athlete doping if they knew the consequence was treatment rather than punishment. Equally, athletes may be more likely to volunteer for drug testing if it was used to monitor health rather than potentially end their career. Such an approach transitions away from the institutional imperatives of compliance through punishment towards appealing to self-interest.

Medically supervised drug use appears to be unpalatable to some, which leads to hybrids of harm minimisation and legalistic prohibition. For example, the Australian Football League uses a harm minimisation approach with its illicit drugs policy.[75] This policy sees the first two drug test positives for illicit drugs place athletes in mandatory treatment for substance misuse or abuse. On the third positive test, the system escalates from treatment to punitive measures. The evidence indicates the combination of harm minimisation and legalistic prohibition reduced the harms associated with illicit drug use in the elite level of that sport.[76] Importantly, such hybrid approaches give some indication that individual compliance can improve by complementing institutional interests, drug control, with individual interests, athlete health and well-being. That being said, there is evidence to suggest that hybrid approaches can also impugn the welfare of athletes, especially in professional sports where institutional interests use harm reduction elements as part of a public relations rather than corporate social responsibility strategy.[77]

Transitioning the Code and its legal framework from breadth to depth of compliance represents a difficult road. Overcoming the assumption that individual compliance is the consequence of organisational compliance represents an important first step. The institutional elements appear to be maturing given the recognition that breadth of compliance now needs to be converted

[73] See Stewart and Smith (n 56).

[74] Carlos D'Angelo and Claudio Tamburrini, 'Addict to Win? A Different Approach to Doping' (2010) 36 *Journal of Medical Ethics* 700.

[75] But see the 2015 revision, which imposes punitive measures on the second positive test: Australian Football League and Australian Football League Players' Association, Illicit Drugs Policy (at 28 October 2015) ss 13(b), (e), 16–18, www.aflplayers.com.au/wp-content/uploads/2014/03/2015-AFL-Illicit-Drugs-Policy.pdf.

[76] Peter Harcourt et al, 'A Strategy to Reduce Illicit Drug Use in Elite Australian Football' (2012) 46 *British Journal of Sports Medicine* 943, 944–45.

[77] Dylan Bennett, 'Harm Reduction and NFL Drug Policy' (2013) 37(2) *Journal of Sport and Social Issues* 160, 161–75.

into depth.[78] It may well be that two separate codes are needed to give effect to drug control in sport: one addressing institutional compliance and the other, drawing on evidence from the social sciences, addressing issues of individual compliance. Of course, reconciling how athletes and support personnel construct the role of drugs in sport in the context of institutional interests will be a complex exercise. While difficult, this approach stands the best chance of slaying the chimera of compliance.

[78] See Houlihan (n 12).

13

The Juridification and Criminalisation of Doping: Time to Revive the Spirit of Sport?

JACK ANDERSON*

Introduction

Academic commentary on the regulation of doping in sport tends to revolve around the policies of the World Anti-Doping Agency (WADA) and awards made by the Court of Arbitration for Sport (CAS). The legal framework within which both WADA and CAS operate is reflective of, and generally discussed within, discourses on the private transnational regulatory framework of international sports law.[1] This chapter seeks to go deeper than that approach, which could be described as broad, normative and a largely descriptive view of sports law. It analyses it in terms of the specific regulatory 'juridification' framework surrounding sports doping investigations. Therefore, it begins with a definition of the term 'juridification', which initially can be taken to include the process by which formal legal principles infuse the conduct and procedural regulation of doping by internal sports dispute resolution mechanisms. In assessing juridification, this chapter implies that, as a concept which has facilitated the 'stress testing' of sporting rules by way of domestic and international arbitration, administrative tribunals, and occasionally the ordinary civil and criminal courts, juridification has been an underplayed factor in the evolution of sports law. In short, an underlying premise of this chapter is that the juridification of sporting disputes is largely responsible for the development of sports law from an area of the law once dismissed as being the ad hoc application of traditional branches of law to its contemporary nature as a recognisably discrete branch of law.

More explicitly, this chapter balances two competing conceptual views of juridifiction. The first is whether an over-juridification of sports doping

* Professor, Queen's University, Belfast.

[1] See most recently Antoine Duval, '*Lex Sportiva*: A Playground for Transnational Law' (2013) 19 *European Law Journal* 822.

investigations, particularly in terms of the procedural and regulatory demands made by appellate bodies such as CAS, is severely hindering the ability of first instance decision-makers in sport to eradicate doping as the antithesis of the spirit of sport. This is a process known in administrative law terms as 'ossification'. The second and competing perspective is that attempts made by CAS to restrict the autonomy of sports bodies in favour of harmonised, legal standards of proof and procedure have not unduly harmed the 'fight' against doping in sport. If anything, this chapter argues that the integration and harmonisation of such legal principles is a necessity in preventing sports bodies from having to engage in lengthy, costly litigation in the ordinary courts of multiple jurisdictions—what is known in terms of alternative dispute resolution theory as a 'pluralistic' approach.

Presenting a further three-dimensional view of 'juridification', the concept is then further illustrated in this chapter by way of a review of the recent xenon doping scandal in sport. Xenon gas has erythropoietin (EPO)-like effects boosting both the inhaling athlete's stamina and powers of recovery from muscle fatigue; however, unlike various synthetic forms of EPO, xenon has not, until recently, appeared on WADA's Prohibited List of substances and methods. The difficulties posed to WADA and sports authorities by the use of substances such as xenon, and indeed hormone and gene therapy treatments that have unintended beneficial uses for athletes' performance, should illustrate that the process of juridification is likely to have to accelerate in instances of doping-related disputes in sport. This in turn raises the issue as to whether the continuing juridification of sports doping disputes is sustainable and what alternatives might be considered. The chapter concludes by briefly assessing the argument that the objectives of current anti-doping policy will only ever be realised when supported by the effective criminalisation of doping and those who dope.

Juridification: An Introduction

The juridification of sporting disputes is not a particularly new concept. Twenty years ago, the term was used as a means of assessing the law's then increasingly prominent role in the regulation of sport, and specifically in evaluating the legitimate role of both the civil and criminal law in controlling the on-field conduct of players in contact sports such as football (soccer).[2] This chapter takes a slightly broader, three-dimensional view of the term.[3] This three-dimensional view as applied to disciplinary, doping-related investigations in sport sees juridification in the following way: first, that such investigations, both in terms of the substance to the dispute and the procedures that surround it, are resolved principally by

[2] Simon Gardiner and Alexandra Felix, 'Juridification of the Football Field: Strategies for Giving Law the Elbow' (1995) 5 *Marquette Sports Law Journal* 189.

[3] This three-dimensional view is adapted from the work of Lars Blichner and Anders Molander, 'Mapping Juridification' (2008) 14 *European Law Journal* 36.

way of reference to legal, as opposed to sporting, norms; second, that the individual athletes involved increasingly see themselves as legal subjects—an accused or a defendant etc—with the 'legitimate expectation', as it might be understood in public law, to lawfulness and fairness in all aspects of their relationship with their sports governing body; and, third, that sporting disputes of this nature are becoming increasingly judicialised. As a result of the last factor, the traditional self-regulatory autonomy of sporting bodies and officials is being *supplanted* rather than *supplemented* by legal norms and, indeed, the legal profession.

In short, and to take the Habermasian view of juridification, it is a process whereby law and key principles of law—fairness, rationality, proportionality etc—have expanded and become embedded in what might hitherto have been an 'informally regulated social matter'.[4] The juridification examples used by Habermas to illustrate both law's expansion and the creation of new, discrete areas of law include family law and labour law.[5] Sports law appears to be following a similar evolutionary pattern from autonomy of regulation to juridification.[6]

This re-affirms the point made in the introduction relating to juridification's hitherto under-appreciated role as an important element in the development of sports law more generally. The response to juridification from sports governing bodies, as supported by the courts, has been to promote greater 'institutionalisation' in the manner in which disputes are heard and processed internally by sport, principally by way of relatively sophisticated alternative dispute resolution mechanisms.[7] The manner in which the key institutions of dispute resolution in sport, such as CAS, interact with the formal legal system and apply general principles of law within a sports-specific regulatory context, such as the World Anti-Doping Code, has led to the development of a recognised corpus of law known to some as *lex sportiva* or sports law.[8]

The Juridification of Sporting Disputes: An Explanation

Explanations for the increased juridification of sports-related disputes are beyond the brief of this chapter, but most likely, and certainly as relating to doping disputes, include the three overlapping factors set out below.

[4] Jürgen Habermas, *The Theory of Communicative Action* (Thomas McCarthy (trans), Boston, MA, Beacon Press, 1987) vol 2, 359 (translation of *Theorie des kommunikativen Handelns, Band 2: Zur Kritik der funktionalistischen Vernunft* (1981)).

[5] ibid 432.

[6] See generally GR Rubin, 'United Kingdom Military Law: Autonomy, Civilianisation, Juridification' (2002) 65 *Modern Law Review* 36.

[7] See generally Penny Brooker, *Mediation Law: Journey through Institutionalism to Juridification* (Abingdon, Routledge, 2013) 33–34.

[8] See, eg, Michael Beloff, 'Is There a *Lex Sportiva*?' [2005] *International Sports Law Review* 49; Lorenzo Casini, 'The Making of a *Lex Sportiva* by the Court of Arbitration for Sport' (2011) 12 *German Law Journal* 1317.

The Commercialisation of Sport

First, the increased commercialisation and professionalisation of sport globally, and particularly since the last quarter of the twentieth century, means that for the professional athlete, a proposed doping-related suspension takes on serious economic and reputational consequences. Although the Lance Armstrong affair is exaggerated in comparison to the prize winnings and endorsements of even the majority of elite athletes, the potential liabilities faced by the cyclist after admitting in 2013 that he used steroids and other performance enhancers to win the Tour de France seven times from 1999 to 2005 hint at the commercial stakes involved. The liabilities for the 'Armstrong Lie' include: a likely £1 million settlement made with the *Sunday Times* in 2013;[9] ongoing claims by two insurance companies to reclaim US$15 million in prize winnings and bonuses fraudulently claimed by Armstrong;[10] and the so-called whistleblower lawsuit in which the US Federal Government wants to recover over US$30 million that the US Postal Service paid, principally in sponsorship, to Armstrong's pro-cycling teams from 1998 to 2004—if found guilty of defrauding the US Government, Armstrong could be fined three times that amount.[11]

Changing Labour Relations in Sport

A second explanation for the increased juridification of sporting disputes, and again related to enhanced revenues streams flowing into sport through corporate sponsorships and TV monies, is the dissipation of the old hierarchical master–servant relationship that existed in many professional sports well into the twentieth century, epitomised by the *Bosman* free agency ruling by the Court of Justice of the European Union (CJEU) in 1995 as applying to professional soccer,[12] and

[9] Armstrong sued the British newspaper in 2004 for libel following an article accusing him of doping. The *Sunday Times* settled the claim in 2006, agreeing to pay Armstrong £300 000, but after his confession, the paper launched a High Court bid to return the money, plus £720 000 in costs. A confidential settlement was reached: Alex Butler, 'Drug Cheat Lance Armstrong Settles with the Sunday Times' *Sunday Times* (25 August 2013) www.thesundaytimes.co.uk/sto/news/uk_news/National/article1305027.ece.

[10] See 'Lance Armstrong Quizzed under Oath for First Time since TV Admission' *The Guardian* (14 June 2014) www.theguardian.com/sport/2014/jun/13/lance-armstrong-under-oath-cycling.

[11] See Liz Clarke, 'US District Judge Rules Federal Whistle-Blower Case vs Lance Armstrong Can Proceed' *Washington Post* (19 June 2014) www.washingtonpost.com/sports/othersports/us-district-judge-rules-federal-whistle-blower-case-vs-lance-armstrong-can-proceed/2014/06/19/685fc25a-f810-11e3-a3a5-42be35962a52_story.html.

[12] Case C-415/93 *Union Royal Belge des Société de Football Association ASBL v Jean-Marc Bosman* [1995] ECR I-4921. Until the mid-1990s, the position in European football (soccer) was that even on the expiry of a player's contract, the club retained that player's registration and might not facilitate the transfer of that player to another club unless a fee was paid. The CJEU found the system in breach of various provisions of European Union (EU) law and notably an unjustified restriction of the free movement of labour within the EU single market.

its replacement with a more nuanced labour relationship where in some sports, epitomised by major league sport in the US, organised player unions are actively involved in the collective bargaining agreements underpinning their sport, including the regulation of anti-doping policy.

The ongoing Biogenesis scandal in US sport is an example of the above. In January 2013, the *Miami New Times* led with a story on how an anti-ageing clinic in South Florida run by Anthony Bosch and trading as Biogenesis had supplied human growth hormone and an array of other performance-enhancing drugs to several high-profile Major League Baseball (MLB) players, among them the Milwaukee Brewers' Ryan Braun and New York Yankees' Alex Rodriguez.[13] By July of that year, Braun had accepted a 65-game ban for his ties to the clinic and had apologised to fans.[14] By the following month, a dozen other players connected to Biogenesis accepted 50-game bans, and Rodriguez was hit with an unprecedented 211-game ban.[15] Rodriguez immediately appealed his suspension under the arbitration process agreed to by MLB and its Players' Association (MLBPA) in its collective bargaining agreement, and its Joint Drug Prevention and Treatment Program.[16] Although the arbitrator reduced the ban to 162 games, Rodriguez still faced serving the longest drug suspension and longest non-lifetime suspension in baseball history.[17] MLB did not initially make the written arbitral award public, but it appeared that the rationale for the unusually long sanction—the MLB's rules at the time called for 50-game bans for first-time doping—was because of evidence, based on the *Miami New Times*' revelations, that Rodriguez had used prohibited substances over a period of years and, moreover, that he had interfered with the MLB investigation into his conduct.

Days after the arbitral appeal had begun in the autumn of 2013, Rodriguez filed a claim against the MLB for tortious interference with his existing contracts and future business dealings, and further accused the MLB of 'buying' the cooperation of Anthony Bosch in pursuit of a MBL-led 'witch hunt' to force him out of the sport.[18] In the immediate aftermath of the arbitration in mid-January 2014,

[13] Tim Elfrink, 'A Miami Clinic Supplies Drugs to Sports' Biggest Names' *Miami New Times* (31 January 2013) www.miaminewtimes.com/2013-01-31/news/a-rod-and-doping-a-miami-clinic-supplies-drugs-to-sports-biggest-names. The story was backed up by hundreds of pages of original documents from the clinic, many of which are available on the *Miami New Times* website.

[14] Steve Eder, 'Doping Tarnishes Baseball Again as Brewers' Braun is Suspended' *New York Times* (22 July 2013) www.nytimes.com/2013/07/23/sports/baseball/ryan-braun-suspended-for-doping.html.

[15] David Lengel and Steve Busfield, 'Alex Rodriguez and 12 Other Players Suspended in Biogenesis PEDs Scandal' *The Guardian* (6 August 2013) www.theguardian.com/sport/2013/aug/05/alex-rodriguez-suspended-mlb-peds-drugs.

[16] Both agreements can be accessed at MLBPA, 'MLBPA Info' (2015) http://mlb.mlb.com/pa/info/cba.jsp.

[17] Steve Eder, 'Arbitrator's Ruling Banishes the Yankees' Alex Rodriguez for a Season' *New York Times* (11 January 2014) www.nytimes.com/2014/01/12/sports/baseball/arbitrators-ruling-banishes-the-yankees-alex-rodriguez-for-a-season.html.

[18] See Steve Eder, 'Rodriguez Sues, Targeting Baseball and Medical Treatment' *New York Times* (4 October 2013) www.nytimes.com/2013/10/05/sports/baseball/rodriguez-sues-mlb-claiming-a-witch-hunt.html?_r=0.

Rodriguez again sued in a federal court, seeking to vacate the arbitration award against him and alleging inter alia that the arbitrator had exhibited a manifest disregard for law and fair procedure, that the MLB had acted in disregard of the essence of its collective agreement with the MLBPA, and that the MLPBA had failed in its duty towards him to represent him fairly at all stages of the process. The filing of this latter suit publicly revealed the findings of Fredric Horowitz, MLB's chief arbitrator, and thus detailed Rodriguez's suspected doping habits 'down to a milligram'.[19] Within a month, the associated negative publicity led to Rodriguez withdrawing his claims in full and accepting his suspension.

This snapshot of the Biogenesis scandal, which has echoes with the infamous Balco scandal a decade earlier,[20] clearly reveals the three-dimensional nature of the juridification process at work: first, the doping investigation in question is premised on a contractual (collective bargaining) agreement; second, the 'defendant' takes an aggressive, adversarial view of the proceedings, preferring to frame his defence in terms of purported due process deficiencies rather than addressing the substantive sporting issue at hand; and, finally, juridification can be seen in the quasi-judicial nature of the resolution of the matter by way of formal arbitration, subject under federal statute to possible judicial scrutiny.

Increased Litigiousness

Third, and finally, juridification may simply be reflective of the increasingly litigious nature of society more generally, as supplemented by greater economic and political consciousness among athletes of human rights and equality provisions relating to their autonomy, dignity and privacy. An illustration of this enhanced awareness by athletes is the fact that two of the better-known doping suspensions in recent years upheld by CAS and subsequently challenged at the Swiss Federal Court have, in 2013, been taken to the European Court of Human Rights—the first time such sports-specific cases has gone to that forum.[21]

[19] The legal basis of the complaint was the Labour Management Relations Act, 29 USC § 185. The original suit filed at the US District Court, Southern District of New York, *Rodriguez v Commission of MLB and MLBPA*, can be read at 'Rodrigues Sues MLB; Arbitrator's Report Revealed' *New York Times* (13 January 2014) www.nytimes.com/interactive/2014/01/14/sports/baseball/14arod-docs.html.

[20] In 2002, US federal investigators in California began investigating Balco, a sports supplement company run by Victor Conte, because it was suspected of supplying and trafficking a range of illegal supplements and steroids. In 2003, US Anti-Doping Agency investigators received a syringe with trace amounts of a mysterious substance, which eventually turned out to be designer anabolic steroid called 'the clear'. The anonymous tipster was Trevor Graham, sprint coach to Marion Jones and Tim Montgomery. A wider investigation implicated Barry Bonds, the then MLB record-holder for home runs in both a single season and a career. See generally Mark Fainaru-Wada and Lance Williams, *Game of Shadows* (New York, Gotham Books, 2006).

[21] The CJEU has been presented with sports-specific cases of interest on a number of occasions. In the context of doping, the most relevant case is Case C-519/04 *Meca-Medina and Majcen v Commission* [2006] ECR I-6991, in which two swimmers unsuccessfully challenged a doping ban on the ground of antitrust law. See the analysis by Stephen Weatherill, 'Anti-doping Revisited: The Demise of the Rule of "Purely Sporting Interest"?' (2006) 27 *European Competition Law Review* 645.

In *Adrian Mutu v Switzerland*,[22] the applicant professional footballer was ordered by Fédération Internationale de Football Association (FIFA) to pay about €17 million in damages to Chelsea Football Club in London for unilateral breach of his employment contract following a positive drugs test. Mutu's subsequent appeal to CAS was dismissed,[23] as was an application for judicial review of that decision at the Swiss Federal Court.[24] The applicant's current case before the European Court of Human Rights is based on alleged violations of various provisions of the European Convention on Human Rights,[25] including Article 6(1) (the right to a fair hearing), Article 8 (the right to respect for private life) and Article 1 (the protection of property).

In *Pechstein v Switzerland*,[26] Claudia Pechstein, a five-time Olympic gold medallist in speed skating, was given a two-year doping-related ban by the Disciplinary Commission of the International Skating Union (ISU). Pechstein's subsequent appeal to CAS was dismissed,[27] as was an application for judicial review of that decision at the Swiss Federal Court.[28] The applicant's current case before the European Court of Human Rights is based on alleged violations of various provisions of the European Convention on Human Rights,[29] including a violation of Article 6(1) (the right to a fair hearing) and Article 6(2) (the presumption of innocence).

Pechstein's determination to legally challenge her ban, despite the fact that she was in her forties, has recently identified a possible weak spot in the current dispute resolution framework surrounding doping in sport. Her contention is that athletes' consent to the binding arbitration clauses in their sporting body's regulations, including its implied waiver of their right of access to courts, is vitiated by the fact that consent is rarely given in a fully informed or voluntary manner.

[22] Communicated Case *Mutu v Switzerland* (European Court of Human Rights, Application No 40575/10, 12 February 2013) http://hudoc.echr.coe.int/sites/eng/pages/search.aspx?i=001-117165.

[23] *Mutu v Chelsea Football Club Ltd* (Award, Court of Arbitration for Sport, Case No CAS 2008/A/1644, 31 July 2009).

[24] *Mutu v Chelsea Football Club Ltd* (Judgment, Swiss Federal Tribunal, Case No 4A_458/2009, 10 June 2010).

[25] Convention for the Protection of Human Rights and Fundamental Freedoms, opened for signature 4 November 1950, 213 UNTS 222 (entered into force 3 September 1953), as amended by Protocol No 14 to the Convention for the Protection of Human Rights and Fundamental Freedoms, opened for signature 13 May 2009, CETS No 194 (entered into force 1 June 2010).

[26] Communicated Case *Pechstein v Switzerland* (European Court of Human Rights, Application No 67474/10, 12 February 2013) http://hudoc.echr.coe.int/sites/eng/pages/search.aspx?i=001-117166.

[27] *Pechstein v International Skating Union* (Award, Court of Arbitration for Sport, Case No CAS 2009/A/1912, 25 November 2009); *Deutsche Eisschnelllauf Gemeinschaft eV v International Skating Union* (Award, Court of Arbitration for Sport, Case No CAS/2009/A/1913, 25 November 2009). See also *Pechstein v Deutscher Olympischer Sportbund* (Award, Court of Arbitration for Sport, Case No CAS OG 10/04, 18 February 2010).

[28] *Pechstein v International Skating Union* (Judgment, Swiss Federal Tribunal, Case No Case 4A_612/2009, 10 February 2010); *Pechstein v International Skating Union* (Judgment, Swiss Federal Tribunal, Case No 4A_144/2010, 28 September 2010).

[29] Convention for the Protection of Human Rights and Fundamental Freedoms, opened for signature 4 November 1950, 213 UNTS 222 (entered into force 3 September 1953), as amended by Protocol No 14 to the Convention for the Protection of Human Rights and Fundamental Freedoms, opened for signature 13 May 2009, CETS No 194 (entered into force 1 June 2010).

Moreover, and pointing to the serious consequences for athletes in terms of access to justice, Pechstein argued that athletes are rarely informed as to the nature or even the existence of arbitration to resolve disputes and, even when they are, they are given no choice in the matter such that the arbitral route to dispute resolution is presented as a fait accompli, which, if rejected, renders them ineligible to compete.[30]

In February 2014, a local court in Munich seems to have been convinced that there was some merit in Pechstein's argument and that the consent given by her to the ISU and CAS to arbitrate her dispute was largely 'illusory' in nature, and thus the arbitral jurisdiction of the sports bodies was questionable.[31] This argument is also likely to feature at the European Court of Human Rights in the sense that Pechstein may argue that the denial of her right of access to courts, by way of an arbitration agreement to which she did not properly consent, is a violation of her right to a court and fair hearing rights pursuant to Article 6 of the European Convention on Human Rights. Authority from the English Court of Appeal[32] and the Swiss Federal Tribunal[33] suggests, however, that the fragmentation of litigation in sport which could follow from pursuing the Pechstein approach to its logical conclusion would have far-reaching and wholly undesirable effects on the efficacious resolution of sports disputes and, indeed, sports administration generally.[34]

The Juridification of Sporting Disputes: The Consequences

At its best, the juridification of sports disputes is the triumph of fairness and certainty over arbitrariness and capriciousness. In addition, the institutionalisation process—whereby doping cases are arbitrated in a quasi-independent manner by reference to globally harmonised disciplinary codes and standards, as regulated by WADA—is a much more efficacious way of dealing with sporting disputes rather than leaving matters vulnerable to a multiplicity of national legal orders and judicial interpretations. Nevertheless, this 'pluralistic'[35] view of the

30 For an assessment of this 'consent to arbitration' issue, see generally Ulrich Haas, 'Role and Application of Article 6 of the European Convention on Human Rights in CAS Procedures' [2012] *International Sports Law Review* 43; Jan Łukomski, 'Arbitration Clauses in Sports Governing Bodies' Statutes: Consent or Constraint? Analysis from the Perspective of Article 6(1) of the European Convention on Human Rights' (2013) 13 *International Sports Law Journal* 60.

31 Landesgericht (German Regional Court), 37 O 28331/12, 26 February 2014.

32 *Stretford v Football Association Ltd* [2007] 1 CLC 256.

33 *Cañas v ATP Tour* (Judgment, Swiss Federal Tribunal, Case No 4P.172/2006, 22 March 2007).

34 See Ian Mill, 'Sports Arbitration: A Matter of Choice for Athletes?' *LawInSport* (27 March 2014) www.lawinsport.com/blog/blackstone-chambers/item/sports-arbitration-a-matter-of-choice-for-athletes?

35 See Jan Paulsson, *The Idea of Arbitration* (Oxford, Oxford University Press, 2014) 38.

resolution of sporting disputes and the enforcement of related sanctions also has a downside. The downside exists in the sense that a consequence of juridification is the replacement of traditional and broad-based allegiances, loyalties and civic virtues—'the spirit of sport'—with an understanding of sport that is legalistically and narrowly rule confined—'the letter of the law'—such that participants understand themselves as parties who are entitled to do anything that is not strictly forbidden.

It is claimed that the former—'the spirit of sport'—is still epitomised in the collegial enforcement system or 'code of honour' that apparently governs golf, even at the highest level.[36] The latter—adherence to 'the letter of the law'—is, however, the more prevalent in doping whereby participants' views on what might or might not be ethically, morally or medically permissible in the spirit of their sport has been replaced by a narrow view of what is or is not on WADA's Prohibited List of performance-enhancing drugs or methods. This might be called the 'Armstrong Phenomenon' in the sense that until his recent qualified confession, Lance Armstrong, the disgraced seven-time winner of the Tour de France bicycle race, proclaimed vociferously and repeatedly that he was the 'most tested athlete on the planet' and was therefore 'clean'.[37] The juridification justification then used subsequently by Armstrong, most famously in his television interview with Oprah Winfrey in January 2013 and in the wake of the US Anti-Doping Agency's Report into Armstrong's US Postal team, was, in effect, that it was not his fault that the various dope testing schemes used by the sport's governing body, the Union Cycliste Internationale (UCI), were inadequately sensitive, or that he coerced and conspired with others to sustain a decade-long culture of doping within the peloton and the sport more generally,[38] because, by the letter of the law, he was 'clean'. Although Armstrong has subsequently admitted that this justification was a 'lie',[39] it must not be forgotten that his was a practical and philosophical approach to doping that was shared by a significant number of his colleagues in the peloton. For example, in the 15 years since 1998, more than a third of the top finishers of the Tour de France have admitted to using performance-enhancing drugs in their careers or have been officially linked to doping.[40]

Accordingly, the 'Prisoner's Paradox' provides an explanation as to what might motivate an athlete to begin doping—although athletes would clearly be better off

[36] See generally Edward J Bird and Gert G Wagner, 'Sport as a Common Property Resource: A Solution to the Dilemmas of Doping' (1997) 41 *Journal of Conflict Resolution* 749.

[37] The 'I passed every test' justification has been used for decades in professional cycling; see David Walsh, *Seven Deadly Sins: My Pursuit of Lance Armstrong* (New York, Simon & Schuster, 2013) 147–48.

[38] On this conspiracy, see Reed Albergotti and Vanessa O'Connell, *Wheelmen: Lance Armstrong, the Tour de France and the Greatest Sporting Conspiracy Ever* (London, Headline Publishing Group, 2013).

[39] See generally Juliet Macur, *Cycle of Lies: The Fall of Lance Armstrong* (London, William Collins, 2014).

[40] See the graphic in Alan McLean, Archie Tse and Lisa Waananen, 'Top Finishers of the Tour de France Tainted by Doping' *New York Times* (24 January 2013) www.nytimes.com/interactive/2012/08/24/sports/top-finishers-of-the-tour-de-france-tainted-by-doping.html.

in a dope-free world, the advantages of doping so outweigh both the likelihood of getting caught and obtaining a meaningful sanction that the system works to ensure that athletes continue to cheat.[41] The 'Armstrong Phenomenon', as based on juridification, provides an explanation as to how a doping athlete is motivated or justifies to himself or herself his or her continued taking of prohibited substances.

It must also be remembered that a process of juridification, once begun, is very difficult to stop; if anything, it begins to accelerate, moving from a self-regulatory, responsive phase to principles-based regulation, to a very complex rules-based regulatory system that requires almost constant monitoring and frequent updating. In short, the system become self-perpetuating in its regulatory density and, to borrow the language of environmental lawyers, regulation of the area in question becomes subject to highly specific and technical rules, ie, heavily legally polluted.[42]

The brief regulatory history of anti-doping policy is illustrative of this juridification process. As originally contemplated, anti-doping policy was premised on three key principles: educating athletes on the chronic health dangers of doping; increasing the chances of 'catching cheats' through improved intelligence and testing mechanisms; and severely applying sanctions as premised on the legal principle of strict liability. Contrast this with the contemporary regulatory framework, which has metamorphosed into the following: a 150-page World Anti-Doping Code, now in its third edition in a little less than 12 years, accompanied by an annually updated 10-page 'Prohibited List' of approximately 200 banned substances and methods; a 100-page document on internationally harmonised standards for testing and investigations of doping; a near 100-page document for internationally harmonised standards for accredited laboratories; a 30-page document on internationally harmonised standards for therapeutic use exemptions; and a 30-page document for internationally harmonised protection of privacy and personal information relating to doping investigations.[43] Furthermore, in realising the objections and policies contained in these documents, WADA has had to develop a Web-based database management system (ADAMS) to collate the generated data and information on laboratory results, therapeutic use exemptions, anti-doping rule violations and athletes' whereabouts.

[41] See Kjetil K Haugen, 'The Performance-Enhancing Drug Game' (2004) 5 *Journal of Sports Economics* 67.

[42] Eric W Orts, 'Reflexive Environmental Law' (1995) 89 *Northwestern University Law Review* 1227, 1239.

[43] The World Anti-Doping Code (1 January 2004) was first adopted in 2003, took effect in 2004 and was then amended in a second edition: WADA, World Anti-Doping Code (1 January 2009). As approved by the WADA Foundation Board in Johannesburg, South Africa on 15 November 2013, the revised third edition of the World Anti-Doping Code has been effective as of 1 January 2015. Since 2004, and as mandated by the World Anti-Doping Code, the list of prohibited substances and methods is published annually by WADA: WADA, The Code (2015) www.wada-ama.org/en/what-we-do/the-code.

Away from the documents and accompanying databases, and taking very recent examples from the past 12 months, the juridification process has made its mark in at least two ways. First, and in practical legal effect, juridification through enhanced awareness by athletes of their legal rights has continued to undermine previously core elements of anti-doping policy such as strict liability, replacing it with a diluted form of presumed fault and one whereby arguments relating to the integrity of testing procedures,[44] mitigating factors[45] and/or (dis)proportionality of sanction[46] have resulted in significant reductions of doping-related sanctions for those athletes who can afford to take their case to CAS.

Second, the demands made by juridification mean that in the necessity to respond in a specific technical and regulatory way to every novel performance-enhancing substance or method, WADA thus appears always to be 'playing catch up' with the cheats, so confidence in the anti-doping system is further undermined. What that might mean, in broader theoretical terms, is that the current trends in sports doping regulations appear to resonate with the 'ossification thesis' in public administration regulation. This thesis—promulgated by scholars working in the fields of public administration, administrative law and political science—asserts that the public administration regulatory process in many Western democracies is suffering for two reasons. The first is because of the procedural constraints imposed on public agencies in legislation. The second is by the courts, which have had the undesirable side-effect of severely hindering the ability of such agencies to regulate in the public interest or to regulate in a timely manner.[47]

Within this ossification thesis, concern with regulatory 'delay' is especially widespread in that legislative and judicial micro-management and interference has so hindered public agency autonomy and discretion with procedural constraints that it has resulted in 'bureaucratic torpidity'. The latter is described by leading scholars as a situation where '[public] agencies are allegedly now

[44] See *Veronica Campbell-Brown v The Jamaica Athletics Administrative Association & The International Association of Athletics Federations* (Award, Court of Arbitration for Sport, Case No CAS 2014/A/3487, 24 February 2014). In that case, a Jamaican sprinter and three-time Olympic gold medallist successfully appeal against a two-year doping ban on the grounds of 'deplorable' flaws in the collection procedures and possible 'environmental contamination' of her urine sample: at 54–55 [177], 56 [182].

[45] See *Dominique Blake v Jamaica Anti-Doping Commission* (Award, Court of Arbitration for Sport, Case No CAS 2013/A/3361, 2 May 2014). In that award, CAS, in view of mitigating factors, reduced the athlete's period of ineligibility by 25 per cent: at 25 [10.1].

[46] *Mads Glasner v Fédération Internationale de Natation* (Award, Court of Arbitration for Sport, Case No CAS 2013/A/3274, 31 January 2014). In that award, CAS held that the disqualification of the athlete from the men's 1500 m freestyle final of the World Swimming Championships (25 m) in Istanbul in 2012, where he won the gold medal, which was based on an in-competition test concerning a prior race at the meeting, for which the athlete's result was rightly annulled, was unnecessary and was thus annulled: at 22 [91].

[47] For a brief introduction to the ossification thesis and related literature, see Jason Webb Yackee and Susan Webb Yackee, 'Administrative Procedures and Bureaucratic Performance: Is Federal Rule-Making "Ossified"?' (2010) 20 *Journal of Public Administration Research and Theory* 261.

unable to readily revise their regulations or to issue new regulations to better suit changing political realities, new scientific understandings, or new facts on the ground'.[48]

An interesting recent and practical example of the ossification thesis at work in sports doping, and the resulting 'bureaucratic torpidity' in WADA, is provided by way of a review of the controversy in 2014 over the use of xenon gas as a performance-enhancing substance.

Case Study: Xenon

Xenon is a colourless, odourless, almost inert gas found in trace amounts, estimated at 0.0000009 per cent of the Earth's atmosphere. It was isolated as late as 1898 and thus was one of the last of the naturally occurring elements on the periodic table to be identified. It has EPO-like features and can boost the formation of oxygen-enriched blood red cells in the body, which means that it has attracted interest, particularly in Russia, as a means of improving athletic performance.[49] Evidence suggests that the use of xenon in this regard has been officially approved by Russian sporting authorities for quite some time. For instance, on 20 March 2006, the President of the Russian Olympic Committee sent a letter to the Director of ZAO Atom-Med Centre, a Russian medical-xenon producer, thanking them for helping to prepare Russian athletes for the 2006 Turin Winter Olympics. Of the 22 Russian athletes that won medals at the Turin Games, 15 had used a xenon-based mixture as part of their preparations. Four years later, the use of xenon-based athletic performance enhancement appears to have received government approval with the publication of a document by the Russian State Research Institute of the Ministry of Defence detailing how best to administer xenon to athletes.[50] Moreover, at the Sochi Winter Olympics of 2014, Russian athletes who won 33 medals, 13 of them gold, have again admitted to the assistance of xenon in their performance.[51]

The principal juridification point here is to consider the Russian attitude to that which is permitted by the letter of WADA law and that which might be contrary to the spirit of sport. Although injecting or ingesting synthetic drug versions of EPO is not permitted under WADA rules, athletes are permitted to live or train at altitudes or sleep in low oxygen hypoxic tents, which similarly, but legally under existing WADA rules, stimulate red-cell production. The Russian view of xenon treatment has been that it merely replicated low oxygen environments by

[48] ibid 263.

[49] 'Breathe it in' *The Economist* (8 February 2014) www.economist.com/news/science-and-technology/21595890-obscure-gas-improves-athletes-performance-breathe-it.

[50] See Ben Koh and Matt de Neef, 'Xenon Gas as a Performance-Enhancing Drug: Doping or Just Hot Air?' *Cycling Tips* (5 March 2014) http://cyclingtips.com.au/2014/03/xenon-gas-as-a-performance-enhancing-drug-doping-or-just-hot-air.

[51] Johnny Watterson, 'Russian Athletes Admit Xenon Doping at Winter Olympics' *Irish Times* (10 September 2014) www.irishtimes.com/sport/other-sports/russian-athletes-admit-xenon-doping-at-winter-olympics-1.1923195.

replacing oxygen with xenon and thus its use to enhance athletic performance was permissible.[52]

The second juridification point is that, although xenon and related substances have now been placed on WADA's Prohibited List, thus necessitating an amendment to the already annually updated list, WADA has also had to admit that an authoritative scientific test for the use of the substances—one that might stand up to legal scrutiny at CAS—has not yet been developed.[53] This means that in pursuing those who use xenon, anti-doping authorities will, for the time being, have to rely on gathering 'non-analytical' evidence—admissions by the athlete, witness statements or other documentary evidence—of the use of the substance in order to prove to the comfortable satisfaction of the anti-doping tribunal that the athlete has used xenon. The founding of a case against a doping athlete on non-analytical evidence is infrequent but not unknown and has been upheld previously by CAS. This was most notably in the aforementioned award against Claudia Pechstein, where the CAS Panel in question was satisfied that the longitudinal blood profiling by way of the athlete's biological passport sufficed as evidence of a scientific pattern indicative of prohibited performance enhancement.[54]

Reliance on the largely circumstantial nature of such evidence, and which might be provided by an athlete who has in effect 'plea-bargained' his or her own doping suspension in reward for cooperation with the authorities,[55] has been questioned as being possibly in violation of fair trial rights protected in Article 6 of the European Convention on Human Rights, especially in circumstances where, as a result of such evidence, the athlete is immediately, if provisionally, suspended pending a full hearing.[56]

[52] In fact, there is an argument that xenon inhalation may be safer than the use of hypoxic tents; see Matt McGrath, 'Wada Brings in Ban on Xenon and Argon, But Has No Test' *BBC News* (1 September 2014) www.bbc.co.uk/news/science-environment-28970855.

[53] See WADA, 'Amended 2014 Prohibited List in Force September 1' (Press Release, 27 August 2014) www.wada-ama.org/en/media/news/2014-08/amended-2014-prohibited-list-in-force-september-1#.VBguYBZZ98E.

[54] *Pechstein v International Skating Union* (Award, Court of Arbitration for Sport, Case No CAS 2009/A/1912, 25 November 2009); *Deutsche Eisschnelllauf Gemeinschaft eV v International Skating Union* (Award, Court of Arbitration for Sport, Case No CAS/2009/A/1913, 25 November 2009). See also *Iourieva and Akhatova v International Biathlon Union* (Award, Court of Arbitration for Sport, Case No CAS 2009/A/1931, 12 November 2009).

[55] WADA, World Anti-Doping Code (1 January 2009) art 10.5.3 holds that where an athlete provides substantial assistance in discovering or establishing anti-doping infractions against others, a disciplinary panel can, in certain circumstances, reduce the usual period of ineligibility, albeit by no more than three-quarters of the otherwise applicable period of ineligibility. The American sprinter Kelli White availed of a reduced period of ineligibility after giving evidence against fellow athletes involved in the so-called Balco scandal (see n 20), leading to their two-year suspensions: *United States Anti-Doping Agency v Montgomery and International Association of Athletics Federation* (Award, Court of Arbitration for Sport, Case No CAS 2004/O/645, 13 December 2005); *United States Anti-Doping Agency v Gaines* (Award, Court of Arbitration for Sport, Case No CAS 2004/O/649, 13 December 2005).

[56] Jérôme de Montmollin and Dmitry Pentsov, 'Do Athletes Really Have the Right to a Fair Trial in "Non-analytical Positive" Doping Cases?' (2011) 22(2) *American Review of International Arbitration* 189.

In sum, although recent pilot testing suggests that detection of xenon use is eminently possible by optimising existing routine sports drug testing procedures—plasma and blood samples in the context of WADA's athlete biological passport scheme[57]—the 'ossified' nature of WADA's response to the use of xenon, and the imagery of WADA being engaged in a Sisyphean task of chasing the cheaters, endures to the detriment of the anti-doping system's credibility as a whole. This, it has been submitted, engenders amongst the watching public a lassitude to, and even a growing tolerance of, doping in sport.[58]

Juridification of Doping in Sport: The Next Step—Criminalisation?

As a result, it has been suggested that only by bringing to bear the full deterrent, prosecutorial and even custodial impact, and support of the criminal law on doping, and dopers in sport, will the objectives of current anti-doing policy ever be realised.[59] A number of European jurisdictions have criminal law provisions relating to doping in sport, many of which were enacted or updated in the aftermath of the 1998 Tour de France. That Tour, which subsequently became known as the Tour de Farce or Tour du Dopage, was characterised by several doping scandals, the most infamous of which became known as the Festina affair. The affair began three days prior to the start of the Tour with the arrest of Willy Voet, the French Festina team's soigneur. Willy Voet was stopped by the French police at the Belgian border with his car full of large quantities of syringes and substances, such as EPO, growth hormones, testosterone and amphetamines.[60] Later, the Festina team headquarters in France was raided by police, and a systematic drug programme for Festina riders and a number of other participating teams was revealed.[61] Other teams were implicated and the extent of doping in that race was later revealed in July 2013 by a French Senate inquiry which, by retrospectively testing the samples of 38 previously tested rider with contemporary technology, suggested that 35 of them (92 per cent) had been using EPO on that Tour.[62]

[57] Mario Thevis et al, 'Measuring Xenon in Human Plasma and Blood by Gas Chromatography/Mass Spectrometry' (2014) 28 *Rapid Communication Mass Spectrometry* 1501.

[58] See Hans Vangrunderbeek and Jan Tolleneer, 'Student Attitudes Towards Doping in Sport: Shifting from Repression to Tolerance?' (2011) 46 *International Review for the Sociology of Sport* 346.

[59] See generally Gregory Ioannidis, 'Legal Regulation of Doping in Sport and the Application of Criminal Law on Doping Infractions: Can a Coercive Response Be Justified?' [2006] *International Sports Law Review* 29.

[60] The Festina team 'pharmacist' subsequently recounted the story in depressing detail in Willy Voet, *Breaking the Chain: Drugs and Cycling, the True Story* (London, Yellow Jersey Press, 2001).

[61] See generally Jeremy Whittle, *Bad Blood: The Secret Life of the Tour de France* (London, Yellow Jersey Press, 2008) chs 1–4; William Fortheringham, *Racing Hard: 20 Tumultuous Years in Cycling* (New York, Faber & Faber, 2013).

[62] The report is available in French: Jean-Jacques Lozach, 'Rapport fait au nom de la Commission d'enquête sur la lutte contre le dopage' (Report No 782, 17 July 2013) www.senat.fr/rap/r12-782-2/r12-782-2.html.

The actions of the French police and legal authorities in 1998 were facilitated by the fact that France has sports-specific legislation criminalising the use of WADA-prohibited substance and methods, the supply and administration of such substances and methods, and any failure to cooperate with anti-doping investigators. Italy and Spain have since enacted similar legislation, as has Austria. The Austrian legislation is of especial interest because it frames the criminal offences—and the analogy here is with the current enactments seeking to criminalise match-fixing in sport—in terms of a conspiracy to commit fraud or gain financial advantage by otherwise deceiving the public. In 2010, an update by the Council of Europe indicated that approximately 30 countries in Europe have laws on doping in sport, although not all were as specific as those in Austrian, French or Italian law, and included regulatory, civil and criminal laws. The offences generally came within the following anti-doping matrix of the illegal procurement, possession, supply, distribution, prescription or administration of WADA-prohibited substances and methods.[63]

Taking a step back from the European approach, other jurisdictions, and particularly those in the common law family, such as the UK and Australia, have preferred a more indirect approach to the use of the criminal law. The UK position was revealed in the answers given by the then UK Minister for Sport to a Westminster House of Commons' Committee Inquiry into Human Enhancement Technologies in Sport in 2006.[64] The Minister was asked to consider whether the UK would enact legislation criminalising doping as part of its legal preparations for the 2012 Olympics. The Minister replied in the negative on two grounds, the first of which was that he considered that any custodial sentences that might result would be 'disproportionate'.

This author agrees with that sentiment: although at first instance criminalisation would, as many of its advocates suggest, carry a significant deterrent effect, the reality of the criminal law and the criminal justice system is that it is a rather blunt instrument to use in combating what is, after all, a relatively narrowly defined, transactional 'deviant' behaviour. Criminalisation could ultimately lead only to the 'scapegoating' of a small number of athletes for what really is a problem for sport as a whole. This echoes with the UK Minister for Sport's second negative response to calls for criminalisation of doping in 2006 and his blunt assertion that it would be better in this instance for sport to 'deal with its own misdemeanours'.[65] Moreover, an unintended side-effect for WADA and international sports authorities might be that if individual jurisdictions proceed to criminalise doping in sport, they will, presumably and understandably, do so in a manner specific to their domestic criminal code and criminal justice system. This may lead to specific problems for sports federations seeking to hold major events across

[63] For a compilation of the relevant national laws, see Council of Europe, *Compilation of National Laws—2010* (August 2012) www.coe.int/t/dg4/sport/Doping/Antidoping_database/Reports/2010/leg/Legislation.asp.

[64] Science and Technology Committee, *Human Enhancement Technologies in Sport* (House of Commons Paper 67, Session 2006–07 (2007)) 35–36.

[65] ibid 35.

jurisdictions, and may also lead more generally to an undermining of the effectiveness of WADA's harmonisation role in anti-doping policy globally and further legal uncertainty for athletes.[66]

Nevertheless, in the UK, and mainly in the context of amendments to and interpretations of the Misuse of Drugs Act 1971—an Act intended to prevent the non-medical use of certain named controlled substances by way of offences, including unlawful possession, supply, intent to supply, import or export (trafficking) and unlawful production—the criminalisation of certain sports doping-related activities can be facilitated and pursued. It is suggested that this approach—built upon in countries such as Australia in the form of an integrated approach favouring statutory 'gateways' of cooperation between sports bodies and drug, law and custom enforcement agencies—is a better way to proceed than one of full criminalisation.[67]

The trafficking of sports doping substances and methods is also of wider societal importance. As revealed by a 2013 Australia Crime Commission Report,[68] and indeed in the continuing arrests made by federal agents investigating the Biogenesis anti-ageing clinic in Florida,[69] the trade in the largely unregulated 'vanity' or anti-ageing products industry (eg, in the US, the market for testosterone is estimated to be worth US$2 billion)[70] poses significant *health dangers* to impressionable users in gyms and significant *integrity dangers* for sport. Drugs might be an attractive entry point for greater involvement by criminal syndicates in sport. In short, if criminalisation of sports doping is to be considered at all, then arguably the legislative debates involved would be better framed within this wider context rather than a constricted targeting of individual athletes.

[66] On other unintended consequences, see generally Jack Anderson, *Modern Sports Law* (Oxford, Hart Publishing, 2010) ch 4; Jack Anderson, 'Doping, Sport and the Law: Time for Repeal of Prohibition' (2013) 9 *International Journal of Law in Context* 135.

[67] To be fair, WADA has recognised the benefits of this approach and since 2008 has worked closely with Interpol to this effect. Further, the International Convention against Doping in Sport 2005, opened for signature 19 October 2015, 2419 UNTS 43649 (entered into force 1 February 2007), should make way for the harmonisation of domestic laws against the manufacture, trafficking and possession of doping substances, since the Convention lists measures for governments to take in this regard at arts 7–8. See also WADA, 'Trafficking' (2015) www.wada-ama.org/en/what-we-do/investigation-trafficking/trafficking.

[68] 'Organised Crime and Drugs in Sport: New Generation Performance and Image Enhancing Drugs and Organised Criminal Involvement in Their Use in Professional Sport' (Report, Australian Crime Commission, February 2013). The study identified the involvement of organised crime groups in the domestic distribution of substances such as peptides and hormones, and that if left unchecked, organised criminals would likely increase their participation in the distribution of such products in Australia: at 7–9, 30–33.

[69] See Michael O'Keeffe, Teri Thompson and Nathaniel Vinton, 'Three More Arrests Made in Connection with Biogenesis Doping Scandal' *New York Daily News* (12 August 2014) www.nydailynews.com/sports/i-team/arrests-made-connection-biogenesis-doping-scandal-article-1.1899690.

[70] David Von Drehle, 'Manopause?! Aging, Insecurity and the $2 Billion Testosterone Industry' *Time Magazine* (18 August 2014) http://time.com/3062889/manopause-aging-insecurity-and-the-2-billion-testosterone-industry.

Conclusion

In conclusion, this chapter suggests that current anti-doping regulation is being influenced and even directed by a juridification process such that the accompanying administrative and legal burdens on all stakeholders—from WADA to national anti-doping agencies, to sports governing bodies and athletes—looks set to increase, thus further ossifying the system as a whole. That being said, it is also necessary to view its legalisation-based approach to doping in an altogether more positive manner. The procedural constraints imposed on sports organisations by juridification and which demand that sport at all levels 'up its game' in delivering due process to athletes accused of doping infractions can also work to the benefit of sport. In administrative law, where a statutory body strictly complies with the rule of law and proceeds in propriety of purpose in a manner, expressly or impliedly, authorised by law, either common law or statutory in basis, that body has the legitimate expectation that any reasonable ruling and proportionate sanction made by it is most unlikely to be overturned on judicial review. Similarly, in sports law, where a sports body strictly complies with its anti-doping regulations, affording the athlete a 'fair go' at every stage of the process, then the room afforded to that athlete to challenge the decision shrinks. Thus, the process of juridification might be seen to be justified.

An excellent illustration of the above occurred in the Federal Court of Australia. An application was made by Essendon Football Club querying the competency of the Chief Executive Officer of the Australian Sports Anti-Doping Authority (ASADA) to carry out an investigation into the possible involvement of Essendon players and personnel in a supplements programme of dubious intent and legality. In rejecting the application, on the ground that ASADA strictly complied with the rule of law in establishing and conducting its investigation,[71] the judge forcefully, if impliedly, supported the juridification process in sports doping disputes.

A brief quote from the judge's summary provides an apt conclusion to this chapter, serving both to underpin WADA's determination to continue its fight against doping and juridification's demand for fairness in decision-making:

> ASADA has very important national and international functions to perform. The fight against doping requires constant vigilance, upgrading of investigatory techniques, and well-resourced and co-ordinated authorised bodies to educate, monitor, investigate and prosecute in appropriate situations. [Provided that ASADA complies with the rule of law] [t]he adoption of innovative processes and methods of investigations [in the fight against doping] is to be strongly supported.[72]

[71] *Essendon Football Club v Chief Executive Officer of the Australian Sports Anti-Doping Authority* (2014) 227 FCR 1, 82 [406] (Middleton J).

[72] ibid 6 [4] (Middleton J). See also Samantha Lane, 'ASADA Trumps Essendon in Federal Court Battle' *The Age* (19 September 2014) www.theage.com.au/afl/afl-news/asada-trumps-essendon-in-federal-court-battle-20140919-10jbok.html.

14

The Commercial Rationale of the World Anti-Doping Code

PAUL J HAYES*

Introduction

The preamble to the 2015 edition of the World Anti-Doping Code (hereinafter the Code)[1] recites the rationale for its existence in terms identical to its previous incarnations in 2009 and 2003. It seeks to preserve 'what is intrinsically valuable about sport … often referred to as the "spirit of sport"' (essentially 'fair play'). Against this backdrop, substances that enhance sports performance, pose an actual or potential health threat to the athlete, or violate the 'spirit of sport' are included on the World Anti-Doping Agency (WADA) List of Prohibited Substances, which is updated annually. WADA is a Swiss private legal foundation legally domiciled in Lausanne, Switzerland and headquartered in Montreal, Canada. It stands as the world's peak sports anti-doping regulation body.[2]

The Code implements and enforces a strict international anti-doping regulatory regime, which sometimes produces harsh or unjust outcomes for athletes, which WADA, the International Olympic Committee (IOC), governments and many international sports commentators argue as being justified. Is the anti-doping rationale, as stated in the Code, the complete rationale for this regime?

The stated rationale expressed in the Code does not explain all of the reasons for the Code's existence in its present form. A rationale broader than that which is explicitly stated and provided for in the Code is at work. The commercial objectives of promoters, broadcasters and sponsors of international sporting events to produce pure or clean 'sporting product', particularly with respect to Olympic sport, also support the strict international anti-doping regime.

* Barrister, Melbourne, London, Singapore and Kuala Lumpur.

[1] World Anti-Doping Authority, World Anti-Doping Code (1 January 2015).

[2] World Anti-Doping Agency, Constitutive Instrument of Foundation of the World Anti-Doping Agency, signed 10 November 1999, arts 1–2; World Anti-Doping Agency, 'Governance' (2015) www.wada-ama.org/en/governance.

Through an examination of both the salient aspects of WADA's history and its structure, and the relationship between the IOC and transnational corporations (TNCs), this chapter identifies how it is that commercial interests also influence the development of international sports anti-doping regulation. In particular, it discusses how the Code and 'pure sport' are not just for the benefit of athletes, but also for the benefit of promoters, broadcasters and sponsors.

Sport, Politics and Money

The Political Power of Sport

Throughout the twentieth century and into the new millennium, sport has played a prominent role in the sphere of international relations, both in terms of political symbolism and also in promoting peace and dialogue between nation states.

The recruitment of sport by states as a means of pursuing and achieving political objectives in the international arena is widely acknowledged.[3] Also: 'Sport is one of the relatively few avenues open for direct mass participation in international relations.'[4]

Under the banner of political symbolism, sport continues to act as a convenient outlet for nationalism[5] and the projection of state power. This can be illustrated by various Olympic Games: Berlin 1936 (Germany's ill-fated experiment with Nazism); Tokyo 1964 (Japan's revival and return to the international community following the Second World War); Sydney 2000 (North and South Korea marching together under the 'unification' flag during the opening ceremony); Beijing 2008 (China's arrival as a global super-power); and Sochi 2014 (Russia's re-emergence as a world power).

Political Power in Sport

As distinct from the mere playing of games for recreation on an ad hoc basis, sport is a rules-based,[6] highly organised social activity requiring governance. This level

[3] Barrie Houlihan, 'Politics and Sport' in Jay Coakley and Eric Dunning (eds), *Handbook of Sports Studies* (London, Sage Publications, 2002) 213; Grant Jarvie, *Sport, Culture and Society: An Introduction* (Abingdon, Routledge, 2006) 113–19; Ellis Cashmore, *Making Sense of Sports* 3rd edn (London, Routledge, 2000) 349–61; Aaron Beacom, 'Sport in International Relations: A Case for Cross-disciplinary Investigation' (2000) 20(2) *The Sports Historian* 1, 4–6.

[4] Christopher Hill, 'Prologue' in Roger Levermore and Adrian Budd (eds), *Sport and International Relations: An Emerging Relationship* (Abingdon, Routledge, 2004) 1, 4.

[5] Geoffrey Blainey, *A Short History of the 20th Century* (Harmondsworth, Penguin, 2005) 484–85.

[6] S Gardiner et al, *Sports Law* 3rd edn (London, Cavendish Publishing, 2005) 15.

of organisation occurs throughout the entire hierarchy of sporting endeavour, ranging from international sports federations (IFs) to national sports federations (NFs), to local sports competitions and teams. Individuals' participation in sport is governed by this hierarchical structure. It is through the organisational character of sport that sport attracts the operation of politics at all levels of operation. Political power in sport is usually achieved with control over the governance of a particular sport (or sporting organisation) or, as suggested below, in the case of the IOC, over sport more generally.

Under the Olympic Charter,[7] the IOC characterises itself as the 'supreme authority' of the Olympic Movement[8] and holds the rights[9] to conduct the quadrennial Olympic Games.[10] The IOC is a private association of 130 members (including honorary members).[11] It is legally constituted in Lausanne, Switzerland as an NGO,[12] and it has United Nations General Assembly observer status.[13]

It is the rights over the Olympic Games (and their related properties)[14] and the commercial value of these rights due to the international popularity of the Olympic Games which supplement the IOC's structural authority over the governance of international sport. For example, the 2012 London Olympic Games were watched by an estimated international television audience of 3.635 billion people in 220 territories and raised US$2.569 billion in broadcast revenue,[15] in addition to US$988 million in ticket sales and US$2.299 billion raised in sponsorship and licensing income.[16] All entities (and their members) wishing to join the Olympic Movement and share the benefits derived from the Olympic Games must

[7] International Olympic Committee, Olympic Charter (2 August 2015).

[8] ibid art 1(1). The Olympic Movement includes IFs (which govern individual sports through their member NFs and ultimately clubs and participants) and National Olympic Committees (which govern Olympic participation of individual citizens of the world's states), as recognised by the IOC under art 3 of the Olympic Charter. These entities (and their members) are contractually bound to the IOC to comprise the Olympic Movement under art 1(2), (3) of the Olympic Charter. See also David Miller, *The Official History of the Olympic Games and the IOC: Athens to Beijing* (Edinburgh, Mainstream Publishing, 2008) 179, quoting former IOC Honorary President Juan Antonio Samaranch, from remarks reported in 'a Spanish magazine article published soon after [Samaranch's] election to the IOC' in 1966, which stated: 'The IOC must occupy the position that is its due through its undoubted merits: that is to say, it must remain the supreme authority in world sport … a position that belongs to the IOC by right and by history, and to it alone.'

[9] Olympic Charter art 7.

[10] ibid art 6.

[11] International Olympic Committee, 'IOC Members' (2015) www.olympic.org/ioc-members-list.

[12] Olympic Charter art 15; James AR Nafziger, *International Sports Law* 2nd edn (London, Transnational Publishers, 2004) 25–26.

[13] *Observer Status for the International Olympic Committee in the General Assembly*, GA Res 64/3, UN GAOR, 64th sess, 21st plen mtg, Agenda Item 167, UN Doc A/RES/64/3 (22 October 2009, adopted 19 October 2009).

[14] Olympic Charter chs 1, 5.

[15] International Olympic Committee, 'Olympic Marketing Fact File' (2014) 23, 26, www.olympic.org/Documents/IOC_Marketing/OLYMPIC_MARKETING_FACT_%20FILE_2014.pdf.

[16] ibid 11, 17 and, 31.

comply with the Olympic Charter and subscribe to the 'fundamental principles of Olympism'[17] as promoted by the IOC.[18]

Mostly, the IOC can dictate unilaterally the terms upon which those who seek to belong to or be involved in the Olympic Movement. This is because the Olympic Games is a highly successful international event. It attracts the attention of many actors in the international community, all seeking the sporting, political and financial rewards of Olympic association. IFs and NFs benefit from belonging to the Olympic Movement because the inclusion of a sport in the Olympic programme will usually result in greater public exposure, high levels of participation and therefore ongoing viability of that sport.[19] National governments seek association with the Olympic Movement because of the international prestige that accompanies the hosting of an Olympic Games and the winning of Olympic medals by athletes who belong to their National Olympic Committees (NOCs). Finally, the commercial advantages which flow to TNCs which broadcast or sponsor the Olympic Games are plainly significant, if the ongoing involvement of the IOC's top sponsors and the broadcast and sponsorship revenue derived by the IOC from the London 2012 Olympic Games are any indications.

International Sports Anti-Doping Regulation: The Code

WADA was established on 10 November 1999.[20] According to its constitution, its primary object or mission is:

> [T]o promote and coordinate at international level the fight against doping in sport in all its forms; to this end, the Foundation will cooperate with intergovernmental organizations, governments, public authorities and other public and private bodies fighting against doping in sport, inter alia the International Olympic Committee (IOC), International Sports Federations (IF), National Olympic Committees (NOC) and the athletes; it will seek and obtain from all of the above the moral and political commitment to follow its recommendations.[21]

WADA pursues this object via the regulatory means of the Code and the International Convention against Doping in Sport (ICADS).[22]

[17] Olympic Charter 13–14. 'Olympism' is essentially the IOC's mission statement and relevantly requires members of the Olympic Movement to adhere to 'universal fundamental ethical principles' and 'fair play'.

[18] ibid 13–14, art 1; International Olympic Committee (n 15) 5, 21, 35–36.

[19] Dick Pound, *Inside the Olympics: A Behind-the-Scenes Look at the Politics, the Scandals and the Glory of the Games* (New York, Wiley, 2004) 251.

[20] World Anti-Doping Agency, 'A Brief History of Anti-doping' (2015) www.wada-ama.org/en/a-brief-history-of-anti-doping.

[21] World Anti-Doping Agency (n 2) art 4(1).

[22] Opened for signature 19 October 2005, 2419 UNTS 201 (entered into force 1 February 2007); World Anti-Doping Agency, 'Governments' (2015) www.wada-ama.org/en/governments.

The Code is a unique document. It is one of the most far-reaching pieces of international legal regulation in force throughout the world. It commenced operation on 1 January 2004.[23] All of the world's NOCs,[24] virtually all of the world's IFs[25] and 182 governments[26] have adopted the Code, which thereby legally binds their members or constituents to the Code within their respective organisations and states. In this way, the Code ultimately regulates most of the world's population who participate in organised sporting activity,

The stated purpose of the Code is to 'protect the Athletes' fundamental right to participate in doping-free sport and thus promote health, fairness and equality for Athletes worldwide' and to 'ensure harmonized, coordinated and effective anti-doping programs at the international and national level with regard to detection, deterrence and prevention of doping'.[27]

The obligations imposed upon persons subject to the Code are significant. Under the strict liability regime imposed by the Code, an athlete must (among other obligations):

— compete in his or her chosen sport drug-free by ensuring that 'no prohibited substance enters his or her body';
— be promptly available to submit to any request to provide a sample for testing (by any entity authorised under the Code to make such a request);
— not possess any substance classified by WADA as a 'prohibited substance'; and
— 'inform medical personnel of their obligation not to Use Prohibited Substances and Prohibited Methods and to take responsibility to make sure that any medical treatment received does not violate anti-doping policies and rules adopted pursuant to the Code'.[28]

Failure to comply with these obligations (subject to an athlete engaging a number of limited exculpatory or mitigation of sanction provisions under the Code) will result in the athlete being declared ineligible to participate in all forms of organised sport at any level for a period of two years or, in the case of a second offence, for life.[29]

The extraordinary global reach of the Code occurs as a result of the hierarchical structure of governance of international sport, and its contractual force as

[23] World Anti-Doping Agency, World Anti-Doping Code (1 January 2015) www.wada-ama.org/en/resources/the-code/world-anti-doping-code.

[24] World Anti-Doping Agency, 'Code Signatories' (2015) www.wada-ama.org/en/code-signatories.

[25] ibid.

[26] United Nations Educational, Cultural and Scientific Organization, International Convention against Doping in Sport: Paris, 19 October 2015, www.unesco.org/eri/la/convention.asp?KO=31037&language=E. Because the Code is essentially a private legal instrument, governments agreed to adopt the Code pursuant to the ICADS. As at 29 July 2015, 182 governments have acceded to, accepted or ratified the ICADS.

[27] Code 11.

[28] ibid arts 2, 21.

[29] ibid art 10.

an instrument of international private law binding all of those organisations in the hierarchy. Similarly, intergovernmental agreement between states achieved through diplomacy has resulted in legislation in the domestic law of subscribing states, as a consequence of the operation of public international law.

In sport, legal obligations between sports organisations and other sports organisations or individuals are created and governed by the private law of contract. So far as individual participants are concerned, usually, a contract comes into being in the form of a membership application/agreement between the participant and the relevant club or sporting organisation, where the individual person agrees to be bound by and submit to the rules and regulations of the club and relevant NF (and sometimes IF). The NF in turn agrees to be bound by the rules and regulations of the applicable IF. Those IFs that are part of the Olympic Movement likewise agree to adopt such rules and regulations of the IOC, as required. It is through this process that IFs agree with the IOC to adopt the Code for their sport and then require their affiliated NFs to correspondingly implement the Code in their respective countries.[30] Additionally, the IOC requires NOCs[31] and IFs[32] to implement and bind their members to the Code. Unlike individual persons, incorporated entities and private associations, which are bound by the private law of contract, governments are bound to the Code through the process of public law. This explains the unanimous adoption of the ICADS by 191 governments in 2005 at the 33rd session of the United Nations Educational, Scientific and Cultural Organization (UNESCO) held in Paris, by which they undertook to adopt the Code in their domestic law.[33]

The WADA and the Code's ideals of seeking to maintain fairness in the sporting contest through eradicating illicit substances which artificially enhance an athlete's performance or which might be injurious to an athlete's health are admirable. However, the Code also preserves the commercial interests of those TNCs invested in the Olympic movement by ensuring that the IOC can deliver a unique 'sporting product' to broadcasters and sponsors. Unlike other professional sport, Olympic sport differentiates itself on the Corinthian ideal of 'pure' sport. Both the IOC's constitutional document, the Olympic Charter, and its marketing record, the 'Olympic Marketing Fact File', make repeated references to 'Olympism' and 'Olympic ideals'.[34] While the breadth of the Code's reach extends well beyond those sports represented at the Olympic Games, the references in the Code to 'Olympism' and 'play[ing] true' (coincidentally, the slogan used by the WADA in

[30] See Figure 1 in the Appendix to this chapter.

[31] Olympic Charter, arts 28, 41, 44–45.

[32] ibid arts 26, 41, 44–46.

[33] United Nations Educational, Cultural and Scientific Organization, 'UNESCO General Conference Adopts international Convention against Doping in Sport' (Press Release No 2005-125, 20 October 2005).

[34] Olympic Charter 13–14, art 1; International Olympic Committee (n 15) 5, 10, 21, 35–36.

its promotion of the Code),[35] as forming a vital component of the Code's stated rationale and the WADA's raison d'etre, betray the power and influence of the IOC in shaping this body of regulation which affects most of the world's sports participants.

TNCs have influenced and can continue to influence the development of the Code in two ways. First, the IOC can effectively control the domain of international anti-doping regulation and, in particular, the Code and its ongoing development. This control is identified through an examination of the historical background to the creation of WADA and the Code's development, along with an analysis of WADA's governing structure. Second, the IOC remains vulnerable to the influence and demands of broadcasters and sponsors in its delivery of Olympic 'sports product', as they provide the income which the IOC needs to stage the Olympic Games as required under the Olympic Charter.

The WADA: An Historical and Structural Analysis

History of International Anti-Doping Regulation

Until the establishment of WADA in 1999, responsibility for anti-doping regulation in sport rested with the IOC and the IFs.

The IOC Medical Commission was established in 1961[36] to address what was then a rise in the incidence of doping among athletes competing in an increasingly globalised sporting environment,[37] in the aftermath of the death of Danish cyclist Knud Jensen during the 100 km road race at the XVII Olympiad held in Rome in 1960. Prior to the establishment of the IOC Medical Commission, there was no private or public legal regulation directly preventing athletes from doping in sporting competition. Although the IOC expressed that it was acting in the interests of athletes by safeguarding their health, it has been argued that the real concern among IOC members was to protect the integrity of the Olympic Games as an amateur competition (as it then was until 1985),[38] as doping was considered to be 'professional' conduct and therefore contrary to the Olympic spirit.[39]

[35] Code 11; World Anti-Doping Agency, 'President's Welcome Message' (2015) www.wada-ama.org/en/presidents-welcome-message.

[36] Miller (n 8) 168.

[37] ibid; Jan Todd and Terry Todd, 'Significant Events in the History of Drug Testing and the Olympic Movement: 1960–1999' in Wayne Wilson and Edward Derse (eds), *Doping in Elite Sport: The Politics of Drugs in the Olympic Movement* (Champaign, IL, Human Kinetics Publishers, 2001) 65, 67.

[38] Nafziger (n 12) 137–46.

[39] Paul Dimeo, *A History of Drug Use in Sport 1876–1976: Beyond Good and Evil* (Abingdon, Routledge, 2007) 13, 54–57, 96.

By 1964, the members of the IOC at its 63rd session held in Tokyo unanimously voted in condemnation of doping by athletes and established the building blocks of what would later form part of a drug-testing regime (rules, sanctions and drug-testing).[40] In 1968, drug-testing was introduced at the XIX Olympiad held in Mexico City and the X Olympic Winter Games held in Grenoble by the IOC Medical Commission, which published the first ever list of prohibited substances in 1971.[41] Yet despite the IOC's early development of an anti-doping regime, the IFs remained responsible for its enforcement outside of the Olympic Games, which in some cases was done 'under considerable pressure from the IOC'.[42]

Sports anti-doping efforts took on a new sense of urgency in the aftermath of the Canadian athlete Ben Johnson (who won the men's 100 metres event at the XXIV Olympiad in Seoul in 1988) testing positive to anabolic steroids, which resulted in his disqualification. Less than a month later, the Canadian Government appointed an Ontario judge, Charles Dubin, to conduct an inquiry into the use of drugs in Canadian sport.[43] The Dubin Inquiry raised substantial doubts as to the 'effectiveness of the IOC testing programme'[44] and its recommendations led to the establishment in Canada and Australia of government-backed anti-doping agencies.[45] The international political environment towards drug use in sport was transforming from one of ignorance and ambivalence to one of disapproval and action.

In response to the changing mood and as sport became ever more global and professional during the 1990s,[46] the IOC, IFs and NOCs implemented the IOC Medical Code (IOCMC) in 1994. This was a model for harmonised anti-doping regulation[47] applicable to Olympic and non-Olympic participation in sport and was the foundation for what was to eventually become the Code.

The year 1998 witnessed the expulsion of the 'Festina' cycling team from the Tour de France after the team car was discovered to have contained significant quantities of performance-enhancing drugs. This culminated in the French police arresting and bringing criminal charges against team manager Bruno Roussel for supplying and trafficking drugs to his cyclists.[48] This incident sparked a worldwide public furore.[49]

[40] Todd and Todd (n 37) 67.

[41] ibid 69; Miller (n 8) 182; Antonio Buti and Saul Fridman, *Drugs, Sport and the Law* (Brighton, Scribblers Publishing, 2001) 31.

[42] Todd and Todd (n 37) 67; Pound (n 19) 60.

[43] Todd and Todd (n 37) 91.

[44] Buti and Fridman (n 41) 34.

[45] Houlihan, 'Doping in Sport' in Barrie Houlihan (ed), *Sport and Society* (London, Sage Publications, 2008) 384.

[46] Andrea Mitchell and Helen Yeates, 'Who's Sorry Now? Drugs, Sports, and the Media Toward 2000' in Kay Schaffer and Sidonie Smith, *The Olympics at the Millennium: Power, Politics, and the Games* (New Brunswick, NJ, Rutgers University Press, 2000) 197, 210.

[47] Buti and Fridman (n 41) 37.

[48] Samuel Abt, 'Tour de France Steadfast in Ouster of Festina Team' *Sports Sunday, New York Times* (19 July 1998) 1.

[49] John J MacAloon, 'Doping and Moral Authority: Sport Organizations Today' in Wilson and Derse (n 37) 203, 214–17.

Following Roussel's arrest, more evidence came to light that doping was widespread among athletes in cycling, a major sport in the Olympic programme. It was suggested that 'a lackadaisical attitude towards prohibited drug use' on the part of the IOC (and more generally the pre-WADA system) was '[possibly] to protect the image of the Olympic Games and that of the IOC'.[50] The IOC's rhetoric, which was reinforced by the then IOC President, Juan Antonio Samaranch, and others during 1998, is certainly consistent with this hypothesis, given that the rise in broadcast and sponsorship revenue since the XXIII Olympiad held in Los Angeles in 1984 had returned the IOC to robust financial health by the 1990s.[51] If this reasoning is applicable to the events of 1998, then strategically the IOC had all the more reason to try and reclaim the initiative of control over sports doping and the enforcement of anti-doping regulation.[52] It lost this control to the authorities of France (and the Netherlands and Italy, which also undertook related investigations) in the Festina scandal.[53] Reclaiming it would keep the IOC's 'sports product' clean, or at least perceived to be clean, to ensure the continuity of its growing revenue stream.

An emergency meeting of the IOC executive board was called in August 1998 amid the ongoing public furore surrounding Samaranch's public statements on doping in sport. Two important decisions were made. First, the IOC requested the IFs forming part of the Olympic Movement to adopt the IOCMC into their own rules. This made the IOCMC applicable not only at the Olympic Games, but at all times each IF's sport was played. The IFs agreed to the IOC's request in November 1998.[54] Second, the Canadian IOC executive board member Richard Pound QC suggested that 'the IOC should create an independent anti-doping agency that would not be controlled by the IOC, nor any other stakeholder in the Olympic Movement'.[55] Such stakeholders included 'persons representing sponsors, the pharmaceutical industry and the sporting goods industry'.[56] Although Pound's initial proposal for commercial stakeholders in sport to be represented on the independent anti-doping entity never came to fruition, his suggestion for the creation of such an entity was crucial for the future survival of the IOC and the Olympic Games if the IOC was to retain its self-appointed role as sport's moral custodian.

As Pound (who at the time was also Chairman of the IOC's commissions for television rights negotiation and marketing)[57] observes: 'What we were selling, what the sponsors and broadcasters wanted, and what the public demanded, were precisely those ethical values that differentiate the Olympics from professional

[50] Mary K FitzGerald, 'The Court of Arbitration for Sport: Dealing with Doping and Due Process during the Olympics' (2000) 7 *Sports Lawyers Journal* 213, 234.

[51] Miller (n 8) 559.

[52] Houlihan (n 45) 386.

[53] ibid; MacAloon (n 49) 213.

[54] Todd and Todd (n 37) 107; Pound (n 19) 71.

[55] Pound (n 19) 71.

[56] Jim Ferstle, 'World Conference on Doping in Sport' in Wilson and Derse (n 37) 275, 277–78, 281.

[57] International Olympic Committee, 'Mr Richard W Pound, QC, AD E' (2015) www.olympic.org/en/content/The-IOC/Members/Mr-Richard-W-POUND-QC.

entertainment sports. We delivered pure sport.'[58] Implicit in Pound's description of the 'Olympic brand'[59] is that 'fair play' informs the Olympic Movement's ethical values, which in its mission and role as described by Article 2 of the Olympic Charter requires the IOC to lead 'the fight against doping in sport'.[60] Accordingly, the IOC convened the inaugural World Conference for Doping in Sport in Lausanne in February 1999 (WCDS 1999), proposing a new international sports anti-doping regime to all of sport's key stakeholders. The years 1998 and 1999 were a critical period in the development of sports anti-doping regulation and for the IOC. Regulatory control could have slipped away from the IOC into the hands of governments and the IFs at a time when governments were showing a greater interest in regulating doping in sport and enforcing these regulations. To protect its interests, the IOC rapidly swung into action to lay out the template for what would in four years' time become the WADA and the Code. It did so by recruiting the IFs to agree to implement the one common anti-doping code (being the IOC's own IOCMC) and then setting the agenda by convening the WCDS 1999 to rally the world's stakeholders in sport to unite in the fight against doping in sport in accordance with its vision. In 1998–99, when power in sports anti-doping regulation hung in the balance, the IOC emphatically seized it. Accordingly, the delegates at the WCDS 1999 agreed to what has since been referred to as the Lausanne Declaration,[61] which provided for an 'independent International Anti-Doping Agency' to be established 'to be fully operational for the Games of the XXVII Olympiad in Sydney in 2000'.[62]

The IOC's seizure of power over anti-doping regulation in 1998–99 also reflected the growing influence of its commercial partners. Because of the increasing scale and cost of staging the Olympic Games, the IOC had to maintain credibility in the international sporting community and satisfy the wishes of those from whom its financial lifeblood flowed—namely, its commercial partners (broadcasters and sponsors) and governments whose support of future host cities was vital if the Olympic Games were to continue in the same vein. By reasserting the Olympic Movement's 'ethical values' through a strengthened stance against drugs in sport—and, in doing so, securing the Olympic brand—the IOC was protecting its revenue stream and thus the future viability of the Olympic Games. No person at the time understood this imperative better than Pound, who not only chaired the IOC's broadcasting and sponsorship commissions, but also led the way towards the establishment of a new international sports anti-doping regime over which the IOC would ultimately retain control.

[58] Pound (n 19) 16.

[59] ibid 163; Michael Payne, *Olympic Turnaround* (London, London Business Press, 2005) 114, 122.

[60] Also, in the preamble to the Olympic Charter, 'universal fundamental ethical principles' and 'fair play' are included in the taxonomy of the 'Fundamental Principles of the Olympism'.

[61] Ferstle (n 56) 285; World Conference on Doping in Sport, Lausanne Declaration on Doping in Sport (4 February 1999) www.sportunterricht.de/lksport/Declaration_e.html.

[62] ibid art 4.

The IOC's dominance over the new international anti-doping initiative was further strengthened by the appointment of Pound as the WADA's inaugural Chairman at the first meeting of the new 'independent' agency, which was held at Olympic House in Lausanne, with many foundation board members representing the 'sports movement' being either existing or future IOC members.[63] Pound's influence in his role as Chairman appears clear, as the WADA Foundation Board resolved that: 'On the basis of the existing Olympic Movement Anti-Doping Code, [WADA] begin work on drafting a WADA Anti-Doping Code.'[64]

In the lead-up to the approval and implementation of the Code at the World Conference on Doping in Sport held in 2003 in Madrid (hereinafter the WCDS 2003), the WADA obtained a legal opinion from three eminent Counsel experienced in the field of international law as to whether the proposed Code conformed to 'commonly accepted principles of international law and human rights'. The Court of Arbitration for Sport (CAS) opined that the Code did so conform.[65] However, in doing so, it observed that, with respect to the policy rationale of the Code: 'The drafters of the Code felt it preferable to set forth only a brief list of values in order to "avoid requests for expansion and clarifications", notably as to whether "sport [should also be considered] entertainment and business".'[66] Taking a broader approach to defining the policy rationale for the Code, CAS considered the social and economic standing of sport and the fact that it provides role models as appropriate justifications for the Code equal to the more conventional policy grounds (that is, the need for sport to be played on a level playing field and the protection of athletes' health). In broadening the moral foundation to justify the strict (and sometimes harsh) effect of the Code, CAS relied upon the decision of the Regional High Court of Munich in the case of *Krabbe v IAAF et al*,[67] where it observed that the '"image of a sports discipline in the public" is a legitimate goal of anti-doping regulation'.[68]

The draft Code considered by CAS was a developed version of the IOC's template for sports anti-doping regulation as set out in the IOCMC. In 2000, the IOCMC was renamed the Olympic Movement Anti-Doping Code (OMADC).[69] The OMADC (as incorporated into the anti-doping policies of the IFs) applied to all participants in Olympic sport between 2000 and 2003.

[63] World Anti-Doping Agency, 'Inaugural Meeting of the Board of the World Anti-Doping Agency (WADA)' (13 January 2000) https://wada-main-prod.s3.amazonaws.com/resources/files/wada_foundationboardminutes_200001_en.pdf; Miller (n 8) 421–23.

[64] World Anti-Doping Agency (n 63) 18.

[65] Gabrielle Kaufmann-Kohler, Antonio Rigozzi and Giorgio Malinverni, 'Legal Opinion on the Conformity of Certain Provisions of the Draft World Anti-Doping Code with Commonly Accepted Principles of International Law' (26 February 2003) 49–53 [166]–[184] https://wada-main-prod.s3.amazonaws.com/resources/files/kaufmann-kohler-full.pdf.

[66] Ibid 13 [26].

[67] *Krabbe v IAAF et al*, Oberlandesgericht München (Munich Court of Appeal), U (K) 3424/95, 28 March 1996.

[68] ibid 15 [32].

[69] Pound (n 19) 71.

Since the commencement of operation of the Code in 2003, international conferences on doping in sport and subsequent revisions to the Code continue to reflect the IOC's power in shaping and driving WADA's sports anti-doping agenda. Examples include:

— Paris 2005—the 33rd session of the UNESCO General Conference unanimously resolved to adopt the ICADS, which provides for the Olympic Movement and governments to equally fund WADA;[70]
— Madrid 2007—IOC gained approval for WADA to amend the Code to acknowledge that the IOC would 'not accept bids to host an Olympic Games from' a country that had not acceded to the ICADS, consistent with the corresponding provision in the Olympic Charter;[71] and
— Johannesburg 2013—increased testing by the WADA, increased penalties for intentional or repeat anti-doping offenders and greater flexibility in terms of reduction of applicable sanctions for unintentional offenders.[72]

Accordingly, two themes emerge from an historical analysis of the development of international sports anti-doping regulation. First, the IOC has been the dominant actor in this field from its beginnings in 1960 to the present date. Second, in being the dominant actor, the IOC has acted from a position of self-interest (in part commercial) in shaping the international anti-doping regime and related rules, through its initiative in the establishment of WADA in 1999, its induction of the IOCMC as the original pre-cursor to the Code and the installation of IOC executive board member Dick Pound as the WADA Foundation Board's first Chairman.

Historically, and contrary to the established rhetoric, the WADA has never been truly independent or an equal partnership between the Olympic Movement and government. The IOC or, more specifically, the IOC executive board, led by Pound during WADA's formative years, has always exercised a significant degree of influence and, at times, control over the regulator and the regulation, both directly when Pound and others from the Olympic Movement have acted as chairperson of WADA and indirectly though the stable bloc influence of the Olympic Movement on WADA's Foundation Board. An important commercial reason lies among the IOC's motives to leverage such influence. Specifically, by preserving the image of the Olympic Games as clean and drug-free, the IOC financially benefits from the sale of the rights to the Olympic Games to its commercial broadcast and sponsorship partners.

[70] ICADS arts 14–15.

[71] World Anti-Doping Agency, World Conference on Doping in Sport Resolution (17 November 2007) [1]–[2]; Code arts 20.1.8, 22; Olympic Charter art 43.

[72] Thomas Bach, 'Fourth World Conference on Doping in Sport' (Speech delivered at Session 1 of the Fourth World Conference on Doping in Sport, Johannesburg, 13 November 2013).

WADA and its Structural Foundations

Under its constitution, WADA is a private '[f]oundation governed by the ... Swiss Civil Code'[73] and its seat is in Lausanne.[74] Its operational headquarters are located in a different location, Montreal, as facilitated by its constitution.[75] The legal domicile and personality of an entity that is not a natural person determine the domestic law which governs it. As WADA is founded in Switzerland, any dispute concerning its constitution and its internal workings is ordinarily justiciable in Switzerland.[76] As pointed out by Pound:

> [WADA] does not conform with the legal format that most governments prefer and with which they are comfortable. Governments are clearly comfortable with public entities and intergovernmental organisations; they are not comfortable with private organisations and are not entirely certain how to deal with such entities.[77]

In creating WADA in the form proposed by the IOC in Lausanne in 1999, the IOC derived two advantages. First, WADA would operate within a private legal structure which suited the IOC (also a Swiss legally domiciled private entity) more so than the government. As a private structure, the IOC was more familiar than governments with WADA's processes and means of governance. WADA was less transparent than a similar public entity and thereby afforded the IOC with a greater level of control as to its operation with less public scrutiny. Second, in practical terms, the rooting of WADA's legal status in the Olympic city of Lausanne provided the IOC with a home ground advantage. That is, it can readily marshal the necessary legal resources in the event of any litigation between the Olympic Movement and governments over WADA in the Swiss Federal Tribunal. WADA's seat in Lausanne is entrenched in Switzerland in another way. Although WADA's place of business can be outside of Lausanne, relocating WADA's seat requires not only a majority vote of the members of the Foundation Board, but also the agreement of the Swiss Federal Department of the Interior.[78]

Governance of WADA is achieved through the Foundation Board and the Executive Committee. The Foundation Board is WADA's ultimate decision-making body. It decides important matters of policy and governance. The Executive Committee has responsibility for WADA's day-to-day operation and the development of policy. Under WADA's constitution, WADA's Foundation Board comprises 19 members appointed by the Olympic Movement (including four places

[73] World Anti-Doping Authority (n 2) art 1.

[74] ibid art 2.

[75] ibid.

[76] ibid art 2.

[77] Richard Pound, 'The World Anti-Doping Agency: An Experiment in International Law' (2002) 2 *International Sports Law Review* 53, 57.

[78] World Anti-Doping Agency (n 2) arts 2, 19.

specifically reserved for IOC members) and 19 members appointed by governments (comprising either ministers or senior bureaucrats), making up a total of 38 members (including the chairperson and vice-chairperson).[79] The all-important position of chairperson (customarily referred to as president) is elected by the Foundation Board members. Candidates are nominated by the Olympic Movement and governments respectively, either within or from outside the Foundation Board, for a three-year term (renewable for a further three years).[80] With the exception of amending WADA's constitution and the relocating WADA's headquarters, decisions made by the Foundation Board and the Executive Committee are made by an absolute majority.[81]

Although overall governance of WADA under its constitution is equally split between the Olympic Movement and governments, membership of the Foundation Board and the Executive Committee is dominated by IOC members. Also, many of the Olympic Movement's members of the Foundation Board and the Executive Committee carry dual responsibilities. In addition to their IOC membership, these persons also hold positions of authority within their respective IFs, NOCs or as members of the IOCAC.

No single stakeholder is better represented on both the Executive Committee and the Foundation Board than the IOC. Although the macro-representation of the Olympic Movement and governments is equal within WADA, governments are a broad and varied group with vast and differing interests (foreign policy, health, economic policy and security). In contrast, the Olympic Movement is a single-interest group ultimately controlled by the IOC and operates in the IOC's interest. In addition, governments are subject to changes in administration (for example, through democratic elections), which results in a higher turnover than the Olympic Movement representatives on WADA's Foundation Board. The IOC's actual level of representation on WADA's Foundation Board and Executive Committee places the IOC in a strongly advantageous position from which it can dominate the other interest blocs within WADA and influence the wielding of WADA's power in its interests. The IOC's power in this respect is even greater when considering that some representatives of government on WADA's Foundation Board may harbour ambitions of hosting the Olympic Games. As the IOC is the owner of this politically valuable currency, it would be naive to think that such governments acting in state self-interest would not otherwise conform to and support the IOC's anti-doping agenda and vote alongside Foundation Board members representing the Olympic Movement.

The IOC keeps a tight rein on its members and the IFs and NOCs that comprise the Olympic Movement by requiring that each act in the IOC's interests, as

[79] World Anti-Doping Agency, 'Foundation Board' (2015) www.wada-ama.org/en/foundation-board.

[80] ibid art 7.

[81] ibid arts 8, 11, 16. Amendment of the constitution and relocation of the WADA headquarters can only occur after a two-thirds majority of votes of the members of the Foundation Board.

prescribed by the Olympic Charter. Upon election to membership of the IOC, members are required to take an oath swearing 'to respect and ensure the respect of all the provisions of the Olympic Charter and the decisions of the International Olympic Committee … and to promote in all circumstances the interests of the International Olympic Committee and those of the Olympic Movement'[82] and 'to inform the [IOC] President, without delay, of all events liable to … adversely affect the Olympic Movement'.[83] IFs within the Olympic Movement are obliged to ensure their rules 'statutes, practice and activities … [are] in conformity with the Olympic Charter, including the adoption and implementation of the World Anti-Doping Code',[84] and NOCs in their countries must 'develop, promote and protect the Olympic Movement … in accordance with the Olympic Charter'.[85] Finally, in the Olympic Charter, the IOC commands that the Code is 'mandatory for the whole Olympic Movement'.[86]

By reason of the structure of the IOC and the Olympic Movement as set out in the Olympic Charter, all members of the WADA Foundation Board representing the Olympic Movement (or the sports movement as it is sometimes more neutrally referred to by WADA) are first and foremost required to act in the interests of the IOC. This is a consequence of either being a member of the IOC or their sports organisation with which they are affiliated belonging to the Olympic Movement. The government members of the Foundation Board, on the other hand, are obliged to act in their respective national interests, which on some occasions for a whole host of foreign policy reasons may be opposed, thereby making the pursuit of common goals or a united position amongst government members almost impossible. This leaves the government representation on the WADA Foundation Board vulnerable to the domination of the relatively more stable and united Olympic Movement bloc of Foundation Board members. It is this enforced unity of purpose among the Olympic Movement members of WADA's Foundation Board which explains the IOC's control of this Board or, more particularly, the Executive Board, which ultimately determines and directs the Olympic Movement's purpose in its relationship with WADA, particularly with respect to the regular revisions to the Code since 2003, which to a large degree has reflected the sports anti-doping policy of the IOC.

The operation of WADA is funded directly by the IOC and government and indirectly by those TNCs which broadcast the Olympic Games.[87] The Olympic Movement's annual financial contribution to WADA is paid by the IOC. This is indicated in each of WADA's annual reports since 2002 and reinforces the cohesive IOC interest among all members of WADA's Foundation Board representing

[82] Olympic Charter art 16.1.3.
[83] ibid art 16.2.7.
[84] ibid art 25.
[85] ibid art 27.
[86] ibid art 43.
[87] See Figure 1 in the Appendix to this chapter.

the Olympic Movement. According to Pound: 'The IOC manages the Olympic Movement portion [payable to the WADA], drawing from the television revenues for the Games.'[88] By way of comparison, governments' financial contribution to the WADA is allocated according to the five Olympic regions (which may be comprised of disparate interests) and in the following proportion: Europe 47.5 per cent; the Americas 29 per cent; Asia 20.46 per cent; Oceania: 2.54 per cent; and Africa: 0.5 per cent.[89]

The IOC is WADA's biggest single financial contributor, matching the total contributions of all governments combined. The IOC also funded the establishment of WADA in 1999. Naturally, this level of financial commitment supports and emphasises the IOC's political weight in the governance of WADA. This ultimately gives the IOC a greater degree of moral authority or control in directing WADA's operations than any other single stakeholder. Also, as the IOC's financial contribution is directly sourced from its television revenue (as opposed to other IOC income sources), the application of these monies to the funding of WADA leaves the IOC open to the suggestion that the TNCs which pay for the rights to broadcast the Olympic Games and which are able to shape the form of the Olympic product they buy (ie, a drug-free and clean image of the Games, nature and timing of events etc)[90] influence the IOC's policy and input in the development and operation of WADA and the Code.

Although WADA is expressed to be a joint partnership between the Olympic Movement and government to combat doping in sport, when WADA's operational, governance and financial structures are examined, it is clear that the IOC is the senior partner for three distinct reasons. First, the nature of WADA's legal personality affords the IOC a strategic advantage through the location of its seat in the Olympic city of Lausanne and WADA's legal status as a private legal foundation, which is able to be controlled by the IOC without being subject to the same level of public scrutiny as a public entity. Second, WADA's governance structure (originally devised by IOC executive board member Richard Pound) reserves half of its Foundation Board's representation for the Olympic Movement (which includes four places specifically reserved for IOC members). There is no representation on the WADA board from non-Olympic sports such as rugby union and cricket. As the IOC controls the Olympic Movement overall, it is also able to control half of WADA's Foundation Board, which effectively represents the singular interest. Third, sourced from its broadcast revenue (thereby implicitly linking its funding contribution to WADA to its commercial imperatives), the IOC

[88] Pound (n 19) 77. See also Pound (n 77) 57.

[89] World Anti-Doping Agency, Copenhagen Declaration on Anti-Doping in Sport (5 March 2003) art 3.2.2.

[90] Directorate-General X, European Commission, 'The European Model of Sport' (Consultation Document, 1999) 12. The Consultation Document addresses the interdependence of sport, television and advertisers generally and cites instances of where IFs have changed their rules to meet the needs of television.

is by far the biggest single financial contributor to WADA. Together with its dominant role in WADA's governance, this level of monetary commitment to the heart of international sports anti-doping regulation equips the IOC with the necessary moral authority to influence the international anti-doping discourse, which it does publicly through the media, through its participation in WADA and through its Olympic Movement representatives who are members of WADA's Foundation Board.

Olympic 'Sports Product' and Commercial Satisfaction

Sport in its purest form is predicated upon fair competition. If there is one universal sporting commandment, it is thou shall not cheat. In classical times at Olympia, cheats were regularly punished and disgraced.[91] This tradition continues today in modern sport, particularly within the Olympic Movement. The Olympic Charter acknowledges and enshrines the principle of fair play[92] and the Olympic Charter's custodian, the IOC, ensures that it is enforced through the Code.

The IOC's role in shaping international anti-doping regulation is influenced by the wishes of the TNCs that are its commercial partners (broadcast and sponsorship) and that purchase from the IOC the Olympic brand or its 'sports product'. According to Payne,[93] the Olympic brand is 'about athletic prowess and fair play, but it is also about trust in the Olympic ideals'.[94] Pound, who was not only the foundation chairman of WADA, but was also a vice-president of the IOC, a long-serving member of the IOC's executive board and chairman of its television rights negotiations and marketing commissions, characterises the Olympic brand as 'pure sport'. Implicit in the IOC's construct of the Olympic Games and, by extension, the Olympic brand is that the Olympic Games is a drug-free event. Such a characterisation is informed by the references to 'fair play', 'the Olympic spirit', 'Olympism' and the recurring anti-doping theme running throughout the Olympic Charter. These themes are also expressly acknowledged in the Code. Pound reinforces this construction by stating that: 'It is the fight against doping in sport that distinguishes Olympic sport from entertainment sport.'[95] Given the confidential nature of commercial arrangements, the argument that the TNCs which are the IOC's commercial partners influence its policy on sports anti-doping

[91] Tony Perrottet, *The Naked Olympics: The True Story of the Ancient Games* (New York, Random House, 2004) 13.

[92] Olympic Charter 11 (Fundamental Principles of Olympism).

[93] Michael Payne was the IOC's Marketing Director from 1988 to 2002 and the IOC's Director of Global Broadcasting and Media Rights from 2002 to 2004.

[94] Payne (n 59) 122.

[95] Pound (n 19) 277.

(albeit indirectly) is a largely circumstantial one, but nevertheless a compelling one, as the relationship between the IOC and its broadcast and sponsorship partners is one of mutual dependence.

Under the Olympic Charter, the IOC is obliged to stage the Olympic Games every four years.[96] Such is the cost of staging an Olympic Games nowadays, even with the backing of a host city's government, that recourse still must be had to commercial means to ensure that the Games proceed.[97] Against this backdrop, commercial support from sponsors and broadcasters is vital to ensuring the viability and continuity of the Olympic Games. As Pound has remarked: 'Without commercial support, sport as we know it today, and the Olympic Games, would simply not exist. Trust me on this.'[98]

The Olympic Charter permits the IOC to 'seek all other resources enabling it to fulfil its tasks' and collect 'revenues from the exploitation of any of its rights, including but not limited to television rights, sponsorships, licences and Olympic properties as well as from the celebration of the Olympic Games'.[99]

The extraordinary financial contribution made by broadcasters and sponsors towards the cost of staging the Olympic Games makes them a stakeholder in the Olympic product that they purchase and, in particular, the Olympic Games. The IOC acknowledges the role and status of these TNCs through the deliberate use of language to refer to some of these entities as its 'worldwide partners'.[100] The role and influence of sponsors has been further recognised by the IOC at the 121st session of the IOC in Copenhagen in 2009, when it recommended that 'the constituents of the Olympic Movement should take into account the role and the opinions of the stakeholders, including sponsors, partners, suppliers and rights holders'.[101] As Pound asserts, 'it is both right and proper that the private sector be actively involved in the Olympic movement and the Olympic Games'.[102] By being a stakeholder in the Olympic Games, those TNCs which are the IOC's commercial broadcast and sponsorship partners can influence the IOC as to the staging of the Olympic Games and the shape of the Olympic product. The IOC depends on TNCs to contribute towards the cost of staging the Olympic Games. At the same time, TNCs depend on IOC delivering the Olympic product to them (drug-free, among other attributes) for their commercial purposes. This symbiotic relationship between the IOC and its TNC commercial partners was highlighted by Coakley and Pike when they referred to the remarks made by a Coca-Cola executive during a presentation to IOC executives prior to the XXVI Olympiad held in Atlanta in 1996, who said: 'Just as sponsors have the responsibility to preserve the integrity of the

[96] Olympic Charter art 2(3).
[97] Pound (n 19) 160.
[98] ibid 166.
[99] Olympic Charter art 25(1).
[100] ibid 14, back cover.
[101] International Olympic Committee, 'The Olympic Movement in Society' (5 October 2009) 11 [24], www.olympic.org/Documents/Congress_2009/Recommendations-eng.pdf.
[102] Pound (n 19) 160–61.

sport, enhance its image, help grow its prestige and its attendance, so too, do you [in sports] have responsibility and accountability to the sponsor.'[103]

According to Pound: 'Corporations, their brands, their products and their services seek to associate themselves with the many evocative images and values of the Olympic movement. These Olympic images add value to their enterprises.'[104] The IOC's longest standing sponsor, the Coca-Cola Company, acknowledges as much on its corporate website:

> The Coca-Cola company shares the Olympic Values, which embody the discovery of one's abilities, the spirit of competition, the pursuit of excellence, a sense of fair play and the building of a better and more-peaceful world. Because of our enormous respect for the integrity of the Olympic Movement and the values of Olympism, we have renewed our historic bond with the IOC through 2020, extending this extraordinary relationship to nearly a full century.[105]

Coca-Cola's embrace of 'Olympic values', a sense of 'fair play' and 'Olympism' tacitly betrays an expectation on its part of a drug-free Olympic Games.

As explained by Richard Moore, Managing Director of sponsorship consultants Capitalize and a board member of the European Sponsorship Association: 'Sponsors want to back clean sport, clean teams, sporting values and athletes who play by the rules.'[106] The withdrawal of sponsorship of professional cycling by TNCs such as Adidas-Salomon, Deutsche Telekom and Audi in light of the multiple doping scandals which plagued the 2007 Tour de France[107] and Kellogg's termination of its sponsorship of Michael Phelps after the swimmer was photographed inhaling from a marijuana pipe[108] only serve to illustrate what is a trite proposition, that being TNCs do not wish to associate with drugs in sport.

Coakley and Pike contend that: 'Commercialization changes the location of control in and over sports. When sports depend on the revenues they generate, the control centre of the sports organizations shifts away from the athletes and towards those who have the resources to produce and promote sports.'[109] The commercialisation of the Olympic Games since 1984 supports the proposition that TNCs which are the IOC's commercial partners not only have the ability to, but in fact do influence the IOC when it comes to formulating its Olympic Games policy. An example of this level of influence over the IOC and the operation of

[103] Jay Coakley and Elizabeth Pike, *Sports in Society: Issues and Controversies* (New York, McGraw-Hill, 2009) 397.

[104] Pound (n 19) 161.

[105] The Coca-Cola Company, 'Coca-Cola Sponsorships: London 2012 Olympic Games' (1 January 2012) www.coca-colacompany.com/stories/coca-cola-sponsorships-london-2012-olympic-games.

[106] Bill Wilson, 'Tour Sponsors Taking Lead on Doping' *BBC News* (27 July 2007) http://news.bbc.co.uk/2/low/business/6917086.stm.

[107] ibid; 'Deutsche Telekom Drops its Sponsorship of Professional Cycling' *New York Times* (27 November 2007) www.nytimes.com/2007/11/27/sports/27iht-CYCLING.4.8499952.html?_r=1.

[108] Juliet Macur, 'Phelps Disciplined over Marijuana Pipe Incident' *New York Times* (5 February 2009) www.nytimes.com/2009/02/06/sports/othersports/06phelps.html.

[109] Coakley and Pike (n 103) 407.

the Olympic Games is seen where the IOC acceded to the demands of NBC (the US licensee of the television broadcast rights of the Olympic Games) not only to reschedule the swimming finals at the 2008 Beijing Olympic Games from the evening session of competition (when swimming finals are conventionally held) to the morning session, but also to reschedule the date of the Olympic Games originally planned for September to August, so as to better fit with the network's live programming schedule.[110]

The Olympic product which broadcasters and sponsors buy from the IOC is of a 'pure sport' and 'fair play' nature. The level of influence that the IOC's major commercial partners (such as NBC) are able to bring to bear upon the IOC as to the operation of the Olympic Games is very high. Events such as doping scandals have the potential to damage the Olympic product and adversely affect the image of the Olympic Games, the IOC and its Olympic broadcasters and sponsors. It would in these circumstances be naive in the extreme to believe that the IOC's commercial partners are not able to influence the IOC to be resolute and proactive in addressing sports doping. Houlihan suggests as much when he observes that 'there are many actors whose attitude towards doping is shaped by non-sports policy objectives, including maintenance of the brand image of the Olympics and other international sports events'.[111] Here, such actors would include the TNCs that are the IOC's commercial partners. The Code (as originally devised and regularly revised), which is harsh in its operation and designed to have a deterrent effect to discourage sports doping, also conveniently serves the mutual commercial objectives of TNCs and the IOC by all but guaranteeing clean or pure 'sports product'.

Influence over the IOC's approach to dealing with drugs in sport from the TNCs which are the IOC's commercial partners and which provide the revenue for the IOC to stage the Olympic Games is one explanation why Pound (who at the critical times of the development of the present international sports anti-doping regime was responsible for the IOC's anti-doping, broadcasting and marketing portfolios) in 1998 sought to obtain representation for sponsors on the governing council of the originally proposed 'independent' anti-doping agency which eventually morphed into WADA. It is also an explanation as to why the IOC sources its annual financial contribution to the budget of WADA from income earned from its broadcast partners, which televise the Olympic brand and rely upon the integrity of that image to attract viewers and advertisers. It is understandable that the IOC's commercial partners would seek to influence the IOC when it comes to sports anti-doping regulation, because it is Olympic or pure sport in which the IOC's broadcast and sponsorship partners are investing, so as to associate their own brands and products with the Olympic image or brand of sport. They have both the opportunity and the commercial motive to do so. At the same time, an anti-doping policy such as the Code, when coupled with a

[110] Bill Carter, 'On TV, Timing is Everything at the Olympics' *Business Day, New York Times* (25 August 2008) 1

[111] Barrie Houlihan, 'Building an International Regime to Combat Doping in Sport' in Levermore and Budd (n 4) 73.

rigorous approach by the IOC towards its enforcement, goes a considerable way towards protecting the integrity of the Olympic brand, which is essential to the mutual financial advantage of both the IOC and its broadcast and sponsorship partners. The references in the Code to 'Olympism' and 'the spirit of sport' as part of its fundamental rationale, which are otiose to the primary goals of eliminating cheating in sport through the use of drugs and ensuring the health of athletes, are consistent with this hypothesis. This is especially clear when considering that CAS in 2003 acknowledged that the public image of sport is a legitimate justification for sports anti-doping regulation.

Ultimately, those TNCs which are the IOC's broadcast and sponsorship partners are able to influence the IOC's stance on sports anti-doping through WADA and the operation of the Code, because of the vast amounts of money they pay for the Olympic brand and because they and the IOC are dependent upon each other and also upon the Olympic brand's integrity. It is through such influence that the TNCs are able to share some of the IOC's power when it comes to the overall control of sports anti-doping regulation.[112]

Conclusion

When analysed from both historical and structural perspectives, the IOC is indisputably the dominant actor in WADA's undertaking. Since the inception of WADA in 1999, the IOC has materially shaped and influenced its operation and the development of the Code in line with the IOC's interests, and continues to do so. These interests of course include the substantial commercial interests from which the IOC benefits, arising from its partnerships with TNCs in the form of broadcasting and sponsorship arrangements. The TNCs, in turn, benefit from the IOC providing the clean or pure 'sports product' that they buy. It is a mutually beneficial relationship. Pure sport is a commodity that benefits both the IOC and also TNCs, which are important stakeholders in Olympic sport and international sport more generally in the professional era and which can and do influence the IOC in its role as the world's most powerful sporting organisation.

Therefore, given the role that TNCs play as broadcasters and sponsors in the staging of international sporting events and, in particular, the Olympic Games, it is difficult to understand why the Code in its fundamental rationale is reticent to identify their interest in 'pure sport' or 'clean sport'. It is also difficult to see why WADA does not explicitly acknowledge the commercial rationale for the Code, given that all stakeholders in the sporting contest, including athletes, benefit from this commercial aspect in the staging of the Olympic Games and other elite sporting contests. Not only would such acknowledgement by WADA appropriately conform to the universal governance ideal of transparency, but it could also lead

[112] See Figure 1 in the Appendix to this chapter.

to a better understanding in the Code's full or complete rationale and inspire greater confidence in the Code's administration, amongst those whom it affects—all things which remain highly desirable outcomes for the international sporting community at large.

Appendix

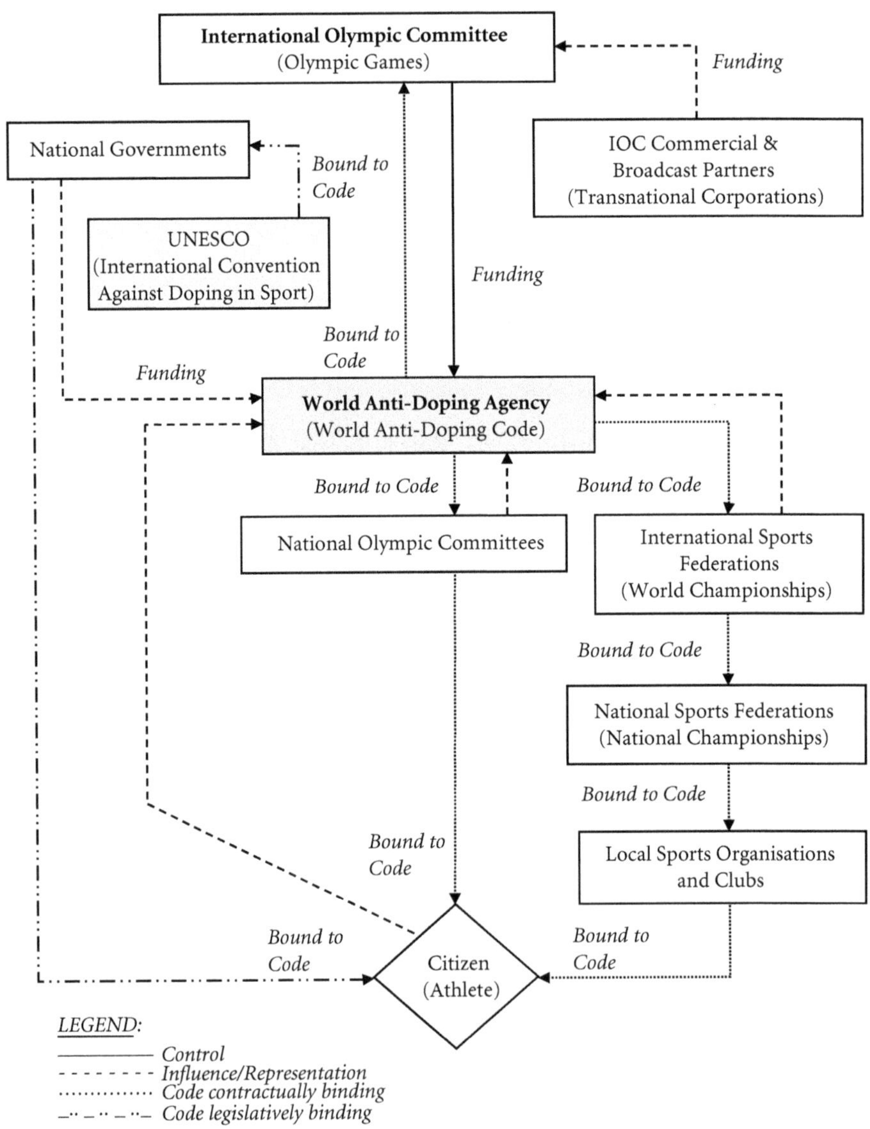

Figure 1: Structure of international sports anti-doping regulation

INDEX

www.ingramcontent.com/pod-product-compliance
Ingram Content Group UK Ltd.
Pitfield, Milton Keynes, MK11 3LW, UK
UKHW020133290926
15471UKWH00003B/466

9 781509 926787